Children's Illustrated Thesaurus

DK UK
Senior Editor Fleur Star
Senior Art Editor Sheila Collins
Editorial Team Tom Booth, Jessica Cawthra,
Anna Fischel, Niki Foreman, Victoria Pyke
US Senior Editor Margaret Parrish
US Editor Jenny Siklos
Design Assistant Kit Lane
Creative Technical Support Tommy Callan
Illustrators Gus Scott, Edwood Burn
Senior Jacket Designer Mark Cavanagh
Jacket Design Development Manager Sophia MTT
Managing Editor Francesca Baines
Managing Art Editor Phil Letsu
Pre-production Jacqueline Street
Producer Gary Batchelor
Publisher Andrew Macintyre
Art Director Karen Self
Publishing Director Jonathan Metcalf

DK India
Senior Editor Anita Kakar
Project Art Editor Shreya Anand
Project Editor Antara Moitra
Art Editors Revati Anand, Heena Sharma
Assistant Art Editor Neetika Malik Jhingan
Jacket Art Editor Dhirendra Singh
Jackets Editorial Coordinator Priyanka Sharma
DTP Designers Vijay Kandwal, Dheeraj Singh
Picture Researcher Jayati Sood
Managing Jackets Editor Sreshtha Bhattacharya
Picture Research Manager Taiyaba Khatoon
Pre-production Manager Balwant Singh
Production Manager Pankaj Sharma
Senior Managing Editor Rohan Sinha
Managing Art Editor Govind Mittal

First American Edition, 2017
Published in the United States by DK Publishing
345 Hudson Street, New York, New York 10014

Based on an original text published by HarperCollins Publishers.
Copyright © 2017 Dorling Kindersley Limited
DK, a Division of Penguin Random House LLC
Original text copyright © HarperCollins Publishers 2009
Revised text copyright © Dorling Kindersley Ltd. 2017
17 18 19 20 21 10 9 8 7 6 5 4 3 2 1
001–299573–June/2017

A catalog record for this book is available from the Library of Congress.
ISBN: 978-1-4654-6237-4

DK books are available at special discounts when purchased in bulk
for sales promotions, premiums, fund-raising, or educational use.
For details, contact: DK Publishing Special Markets,
345 Hudson Street, New York, New York 10014
SpecialSales@dk.com

Printed in China

All images © Dorling Kindersley Limited
For further information see: www.dkimages.com

A WORLD OF IDEAS:
SEE ALL THERE IS TO KNOW

www.dk.com

Children's Illustrated Thesaurus

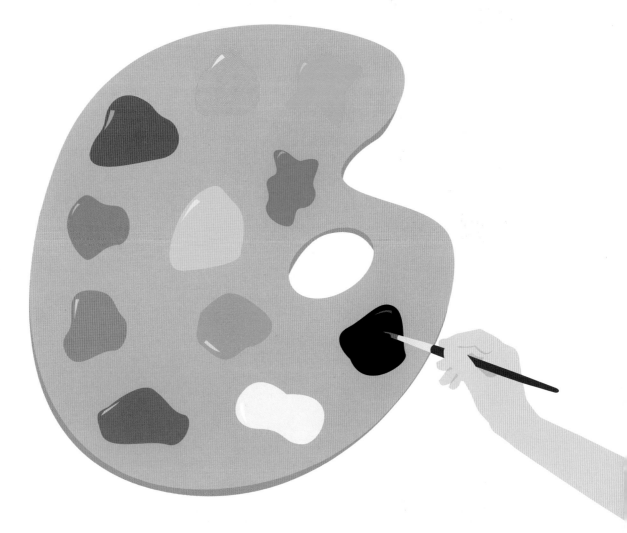

How to use this book

The *Children's Illustrated Thesaurus* is easy to use when you want to find a synonym to improve your writing. Synonyms are words that can have the same meaning as other words – see page 6 for more information.

Related words
Words that relate to the entry to expand your vocabulary even further come at the end.

Entry
This is the word you want to find a synonym for.

Guideword
The word on the top left shows you the first entry on the page.

>> **ab**andon

Aa

Synonym
*Alternative words you can use instead of the entry word are shown in **bold**.*

Definition
What the word means.

Example sentence
Helping you find the right word by putting it in context.

abandon ①
verb to leave someone or something » *The child abandoned her toy.*
desert, jilt, leave, leave behind, forsake, leave in the lurch

*The child **abandoned** her toy.*

abandon ②
noun lack of restraint » *Raj began to laugh with abandon.*
recklessness, wildness
antonym: **control**

abate
verb to become less » *The four-day flood abated and the road became visible.*
decrease, diminish, ebb, lessen, subside, wane

ability
noun the skill needed to do something » *Sheila has the ability to get along with others.*
capability, competence, expertise, skill, talent, aptitude, dexterity, proficiency
antonym: **inability**

able
adjective good at doing something » *Luca proved himself to be an able teacher when all his students passed the exam.*
accomplished, capable, efficient, expert, first-rate, skilled, talented, competent, proficient

abolish
verb to do away with something » *The children wanted to abolish the school's homework policy.*
annul, do away with, overturn, put an end to, quash, rescind, revoke

about ①
preposition relating to or concerning » *Laura was happy about her excellent exam score.*
concerning, on, regarding, relating to

about ②
adverb not exactly » *I think the movie lasts about one hour.*
almost, approximately, around, nearly, roughly

above ①
preposition over or higher than something » *The bird flew above the clouds.*
higher than, over
antonym: **below**
related words: prefixes **super-, supra-, sur-**

*The bird flew **above** the clouds.*

above ②
preposition greater than a certain level or amount » *The number of visitors will rise above the 100 mark.*
beyond, exceeding

abrupt ①
adjective sudden or unexpected » *They were surprised by the teacher's abrupt departure.*
sudden, unexpected, unforeseen, precipitate, unanticipated

abrupt ②
adjective unfriendly and impolite » *He was surprised by her abrupt manner.*
curt, rude, short, terse, brusque, unceremonious
antonym: **polite**

absent
adjective not present » *Hugo was absent from school yesterday, so he missed the practice test.*
away, elsewhere, gone, missing
antonym: **present**

absent-minded
adjective forgetful or not paying attention » *Nora's absentminded father left the camera under the seat.*
distracted, forgetful, inattentive, mindless, out to lunch (informal)

absolute ①
adjective total and complete » *I can't understand him, he is talking absolute nonsense.*
complete, downright, pure, sheer, thorough, total, utter, unmitigated, unqualified

accommodation
noun a house or room for living in
» *What kind of **accommodation** are you staying in?*

cottage
*A **cottage** is a small house for vacations.*

house
*Each **house** has its own yard.*

crib
(slang)
*The actors stayed in a great **crib** as they toured the city.*

mobile home
*A **mobile home** is more affordable than a house.*

penthouse
*I live in the **penthouse** on the top floor.*

8

Entry number

If there is more than one sense of the word, each one has a separate entry.

Part of speech

For example, noun, verb, or adjective. See page 7 for more about parts of speech.

More synonyms

Shown in gray, these are slightly more complicated or advanced synonyms.

Shades of

Instead of a definition, color entries have a list of shades.

Guideword

The word on the top right shows you the last entry on the page.

yellow
noun or adjective
- Shades of yellow:
amber, canary yellow, citrus yellow, daffodil, gold, lemon, mustard, primrose, saffron, sand, straw, topaz

Alphabet bars

The highlighted letter shows you which section you're in.

Antonym

A word that means the opposite from the entry.

▼, ▲, ◀◀, ▶▶

See below/above/ left/right: Look at the big illustration for this entry.

Usage

Shows when and how some synonyms are used.

Example sentence

These show each synonym in a sentence.

---

accompany »

absolute ②
adjective having total power » *Louis XIV of France was an absolute monarch and had complete authority on all state matters.*
dictatorial, supreme, tyrannical

absorb
verb to soak up or take in something » *A sponge can absorb a lot of water.*
digest, soak up, take in

abstain
verb to choose not to do something » *Vegetarians abstain from eating meat.*
avoid, deny yourself, forgo, give up, refrain, desist, forbear, renounce

absurd
adjective ridiculous or nonsensical » *The movie's plot was absurd, I couldn't make sense of it.*
crazy (informal)**, illogical, ludicrous, nonsensical, ridiculous, incongruous, preposterous**

abundance
noun a great amount of something » *There is an abundance of wildlife in the rain forest.*
affluence, bounty, plenty, cornucopia, plethora
antonym: **shortage**

*There was an **abundant** supply of cakes at the party.*

abundant
adjective present in large quantities » *There was an abundant supply of cakes at the party.*
ample, copious, full, plentiful
antonym: **scarce**

abuse ①
noun cruel treatment of someone » *Animal abuse is rightly illegal.*
exploitation, harm, hurt, ill-treatment, oppression

abuse ②
noun unkind remarks directed toward someone » *The cyclist shouted abuse at the man driving dangerously.*
censure, derision, insults, invective

abuse ③
verb to speak insultingly to someone » *The fans verbally abused the rival football team.*
curse, insult, scold, slate (Britain; informal)

abusive
adjective rude and unkind » *Don't use abusive language when speaking to people, it will offend them.*
disparaging, insulting, offensive, rude, scathing, censorious, vituperative

abyss
noun a very deep hole » *He peered over the edge of the abyss.*
chasm, fissure, gorge, pit, void

*He peered over the edge of the **abyss**.*

accelerate
verb to go faster » *The car accelerated to reach the higher speed limit.*
hurry, quicken, speed up
antonym: **decelerate**

accept
verb to receive or agree to something » *Lucas accepted the party invitation.*
acknowledge, agree to, concur with, consent to, take
antonym: **refuse**

acceptable
adjective good enough to be accepted » *His messy handwriting was not acceptable.*
adequate, all right, fair, good enough, passable, satisfactory, tolerable

accidental
adjective happening by chance » *The fire was accidental.*
casual, chance, inadvertent, random
antonym: **deliberate**

accommodate
verb to provide someone with a place to stay » *A hotel was built to accommodate guests for weddings.*
house, put up, shelter

accommodating
adjective willing to help » *The waiter was very accommodating and found us a new table.*
considerate, helpful, hospitable, kind, obliging

accommodation
noun a house or room for living in
▼ SEE BELOW

accompany ①
verb to go somewhere with someone » *Children must be accompanied by an adult.*
conduct (formal)**, escort, go with, usher**

---

apartment
*How many **apartments** are in the building?*

housing
*This **housing** is perfect for families.*

studio
*He lives in a one-room **studio**.*

condominium
*My **condominium** has a snow removal service.*

garden apartment
*A **garden apartment** is an apartment on the first floor with a garden or yard.*

dormitory
*The student **dormitory** needed decorating.*

mansion
*The **mansion** has seven bedrooms.*

9

a b c d e f g h i j k l m n o p q r s t u v w x y z

Why use a thesaurus?

The main reason for using a thesaurus is to find synonyms, or alternative words, to help you with your writing. In addition, this thesaurus will identify what kind of word (part of speech) it is and provide helpful definitions and examples. It will also give antonyms, or words that mean the opposite of the one you look up, wherever possible.

What is a synonym?

A synonym is a word that means the same—or almost the same—as another word, for example "little" and "small." Most of the time, there is no such thing as a true synonym. If two words mean exactly the same thing, then why bother having both? Rather, a synonym can or could mean the same thing as another word depending on how you use it. Usually, however, synonyms have little differences in meaning that make one word more suitable to use than another. For example, "little girl" usually means a young girl, but a "small girl" suggests she is not big in size.

*This puppy could be described as **little** or **small**.*

*The **little** girl is the young girl on the right.*

*The **small** girl is the short girl on the left.*

Improve your vocabulary

Synonyms can help you improve your writing by using more interesting words. For example, instead of putting "she said" in a story, using "she shouted" can tell the reader that she might be angry or in a noisy room. It is also much more interesting to use and read a variety of words than writing "she said" all the time!

He **said**

She **shouted**

What is an antonym?

An antonym is a word that means the opposite of another word, for example "big" is an antonym of "small."

*A **small** frog*

*A **big** elephant*

Parts of speech

To help you find the right entry in the thesaurus, it can help to know the type of word (or "part of speech") you're looking up. Some words can be used in different ways, such as "bend"—this can be a verb (to bend over) or a noun (a bend in the river). Here are the main parts of speech and how they fit together.

*Grace **bent** over to pick a flower.*　　*The river has many **bends**.*

Noun

An object, person, or place. A noun doesn't have to be a visible thing—"fact" and "history" are also nouns. Things with a name (such as a country or a person) are known as proper nouns.

Adjective

A describing word, such as green, big, or old. Adjectives are used to describe nouns.

*The amusement park has **bright** lights and fun rides.*

*Lei wrinkled her nose when she tasted the **bitter** lemon.*

Verb

An action (or "doing word"). These include any kind of action—such as run, breathe, and sleep—and also "helping" verbs, which may be used with other verbs to show how possible or necessary an action is. These include: have, will, be, must, may, and do. For example, he must run to catch the bus; she will come to the party.

*John **ran** to catch the bus.*

Adverb

A word that gives more information about a verb, adjective, or another adverb. These often end in "ly," such as quietly and helpfully, but don't have to— today, very, and forward are all adverbs.

*Pat arrived at **exactly** 8 o'clock.*　　*The dog leaped **high** in the air.*

Preposition

A word that shows how one noun (person or thing) relates to another, such as "in," "with," and "in spite of."

Interjection

A word that can be used on its own without a full sentence, such as "ouch" and "hello."

Sentence formation

This is how the parts of speech fit together in a sentence.

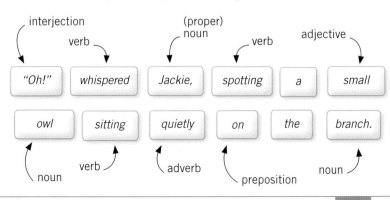

| interjection | verb | (proper) noun | verb | | adjective |
| "Oh!" | whispered | Jackie, | spotting | a | small |

| owl | sitting | quietly | on | the | branch. |
| noun | verb | adverb | preposition | | noun |

Aa

abandon [1]

verb to leave someone or something » *The child abandoned her toy.*
desert, jilt, leave, leave behind, forsake, leave in the lurch

*The child **abandoned** her toy.*

abandon [2]

noun lack of restraint » *Raj began to laugh with abandon.*
recklessness, wildness
antonym: **control**

abate

verb to become less » *The four-day flood abated and the road became visible.*
decrease, diminish, ebb, lessen, subside, wane

ability

noun the skill needed to do something » *Sheila has the ability to get along with others.*
capability, competence, expertise, skill, talent, aptitude, dexterity, proficiency
antonym: **inability**

able

adjective good at doing something » *Luca proved himself to be an able teacher when all his students passed the exam.*
accomplished, capable, efficient, expert, first-rate, skilled, talented, competent, proficient

abolish

verb to do away with something » *The children wanted to abolish the school's homework policy.*
annul, do away with, overturn, put an end to, quash, rescind, revoke

about [1]

preposition relating to or concerning » *Laura was happy about her excellent exam score.*
concerning, on, regarding, relating to

about [2]

adverb not exactly » *I think the movie lasts about one hour.*
almost, approximately, around, nearly, roughly

above [1]

preposition over or higher than something » *The bird flew above the clouds.*
higher than, over
antonym: **below**
related words: prefixes **super-, supra-, sur-**

*The bird flew **above** the clouds.*

above [2]

preposition greater than a certain level or amount » *The number of visitors will rise above the 100 mark.*
beyond, exceeding

abrupt [1]

adjective sudden or unexpected » *They were surprised by the teacher's abrupt departure.*
sudden, unexpected, unforeseen, precipitate, unanticipated

abrupt [2]

adjective unfriendly and impolite » *He was surprised by her abrupt manner.*
curt, rude, short, terse, brusque, unceremonious
antonym: **polite**

absent

adjective not present » *Hugo was absent from school yesterday, so he missed the practice test.*
away, elsewhere, gone, missing
antonym: **present**

absent-minded

adjective forgetful or not paying attention » *Nora's absentminded father left the camera under the seat.*
distracted, forgetful, inattentive, mindless, out to lunch (informal)

absolute [1]

adjective total and complete » *I can't understand him, he is talking absolute nonsense.*
complete, downright, pure, sheer, thorough, total, utter, unmitigated, unqualified

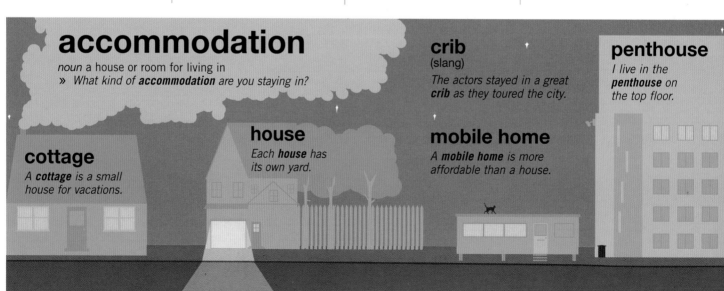

accommodation

noun a house or room for living in » *What kind of **accommodation** are you staying in?*

cottage

A **cottage** is a small house for vacations.

house

Each **house** has its own yard.

crib

(slang)
The actors stayed in a great **crib** as they toured the city.

mobile home

A **mobile home** is more affordable than a house.

penthouse

I live in the **penthouse** on the top floor.

absolute ☑

adjective having total power
» *Louis XIV of France was
an absolute monarch and
had complete authority
on all state matters.*
**dictatorial, supreme,
tyrannical**

absorb

verb to soak up or take
in something » *A sponge
can absorb a lot of water.*
digest, soak up, take in

abstain

verb to choose not to do
something » *Vegetarians
abstain from eating meat.*
**avoid, deny yourself, forgo,
give up, refrain,** desist,
forbear, renounce

absurd

adjective ridiculous
or nonsensical » *The
movie's plot was absurd,
I couldn't make sense of it.*
crazy (informal)**, illogical,
ludicrous, nonsensical,
ridiculous,** incongruous,
preposterous

abundance

noun a great amount
of something
» *There is an abundance
of wildlife in the rain forest.*
affluence, bounty, plenty,
cornucopia, plethora
antonym: **shortage**

*There was an **abundant** supply
of cakes at the party.*

abundant

adjective present in large
quantities » *There was
an abundant supply of
cakes at the party.*
**ample, copious,
full, plentiful**
antonym: **scarce**

abuse ☐

noun cruel treatment
of someone » *Animal
abuse is rightly illegal.*
**exploitation, harm, hurt,
ill-treatment, oppression**

abuse ☑

noun unkind remarks directed
toward someone » *The cyclist
shouted abuse at the man
driving dangerously.*
**censure, derision,
insults, invective**

abuse ☒

verb to speak insultingly to
someone » *The fans verbally
abused the rival football team.*
**curse, insult, scold,
slate** (Britain; informal)

abusive

adjective rude and unkind
» *Don't use abusive language
when speaking to people, it will
offend them.*
**disparaging, insulting,
offensive, rude, scathing,**
censorious, vituperative

abyss

noun a very deep hole
» *He peered over the edge
of the abyss.*
**chasm, fissure, gorge,
pit, void**

*He peered over the edge
of the **abyss**.*

accelerate

verb to go faster » *The car
accelerated to reach the
higher speed limit.*
hurry, quicken, speed up
antonym: **decelerate**

accept

verb to receive or agree
to something » *Lucas
accepted the party invitation.*
**acknowledge,
agree to, concur with,
consent to, take**
antonym: **refuse**

acceptable

adjective good enough
to be accepted
» *His messy handwriting
was not acceptable.*
**adequate, all right, fair,
good enough, passable,
satisfactory, tolerable**

accidental

adjective happening by chance
» *The fire was accidental.*
**casual, chance,
inadvertent, random**
antonym: **deliberate**

accommodate

verb to provide someone with
a place to stay » *A hotel was
built to accommodate guests
for weddings.*
house, put up, shelter

accommodating

adjective willing to help » *The
waiter was very accommodating
and found us a new table.*
**considerate, helpful,
hospitable, kind, obliging**

accommodation

noun a house or room
for living in
▼ SEE BELOW

accompany ☐

verb to go somewhere with
someone » *Children must
be accompanied by an adult.*
conduct (formal)**, escort,
go with, usher**

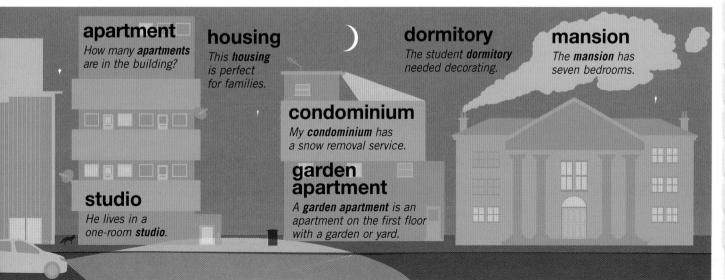

apartment
*How many **apartments**
are in the building?*

studio
*He lives in a
one-room **studio**.*

housing
*This **housing**
is perfect
for families.*

condominium
*My **condominium** has
a snow removal service.*

**garden
apartment**
*A **garden apartment** is an
apartment on the first floor
with a garden or yard.*

dormitory
*The student **dormitory**
needed decorating.*

mansion
*The **mansion** has
seven bedrooms.*

a b c d e f g h i j k l m n o p q r s t u v w x y z

act
② *verb* to perform in a play or movie

Get ready to start **acting!**

But I want to **perform** *that role!*

I will **act out** *the part of the king!*

accompany ②
verb to occur with something » *A cold is often accompanied by a cough.*
come with,
go together with

accomplish
verb to manage to do something » *The whole team worked together to accomplish its goal.*
achieve, bring about, complete, do, fulfill, manage, effect, execute, realize

accurate
adjective correct to a detailed level » *Use a ruler to make the drawing more accurate.*
correct, exact, faithful, precise, right, strict, true
antonym: **inaccurate**

accuse
verb to charge someone with doing something wrong » *Jack was accused of losing the office keys again.*
blame, censure, charge, cite, denounce, impeach, incriminate, indict

*Jack was **accused** of losing the office keys again.*

accustomed
adjective used to something » *Students become accustomed to early morning starting times for school.*
adapted, familiar, used
antonym: **unaccustomed**

achieve
verb to gain through hard work or ability » *She achieved the highest scores in the competition.*
accomplish, carry out, complete, do, fulfill, perform

*She **achieved** the highest scores in the competition.*

achievement
noun something which someone has succeeded in doing » *Finishing a marathon is a huge achievement.*
accomplishment, deed, exploit, feat

acquire
verb to get something » *I have recently acquired a digital camera.*
attain, gain, get, obtain, pick up, procure, secure

act ①
verb to do something » *The referee acted correctly in giving a penalty for the bad tackle.*
function, operate, perform, work

act ②
verb to perform in a play or movie
▲ **SEE ABOVE**

act ③
noun a single thing someone does » *Adopting the stray dog was an act of kindness.*
accomplishment, achievement, deed, feat, undertaking

action ①
noun the process of doing something » *This letter requires immediate action—please do not ignore it.*
activity, operation, process

action ②
noun something that is done » *He did not like his actions to be questioned.*
accomplishment, achievement, deed, exploit, feat

active ①
adjective full of energy » *Andrea was always so active and fun to be around.*
energetic, lively, restless, sprightly, vivacious, dynamic, indefatigable

active ②
adjective busy and hardworking » *Parents were very active in the school community.*
busy, engaged, enthusiastic, hardworking, industrious, involved, occupied

activity ①
noun a situation in which lots of things are happening » *There is an extraordinary level of activity in the school.*
action, bustle, energy, liveliness

activity ②
noun something you do for pleasure » *The gym offers activities like jogging on the treadmill or swimming.*
hobby, interest, pastime, pursuit

*The gym offers **activities** like jogging on the treadmill or swimming.*

actual
adjective real, rather than imaginary or guessed » *That is the estimate—the actual figure is much higher.*
authentic, genuine, realistic, true, verified

A B C D E F G H I J K L M N O P Q R S T U V W X Y Z

acute ①

adjective severe or intense
» *He suddenly had an acute pain in his back.*
critical, extreme, grave, great, intense, serious, severe

*He suddenly had an **acute** pain in his back.*

acute ②

adjective very intelligent
» *She has an acute mind and was always the best at problem-solving.*
alert, astute, bright, keen, perceptive, quick, sharp, shrewd, discriminating, discerning, perspicacious

adapt

verb to alter for a new use
» *The offices were adapted for use as a library.*
adjust, alter, change, convert, modify

add ①

verb to put something with something else » *She added more pages to the book.*
attach, augment, supplement, adjoin, affix, append

add ②

verb to combine numbers or quantities » *Add all the items together to find out how much you have bought.*
add up, count up, total
antonym: **subtract**

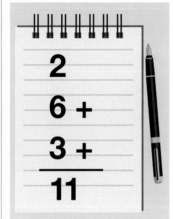

***Add** all the items together to find out how much you have bought.*

addition

noun something that has been added to something else
» *The showroom revealed recent additions to their range of cars.*
increase, supplement, addendum, adjunct, appendage

adequate

adjective enough in amount or quality for a purpose
» *Adequate protein is part of a balanced diet.*
acceptable, ample, enough, satisfactory, sufficient
antonym: **insufficient**

administer ①

verb to be responsible for managing something
» *It must be hard work to administer a large company.*
be in charge of, command, control, direct, manage, run, supervise

administer ②

verb to inflict or impose something on someone
» *He administered strict curfews on the boys.*
carry out, deal, dispense, execute, impose, inflict, perform, mete out

admiration

noun a feeling of great liking and respect » *I have always had the greatest admiration for her.*
appreciation, approval, esteem, regard, respect

admire

verb to like and respect someone or something
» *They admired him for his work.*
appreciate, look up to, respect, value, esteem, venerate
antonym: **scorn**

admit ①

verb to agree that something is true » *The driver admitted that he was lost.*
accept, acknowledge, grant
antonym: **deny**

admit ②

verb to allow to enter
» *Pablo was admitted to the university.*
accept, let in, receive, take in
antonym: **exclude**

adult

noun a grown-up person
» *A family ticket covers two adults and three children.*
grown-up, man, woman
antonym: **child**

*A family ticket covers two **adults** and three children.*

advance ①

verb to move forward or develop » *The forces advanced on the battlefield.*
make inroads, press on, proceed, progress

advance ②

noun progress in something
» *Scientific advances help us explore the Solar System in ever greater detail.*
breakthrough, development, gain, progress, step

a b c d e f g h i j k l m n o p q r s t u v w x y z

A
B C D E F G H I J K L M N O P Q R S T U V W X Y Z

advantage
noun a more favorable position or state » *Sara had the advantage of knowing his favorite hiding place.*
ascendancy, benefit, dominance, superiority
antonym: **disadvantage**

advertise
verb to present something to the public in order to sell it » *Printed bags are a good way to advertise a store.*
plug (informal), **promote, publicize, push, blazon, promulgate**

advertisement
noun a public announcement to sell or publicize something » *Mia placed an advertisement in the local newspaper.*
ad (informal), **banner ad, commercial, notice, plug** (informal)

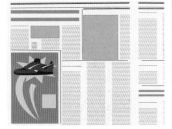

*Mia placed an **advertisement** in the local newspaper.*

advice
noun a suggestion as to what to do » *Take my advice and don't order the apple pie.*
counsel (formal), **guidance, opinion, suggestion**

advise ①
verb to offer advice to someone » *His friend advised him to leave as soon as possible.*
caution, counsel, recommend, suggest, urge, commend, prescribe

advise ②
verb to notify someone » *I would like to advise you of my decision to change classes.*
inform, make known, notify

adviser
noun a person whose job is to give advice » *My mother spent the day in meetings with her advisors.*
aide, consultant, guru, mentor, tutor

advocate
verb to publicly support a plan or course of action » *Tom advocates Mr. Johnson to be the new governor.*
back, champion, endorse, favor, promote, recommend, support, uphold

affair
noun an event or series of events » *The wedding was a large affair.*
business, event, issue, matter, question, situation, subject

affect
verb to influence something or someone » *More than 7 million people have been affected by the drought.*
act on, alter, change, impinge on

affection
noun a feeling of fondness for someone or something » *She thought of him with affection.*
attachment, fondness, liking, love, warmth
antonym: **dislike**

affectionate
adjective full of fondness for someone » *Elsa gave her dog an affectionate stroke.*
caring, fond, loving, tender
antonym: **cold**

*Elsa gave her dog an **affectionate** stroke.*

afraid
adjective scared of something unpleasant happening
▶▶ **SEE RIGHT**

after
adverb at a later time » *After the main course, you can choose a dessert.*
afterward, following, later, subsequently
antonym: **before**
related word: *prefix* **post-**

again
adverb happening one more time » *When he didn't get a reply, Carlos texted his best friend again.*
afresh, anew, once more

against ①
preposition in opposition to » *We are against the new construction project.*
averse to, hostile to, in opposition to, versus
related words: *prefixes* **anti-, contra-, counter-**

*We are **against** the new construction project.*

against ②
preposition in preparation for or in case of something » *When you go out, dress well to protect yourselves against the cold.*
in anticipation of, in expectation of, in preparation for

aggressive
adjective full of hostility and violence » *Hungry sharks can be very aggressive.*
hostile, quarrelsome, belligerent, pugnacious
antonym: **peaceful**

agile
adjective able to move quickly and easily » *He is as agile as a cat.*
lithe, nimble, sprightly, supple, limber, lissom, lissome
antonym: **clumsy**

agitate ①
verb to campaign energetically for something » *The workers had begun to agitate for better conditions in the office.*
campaign, demonstrate, protest, push

agitate ②
verb to worry or distress someone » *Everything she said agitated me.*
bother, distress, disturb, trouble, upset, worry, discompose, faze, perturb

agree ①
verb to have the same opinion as someone » *They all agreed to go bowling.*
assent, be of the same opinion, concur, see eye to eye
antonym: **disagree**

agree ②
verb to match or be the same as something » *His statement agrees with the facts given by other witnesses.*
accord, conform, match, square, tally

agreeable ①
adjective pleasant or enjoyable » *I've just had the most agreeable vacation, I want to go back!*
delightful, enjoyable, lovely, nice, pleasant, pleasurable
antonym: **disagreeable**

afraid

adjective scared of something unpleasant happening » *The children felt **afraid** of the house on top of the hill.*

apprehensive

*He felt **apprehensive** approaching the house— there was something very strange about it.*

fearful

*Anyone would be **fearful** near a haunted house, it gives you goose bumps.*

frightened

*She was so **frightened**, she stood rooted to the spot.*

nervous

*Being **nervous** made her tremble like a leaf.*

scared

*He told her not to be **scared**, although he was also shaking in his boots.*

antonym: unafraid

*Walking toward the gloomy house, she was surprised that she felt completely **unafraid**.*

spooked

*They felt **spooked**—the haunted house gave them the shivers.*

a b c d e f g h i j k l m n o p q r s t u v w x y z

alike

1 *adjective* similar in some way
» *The snakes look so **alike**.*

similar
These snakes have **similar** patterns.

close
A king snake is **close** in appearance to a coral snake.

the same
All snakes have **the same** body shape.

identical
Their colors are **identical**, just in a different order.

indistinguishable
The two snakes are almost **indistinguishable** from each other.

antonym:
different
The butterflies are **different** in color and shape.

agreeable 2
adjective willing to allow or do something » *Pooja said she was **agreeable** to this plan.*
game, happy, prepared, ready, willing,
amenable, compliant

agreement
noun a decision reached by two or more people » *The two countries have signed agreements on fishing and oil rights.*
arrangement, contract, deal (informal), pact, settlement, treaty,
compact, covenant

aim 1
verb to plan to do something » *The school aims to recruit three new teachers next year.*
aspire, attempt, intend, plan, propose, strive

aim 2
noun what someone intends to achieve » *My main aim is to be captain of the hockey team.*
ambition, goal, intention, objective, plan, target

alarm 1
noun a feeling of fear » *The cat sprang back in alarm.*
anxiety, apprehension, fright, nervousness, panic, scare,
consternation, trepidation
antonym: **calm**

*The cat sprang back in **alarm**.*

alarm 2
noun a device used to warn people of something
» *The burglar alarm woke up the whole street.*
distress signal, siren, warning

alarm 3
verb to fill with fear
» *We could not see what had alarmed him.*
distress, frighten, panic, scare, startle, unnerve
antonym: **calm**

alert 1
adjective paying full attention
» *The alert guard caught the shoplifter red-handed.*
attentive, observant, on guard, vigilant, wary
antonym: **unaware**

alert 2
verb to warn of danger
» *The swimmers alerted the passerby that they needed help.*
forewarn, inform, notify, warn

*The swimmers **alerted** the passerby that they needed help.*

alike 1
adjective similar in some way
◀◀ **SEE LEFT**

alike 2
adverb in a similar way
» *All the children taking part in the parade were dressed alike—it was hard to tell them apart.*
equally, in the same way, similarly, uniformly

alive 1
adjective having life
» *Doctors worked around the clock to keep the patient alive.*
animate, breathing, living
antonym: **dead**

alive 2
adjective lively and active
» *After jogging up the hill, Juan felt alive with energy.*
active, alert, animated, energetic, full of life, lively, vivacious
antonym: **dull**

*After jogging up the hill, Juan felt **alive** with energy.*

all
pronoun the whole of something
» *Did you eat all the cookies?*
each, every one, everything, the whole amount, the (whole) lot
related words:
prefixes **pan-, panto-**

allow 1
verb to permit someone to do something
» *Jane's mother allowed her to go to the party.*
approve, authorize, let, permit, stand for, tolerate,
brook, give leave, sanction
antonym: **forbid**

allow 2
verb to set aside for a particular purpose
» *Allow four hours for the paint to dry.*
allocate, allot, assign, grant, set aside

all right
adjective acceptable » *It was all right, but nothing special.*
acceptable, adequate, average, fair, okay or OK (informal)

almost
adverb very nearly
» *The number of children in each class has almost doubled in less than a decade.*
about, approximately, close to, nearly, not quite, practically

alone
adjective not with other people or things » *He was all alone in the middle of the hall.*
detached, isolated, separate, single

aloud
adverb out loud
» *Our father read aloud to us.*
audibly, out loud

also
adverb in addition
» *Carlos is also an excellent basketball player.*
as well, besides, furthermore, into the bargain, moreover, too

always
adverb all the time or forever
» *Zoe's always singing, she never stops!*
continually, every time, forever, invariably, perpetually

amaze
verb to surprise greatly
» *Noah amazed us with his knowledge of local history.*
astonish, astound, shock, stagger, stun, surprise,
dumbfound, flabbergast, stupefy

amazement
noun complete surprise
» *Much to my amazement, Yasmin arrived on time.*
astonishment, shock, surprise, wonder,
perplexity, stupefaction

*Kirsten surfed the most **amazing** wave.*

amazing
adjective very surprising or remarkable » *Kirsten surfed the most amazing wave.*
astonishing, astounding, staggering, startling, stunning, surprising

among 1
preposition surrounded by
» *The broken bike lay among piles of chains and pedals.*
amid, in the middle of, in the thick of, surrounded by

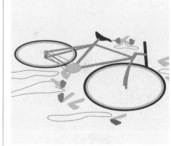

*The broken bike lay **among** piles of chains and pedals.*

among 2
preposition between more than two » *The donations will be divided among seven charities.*
to each of

amount
noun how much there is of something
» *My teachers assign a huge amount of homework every weekend.*
expanse, quantity, volume

*There was **ample** space in the tent for both children and the dog.*

A B C D E F G H I J K L M N O P Q R S T U V W X Y Z

ample
adjective of an amount: more than enough » *There was ample space in the tent for both children and the dog.*
abundant, enough, plenty of, sufficient

ancestor
noun a person from whom someone is descended » *Leon could trace his ancestors back 100 years.*
forebear, forefather, precursor, progenitor

anger ①
noun extreme annoyance » *She vented her anger at the umpire.*
fury, outrage, rage, wrath, furor, indignation, ire, pique, vexation

anger ②
verb to make someone angry » *The politician's remarks angered his critics.*
enrage, infuriate, outrage
antonym: **calm**

angry
adjective very annoyed
▶▶ SEE RIGHT

animal
noun a living creature » *Dogs and cats are the nation's favorite animals.*
beast, creature
related word: *prefix* **zoo-**

animosity
noun a feeling of strong dislike toward someone » *There is no animosity between the two players—they get along well.*
antagonism, antipathy, dislike, hatred, hostility, ill will, malice, resentment

announce
verb to make known something publicly » *He announced the winner of the competition live on the radio.*
advertise, make known, proclaim, reveal, tell, tweet, promulgate, propound

*He **announced** the winner of the competition live on the radio.*

announcement
noun a statement giving information about something » *There has been no formal announcement about the school trip.*
advertisement, broadcast, bulletin, declaration, report, statement

annoy
verb to irritate or displease someone » *Try making a note of the things that annoy you.*
aggravate, bother, displease, get on someone's nerves (informal), **hack off** (Britain; slang), **hassle** (informal), **irritate, plague, vex**

annoyance ①
noun a feeling of irritation » *Isaac made no secret of his annoyance at bad grammar.*
displeasure, irritation

annoyance ②
noun something that causes irritation » *Snoring can be more than an annoyance.*
bore, drag (informal), **nuisance, pain** (informal), **pain in the neck** (informal), **pest**

answer ①
verb to reply to someone » *I waited all day for him to answer my question.*
reply, respond, retort
antonym: **ask**

answer ②
noun a reply given to someone » *He walked away without waiting for an answer.*
reply, response, retort, rejoinder, riposte
antonym: **question**

anxiety
noun nervousness or worry » *It's natural to have some anxiety before starting at a new school.*
apprehension, concern, fear, misgiving, nervousness, unease, worry, perturbation, trepidation

anxious
adjective nervous or worried » *Nicole was very anxious before starting the exam.*
apprehensive, bothered, concerned, fearful, nervous, troubled, uneasy, worried

*Nicole was very **anxious** before starting the exam.*

apathetic
adjective not interested in anything » *He was apathetic about politics.*
cool, indifferent, passive, uninterested
antonym: **enthusiastic**

apologize
verb to say sorry for something » *I apologize for being late.*
ask forgiveness, beg someone's pardon, express regret, say sorry

*Lily **appealed** for people to sign her petition.*

appeal ①
verb to make an urgent request for something » *Lily appealed for people to sign her petition.*
beg, call upon, plead, request, entreat, implore, pray

appeal ②
verb to attract or interest » *The idea of getting a sports car appealed to him.*
attract, fascinate, interest, please

appeal ③
noun a formal request for something » *The speaker made an appeal for quiet.*
petition, plea, request, entreaty, supplication

appear ①
verb to become visible or present » *A woman appeared at the far end of the street.*
come into view, crop up (informal), **emerge, show up** (informal), **surface, turn up**
antonym: **disappear**

appear ②
verb to begin to exist » *Small white flowers appear in the spring.*
become available, be invented, come into being, come into existence, come out

appearance ①
noun the time when something begins to exist » *We were surprised but pleased at the new girl's appearance in our class.*
advent, arrival, coming, debut, emergence, introduction

*Sofia really cares about her **appearance**.*

appearance ②
noun the way that a person looks » *Sofia really cares about her appearance.*
bearing, image, look, looks, demeanor, mien

application
noun a computer program designed for a particular purpose » *This application runs on all tablets.*
app, software

appointment ①
noun an arrangement to meet someone » *Valeria has an appointment with the dentist.*
date, interview, meeting, rendezvous

appointment ②
noun the choosing of a person to do a job » *Roy was pleased with his appointment as the new class president.*
election, naming, nomination, selection

appointment ③
noun a job » *He applied for an appointment in Russia.*
assignment, job, place, position, post

appreciate ①
verb to value something highly » *Joe appreciates good food.*
admire, prize, rate highly, respect, treasure, value
antonym: **scorn**

appreciate ②
verb to understand a situation or problem » *I didn't appreciate the seriousness of it at the time.*
be aware of, perceive, realize, recognize, understand

angry
adjective very annoyed » *The **angry** bull charged across the field.*

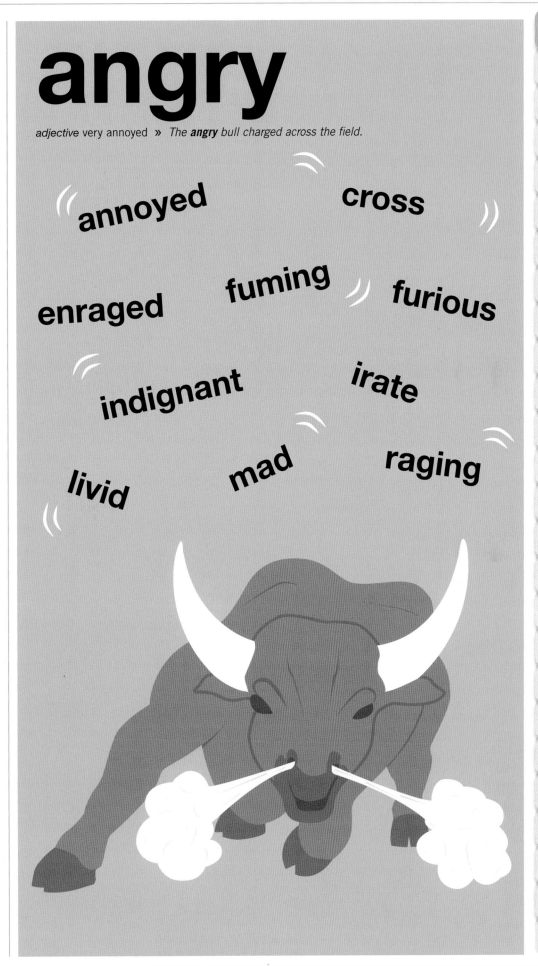

annoyed

cross

enraged

fuming

furious

indignant

irate

livid

mad

raging

a b c d e f g h i j k l m n o p q r s t u v w x y z

A B C D E F G H I J K L M N O P Q R S T U V W X Y Z

*Jeans are not **appropriate** clothes for a formal occasion.*

appropriate

adjective suitable or acceptable for a given situation
» *Jeans are not appropriate clothes for a formal occasion.*
apt, correct, fitting, proper, suitable, apposite, congruous, germane
antonym: **inappropriate**

approval [1]

noun agreement given to something » *The idea will require approval from teachers and parents.*
agreement, authorization, blessing, endorsement, permission, sanction, assent, imprimatur, mandate, ratification

approval [2]

noun liking and admiration of a person or thing
» *He wanted to gain his father's approval.*
admiration, esteem, favor, praise, respect
antonym: **disapproval**

approve [1]

verb to think something or someone is good
» *Not everyone approved of the choice of players.*
admire, favor, praise, respect, think highly of
antonym: **disapprove**

approve [2]

verb to agree formally to something » *They approved the plan for a new playground.*
authorize, consent to, endorse, permit, sanction
antonym: **veto**

approximate

adjective close but not exact
» *The approximate time the concert ends is 10pm.*
estimated, inexact, loose, rough
antonym: **exact**

ardent

adjective full of enthusiasm and passion » *Stefan was an ardent performer.*
avid, devoted, enthusiastic, fervent, intense, keen, passionate, zealous
antonym: **apathetic**

*Stefan was an **ardent** performer.*

area [1]

noun a particular part of a place » *Elena lived in an exclusive area of the city.*
district, locality, neighborhood, region, zone

area [2]

noun the size of a two-dimensional surface
» *The islands cover a total area of 241 square miles.*
expanse, extent, range, size

argue [1]

verb to disagree with someone in an angry way » *They argued over the cost of the taxi fare.*
bicker, disagree, fall out (informal), **feud, fight, quarrel, squabble, wrangle**

argue [2]

verb to try to prove
» *Lena argued that the dog could not have scratched the table.*
assert, claim, debate, maintain, reason, contend, plead, propose, submit

argument [1]

noun an angry disagreement
» *He got into an argument with one of the protesters.*
altercation, barney (Britain; informal), **brawl, clash, disagreement, dispute, feud, fight, row, squabble**

argument [2]

noun a set of reasons presented for something
» *There's a strong argument for going home now.*
case, grounds, logic, reasoning

arrange [1]

verb to make plans to do something » *Why don't you arrange to meet him later?*
fix up, organize, plan, schedule

arrange [2]

verb to set things out in a particular order
» *Lucy's sister arranged the books on the shelves.*
classify, group, order, organize, sort, array, systematize

*Lucy's sister **arranged** the books on the shelves.*

arrest [1]

verb to take someone into custody » *Police arrested five men.*
apprehend, capture, seize, take prisoner

arrest [2]

noun the act of arresting someone » *The police made two arrests.*
apprehension, capture, seizure

article [1]

noun a piece of writing in a newspaper or magazine
» *There's an article about the new park in today's paper.*
feature, item, piece, story

article [2]

noun a particular item
» *How many articles are on the table?*
item, object, thing

ashamed

adjective feeling embarrassed or guilty » *He was not ashamed of what he had done.*
embarrassed, guilty, humiliated, sheepish, sorry, chagrined, mortified
antonym: **proud**

ask [1]

verb to put a question to someone » *Erin asked me if I'd enjoyed my dinner.*
inquire, interrogate, query, question, quiz
antonym: **answer**

ask [2]

verb to make a request to someone » *We had to ask him to leave.*
appeal, beg, demand, implore, plead, seek, beseech, entreat

ask [3]

verb to invite someone
» *Everybody in the class had been asked to the party.*
bid (literary), **invite**

aspect

noun a feature of something
» *Exam scores are only one aspect of a school's success.*
consideration, element, factor, feature, part, point, side

assemble [1]

verb to fit the parts of something together
» *The children were assembling model planes.*
build, construct, erect, make, put together

*The tourists **assembled** in a line next to the bus.*

assemble ②
verb to gather together in a group » *The tourists assembled in a line next to the bus.*
collect, come together, congregate, convene, gather, mass

assistant
noun a person who helps someone » *The assistant took notes as his boss listed what meetings he needed.*
aide, ally, colleague, helper, right-hand man

associate ①
verb to connect one thing with another » *Dark clouds are associated with rain.*
connect, couple, identify, link

associate ②
verb to spend time with a person » *I began associating with different groups of people.*
hang out (informal), **mingle, mix, run around** (informal), **socialize, consort, fraternize**

associate ③
noun a person known through work » *After arriving late, she joined her business associates at the meeting.*
colleague, coworker, workmate

association ①
noun an organization » *Many schools have a parents' association.*
body, club, company, confederation, group, institution, league, society, syndicate, fraternity

association ②
noun a connection or involvement with a person or group » *Did you know about his association with the band?*
affiliation, attachment, bond, connection, relationship, tie, affinity, liaison

assume ①
verb to accept that something is true » *Lewis assumed that John knew what he was doing.*
believe, guess (informal), **imagine, suppose, think**

assume ②
verb to take responsibility for something » *I will assume the role of team leader.*
accept, shoulder, take on, undertake

astute
adjective very intelligent or perceptive » *Amy's an astute judge of character.*
alert, clever, keen, perceptive, quick, sharp, shrewd, smart, discerning

attach
verb to join or fasten things together » *The gadget can be attached to any surface.*
affix, connect, couple, fasten, join, link, tie
antonym: **separate**

attachment ①
noun a feeling of love and affection » *A mother and child form a close attachment.*
affection, bond, fondness, liking, love

attachment ②
noun a part that connects to something else » *The drill comes with a wide range of attachments.*
accessory, component, fitting, fixture, part, unit

attack ①
verb to use violence against someone or something
▼ SEE BELOW

attack
① *verb* to use violence against someone or something » *The king's army **attacked** the invaders.*

I really didn't want to be involved in this **raid**.

What if they decide to **invade** *our country?*

I've always wanted to **storm** *a castle.*

Your **assault** *will go down in history.*

Forward, men, and **set upon** *the cavalry.*

Charge!

a b c d e f g h i j k l m n o p q r s t u v w x y z

attack [2]
verb to criticize someone strongly » *She attacked the minister's views on education.*
blast, censure, criticize, put down (informal), **vilify** (formal)**, berate, dress down, lambaste, revile**

attack [3]
noun violent physical action against someone or something » *It was an unprovoked attack on the surprised man.*
assault, charge, invasion, offensive, onslaught, raid

attempt [1]
verb to try to do something » *They attempted to escape.*
endeavor, seek, strive, try, try your hand at

attempt [2]
noun an act of trying to do something » *It was Ryan's third attempt at the pole vault.*
bid, crack (informal), **go** (informal), **shot** (informal), **stab** (informal), **try**

*It was Ryan's third **attempt** at the pole vault.*

attitude
noun someone's way of thinking and behaving » *Having a positive attitude helps you achieve your dreams.*
outlook, perspective, point of view, position, stance

attract
verb to appeal to or interest » *The trial races have attracted many leading riders.*
appeal to, draw, entice, lure, pull (informal), **tempt**
antonym: **repel**

*The leading star is very **attractive**.*

attractive
adjective pleasant, especially to look at » *The leading star is very attractive.*
appealing, charming, fetching, handsome, lovely, pretty, comely, prepossessing, winsome
antonym: **unattractive**

attribute
noun a quality or feature » *Anna's main attribute is her unfailing generosity.*
characteristic, feature, property, quality, trait, idiosyncrasy, peculiarity

augment
verb to add something to something else » *Sally augmented her pocket money by dogsitting for the neighbors when they went out for the day.*
add to, boost, complement, increase, reinforce, supplement, top up

authentic
adjective real and genuine » *The cake was made from an authentic French recipe.*
bona fide, certifiable, genuine, legitimate, real, true
antonym: **fake**

automatic [1]
adjective operating mechanically by itself » *Modern trains have automatic doors.*
automated, mechanical, robot, self-propelled

automatic [2]
adjective without conscious thought » *Breathing is an automatic physical function.*
instinctive, involuntary, natural, reflex

automobile
noun a vehicle for carrying a few people » *After thinking about it, Ali decided to buy an expensive automobile.*
car, motor vehicle, vehicle

*After thinking about it, Ali decided to buy an expensive **automobile**.*

available
adjective ready for use » *There are three small apartments available for rent.*
accessible, at hand, at someone's disposal, free, handy, to hand
antonym: **unavailable**

average [1]
adjective standard or normal » *I get up at 7am on an average weekday, but tomorrow is a holiday, so I'll sleep longer.*
normal, regular, standard, typical, usual

average [2]:
on average
adverb for the most part » *Men are, on average, taller than women.*
as a rule, generally, normally, typically, usually

avoid [1]
verb to keep away from someone or something » *She thought he was trying to avoid her.*
dodge, elude, eschew (formal)**, evade, shun, sidestep, steer clear of**

avoid [2]
verb to make an effort not to do something » *Liam avoided going out by pretending to be sick.*
dodge, duck out of (informal), **fight shy of, refrain from, shirk, circumvent, give a wide berth to**

aware [1]: **aware of**
adjective conscious of something » *Ava was acutely aware of the noise of the city.*
acquainted with, conscious of, familiar with, mindful of
antonym: **unaware**

aware [2]
adjective knowing about something » *Keep me aware of any developments.*
informed, in the picture, knowledgeable, in the loop

awful
adjective very unpleasant or very bad » *The weather this morning is awful.*
appalling, dreadful, frightful, ghastly, horrendous, terrible, abysmal, deplorable

*The weather this morning is **awful**.*

Bb

babble
verb to talk in an excited way
» *Tim babbled on and on about how much fun he'd had at the party.*
chatter, drivel, gabble, gibberish, prattle

baby
noun a very young child
» *Jia enjoyed playing with her baby brother.*
babe, bambino, child, infant, kid, squirt, tot, tyke

*Jia enjoyed playing with her **baby** brother.*

back ①
noun the part that is behind the front » *Write a message on the back of a postcard.*
aft, end, rear, reverse
antonym: **front**

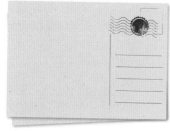

*Write a message on the **back** of a postcard.*

back ②
verb to support a person or organization
» *Mina's friends backed her campaign for school president.*
advocate, encourage, endorse, favor, promote, support, champion, second
antonym: **oppose**

background
noun where you come from; your class, education, training, or experience » *Marianne came from a rich background.*
culture, environment, history, upbringing

bad ①
adjective harmful, unpleasant, or upsetting » *I have bad news—our vacation is canceled.*
damaging, destructive, detrimental, distressing, disturbing, grim, harmful, painful, traumatic, unhealthy, unpleasant, unsettling, upsetting
antonym: **good**

bad ②
adjective of poor quality
» *The roads were bad and full of potholes.*
defective, deficient, faulty, imperfect, inadequate, inferior, pathetic, poor, sorry, unsatisfactory
antonym: **satisfactory**

bad ③
adjective evil in character
» *Superheroes always win over the bad guys.*
corrupt, criminal, depraved, evil, immoral, sinful, villainous, wicked, wrong
antonym: **good**

badly ①
adverb in an inferior way
» *This essay is badly written, with poor grammar.*
inadequately, ineptly, poorly, shoddily, unsatisfactorily
antonym: **well**

badly ②
adverb seriously
» *Ben was badly hurt in a fall.*
deeply, desperately, gravely, seriously
antonym: **slightly**

badly ③
adverb in a cruel manner
» *Jim would never treat his dog badly—he adores her.*
brutally, callously, cruelly, savagely, viciously
antonym: **well**

bait
noun something used to catch something » *Charles used worms as bait to catch fish.*
bribe, decoy, inducement, lure, temptation

balance ①
verb to make or remain steady
» *The gymnast balanced gracefully on one leg.*
level, stabilize, steady

*The gymnast **balanced** gracefully on one leg.*

balance ②
noun a stable relationship between things » *There must be a balance between study and play time.*
equilibrium, equity, equivalence, parity

*The dog loved playing with the **ball**.*

ball
noun a round object
» *The dog loved playing with the ball.*
drop, globe, pellet, sphere, egg, globule, orb, wad

ban ①
verb to disallow something
» *Adults are banned from taking part in the kids' race.*
bar, disqualify, exclude, forbid, outlaw, prohibit, banish, deter, disuade, suppress
antonym: **permit**

ban ②
noun a rule disallowing something » *There is a ban on chewing gum in school.*
disqualification, embargo, prohibition, suppression
antonym: **permit**

band ①
noun a group of musicians who play together
» *Luiz was a singer in a rock-and-roll band.*
group, orchestra, combo, ensemble

band ②
noun a group of people who share a common purpose
» *The protest was led by a band of angry students.*
bunch, company, crowd, gang, party, troupe

*The protest was led by a **band** of angry students.*

a b c d e f g h i j k l m n o p q r s t u v w x y z

A
B
C
D
E
F
G
H
I
J
K
L
M
N
O
P
Q
R
S
T
U
V
W
X
Y
Z

hammer
Mike **hammered** on the door to be let in.

knock
I **knocked** on the window, but they didn't hear me.

pound
We **pounded** on the walls.

hit
The ball **hit** the post.

thump
The children cheered and **thumped** on their desks.

beat
The group sat in a circle, **beating** small drums.

slam
I **slammed** down the phone.

bang

1 *verb* to hit or put something down hard, with a loud noise
» *Charlie* **banged** *the drums so loudly, my ears hurt.*

bang ①

verb to hit or put something down hard, with a loud noise
◀◀ **SEE LEFT**

bang ②

noun a sudden, short, loud noise » *The microwave exploded with a bang.*
blast, boom, crack, detonation, explosion, thump

bang ③

noun a hard or painful bump against something » *I got a nasty bang on the elbow.*
blow, clout (informal)**, knock, thump, whack**

banish ①

verb to exile someone » *Alison banished Doug from the house until he took off his muddy shoes.*
deport, eject, evict, exile, expel, transport

banish ②

verb to get rid of something or someone » *The kids finally banished their boredom with a game of hide and seek.*
discard, dismiss, dispel, eliminate, eradicate, remove

bank ①

noun the edge of a river or lake » *Ed fished on the river bank all afternoon.*
brink, edge, shore, side

*Ed fished on the river **bank** all afternoon.*

bank ②

noun a store of something » *Supplies are running low at the blood bank.*
fund, hoard, reserve, stock, store, reservoir, stockpile

bar ①

noun a piece of metal » *The prison cell had bars across the window.*
pole, rail, rod, shaft

bar ②

verb to stop someone » *Bryan's bodyguards barred the way as his fans rushed toward him.*
obstruct, prevent

*Bryan's bodyguards **barred** the way as his fans rushed toward him.*

bare ①

adjective not covered » *Stella wore shorts to the beach, and she burned her bare legs in the sun.*
exposed, uncovered
antonym: **covered**

bare ②

adjective with nothing on top or inside » *Lil forgot to buy groceries, so the pantry was bare.*
empty, open, spartan, vacant

barely

adverb only just » *It's too early in the morning for Lisa to join us for a walk— she'll be barely awake.*
almost, hardly, just, scarcely

*The Sahara is a **barren** desert.*

barren

adjective with nothing growing on it » *The Sahara is a barren desert.*
arid, desert, desolate, dry, empty, waste, unfruitful, unproductive
antonym: **fertile**

barrier ①

noun something preventing entry » *There were barriers to prevent the audience from getting onto the stage.*
barricade, fence, obstruction, wall, fortification, obstacle

barrier ②

noun something that prevents progress » *A lack of funds is the biggest barrier preventing me from traveling to South Africa in the summer.*
handicap, hindrance, hurdle, obstacle

barter

verb to exchange goods or services without money » *I bartered my comic book for Wayne's baseball.*
bargain, exchange, swap, trade, trade off

base ①

noun the lowest part of something » *They played at the base of the cliffs.*
bed, bottom, foot, foundation, pedestal, stand
antonym: **top**

base ②

noun the place you work from » *He lived at the military base.*
camp, center, headquarters, post, station

base ③

verb to use as a foundation » *The movie is based on a true story.*
build, derive, found, ground, hinge

basic

adjective most necessary » *A basic first aid kit usually includes bandages, gauze, and antiseptic.*
elementary, essential, fundamental, key, necessary, vital, central, indispensable, primary

basis

noun the main principle of something » *An old fairy tale forms the basis of the new fantasy movie.*
core, fundamental, heart, premise, principle

bay ①

noun a curve, or inlet, on the coastline of a lake or sea » *Monterey Bay, famous for its sea otters and whales, is on the coast in California.*
cove, gulf, inlet, sound

bay ②

verb to make a howling noise » *The wolf bayed in the moonlight.*
bark, cry, howl, yelp

*The wolf **bayed** in the moonlight.*

a
b
c
d
e
f
g
h
i
j
k
l
m
n
o
p
q
r
s
t
u
v
w
x
y
z

A B C D E F G H I J K L M N O P Q R S T U V W X Y Z

beach
noun an area by the sea
▼ SEE BELOW

bear 1
verb to carry something
» *The lake's ice wasn't thick enough to bear their weight, and it began to crack.*
carry, convey, shoulder, support, take

bear 2
verb to have or show something
» *The room bore the signs of a lively party.*
exhibit, harbor, have

*The room **bore** the signs of a lively party.*

bear 3
verb to accept something
» *Jim can't bear the sound of forks scraping on a plate.*
abide, endure, stomach, suffer, tolerate

beat 1
verb to hit someone or something hard
» *Sheila beat the drum.*
batter, buffet, hit, pound, strike, thrash

beat 2
verb to defeat
» *Ethan is a slow runner and was easily beaten in the race.*
defeat, outdo, outstrip, overcome, overwhelm, vanquish, conquer, master, surpass

beat 3
noun a rhythm » *Rock music often has a thumping beat.*
cadence, meter, rhythm, stress, time

beautiful
adjective attractive or pleasing
» *A beautiful picture can brighten up a room.*
attractive, delightful, fine, gorgeous, lovely, pleasing, exquisite, fair
antonym: **ugly**

*The coast is an area of outstanding natural **beauty**.*

beauty 1
noun the quality of being beautiful » *The coast is an area of outstanding natural beauty.*
attractiveness, charm, elegance, loveliness
antonym: **ugliness**

beauty 2
noun a good-looking person
» *She was a dark-eyed beauty.*
babe, doll, knockout, looker, stunner (informal)

beauty 3
noun an attractive feature
» *The beauty of the plan is its simplicity.*
advantage, asset, attraction, benefit

because
conjunction for the reason that
» *I didn't go to the party because I was tired.*
as, since, in that, on account of, owing to

before
adverb at a previous time
» *Have you ever been to Mexico before?*
earlier, formerly, in advance, previously, sooner
antonym: **after**
related words: *prefixes* **ante-, fore-, pre-**

beg
verb to ask anxiously for something
» *The girl begged her dad for some more ice cream.*
appeal to, implore, petition, plead, entreat, request

*The girl **begged** her dad for some more ice cream.*

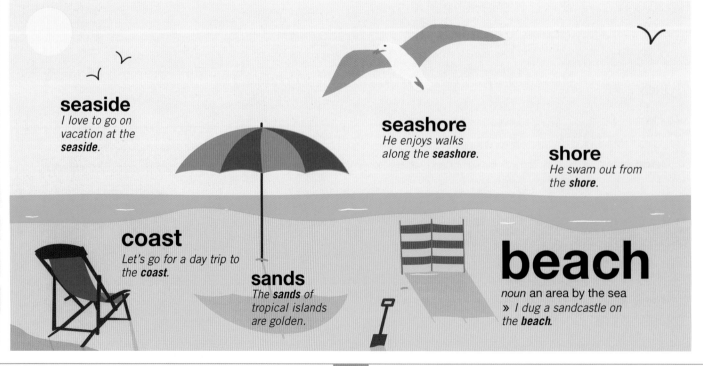

seaside
*I love to go on vacation at the **seaside**.*

seashore
*He enjoys walks along the **seashore**.*

shore
*He swam out from the **shore**.*

coast
*Let's go for a day trip to the **coast**.*

sands
*The **sands** of tropical islands are golden.*

beach
noun an area by the sea
» *I dug a sandcastle on the **beach**.*

begin

verb to start or cause to start
» *When did the show begin?*
commence (formal), **initiate, originate, set about, start,** inaugurate, instigate, launch
antonym: **end**

beginner

noun someone learning to do something
» *Ali joined the "Spanish for beginners" class.*
apprentice, learner, novice, starter, trainee
antonym: **expert**

beginning

noun where something starts
» *The audience quieted down at the beginning of the play.*
birth, commencement (formal), **opening, origin, outset, start,** inauguration, initiation, onset
antonym: **end**

behave

verb to act in a certain way
» *If you don't behave politely, we'll have to leave the party.*
act, function, operate, work

belief 1

noun the certainty something is true » *Miriam's belief that it was going to be a gorgeous summer turned out to be right.*
confidence, conviction, judgment, opinion, trust, view

belief 2

noun a principle of a religion or system » *His religion gave him a strong set of beliefs.*
creed, doctrine, dogma, faith, ideology, principle, tenet

believable

adjective possible or likely to be the case » *The book is full of believable characters that I can relate to.*
credible, imaginable, likely, plausible, possible, probable
antonym: **unbelievable**

believe

verb to accept something is true » *Don't believe everything you hear on TV news.*
accept, assume, presume, swallow (informal), **trust**
antonym: **doubt**

belittle

verb to make someone or something seem or feel less important » *Ted always belittles me in front of my friends—it really shakes my confidence.*
deride, detract from, downgrade, scorn, undervalue, disparage, minimize
antonym: **praise**

beloved

adjective dearly loved
» *Anthony proposed to his beloved girlfriend.*
adored, cherished, darling, dearest, precious
antonym: **despised**

*Anthony proposed to his **beloved** girlfriend.*

below

preposition or *adverb* lower down » *The basement is below the first floor.*
beneath, down, lower, under, underneath
antonym: **above**

bend 1

verb to make or become curved » *Bend the bar into a horseshoe.*
buckle, curve, turn, twist, warp

bend 2

verb to curve the body downward » *I bent over and kissed her cheek.*
arch, bow, crouch, incline, lean, stoop

bend 3

noun a curve in something
» *Watch out for the sharp bend in the road.*
arc, corner, curve, loop, turn, angle, arch, twist

beneficial

adjective giving some benefit
» *Eating fruit is beneficial to your health.*
advantageous, good for you, healthy, helpful, useful, wholesome

benefit 1

noun an advantage » *Meeting interesting people is one of the benefits of joining a club.*
advantage, asset, boon, gain, good, help, profit, use
antonym: **disadvantage**

benefit 2

verb to help in something
» *The experience will benefit you when you take the test.*
aid, assist, enhance, further, help, profit
antonym: **harm**

benevolent

adjective kind and helpful
» *Arthur was a benevolent king who cared about his people.*
benign, charitable, compassionate, humane, kind, altruistic, beneficent, philanthropic

beside

preposition next to » *We sat beside each other watching TV.*
adjacent to, alongside, close to, near, next to

*We sat **beside** each other watching TV.*

best 1

adjective of the highest standard » *That was the best movie I have seen in a long time.*
finest, first-rate, foremost, greatest, leading, outstanding, preeminent, principal, superlative, supreme, top
antonym: **worst**

best 2

adjective most desirable
» *Offering to pay for the broken window was the best thing to do.*
correct, most fitting, right
antonym: **worst**

best 3

noun the preferred thing
» *Of all my presents, this looks like the best—can I open it first?*
cream, elite, finest, pick
antonym: **worst**

*Of all my presents, this looks like the **best**—can I open it first?*

betray 1

verb to break someone's trust
» *I was betrayed by someone I thought was a friend.*
break your promise, double-cross (informal), **inform on**

betray 2

verb to show feelings
» *Jeremy's voice betrayed little emotion over the phone.*
expose, manifest, reveal, show

a b c d e f g h i j k l m n o p q r s t u v w x y z

A
B
C
D
E
F
G
H
I
J
K
L
M
N
O
P
Q
R
S
T
U
V
W
X
Y
Z

large great significant enormous huge immense

big

1 *adjective* of a large size
» *The diplodocus was a **big** dinosaur...*

better 1
adjective of more worth than another » *The weather today was better than yesterday.*
finer, grander, greater, higher-quality, nicer, preferable, superior, surpassing, worthier
antonym: **inferior**

better 2
adjective well after being sick
» *I hope you feel better soon.*
cured, fitter, fully recovered, healthier, improving, on the mend (informal)**, recovering, stonger, well**
antonym: **worse**

beware
verb to be cautious » *The sign warned us to beware of the dog.*
be careful, be cautious, be wary, guard against, look out, watch out

*The sign warned us to **beware** of the dog.*

bias
noun prejudice for or against a person, group, or idea
» *The boss had a bias for hiring staff who spoke Spanish.*
bigotry, favoritism, one-sidedness, prejudice

biased
adjective showing prejudice
» *The basketball team were biased against short players.*
one-sided, partial, prejudiced, slanted, weighted
antonym: **neutral**

big 1
adjective of a large size
▲ SEE ABOVE

big 2
adjective someone of great importance » *My cousin met some of the biggest Hollywood stars at the film festival.*
eminent, important, influential, leading, major, powerful, principal, prominent, significant
antonym: **unimportant**

big 3
adjective an important issue or problem » *Moving to a new city was a big decision.*
critical, grave, momentous, serious, urgent, weighty
antonym: **minor**

bill
noun a statement of how much is owed » *The party of 20 ran up a huge bill in the restaurant.*
account, charges, invoice, statement

bit
noun a small amount
» *A bit of his pie fell on the floor while Stan was eating it.*
crumb, fragment, grain, part, piece, scrap, iota, jot, speck

bite
verb to cut into something with your teeth
» *Rachel's cat bit me when I tried to stroke it.*
chew, gnaw, nibble, nip

*Matt and Joe had a **bitter** argument over the accident.*

bitter 1
adjective angry and resentful
» *Matt and Joe had a bitter argument over the accident.*
acrimonious, begrudging, embittered, rancorous, resentful, sour

bitter 2
adjective tasting or smelling sharp » *Something in the meal had a bitter taste.*
acid, acrid, astringent, sharp, sour, tart
antonym: **sweet**

gigantic massive colossal **vast**

antonym:
little
*… But compsognathus was a **little** beast!*

bizarre
adjective very strange or eccentric » *Chang has some bizarre ideas about what to do on a vacation.*
curious, eccentric, extraordinary, odd, outlandish, peculiar, queer, strange, weird
antonym: **ordinary**

black
noun or adjective
Shades of black:
coal-black, ebony, inky, jet, jet-black, pitch-black, raven, sable, sooty

blame ①
verb to believe someone caused something » *Don't blame me for losing the house key.*
accuse, charge, hold responsible

blame ②
noun the responsibility for something bad » *I'm not going to take the blame for forgetting the tickets!*
accountability, fault, guilt, liability, rap (slang), **responsibility, culpability, incrimination**

blank ①
adjective with nothing on it » *Use a blank sheet of paper.*
bare, clean, clear, empty, plain, unmarked

blank ②
adjective showing no feeling » *John just looked blank upon hearing the news.*
deadpan, dull, empty, expressionless, impassive, vacant

blend ①
verb to mix things so as to form a single item or substance » *Jill used a mixer to blend the ingredients.*
combine, merge, mix
antonym: **separate**

*Jill used a mixer to **blend** the ingredients.*

blend ②
verb to combine in a pleasing way » *The colors blend in with the rest of the decor.*
complement, coordinate, go well, harmonize, match, suit

blend ③
noun a mixture or combination of things » *The menu was a blend of French and Chinese flavors.*
alloy, amalgamation, combination, compound, fusion, mix, mixture

bless
verb to hope for care, protection, and good will » *The mayor blessed the new ship by breaking a bottle of champagne on its bow.*
anoint, consecrate, dedicate, hallow
antonym: **curse**

blessing ①
noun something good » *Good health is a blessing.*
benefit, boon, gift, godsend, help
antonym: **disadvantage**

blessing ②
noun approval or permission to do something » *Fiona got married with her parents' blessing.*
approval, backing, consent, leave, permission, support, approbation, sanction
antonym: **disapproval**

blob
noun a small amount of a thick or sticky substance » *The artist squeezed out a blob of pink paint.*
bead, dab, drop, droplet

*The artist squeezed out a **blob** of pink paint.*

block ①
noun a large piece » *A block of wood fell near his foot.*
bar, brick, chunk, lump, piece

a b c d e f g h i j k l m n o p q r s t u v w x y z

A B **B** C D E F G H I J K L M N O P Q R S T U V W X Y Z

block 2
verb to close by putting something across
» *Rubble blocked the river.*
choke, clog, obstruct, plug
antonym: **unblock**

block 3
verb to prevent something happening » *The neighbors blocked his plan to build a high fence around his yard.*
bar, check, halt, obstruct, stop, thwart

blockage
noun a thing that clogs something » *There was a blockage in the pipe.*
block, obstruction, stoppage

blog
noun a journal written on the internet » *Have you seen Mandy's new fashion blog?*
microblog, vlog, weblog

blow 1
verb to move or cause to move in the wind » *The wind blew Gary's papers away.*
buffet, drive, flutter, sweep, waft, whirl

blow 2
noun a hit from something » *Danny gave the punchbag a mighty blow.*
bang, clout (informal)**, knock, smack, thump, whack**

*Danny gave the punchbag a mighty **blow**.*

blow 3
noun something disappointing or upsetting » *Losing the game was a terrible blow.*
bombshell, disappointment, misfortune, setback, shock, upset, calamity, catastrophe, jolt

blue
noun or *adjective*
Shades of blue:
aqua, aquamarine, azure, baby blue, cerulean, cobalt, cyan, duck-egg, electric blue, gentian, indigo, lapis lazuli, midnight blue, navy, Nile blue, peacock blue, periwinkle, petrol blue, powder blue, royal blue, sapphire, sky blue, teal, turquoise, ultramarine

blunt 1
adjective having rounded edges » *Blunt scissors can't cut through cardboard.*
dull, rounded, unsharpened
antonym: **sharp**

blunt 2
adjective saying what you think » *Steve's speech was blunt and to the point.*
bluff, brusque, forthright, frank, outspoken, straightforward, explicit, tactless, trenchant
antonym: **tactful**

blush 1
verb to go red in the face » *Fatima blushed when her name was called out to receive an award.*
color, go crimson, flush, go red, turn red, turn scarlet

boar
noun a wild pig » *The boars in the nearby woods can be quite aggressive.*
swine, porker, warthog

boast
verb to talk proudly » *Carol boasted about her expensive costume.*
blow, bluster, brag, crow, flaunt

boastful
adjective tending to brag about things » *The boastful liar told us he was a millionaire.*
bragging, cocky, conceited, crowing, egotistical, swaggering
antonym: **modest**

*Exercise is good for your **body** and mind.*

body 1
noun all your physical parts » *Exercise is good for your body and mind.*
build, figure, form, frame, physique, shape
related words: *adjectives*
corporal, physical

body 2
noun a dead body » *The body of the former president lay in state.*
carcass, corpse, dead body, remains

body 3
noun an organized group of people » *Local bodies worked together to put on a successful summer fair.*
association, band, company, confederation, organization, society, bloc, collection, corporation

boil 1
verb to bubble » *The water is boiling in the pan.*
bubble, fizz, foam, froth, effervesce, seethe

boil 2
noun a swelling on the skin » *Ted had a boil on his neck.*
blister, swelling, papule, pimple, tumor, pustule

bold 1
adjective confident and not shy » *It was a bold move to invite the entire school to her party.*
brash, brazen, confident, daring, forward, impudent, barefaced,
antonym: **shy**

bold 2
adjective unafraid of risk or danger » *The crew made a bold attempt at rescuing the boat.*
adventurous, brave, courageous, daring, fearless, intrepid, audacious, heroic, valiant
antonym: **cowardly**

bold 3
adjective clear and noticeable » *Emily and Kathy's outfits were a riot of bold colors.*
bright, flashy, loud, striking, strong, vivid, conspicuous, prominent, pronounced
antonym: **dull**

*Emily and Kathy's outfits were a riot of **bold** colors.*

bolt
verb to escape or run away » *The horse bolted from the stable after Claude left the door open.*
dash, escape, flee, fly, run away, run off, rush

bomb 1
noun an explosive device » *Luckily, the bomb failed to detonate, so no one was hurt.*
device, explosive, missile, rocket, shell, torpedo, grenade, mine, projectile

bomb 2
verb to attack with bombs » *The old factory was bombed during the war.*
attack, blow up, bombard, destroy, shell, torpedo

bond 1
noun a close relationship » *There is a special bond between parent and child.*
attachment, connection, link, relation, tie, union, affiliation, affinity

bond [2]

noun a pledge or promise made between people » *Marriage is a solemn bond between two people who love one other.*
agreement, contract, obligation, pledge, promise, word, compact, covenant, guarantee

bond [3]

verb to attach separate things » *The strips of wood are bonded together to form a stronger, solid block.*
bind, fasten, fuse, glue, paste

book [1]

noun a number of written pages in a cover » *I'm reading a great book at the moment.*
eBook, publication, textbook, volume, work
▼ SEE BELOW

book [2]

verb to arrange to have or use » *The theater tickets are booked for Tuesday evening.*
charter, engage, organize, reserve, schedule

border [1]

noun a dividing line between things or places » *There were long lines of traffic waiting to cross the border between the two countries.*
borderline, boundary, frontier, line

border [2]

noun an edge of something » *Draw a border around your picture.*
bounds, edge, limits, margin, rim

border [3]

verb to form an edge » *Tall trees bordered the fields.*
edge, fringe, hem, rim, trim

bored

adjective impatient and not interested in something » *I am bored with this subject.*
fed up, tired, uninterested, wearied
antonym: **interested**

*I am **bored** with this subject.*

boredom

noun a lack of interest » *Boredom can set in quickly on long road trips.*
apathy, dullness, flatness, monotony, tedium, weariness
antonym: **interest**

boring

adjective dull and uninteresting » *Garth couldn't wait for the boring movie to end.*
dull, flat, humdrum, monotonous, tedious, tiresome, insipid, repetitious, stale
antonym: **interesting**

boss

noun a person in charge of employees » *The boss had to make some difficult decisions.*
chief, director, employer, head, leader, manager

bossy

adjective telling people what to do » *Sophia is quite a bossy little girl.*
arrogant, authoritarian, dictatorial, domineering, imperious, overbearing

botch

verb to do something badly » *Dad botched decorating the cake so we had to get one from the bakery.*
bungle, foul up, mess up

bother [1]

verb to annoy or intrude on someone » *Stop bothering your mother when she's busy working!*
annoy, concern, disturb, get on someone's nerves (informal), **trouble, worry,** harass, inconvenience

bother [2]

noun trouble and difficulty » *Getting dressed at the gym after exercising is such a bother.*
annoyance, difficulty, inconvenience, irritation, trouble, worry, nuisance, strain

bottom [1]

noun the lowest part of something » *The dog sat at the bottom of the stairs.*
base, bed, depths, floor, foot
antonym: **top**

*The dog sat at the **bottom** of the stairs.*

bottom [2]

adjective in the lowest place or position » *I keep my socks in the bottom drawer.*
base, basement, ground, lowest
antonym: **highest**

bounce [1]

verb to spring back » *The ball bounced against the wall.*
bump, ricochet, rebound, recoil

book

[1] types of books

anthology · atlas · autobiography · biography · dictionary · directory · encyclopedia · gazeteer · glossary · guidebook · manual · novel · phrasebook · thesaurus

a b c d e f g h i j k l m n o p q r s t u v w x y z

A B C D E F G H I J K L M N O P Q R S T U V W X Y Z

*Sue **bounced** across the field.*

bounce ②
verb to move up and down
» *Sue bounced across the field.*
bob, bound, jump

box
noun a container with a firm base and sides
» *Sara's things were packed in boxes, ready to move.*
carton, case, chest, container, trunk

boy
noun a male child » *I knew Adam when he was a boy.*
fellow, kid, schoolboy, youngster, youth

boycott
verb to refuse to do or buy something » *They boycotted the company due to its policies.*
blacklist, embargo, exclude, reject, spurn, proscribe, refrain from

brag
verb to boast about something » *People who brag about their achievements are really annoying.*
boast, crow, swagger, prepare, prime

braggart ①
noun a person who boasts » *David was a braggart, telling everyone about his amazing new sports car.*
bigmouth (slang), blowhard, boaster, bragger, self-promoter, show-off

brave ①
adjective willing to do dangerous things » *Rescuing the girl from the water was a brave act.*
bold, courageous, fearless, heroic, plucky, valiant, daring, intrepid, valorous
antonym: **cowardly**

brave ②
verb to face something without fear » *Fans braved the rain to hear the star sing.*
face, stand up to

bravery
noun the quality of being courageous » *The knight was rewarded for his bravery.*
boldness, courage, daring, fortitude, heroism, valor, fearlessness, gallantry, mettle
antonym: **cowardice**

breach ①
noun a breaking of a law or agreement » *Coming into work late is a breach of contract.*
infringement, offense, trespass, violation, contravention, transgression

breach ②
noun a gap in something » *The dog stuck his head through a breach in the fence.*
crack, gap, hole, opening, rift, split, chasm, fissure, rupture

*The dog stuck his head through a **breach** in the fence.*

break ①
verb to separate into pieces
▶▶ **SEE RIGHT**

break ②
verb to fail to keep a rule or promise » *Sal broke his promise to attend the party.*
breach, contravene, infringe, violate

break ③
noun a short period of rest or change » *I took a five-minute break from writing.*
interlude, interval, pause, recess, respite, rest

breed ①
noun a type of animal » *The farm specialized in rare breeds of cattle.*
kind, species, stock, strain, type, variety

breed ②
verb to reproduce and take care of » *Daniel breeds dogs for the police.*
cultivate, develop, keep, nurture, raise, rear

breed ③
verb to produce offspring » *Chickens can breed throughout the year.*
multiply, produce, propagate, reproduce, engender, procreate

*Chickens can **breed** throughout the year.*

brief ①
adjective lasting for a short time » *Ethan made a brief appearance on television*
fleeting, momentary, quick, short, swift, ephemeral, temporary, transitory
antonym: **long**

brief ②
verb to give necessary information » *The teacher briefed the class on the project.*
advise, fill in (informal), inform, instruct, prepare, prime

bright ①
adjective strong and startling » *Lighthouses emit a bright light that is visible from a distance.*
brilliant, dazzling, glowing, luminous, radiant, vivid, blazing, illuminated, resplendent
antonym: **dull**

*Lighthouses emit a **bright** light that is visible from a distance.*

bright ②
adjective intelligent and alert » *You are one of my brightest students—you always get good grades.*
brainy (informal), brilliant, clever, ingenious, intelligent, smart, acute, astute, sharp
antonym: **dim**

bright ③
adjective cheerful and lively » *Lily always has a bright smile on her face.*
cheerful, happy, jolly, light-hearted, lively, merry

brilliant ①
adjective very bright » *The diamond reflected a brilliant light.*
bright, dazzling, gleaming, glowing, luminous, radiant, sparkling, vivid
antonym: **dull**

break

[1] *verb* to separate into pieces
» He **broke** the ice with a hammer

crack
The wall **cracked** from top to bottom.

disintegrate
*Tissue paper **disintegrates** in water.*

crumble
Crumble the stock cube into the water.

demolish
The derelict house needed **demolishing**.

fragment
The picture **fragmented** into tiny pieces.

fracture
She **fractured** her arm.

shatter
The dropped plate **shattered**.

splinter
The wood **splintered** as he cut it.

smash
The ball **smashed** the window.

snap
The pencil **snapped** in half.

split
Split the apple to share it.

wreck
The iceberg **wrecked** the ship's hull.

a b c d e f g h i j k l m n o p q r s t u v w x y z

brilliant ②

adjective very intelligent
» *Ed is a brilliant student, and grasps complex ideas easily.*
acute, brainy (informal), **bright, clever, intelligent, perceptive, sharp, smart**
antonym: **stupid**

brilliant ③

adjective wonderful or superb
» *It's a brilliant movie.*
first-class, great, magnificent, marvelous, outstanding, superb, tremendous, wonderful
antonym: **terrible**

bring ①

verb to take somewhere
» *Can you please bring the laundry downstairs?*
bear, carry, convey, lead, take, transport

*Can you please **bring** the laundry downstairs?*

bring ②

verb to cause to happen
» *The new factory will bring more jobs to the city.*
cause, create, inflict, produce, result in, wreak, effect, occasion

bring about

verb to cause something to happen » *It was Donald's arrogance that brought about his downfall.*
cause, create, generate, make happen, produce, provoke

broad ①

adjective large, especially from side to side » *The bodybuilder had broad shoulders.*
expansive, extensive, large, thick, vast, wide, ample, spacious
antonym: **narrow**

broad ②

adjective including or affecting many different things or people
» *We discussed a broad range of issues.*
comprehensive, extensive, general, sweeping, universal, wide, wide-ranging

broad ③

adjective general rather than detailed » *The documents provided a broad outline of the plan.*
approximate, general, nonspecific, rough, sweeping, vague

broadcast ①

noun a program on radio or television » *The news broadcast starts at 6pm.*
podcast, program, show, transmission, webcast

broadcast ②

verb to send out so that it can be seen or heard » *You can hear the concert broadcast live on the radio.*
air, show, stream, transmit

broadcast ③

verb to make known publicly
» *You don't need to broadcast your feelings to the entire world.*
advertise, announce, blare, make public, proclaim, tweet

broken ①

adjective in pieces
» *Jo called the police when she saw the broken window.*
burst, demolished, fractured, fragmented, shattered, smashed

*Jo called the police when she saw the **broken** window.*

broken ②

adjective not kept
» *Frank had heard so many broken promises, he no longer believed what Sally said.*
infringed, violated, disobeyed, transgressed

brown

noun or *adjective*
Shades of brown:
auburn, bay, beige, bronze, brunette, buff, burnt sienna, burnt umber, café au lait, camel, chestnut, chocolate, cinnamon, coffee, dun, fawn, ginger, hazel, khaki, mahogany, mocha, oatmeal, ocher, putty, russet, rust, sandy, sepia, tan, taupe, tawny, terracotta, umber

build ①

verb to make something
» *Simon used brick and mortar to build a new garden wall.*
assemble, construct, erect, fabricate, form, make
antonym: **dismantle**

*Simon used brick and mortar to **build** a new garden wall.*

build ②

verb to develop gradually
» *I want to build a relationship with the new neighbors.*
develop, extend, increase, intensify, strengthen, augment, enlarge, escalate

build ③

noun the size of a person's body
» *Pedro is of medium build.*
body, figure, form, frame, physique, shape

building

noun a structure with walls
» *The office building had 14 floors.*
edifice, structure

bulge ①

verb to swell out » *The frog's vocal sac bulges as it sings to attract a mate.*
expand, protrude, stick out, swell

*The frog's vocal sac **bulges** as it sings to attract a mate.*

bulge ②

noun a lump in something
» *My wallet made a bulge in my pocket.*
bump, hump, lump, protrusion, swelling

bully ①

noun someone who deliberately frightens or hurts others
» *No one likes the class bully.*
abuser, hood, intimidator, oppressor, persecutor, roughneck, taunter, teaser, thug

bully ②

verb to frighten or hurt someone deliberately and repeatedly » *I wasn't going to let him bully me anymore.*
abuse, harass, intimidate, oppress, persecute, pick on, tease, torment

bully ③

verb to make someone do something by using force
» *Sarah used to bully me into doing her homework.*
bulldoze, force, intimidate, pressurize, push, strong-arm, coerce, terrorize

bump 1

verb to hit something » *Ted bumped his elbow on the wall.*
bang, collide, hit, jolt, knock, strike

bump 2

noun a dull noise
» *Layla heard a bump upstairs.*
bang, knock, thud, thump

bump 3

noun a raised part of something » *Watch out for the bump in the road.*
bulge, hump, knob, lump, swelling, contusion, node, protuberance

bunch 1

noun a group of people
» *The volunteers were a great bunch of people.*
band, clique, crowd, gaggle, gang, group

bunch 2

noun several cut flowers held together » *Wyatt had left a bunch of flowers in her hotel room.*
bouquet, posy, spray

*Wyatt had left a **bunch** of flowers in her hotel room.*

bunch 3

noun a group of things
» *George took out a bunch of keys and found the right one for the lock.*
batch, bundle, cluster, heap, load, pile, set

burden 1

noun a load that is carried
» *My bags of groceries turned out to be a real burden.*
load, weight

burden 2

noun something that worries you » *Becky had the added burden of taking care of a sick pet.*
anxiety, care, strain, stress, trouble, worry, affliction, millstone, trial
related word:
adjective **onerous**

bureaucracy

noun complex rules and procedures » *Is there too much bureaucracy in government?*
administration, officialdom, red tape, regulations

burn 1

verb to be on fire » *A fire burned in the fireplace.*
be ablaze, be on fire, blaze, flame, flare, flicker

*A fire **burned** in the fireplace.*

burn 2

verb to destroy with fire » *The rioters burned the house down.*
char, incinerate, scorch, singe

burst 1

verb to split apart » *Bella blew too much air into the balloon and it burst.*
break, crack, explode, puncture, rupture, split

burst 2

verb to happen or appear suddenly » *Marco burst into the room with important news.*
barge, break, erupt, rush

burst 3

noun a short period of something » *After a burst of energy, the dog fell asleep.*
fit, outbreak, rush, spate, surge, torrent

business 1

noun the buying and selling of goods or services » *Leah made a career in business.*
commerce, dealings, industry, trade, trading, transaction

business 2

noun an organization selling goods or services
» *Monica wanted to work for the family business.*
company, corporation, enterprise, establishment, firm, organization, conglomerate, venture

business 3

noun any event or situation
» *This business has upset me.*
affair, issue, matter, problem, question, subject

bustle 1

verb to move hurriedly
» *My mother bustled around the room putting things in place.*
dash, fuss, hurry, rush, scurry, scuttle

bustle 2

noun busy and noisy activity
» *The city is full of the bustle of modern life.*
activity, commotion, excitement, flurry, fuss, hurry
antonym: **peace**

*The city is full of the **bustle** of modern life.*

busy 1

adjective doing something
» *I can't go out tonight, I'm busy.*
active, employed, engaged, engrossed, occupied, working
antonym: **idle**

busy 2

adjective full of activity
» *The station was busy with commuters.*
active, full, hectic, lively, restless

*The station was **busy** with commuters.*

busy 3

verb to occupy or keep busy
» *Jamie busied himself in the kitchen with a new recipe.*
absorb, employ, engage, immerse, occupy

but 1

conjunction although
» *Heat the water until it is very hot, but not boiling.*
although, though, while, yet

but 2

preposition with the exception of » *I packed everything but my hairdryer for my vacation.*
except, except for, other than, save

buy

verb to obtain with money
» *I'd like to buy that bag.*
acquire, invest in, obtain, pay for, procure, purchase
antonym: **sell**

a
b
c
d
e
f
g
h
i
j
k
l
m
n
o
p
q
r
s
t
u
v
w
x
y
z

Cc

calculate

verb to work out a number or amount » *Cathy wanted to calculate the cost of the trip.*
add up, average, count, determine, tally, work out

*Cathy wanted to **calculate** the cost of the trip.*

calculated

adjective deliberately planned » *Although it was winter, Anthony took a calculated risk and took the road through the mountains.*
aimed, designed, intended, planned
antonym: **unplanned**

call 1

verb to give a name » *He was called Jeff.*
baptize, christen, designate, dub, name

call 2

verb to phone » *Ruby called me at home.*
contact, phone, ring, telephone

call 3

verb to say loudly » *I heard someone calling my name.*
announce, cry, cry out, shout, yell

call 4

noun an instance of someone shouting out » *There was a call for volunteers.*
cry, shout, yell

callous

adjective not concerned about other people » *He was mean and had a callous disregard for other people.*
cold, heartless, indifferent, insensitive, hard-bitten, hardhearted, unsympathetic
antonym: **caring**

calm 1

adjective not worried or excited » *Mia found that practicing yoga helped her to keep calm.*
collected, composed, cool, impassive, relaxed, imperturbable, unemotional, unruffled
antonym: **worried**

*Mia found that practicing yoga helped her to keep **calm**.*

calm 2

adjective still because there is no wind » *Tuesday was a fine, clear, and calm day.*
balmy, mild, still, tranquil
antonym: **rough**

calm 3

noun the state of being peaceful » *In the calm of the night, the bats emerged from the cave.*
calmness, peace, peacefulness, quiet, serenity, stillness

calm 4

verb to make less upset or excited » *He tried to calm the baby when it cried.*
quieten, relax, soothe, mollify, placate

campaign

noun actions planned to get a certain result » *She went on a campaign, seeking votes to be elected president.*
crusade, movement, operation, push

*She went on a **campaign**, seeking votes to be elected president.*

cancel 1

verb to stop something from happening » *We're going to have to cancel our picnic since it's raining.*
abandon, call off

cancel 2

verb to stop something from being valid » *Peter needed to cancel his lost credit card.*
annul, quash, repeal, revoke, abrogate, countermand, rescind

candid

adjective honest and frank » *She gave a candid interview and revealed many secrets.*
blunt, frank, honest, open, straightforward, truthful

candidate

noun a person being considered for a position » *Hugh was the best candidate for the job.*
applicant, competitor, contender, nominee, possibility, runner

capable

adjective able to do something well » *Miguel was a capable leader and brought out the best in his team.*
able, accomplished, adept, competent, efficient, proficient, skillful
antonym: **incompetent**

capacity 1

noun the maximum amount that something holds or produces » *What is the capacity of the glass?*
dimensions, room, size, space, volume

capacity 2

noun a person's power or ability to do something » *Her capacity to help was limited by being so far away.*
ability, capability, facility, gift, potential, power

capture 1

verb to take prisoner » *Sharon's knight captured Ian's king on the chessboard.*
apprehend, arrest, catch, seize, take
antonym: **release**

capture 2

noun the act of capturing » *The fish couldn't escape its capture by the bear.*
arrest, seizure, taking, trapping

*The fish couldn't escape its **capture** by the bear.*

A B C D E F G H I J K L M N O P Q R S T U V W X Y Z

car

noun a vehicle for carrying a few people » *Dad drove the car to the station to pick us up.*
automobile, motor vehicle, wheels (slang)

care [1]

verb to be concerned about something » *I care about the environment.*
be bothered, be concerned, be interested, mind

care [2]

noun something that causes you to worry » *Luke didn't have a care in the world.*
anxiety, concern, stress, trouble, woe, worry, tribulation, vexation

care [3]

noun close attention when doing something » *We took great care to make him feel at home.*
attention, caution, pains, circumspection, forethought

careful [1]

adjective acting with care » *Be careful with that vase.*
attentive, cautious, prudent, vigilant
antonym: **careless**

careful [2]

adjective complete and well done » *The experiment needs careful planning.*
meticulous, painstaking, precise, thorough
antonym: **careless**

careless [1]

adjective not taking enough care » *Heather had careless and messy handwriting.*
irresponsible, neglectful, sloppy (informal), **cavalier, lackadaisical, slapdash, slipshod**
antonym: **careful**

careless [2]

adjective relaxed and unconcerned » *Sam shrugged and gave a careless laugh.*
casual, nonchalant, offhand

He carried the heavy box.

carry

verb to hold and take something somewhere » *He carried the heavy box.*
bear, convey (formal), **haul, lug, take, transport**

carry out

verb to do and complete something » *The surgeon carried out the operation.*
accomplish, achieve, fulfil, perform, execute, implement

carve

verb to make something by cutting
▼ SEE BELOW

case [1]

noun a particular situation or example » *There have been six cases of chicken pox in my class this year.*
example, illustration, instance, occasion, occurrence

case [2]

noun a container for holding something » *Kay kept her glasses in a red case.*
box, container, holder, receptacle

Kay kept her glasses in a red case.

case [3]

noun a trial or inquiry » *The court case was heard behind closed doors.*
action, lawsuit, proceedings, trial

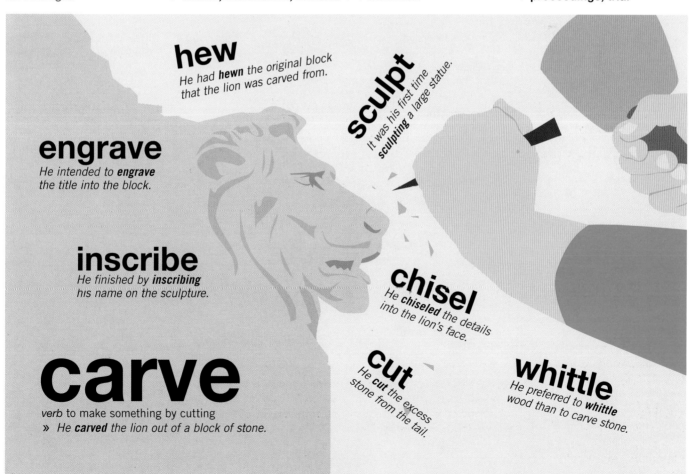

hew He had **hewn** the original block that the lion was carved from.

sculpt It was his first time **sculpting** a large statue.

engrave He intended to **engrave** the title into the block.

inscribe He finished by **inscribing** his name on the sculpture.

chisel He **chiseled** the details into the lion's face.

carve *verb* to make something by cutting » *He **carved** the lion out of a block of stone.*

cut He **cut** the excess stone from the tail.

whittle He preferred to **whittle** wood than to carve stone.

a b c d e f g h i j k l m n o p q r s t u v w x y z

A B C D E F G H I J K L M N O P Q R S T U V W X Y Z

celebration

noun an event in honor of a special occasion
» *The family dinner was a birthday* **celebration**.

party
Would you like to come to my **party**?

festival
They went to the big music **festival**.

gala
The music contest finished with a **gala**.

festivity
The wedding **festivities** *went on for a week.*

revelry
She joined in the **revelry** *with lots of enthusiasm.*

casual ①
adjective happening by chance » *The casual meeting led to a great friendship.*
accidental, chance, incidental, fortuitous, serendipitous, unintentional, unpremeditated
antonym: **deliberate**

casual ②
adjective showing no concern or interest » *Mick gave a casual glance over his shoulder.*
careless, cursory, nonchalant, offhand, relaxed, blasé, insouciant, lackadaisical, perfunctory
antonym: **concerned**

cat
noun a small animal kept as a pet » *Fiona had three long-haired cats.*
alley cat, feline, kitty, puss or **pussy** or **pussycat** (informal), **tomcat**
related words:
adjective **feline**; *male* **tom**; *female* **queen**; *young* **kitten**

Fiona had three long-haired **cats**.

catch ①
verb to capture an animal or fish » *Mom went fishing to catch some trout for dinner.*
capture, snare, trap

catch ②
verb to capture a person » *The police planned a way to catch the suspects.*
apprehend, arrest

catch ③
noun a device that fastens something » *The windows were fitted with safety catches so children could not fall out.*
bolt, clasp, clip, latch

catch ④
noun a hidden difficulty or negative
» *The catch for this great price is that the book will take a month to arrive.*
disadvantage, drawback, gimmick, hitch, pitfall, snag, fly in the ointment, stumbling block

category
noun a set of things with something in common
» *The items were organized into six different categories.*
bracket, class, classification, division, group, league, set, sort, tier, type

cause ①

noun what makes something happen » *The cause of the fire was unknown.*
origin, root, source

cause ②

noun an aim supported by a group » *Sarah took up the cause to save the old library.*
aim, ideal, movement

cause ④

verb to make something happen » *The broken-down train caused delays.*
bring about, create, effect, draw on, generate, produce, provoke, effect, engender, **give rise to, lead to, result in**

caution ①

noun great care taken in order to avoid danger » *Use caution when skating.*
care, prudence, forethought, circumspection

*Use **caution** when skating.*

caution ②

verb to scold or warn someone against doing something » *The policeman cautioned that riding a bike without a helmet is dangerous.*
advise, alert, inform, reprimand, warn

cautious

adjective acting very carefully to avoid danger » *The zookeeper was cautious in the crocodile enclosure.*
careful, guarded, tentative, wary, prudent
antonym: **daring**

cease ①

verb to stop from happening » *The noise ceased and peace was restored.*
be over, come to an end, die away, end, finish, stop
antonym: **begin**

cease ②

verb to stop doing something » *He ceased talking when the teacher called for quiet.*
desist from, discontinue, finish, give up, stop, suspend
antonym: **start**

celebrate

verb to do something special to mark an event » *It's my birthday—let's celebrate!*
commemorate, party, rejoice

celebration

noun an event in honor of a special occasion
◀◀ SEE LEFT

celebrity

noun a famous person » *The presenter interviewed the celebrity on the red carpet.*
big name, name, personality, star, superstar, VIP

*The presenter interviewed the **celebrity** on the red carpet.*

censure ①

noun strong disapproval » *His bad behavior led to censure from his parents.*
blame, condemnation, criticism, disapproval, reproach

censure ②

verb to criticize severely » *The school censured Mike for his graffiti.*
condemn, criticize, denounce, reproach, berate, castigate

center ①

noun the mid-point of a circle or activity » *Downtown is the center of night life in this city.*
core, focus, heart, hub, middle
antonym: **edge**

center ②

verb to have as the main subject » *The party centered on the birthday girl.*
concentrate, focus, revolve

ceremony ①

noun formal actions done for a special occasion » *They had a traditional wedding ceremony.*
observance, pomp, rite, ritual, service, tradition

*They had a traditional wedding **ceremony**.*

ceremony ②

noun formal and polite behavior » *We stood on ceremony to greet the mayor.*
decorum, etiquette, formality, niceties, protocol

certain ①

adjective definite or reliable » *It is certain to rain.*
definite, established, guaranteed, inevitable, known, sure, undeniable
antonym: **uncertain**

certain ②

adjective having no doubt in your mind » *Lily's certain that she will succeed.*
clear, confident, convinced, definite, positive, satisfied, sure
antonym: **uncertain**

certainly

adverb without any doubt » *I'll certainly do all I can to help.*
definitely, undeniably, undoubtedly, unquestionably, without doubt

challenge ①

noun a suggestion to try something » *The coach gave the team a series of challenges.*
dare, face-off (informal)

challenge ②

verb to give someone a challenge » *Sue challenged me to a game of tennis.*
dare, defy

challenge ③

verb to question the truth or value of something » *I challenged Jeff's story about where he had been.*
dispute, question

champion ①

noun a person who wins a competition » *She won the contest to become the regional judo champion.*
hero, title holder, victor, winner

*She won the contest to become the regional judo **champion**.*

a b c d e f g h i j k l m n o p q r s t u v w x y z

champion [2]

noun someone who supports a group, cause, or principle » *Judith became a champion for animal rights.*
advocate, defender, guardian, protector

champion [3]

verb to support a group, cause, or principle » *We championed the school's request for new sports equipment.*
defend, fight for, promote, stick up for (informal), **support, uphold,** advocate, espouse

chance [1]

noun a possibility of something happening » *Lucy had a good chance of success in college.*
likelihood, odds, possibility, probability, prospect

chance [2]

noun an opportunity to do something » *Please give me a chance to explain why I'm late.*
occasion, opening, opportunity, time

chance [3]

noun the way things happen without being planned » *We met up by chance.*
accident, coincidence, fortune, luck
related word:
adjective **fortuitous**

change [1]

noun an alteration in something » *There was a change in her attitude from sulky to helpful.*
alteration, difference, modification, transformation, metamorphosis, mutation, transition, transmutation

change [2]

verb to make or become different » *We changed the garage into a TV room.*
alter, convert, moderate, modify, reform, transform, metamorphose, mutate, transmute

change [3]

verb to exchange one thing for another » *Can I change the red T-shirt for a black one?*
barter, exchange, interchange, replace, substitute, swap, trade

*Can I **change** the red T-shirt for a black one?*

changeable

adjective likely to change all the time » *The weather was changeable—hot one minute and cold the next.*
erratic, fickle, irregular, unpredictable, unstable, variable, volatile, mercurial, mutable, protean
antonym: **constant**

character [1]

noun the qualities of a person » *She has a sunny character.*
nature, personality, temperament, disposition, make-up, quality, temper

character [2]

noun an honorable nature » *Mark showed great character in handling a tricky situation.*
honor, integrity, strength

characteristic [1]

noun a typical quality » *Mark's chief characteristic is honesty.*
attribute, feature, property, quality, trait, idiosyncrasy, peculiarity, quirk

characteristic [2]

adjective typical of a person or thing » *Jack responded with characteristic generosity.*
distinctive, distinguishing, typical, idiosyncratic, peculiar, singular, symptomatic
antonym: **uncharacteristic**

charge [1]

verb to ask someone for money as a payment » *The store charged me a fair price.*
ask (for), bill, levy

charge [2]

noun the price you have to pay for something » *There was an additional charge for a bag.*
cost, fee, payment, price

charge [3]

verb to rush forward, often to attack someone » *The rhino charged toward us.*
dash, rush, stampede, storm

*The rhino **charged** toward us.*

charm [1]

noun an attractive quality » *The house has real charm.*
allure, appeal, attraction, magnetism, fascination

charm [2]

verb to use charm to please someone » *He charmed the audience with his smile.*
bewitch, captivate, delight, entrance, beguile, enchant, enrapture

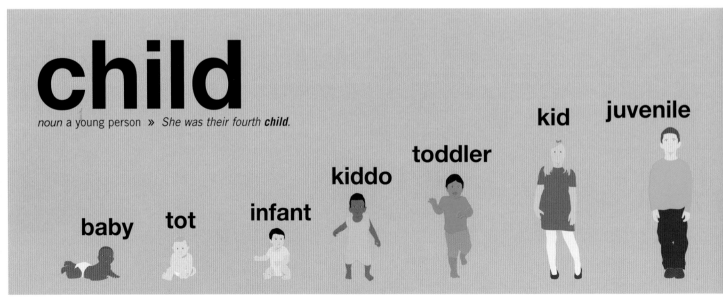

child

noun a young person » *She was their fourth **child**.*

baby   tot   infant   kiddo   toddler   kid   juvenile

chase 1
verb to try to catch someone or something » *My sister chased me until I gave up.*
hunt, pursue

chase 2
verb to force to go somewhere » *The dog chased the mail carrier out of the neighborhood.*
drive, hound, expel, put to flight

chat 1
noun a friendly talk » *Ellie came over and joined us for a chat.*
conversation, gossip, chin-wag (informal), **talk**

chat 2
verb to talk in a friendly way » *Dan chatted to his father.*
gab, small talk, talk

cheap 1
adjective costing very little » *Cheap flights are available.*
bargain, economical, inexpensive, reasonable, cut-price, low-cost, low-priced
antonym: **expensive**

cheap 2
adjective inexpensive but of poor quality » *His cheap jeans ripped when he sat down on the chair.*
budget, cheapo, inferior, low-end, second-rate

*He **cheated** on the exam.*

cheat
verb to get something from someone dishonestly » *He cheated on the exam.*
con (informal), **deceive, defraud, dupe, fleece, rip off** (slang), **swindle,** hoodwink

check 1
verb to examine something » *Please check all the details before signing.*
check out (informal), **examine, inspect, test,** inquire into, look over, scrutinize

check 2
verb to reduce or stop something » *Hand washing will check the spread of germs.*
control, curb, halt, inhibit, restrain, stop

check 3
noun an examination » *The technician performed a thorough check of all of the equipment.*
examination, inspection, test

cheek
noun (Britain) speech or behavior that is rude or disrespectful » *I'm amazed they had the cheek to ask.*
audacity, gall, impudence, insolence, nerve, rudeness, effrontery, temerity

cheeky
adjective (Britain) rude and disrespectful » *The children were cheeky to their mom.*
impertinent, impudent, insolent, rude
antonym: **polite**

cheerful
adjective in a happy mood » *Eliza was feeling cheerful, despite the rain.*
bright, buoyant, cheery, happy, jaunty, jolly, light-hearted, merry
antonym: **miserable**

*Eliza was feeling **cheerful**, despite the rain.*

cheery
adjective happy and cheerful » *Jill sounded very cheery on the phone.*
cheerful, chirpy, good-humored, happy, jolly, sunny, upbeat, genial, jovial
antonym: **gloomy**

chew
verb to break food up with the teeth » *My mom always told me to eat slowly and chew well with my mouth closed.*
crunch, gnaw, munch, champ, chomp, masticate

chief 1
noun the leader of a group or organization » *He was the new chief of police.*
boss, chieftain, director, governor, head, leader, manager

chief 2
adjective most important » *The job went to one of his chief rivals.*
foremost, key, main, prevailing, primary, prime, principal, preeminent, premier

child
noun a young person
▼ SEE BELOW

minor **youngster** **teenager** **youth**

antonym: **adult**

A B C D E F G H I J K L M N O P Q R S T U V W X Y Z

childish
adjective immature and foolish
» *Sulking and stamping your feet when you don't get your own way is childish behavior.*
immature, infantile, juvenile, puerile
antonym: **mature**

choice ①
noun a range of things to choose from » *The hat is available in a choice of colors and sizes.*
range, selection, variety

choice ②
noun the power to choose » *Paul was given a choice about what to eat.*
alternative, option, say

choose
verb to decide to have or do something » *There were so many flavors of ice cream to choose from.*
opt for, pick, select, take, elect, fix on, settle on

chop
verb to cut down or into pieces » *I saw him chopping wood with an ax.*
cut, fell, hack, lop, cleave, hew

*I saw him **chopping** wood with an ax.*

circulate
verb to pass around » *Grandpa's birthday card was circulated around the family for everyone to sign.*
distribute, propagate, spread, disseminate, promulgate

*The **city** was built on the banks of a river.*

city
noun a large town » *The city was built on the banks of a river.*
metropolis, town, conurbation, municipality
related word: *adjective* **civic**

civilized
adjective having an advanced society » *We live in a civilized country.*
cultured, enlightened

claim ①
verb to say something is the case » *Mr. Brown claims to have lived here all his life.*
allege, assert, hold, insist, maintain, profess

claim ②
noun a statement that something is the case » *Emma admitted that the claims about her were true.*
allegation, assertion, pretension, protestation

clash ①
verb to fight or argue with another person » *My brother and sister constantly clash, but they always make up.*
battle, fight, quarrel, wrangle

clash ②
verb of two things: to be so different that they do not go together » *David's plan to stay in the playground clashed with the teacher's demand that he come into the classroom.*
conflict, contradict, differ, disagree, go against, jar

clash ③
noun a fight or argument » *The latest clash between the two teams ended in players being sent off.*
battle, conflict, confrontation, contest, fight, skirmish (informal), **squabble, struggle**

clasp ①
verb to hold something tightly » *Helena clasped her locket in her hands.*
clutch, embrace, grip, hold, hug, press, squeeze

clasp ②
noun a fastening such as a hook or catch » *Miriam undid the clasp on her coat.*
buckle, catch, clip, fastener, fastening

class ①
noun a group of a particular type » *Animals are grouped into classes including mammals, birds, fish, reptiles, and amphibians.*
category, genre, grade, group, kind, set, sort, type

class ②
verb to regard as being in a particular group » *The children were classed into different team colors.*
categorize, classify, designate, grade, rank, rate

*The children were **classed** into different team colors.*

classify
verb to arrange similar things in groups » *We can classify the books into fiction and nonfiction.*
arrange, categorize, grade, rank, sort, pigeonhole, systematize, tabulate

clean ①
adjective free from dirt or marks » *Patrick's clothes are always very clean.*
immaculate, impeccable, laundered, spotless, washed
antonym: **dirty**

clean ②
adjective free from germs or infection » *There was a source of clean drinking water.*
antiseptic, hygienic, purified, sterilized, uncontaminated, unpolluted
antonym: **contaminated**

clean ③
verb to remove dirt from
▶▶ SEE RIGHT

clear ①
adjective easy to see or understand » *It was clear from her tearful voice that she was upset.*
apparent, blatant, conspicuous, definite, evident, explicit, obvious, plain, incontrovertible, manifest, palpable, patent, unequivocal

clear ②
adjective easy to see through » *The liquid inside the glass beaker was clear.*
crystalline, glassy, translucent, transparent, limpid, pellucid, see-through
antonym: **cloudy**

*The liquid inside the glass beaker was **clear**.*

clear ③

verb to prove someone is not guilty » *Beth was cleared of having any part in the incident.*
absolve, acquit
antonym: **convict**

clever

adjective very intelligent » *Luis was clever and always got high grades on his exams.*
brainy (informal)**, bright, intelligent, shrewd, smart, astute, quick-witted, sagacious**
antonym: **stupid**

climb

verb to move upward over something » *We climbed the mountain in a day.*
ascend, clamber, mount, scale, scrabble

close ①

verb to shut something » *Clare closed the gate behind her when she left.*
secure, shut
antonym: **open**

*Clare **closed** the gate behind her when she left.*

close ②

verb to block so that nothing can pass » *All the roads out of town are closed.*
bar, block, obstruct, seal

close ③

adjective near to something » *We went to a restaurant close to our home.*
adjacent, adjoining, at hand, handy, near, nearby, neighboring
antonym: **distant**

cleanse
There are lotions to **cleanse** the skin.

dust
I vacuumed, **dusted**, and polished the living room.

scour
He **scoured** the sink.

sponge
Sponge down the surfaces.

scrub
I started to **scrub** off the dirt.

swab
The sailor **swabbed** the deck.

wipe
She **wiped** the windows with a dry cloth.

wash
He **washed** dishes in a restaurant.

clean
③ *verb* to remove dirt from » *She **cleaned** the house from top to bottom.*

antonym: **soil**
*Using a dirty mop can **soil** the floor.*

A B C D E F G H I J K L M N O P Q R S T U V W X Y Z

apparel
She often chose bright **apparel** *in the summer.*

clothing
She bought the shirt from the men's **clothing** *department.*

attire
The T-shirt was not suitable **attire** *for work.*

dress
She liked to wear her party **dress**.

wear
She didn't have much winter **wear**.

outfit
The red shirt was an essential part of her **outfit**.

gear
She had some sports **gear** *including a tennis dress.*

wardrobe
In the spring, she would buy herself a whole new **wardrobe**.

garments
There were too many **garments** *in her closet.*

costume
Her favorite **costume** *came from her sister.*

garb
She preferred colorful **garb**.

clothes

plural noun the things people wear
» *Alicia spends all her money on* **clothes**.

---

close 4
adjective friendly and loving
» *We became close friends.*
attached, dear, devoted, familiar, friendly, intimate, loving
antonym: **distant**

cloth
noun woven or knitted fabric
» *The sofa was covered in bright red cloth.*
fabric, material, textile

clothes
plural noun the things people wear
▲ SEE ABOVE

cloud 1
noun a mass of vapor or smoke » *The sky was dark with clouds.*
billow, fog, haze, mist, vapor

cloud 2
verb to make something confusing » *Anger has clouded his judgment.*
confuse, distort, muddle

cloudy 1
adjective full of clouds
» *It's a very cloudy sky today.*
dull, gloomy, leaden, overcast
antonym: **clear**

cloudy 2
adjective difficult to see through » *The liquid in the glass was cloudy.*
muddy, murky, opaque
antonym: **clear**

club 1
noun an organization for people with a special interest
» *We joined the swimming club today.*
association, circle, group, guild, society, union

club [2]
noun a heavy stick
» Andy dressed up as a caveman and carried a club to the costume party.
bat, stick, truncheon

clue
noun something that helps to solve a problem or mystery
» The police looked for clues to solve the crime.
hint, indication, lead

clumsiness
noun awkwardness of movement » Meg's usual clumsiness was made worse by her high-heeled shoes.
awkwardness, ungainliness

Meg's usual **clumsiness** was made worse by her high-heeled shoes.

clumsy
adjective moving awkwardly
» Rob is big and clumsy in his movements.
awkward, gauche, lumbering, uncoordinated, ungainly, accident-prone, bumbling, gawky, maladroit
antonym: **graceful**

coast
noun the land next to the ocean » We had a vacation on the coast this year.
beach, border, coastline, seaside, shore, strand

coat [1]
noun an animal's fur or hair
» Anna gave the dog's coat a brush.
fleece, fur, hair, hide, pelt, skin, wool

coat [2]
noun a warm piece of outerwear clothing » You'll need a coat; it's cold outside.
jacket, overcoat, raincoat, mac (Britain)

coating
noun a layer of something
» The lake had a thin coating of ice.
coat, covering, layer

The lake had a thin **coating** of ice.

coax
verb to persuade gently
» We coaxed her into coming to the mall with us.
butter up, cajole, persuade, sweet-talk, talk into, flatter, woo

coil
verb to wind in loops
» The snake coiled its body around the tree.
curl, loop, spiral, twine, twist, wind

cold [1]
adjective having a low temperature » The spring weather felt so cold that it felt more like winter.
arctic, biting, bitter, bleak, chilly, freezing, icy, raw, wintry
antonym: **hot**

cold [2]
adjective not showing affection
» Uncle John was a cold, unfeeling person who loved his dog more than people.
aloof, distant, frigid, lukewarm, reserved, stony, standoffish, undemonstrative
antonym: **warm**

collapse [1]
verb to fall down » Stand back—the old building looks like it could collapse at any minute.
fall down, give way

collapse [2]
verb to fail » The business collapsed due to a lack of money.
fail, fold, founder

collapse [3]
noun the failure of something
» The collapse of the project was caused by a disagreement within the team.
downfall, failure

colleague
noun a person someone works with » My colleagues all worked extremely hard on the latest project.
associate, coworker, partner, workmate

collect
verb to gather together
» My brother Timothy collects stamps that come from all over the world.
accumulate, assemble, gather, raise, aggregate, amass
antonym: **scatter**

My brother Timothy **collects** stamps that come from all over the world.

We visited the **collection** of paintings in the gallery.

collection
noun a group of things collected together
» We visited the collection of paintings in the gallery.
assortment, group, store

colloquial
adjective used in everyday conversation » Clare used colloquial expressions like: "He's gone nuts."
conversational, everyday, informal, demotic, idiomatic, vernacular

colony [1]
noun a country controlled by another country
» Many European countries used to have colonies around the world.
dependency, dominion, territory

colony [2]
noun a group of settlers in a place » Many settlers from the East moved to the American West in the 1800s.
community, outpost, settlement

color [1]
verb to give something a color
» Jules used hair dye to color his hair.
dye, paint, stain, tint

color [2]
verb to affect the way you think
» The rainy weather colored her opinion of the trip.
bias, distort, prejudice, slant

a b c d e f g h i j k l m n o p q r s t u v w x y z

color ③
noun a shade or hue
» Joe's favorite color is blue.
hue, pigmentation, shade, tint
▶▶ SEE RIGHT

color ④
noun a substance used to give color » She added a few drops of red food color to the icing.
dye, paint, pigment

colorful ①
adjective full of color
» The lorikeets have such colorful feathers.
bright, brilliant, intense, jazzy (informal)**, rich, vibrant, vivid,** kaleidoscopic, multicolored, psychedelic
antonym: **dull**

colorful ②
adjective interesting or exciting
» The girls gave a colorful account of their school field trip to the farm.
graphic, interesting, lively, rich, vivid
antonym: **dull**

colossal
adjective very large indeed
» The statue was colossal.
enormous, gigantic, huge, immense, mammoth, massive, vast
antonym: **tiny**

combination
noun a mixture of things
» Green is a combination of yellow and blue.
amalgamation, blend, mix, mixture, amalgam, composite, meld

Green is a **combination** of yellow and blue.

combine
verb to join or mix together
» The performer combined magic and dance in his act.
amalgamate, blend, fuse, integrate, merge, mix, unite, meld, synthesize
antonym: **separate**

come ①
verb to move or arrive somewhere » The teacher came into the room.
appear, arrive, enter, materialize, show up (informal)**, turn up** (informal)

come ②
verb to happen or take place
» The opportunity to audition comes only twice a year.
happen, occur, take place

comfort ①
noun a state of ease
» The seating in the airy sitting room was designed for comfort.
ease, luxury, wellbeing

The seating in the airy sitting room was designed for **comfort**.

comfort ②
noun relief from worry or unhappiness » Jan's reassuring words gave him some comfort.
consolation, help, relief, satisfaction, support

comfort ③
verb to give someone comfort
» The woman tried to comfort her screaming baby.
cheer, console, reassure, soothe

Trish made herself **comfortable** and read a book.

comfortable ①
adjective physically relaxing
» Trish made herself comfortable and read a book.
cosy, easy, homely, relaxing, restful
antonym: **uncomfortable**

comfortable ②
adjective feeling at ease
» The couple sat together in comfortable silence.
at ease, at home, contented, happy, relaxed
antonym: **uneasy**

command ①
verb to order someone to do something » The sports coach commanded the team to run around the field.
bid, demand, direct, order, charge

command ②
verb to be in charge of
» The politician asked to meet the general who had commanded the rescue mission.
control, head, lead, manage, supervise

command ③
noun an order to do something
» Everyone in the class jumped up and down at the gym teacher's command.
bidding, decree, directive, injunction, instruction, order, behest, edict

command ④
noun knowledge and ability
» Ned had a good command of several languages.
grasp, knowledge, mastery

commemorate
verb to do something in memory of » A concert was held to commemorate the anniversary of the victory.
celebrate, honor, memorialize, pay tribute to

comment ①
verb to make a remark
» She was asked to comment on the situation.
mention, note, observe, point out, remark, say, weigh in, reflect, opine

She was asked to **comment** on the situation.

comment ②
noun something you say
» Mary made a nice comment about my new hairstyle.
observation, remark, statement

commit
verb to do something
» It appears that a crime has been committed.
carry out, do, perform, perpetrate

common ①
adjective of many people
» The statue was a common stop for tourists.
general, popular, prevailing, prevalent, universal, widespread
antonym: **rare**

color

3 shades of different colors

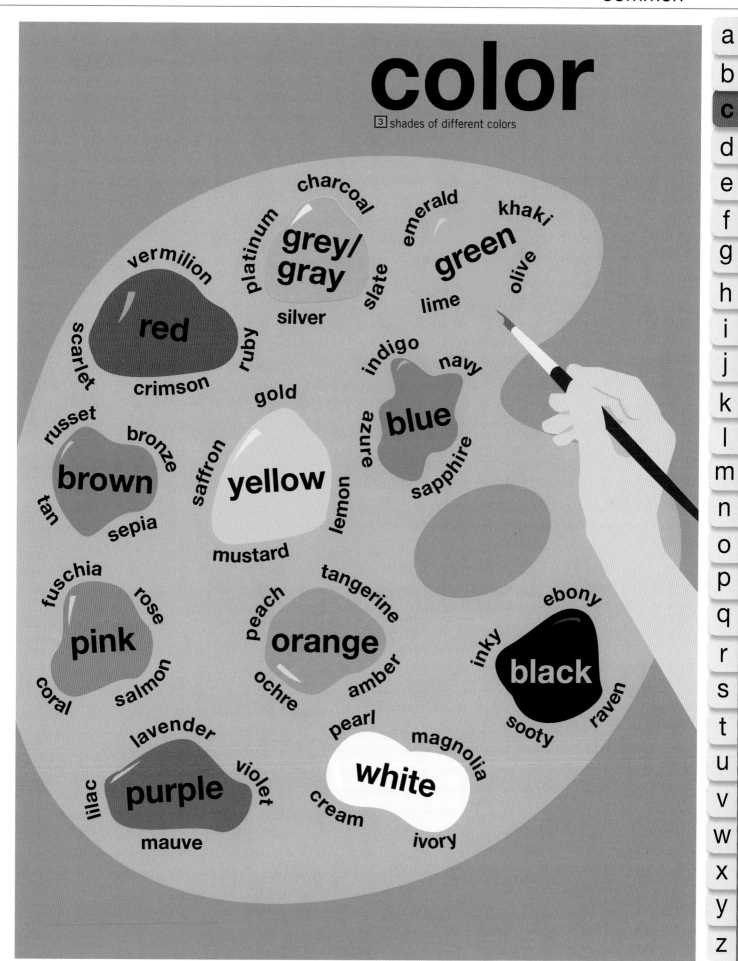

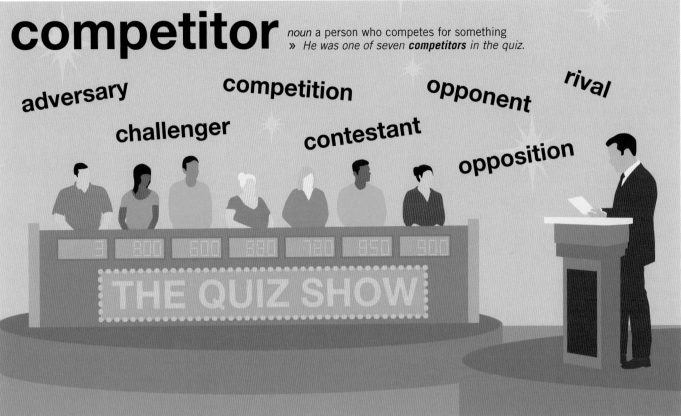

competitor
noun a person who competes for something
» *He was one of seven* **competitors** *in the quiz.*

adversary

competition

opponent

rival

challenger

contestant

opposition

THE QUIZ SHOW

common 2
adjective not special
» *Sparrows are common birds.*
average, commonplace, everyday, ordinary, plain, standard, usual
antonym: **special**

common 3
adjective being related to the whole of something » *It is common knowledge that smoking is not allowed on airplanes.*
across-the-board, broad, comprehensive, general

common sense
noun good judgment in practical matters » *Use your common sense to find the clue.*
good sense, judgment, level-headedness, wit

communicate 1
verb to be in touch with someone » *We communicate mainly by text message.*
be in contact, be in touch, correspond

communicate 2
verb to pass on information
» *The results will be communicated by mail.*
convey, impart, inform, pass on, retweet, spread, transmit, tweet,
disseminate, make known

companion
noun someone you travel with or spend time with » *Matt has been her constant companion for the last six years.*
comrade, crony (old-fashioned), friend, mate, pal (informal), partner

company 1
noun a business » *The store was run by a large company.*
business, corporation, establishment, firm, house

company 2
noun a group of people
» *A company of actors performed a play.*
assembly, band, circle, community, crowd, ensemble, group, party, troupe, concourse, coterie

company 3
noun the act of spending time with someone » *I really enjoy your company.*
companionship, presence

compare
verb to look at things for similarities or differences
» *Compare the two pictures and spot the differences.*
contrast, juxtapose, weigh

compartment 1
noun one of the separate parts of an object
» *The fridge has a freezer compartment at the top.*
bay, chamber, division, section

The fridge has a freezer **compartment** *at the top.*

The passengers in the **compartment** *waited for the train to move.*

compartment 2
noun a section of a train car
» *The passengers in the compartment waited for the train to move.*
car, carriage (Britain)

compassionate
adjective feeling or showing sympathy and pity for others
» *The compassionate man adopted the stray dog.*
caring, humane, kind, kind-hearted, merciful, sympathetic, tender, benevolent, humanitarian

compensate 1

verb to repay someone for loss or damage » *The company offered to compensate the customer for the broken laptop plus the inconvenience.*
atone, refund, repay, reward, make amends, make restitution, recompense, reimburse, remunerate

compensate 2

verb to cancel out » *Theo's enthusiasm compensated for his lack of skill at knitting.*
balance, cancel out, counteract, make up for, offset, counterbalance, redress

compensation

noun something that makes up for loss or damage » *She received compensation for the damage to her property.*
amends, atonement, damages, payment, recompense, reimbursement, remuneration, reparation, restitution

compete

verb to try to win » *The teams competed for the title in the final game of the season.*
contend, contest, fight, vie

*The teams **competed** for the title in the final game of the season.*

competition 1

noun an attempt to win » *There's a lot of competition for places.*
contention, contest, opposition, rivalry, struggle

competition 2

noun a contest to find the winner in something » *Jenny won the surfing competition.*
championship, contest, event, tournament

competitor

noun a person who competes for something
◄◄ SEE LEFT

complain

verb to express dissatisfaction » *Poppy complained to the teacher that John had taken her pencil.*
bellyache, carp, find fault, gripe, grouse, grumble, kick up a fuss (informal), **moan, whine, whine,** bemoan, bewail

*Poppy **complained** to the teacher that John had taken her pencil.*

complaint

noun an instance of complaining about something » *There have been a number of complaints about the noise from the road construction.*
criticism, grievance, grumble, objection, protest

complete 1

adjective to the greatest degree possible » *The garden had undergone a complete transformation.*
absolute, consummate, outright, perfect, thorough, total, utter

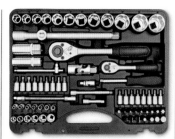

*Lesley owned a **complete** set of tools with all the attachments.*

complete 2

adjective with nothing missing » *Lesley owned a complete set of tools with all the attachments.*
entire, full, intact, undivided, whole
antonym: **incomplete**

complete 3

verb to finish » *Tim has just completed his first fun run.*
conclude, end, finish

complex 1

adjective having many different parts » *The complex puzzle took a long time to solve.*
complicated, difficult, intricate, involved, tangled, convoluted, tortuous
antonym: **simple**

complex 2

noun an emotional problem » *Vincent has a complex about being bad at math.*
fixation, obsession, phobia, preoccupation, problem, thing

complicated

adjective complex and difficult » *The questions in the test were so complicated that he couldn't understand them.*
complex, convoluted, elaborate, intricate, involved, labyrinthine, perplexing
antonym: **simple**

compose

verb to create or write » *Stephen has composed many songs.*
create, devise, invent, produce, write

comprehend

verb to understand or appreciate something » *It took me a moment to comprehend what Lewis was saying.*
appreciate, fathom, grasp, see, take in, understand, work out

compulsory

adjective required by law » *School attendance is compulsory.*
mandatory, obligatory, required, requisite
antonym: **voluntary**

computer

noun an electronic machine that stores and processes data » *Ana used a computer to work out the company's profits.*
laptop, PC, tablet

*Ana used a **computer** to work out the company's profits.*

con 1

verb to trick someone into doing or believing something » *Joshua conned me into buying his broken bike.*
cheat, deceive, mislead, swindle, trick, defraud, dupe

con 2

noun a trick intended to mislead or hurt someone » *The packaging is a con—it makes the contents look twice as big as they are.*
bluff, deception, fraud, swindle, trick

conceit

noun excessive pride » *The singer made so many demands; his conceit was insufferable.*
conceitedness, egotism, pride, self-importance, vanity, narcissism, vainglory

a b c d e f g h i j k l m n o p q r s t u v w x y z

conceited

adjective too proud **»** *She was conceited and too full of herself.*
bigheaded (informal), **cocky, egotistical, self-important, vain,** narcissistic, swollen-headed, vainglorious
antonym: **modest**

concentrate ①

verb to give something all your attention **»** *Julie was trying hard to concentrate on her studies.*
be engrossed in, focus your attention on, give your attention to, put your mind to

Julie was trying hard to concentrate on her studies.

concentrate ②

verb to be found in one place **»** *The music stores are concentrated in one street.*
accumulate, collect, gather

concern ①

noun a feeling of worry **»** *Martin's timing was a concern—he was always late.*
anxiety, apprehension, disquiet, worry

concern ②

noun someone's duty or responsibility **»** *A child's health is a parent's concern.*
affair, business, responsibility

concern ③

verb to make someone worried **»** *It concerns me that Leo doesn't want to talk to the teacher about the problem.*
bother, distress, disturb, trouble, worry, disquiet, perturb

concern ④

verb to affect or involve **»** *This concerns both of you.*
affect, apply to, be relevant to, involve, bear on, pertain to, touch

concise

adjective using no unnecessary words **»** *The report was short and concise.*
brief, short, succinct, terse, laconic, pithy
antonym: **long**

conclude ①

verb to decide something **»** *Dad concluded that I had been right after all.*
decide, deduce, determine, infer, judge, suppose, surmise

conclude ②

verb to finish something **»** *She concluded the letter by signing her name.*
close, end, finish, round off, wind up
antonym: **begin**

She concluded the letter by signing her name.

conclusion ①

noun a decision made after thinking carefully about something **»** *I've come to the conclusion that she was lying.*
deduction, inference, judgment, verdict

conclusion ②

noun the finish or ending of something **»** *A period marks the conclusion of a sentence.*
close, end, ending, finish, termination
antonym: **beginning**

condemn ①

verb to say that something is bad or unacceptable **»** *The scheme was condemned for being a waste of money.*
blame, censure, criticize, damn, denounce

condemn ②

verb to give a punishment **»** *The thief was condemned to five years in prison.*
damn, doom, sentence

condition ①

noun the state of something **»** *The house is in good condition and needs no repairs.*
form, shape, state

condition ②

noun something required for something else to be possible **»** *Emily was allowed to go to the party on the condition that she first cleaned her room.*
prerequisite, provision, proviso, qualification, requirement, requisite, stipulation, terms

conduct ①

verb to carry out an activity or task **»** *We conducted an experiment in science class.*
carry out, direct, do, manage, organize, perform, run, execute, implement, orchestrate

We conducted an experiment in science class.

conduct ②

noun the way someone behaves **»** *Mary's conduct was a good example to others.*
attitude, behavior, manners, ways, comportment, demeanor

conduct yourself

verb to behave in a particular way **»** *The way you conduct yourself reflects on the school.*
act, behave, acquit yourself

conference

noun a meeting for discussion **»** *The team held a conference to discuss the new project.*
congress, convention, discussion, forum, meeting, colloquium, convocation, symposium

The team held a conference to discuss the new project.

confess

verb to admit to something **»** *The boy confessed to eating the entire package of cookies.*
acknowledge, admit, own up
antonym: **deny**

confession

noun the act of confessing **»** *I have to make a confession—I borrowed your dress without asking first.*
acknowledgment, admission

confidence ①

noun a feeling of trust **»** *I have complete confidence that you will do well.*
belief, faith, reliance, trust
antonym: **distrust**

confidence ②

noun sureness of yourself **»** *I've never had much confidence about speaking in class.*
aplomb, assurance, self-assurance, self-possession
antonym: **shyness**

confident [1]

adjective sure about something
» *Angela had worked hard and was confident of success.*
certain, convinced, positive, satisfied, secure, sure
antonym: **uncertain**

confident [2]

adjective sure of yourself
» *Hari was a confident actor.*
assured, self-assured, self-possessed
antonym: **shy**

*Hari was a **confident** actor.*

confine [1]

verb to limit to something specified » *We confined our discussion to tennis rather than sports in general.*
limit, restrict

confine [2]

verb to prevent from leaving
» *His flu confined him to bed for two days.*
hem in, imprison, restrict, shut up, immure, incarcerate, intern

confirm [1]

verb to say or show that something is true » *Kate was given a certificate to confirm that she had passed the test.*
bear out, endorse, prove, substantiate, validate, verify, authenticate, corroborate

confirm [2]

verb to make something definite » *The date of the election was confirmed.*
fix, formalize, settle

*Will resolved the **conflict** between the friends.*

conflict [1]

noun disagreement and argument » *Will resolved the conflict between the friends.*
antagonism, disagreement, discord, friction, hostility, opposition, strife

conflict [2]

noun a war or battle
» *The man reported on the conflict in the Middle East.*
battle, combat, fighting, strife, war

conflict [3]

verb to differ or disagree
» *The team leaders conflicted over who should go first.*
battle, be incompatible, clash, collide, combat, differ, disagree, jar

confuse [1]

verb to mix two things up
» *It is possible to confuse fact with fiction.*
confound, mistake, mix up, muddle up

confuse [2]

verb to puzzle or bewilder
» *The complicated instructions confused me.*
baffle, bewilder, mystify, puzzle, bemuse, faze, nonplus, perplex

confused [1]

adjective puzzled or bewildered
» *Hattie was confused—the information didn't make sense.*
baffled, bewildered, confounded, muddled, perplexed, puzzled, at a loss, flummoxed, nonplussed

confused [2]

adjective in an unorganized mess » *The papers were in a confused heap on the floor.*
chaotic, disordered, disorganized, untidy
antonym: **orderly**

confusing

adjective bewildering or puzzling » *Trying to find our way in the city was confusing.*
baffling, bewildering, complicated, puzzling

confusion

noun an untidy mess
» *The room was in a state of confusion with furniture all over the place.*
chaos, disarray, disorder, disorganization, mess
antonym: **order**

connect [1]

verb to join together
» *The firefighter connected the hose to the faucet.*
affix, attach, couple, fasten, join, link
antonym: **separate**

*The firefighter **connected** the hose to the faucet.*

connect [2]

verb to associate one thing with another » *Laughter is connected to happiness.*
ally, associate, link, relate

connection [1]

noun a link or relationship
» *Bridget had connections to a large number of people.*
affinity, affiliation, association, bond, correlation, correspondence, link, relation, relationship

*He fixed the loose **connection** in the circuit board.*

connection [2]

noun a point where things are joined » *He fixed the loose connection in the circuit board.*
coupling, fastening, junction, link

conscience

noun a sense of right and wrong » *Phil's conscience told him the right thing to do.*
principles, scruples, sense of right and wrong

conservative

adjective unwilling to change
» *People often get more conservative as they grow older.*
conventional, traditional, hidebound, reactionary
antonym: **radical**

consider [1]

verb to judge someone or something » *We consider him the perfect candidate.*
believe, judge, rate, regard as, think, deem, hold to be

consider [2]

verb to think carefully
» *I will consider your offer.*
contemplate, deliberate, kick around (informal), **meditate, muse, ponder, reflect, think about, cogitate, mull over**

consider [3]

verb to take into account
» *You should consider Ruth's feelings when making your decision.*
bear in mind, make allowances for, respect, take into account, think about

a b c d e f g h i j k l m n o p q r s t u v w x y z

A B C D E F G H I J K L M N O P Q R S T U V W X Y Z

consideration 1
noun careful thought about something » *Ramon's decision required careful consideration.*
attention, contemplation, deliberation, study, thought

consideration 2
noun concern for someone » *Please show consideration for others and work quietly.*
concern, kindness, respect, tact

consideration 3
noun something to be taken into account » *Safety is a major consideration at music festivals.*
factor, issue, point

consist: consist of
verb to be made up of » *The brain consists of millions of nerve cells.*
be composed of, be made up of, comprise

conspicuous
adjective easy to see or notice » *Sarah wore her bright red coat to be conspicuous.*
apparent, blatant, evident, noticeable, obvious, perceptible, patent

Sarah wore her bright red coat to be **conspicuous**.

constant 1
adjective going on all the time » *There was constant barking from the dog next door.*
continual, continuous, eternal, nonstop, perpetual, relentless, incessant, interminable, sustained, unremitting
antonym: **periodic**

constant 2
adjective staying the same » *The thermometer showed the temperature was constant.*
even, fixed, regular, stable, steady, uniform, immutable, invariable
antonym: **changeable**

construct
verb to build or make something » *He's constructing a compost bin.*
assemble, build, create, erect, make, put together, put up

He's **constructing** a compost bin.

consult
verb to go to for advice » *Consult your doctor before training for the race.*
ask for advice, confer with, refer to

contact 1
noun the state of being in touch with someone » *We must keep in contact.*
communication, in touch

contact 2
noun someone you know » *He had a contact in the music business.*
acquaintance, connection

contact 3
verb to get in touch with » *Abbey contacted the company to complain.*
approach, communicate with, get hold of, get in touch with, reach

Abbey **contacted** the company to complain.

contain 1
verb to include as a part of » *The glass contains the juice from 10 oranges.*
comprise, include

contain 2
verb to keep under control » *Hans was finding it difficult to contain his excitement.*
control, curb, repress, restrain, stifle

container
noun something that holds things » *Gail used a plastic container for her food.*
holder, vessel, receptacle, repository

contemplate 1
verb to think carefully about something » *Maria paused to contemplate her options.*
consider, examine, muse on, ponder, reflect on, think about

contemplate 2
verb to consider doing something » *He contemplated becoming a doctor.*
consider, envisage, plan, think of

contempt
noun complete lack of respect » *Rick's contempt for the club's rules made him lose his membership.*
derision, disdain, disregard, disrespect, scorn
antonym: **respect**

contest 1
noun a competition or game » *It was a thrilling contest between two strong teams.*
competition, game, match, tournament

contest 2
noun a struggle for power » *There was a bitter contest over who should control the nation's future.*
battle, fight, struggle

boil   **fry**   **grill**

cook
verb to prepare food for eating by heating it in some way » *I enjoy cooking for friends.*

bake

contest 3

verb to object formally
to a statement or decision
» *You have 14 days to contest
the results of the election.*
**challenge, dispute, oppose,
question**
antonym: **accept**

continual 1

adjective happening all
the time without stopping
» *There was continual rain
the afternoon of the fair.*
**constant, continuous,
endless, eternal, nagging,
perpetual, uninterrupted,**
incessant, interminable,
unremitting

continual 2

adjective happening again and
again » *Paolo received
continual reminders to renew
his membership of the club.*
**frequent, recurrent, regular,
repeated**
antonym: **occasional**

continue 1

verb to keep doing something
» *She continued talking even
though no one was listening.*
**carry on, go on, keep on,
persist**

*She **continued** talking even though
no one was listening.*

continue 2

verb to go on existing
» *Their friendship continued
even when one of them
moved abroad.*
**carry on, endure, last,
persist, remain, survive**

continue 3

verb to start doing again
» *When he returned from
school, Ron continued to work
on his art project.*
**carry on, recommence,
resume**

continuous

adjective going on without
stopping » *The continuous
building work went on
for weeks.*
**constant, continued,
extended, prolonged,
uninterrupted**
antonym: **periodic**

control 1

noun power over something
» *The city was under the
control of a very powerful
new mayor.*
**authority, command,
direction, government,
management, power, rule,
supremacy,** jurisdiction,
mastery, superintendence

control 2

verb to be in charge of
» *Camilla controlled the rota
for cleaning the bathroom.*
**administer, be in charge of,
command, direct, govern,
have power over,
manage, rule**

convenient

adjective helpful or easy to use
» *Cycling was a convenient
way to get around the busy city.*
**handy, helpful, useful,
user-friendly,**
labor-saving, serviceable
antonym: **inconvenient**

convention 1

noun an accepted way of
behaving or doing something
» *The convention is to shake
hands when you strike a deal.*
**code, custom, etiquette,
practice, tradition,**
propriety, protocol

*The **convention** is to shake hands
when you strike a deal.*

convention 2

noun a large meeting of an
organization or group » *The
society hosted a convention
of children's authors every year.*
**assembly, conference,
congress, meeting**

conventional 1

adjective relating to what
is normally done or believed
» *His uniform was
conventional school wear.*
**conformist, conservative,
unadventurous,** bourgeois,
staid

conventional 2

adjective familiar, or generally
used » *The coach taught us
all a conventional tennis serve.*
**customary, ordinary,
orthodox, regular,
standard, traditional**

convey

verb to cause information
or ideas to be known »
*She conveyed her thoughts
on global warming to the class.*
**communicate, express,
get across, impart**

convince

verb to persuade
that something is true
» *I convinced him to come
to the concert with me.*
assure, persuade, satisfy

convincing

adjective persuasive » *Jackie
had a convincing argument.*
**conclusive, effective,
persuasive, plausible,
powerful, telling,**
cogent, incontrovertible
antonym: **unconvincing**

cook

verb to prepare food for eating
by heating it in some way
▼ SEE BELOW

cool 1

adjective having a low
temperature » *There was
a gust of cool air.*
**chilled, chilly, cold,
refreshing**
antonym: **warm**

a b c d e f g h i j k l m n o p q r s t u v w x y z

microwave | poach | steam | toast | barbecue
roast | stew

A B C D E F G H I J K L M N O P Q R S T U V W X Y Z

cool 2
adjective staying calm
» *José kept cool through the whole incident.*
calm, collected, composed, level-headed, relaxed, serene, dispassionate, imperturbable, unemotional, unexcited, unruffled
antonym: **nervous**

cool 3
verb to make or become cool
» *Elsa put the cupcakes on a rack to cool.*
chill, cool off, freeze, refrigerate
antonym: **heat**

Elsa put the cupcakes on a rack to cool.

cooperate
verb to work together » *Laura cooperated with the rest of the team to finish the task.*
collaborate, join forces, pull together, work together

copy 1
noun something made to look like something else
» *Tony made a copy of his favorite painting*
counterfeit, duplicate, fake, forgery, imitation, replica, reproduction, facsimile, likeness, replication

copy 2
verb to do the same thing as someone else » *My little brother copies everything that I do.*
ape, emulate, follow, imitate, mimic, follow suit, parrot, simulate

copy 3
verb to make a copy of
» *The teacher copied the handout and gave a sheet of it to each pupil.*
counterfeit, duplicate, reproduce

corny
adjective unoriginal or sentimental » *Dad always listens to corny music.*
banal, hackneyed, maudlin, sentimental, stale, stereotyped, trite, mawkish, old hat, unoriginal

correct 1
adjective without mistakes
» *Jonathan's calculations were correct.*
accurate, exact, faultless, flawless, precise, right, true

correct 2
adjective socially acceptable
» *Our teacher said the correct way to greet the principal was "Good morning, Mr. Brown."*
acceptable, appropriate, fitting, okay or **OK** (informal), **proper, seemly**
antonym: **wrong**

correct 3
verb to make right » *Gina corrected the errors in her work.*
amend, cure, improve, rectify, reform, remedy, right, emend, redress

correction
noun the act of making something right » *We made a correction to our design project.*
adjustment, amendment, righting, rectification

*We made a **correction** to our design project.*

correspond
verb to be similar or connected to something else » *The two maps correspond—they both show the old tower at the top of the hill.*
agree, be related, coincide, correlate, fit, match, tally

corrupt 1
adjective acting dishonestly or illegally » *Her scheme was unfair and showed her to be corrupt.*
crooked, dishonest, fraudulent, shady (informal), **unscrupulous,** unethical, unprincipled, venal
antonym: **honest**

corrupt 2
verb to change a computer file by introducing errors
» *I should take a back-up copy in case the original is corrupted.*
alter, contaminate, falsify, manipulate, doctor

corruption
noun dishonest and illegal behavior » *The police arrested him on charges of corruption.*
bribery, dishonesty, fraud, extortion, profiteering, venality

cost 1
noun the amount of money needed » *The cost of chocolate has gone up.*
charge, expense, outlay, payment, price, rate

cost 2
noun loss or damage
» *They added on to the house at the cost of most of the yard.*
detriment, expense, penalty

cost 3
verb to involve a cost of
» *The air fares were going to cost a lot of money.*
come to, sell at, set someone back (informal)

cosy 1
adjective warm and comfortable
» *Guests can relax in the cosy lounge.*
comfortable, snug, warm

cosy 2
adjective pleasant and friendly » *She enjoyed the cosy chat with her friends.*
friendly, informal, intimate, relaxed

council
noun a governing group of people » *The city council had ordered the road closure.*
assembly, board, committee, panel, conclave, convocation

count 1
verb to add up
» *I counted the money.*
add up, calculate, tally, compute, enumerate

*I **counted** the money.*

count 2
verb to be important
» *Your opinions count.*
carry weight, matter, rate, signify, weigh

count 3
noun a counting or number counted » *The count revealed that our group had the most votes.*
calculation, reckoning, sum, tally, computation, enumeration

counteract

verb to reduce the effect of something » *Water the plants to counteract the drying effect of the sun.*
act against, offset, counterbalance, countervail, negate, neutralize

countless

adjective too many to count » *She was the star of countless movies.*
infinite, innumerable, myriad, untold, incalculable, limitless, measureless, multitudinous

country ①

noun a political area » *He drove over the border between the two countries.*
kingdom, land, state

country ②

noun land away from towns and cities » *My friend lives right out in the country.*
backwoods, boondocks, bush, countryside, outback, outdoors, sticks
related words:
adjectives **pastoral, rural**

My friend lives right out in the country.

courage

noun lack of fear
▶▶ **SEE RIGHT**

course ①

noun a policy of action » *Jen took the only course left open to her.*
plan, policy, procedure

She taught a course on algebra.

course ②

noun a series of lessons » *She taught a course on algebra.*
classes, curriculum

course ③

noun a way taken to get somewhere » *The sailor changed the yacht's course to avoid the rocks.*
direction, line, path, route, trajectory, way

court ①

noun a place where legal matters are decided » *He ended up in court for theft.*
bench, law court, tribunal

court ②

verb (old-fashioned) to hope to marry » *Grandpa said he courted grandma for years before she agreed to marry him.*
go steady, woo

courtesy

noun polite and considerate behavior » *He showed courtesy to other drivers, giving way to them on the busy road.*
civility, courteousness, gallantry, good manners, grace, graciousness, politeness

cover ①

verb to protect or hide » *He covered his face.*
cloak, conceal, cover up, hide, mask, obscure, screen, shade
antonym: **reveal**

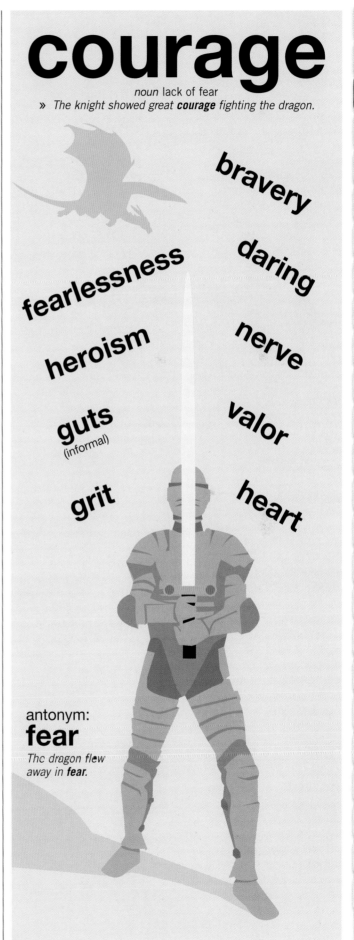

courage
noun lack of fear
» *The knight showed great **courage** fighting the dragon.*

bravery

daring

fearlessness

heroism

nerve

guts
(informal)

valor

grit

heart

antonym:
fear
*The dragon flew away in **fear**.*

a b c d e f g h i j k l m n o p q r s t u v w x y z

cover [2]
verb to form a layer over
» *The fish was covered with bread crumbs.*
coat, overlay

cover [3]
noun something which protects or hides » *They snuggled down under the covers.*
case, coating, covering, jacket, mask, screen, wrapper

*They snuggled down under the **covers**.*

cow
noun a farm animal kept for milk or meat » *A group of dairy cows stood in the field.*
bovine, cattle

coward
noun someone who is easily scared » *I'm a coward when it comes to the dark, so Dad leaves the porch light on.*
chicken (slang), **wimp** (informal)

cowardly
adjective easily scared » *She was too cowardly to get the spider out of the bathtub.*
chicken (slang), **faint-hearted, gutless** (informal), **craven, lily-livered, pusillanimous, spineless, timorous**
antonym: **brave**

cower
verb to crouch with fear » *To our surprise, the dog cowered in front of the cat.*
cringe, grovel, quail, recoil, shrink

crack [1]
verb to become damaged, with lines on the surface » *The road surface cracked in the intense heat.*
break, fracture, snap

crack [2]
verb to find the answer to something » *We've managed to crack the problem.*
decipher, solve, work out

crack [3]
noun a line or gap caused by damage » *There was a large crack in the wall.*
break, cleft, crevice, fracture, fissure, interstice

crafty
adjective smart and rather dishonest » *The crafty kid managed to get both his parents to give him his allowance that week.*
artful, cunning, devious, scheming, slippery, sly, wily

cram
verb to stuff something into a container or place » *Mary crammed chips into her mouth.*
jam, pack, squeeze, stuff

crash [1]
noun an accident involving a moving vehicle » *No one was hurt in the car crash.*
accident, bump, collision, pile-up (informal), **smash**

*No one was hurt in the car **crash**.*

crash [2]
noun a loud noise » *I heard a crash coming from outside.*
bang, clash, din, smash

crash [3]
noun the failure of a business or money-related activity » *There was a stock market crash overnight.*
bankruptcy, collapse, depression, failure, ruin

crash [4]
verb to have an accident » *His car crashed into the back of a van.*
bump, collide, drive into, have an accident, hurtle into, plow into, wreck

crawl [1]
verb to move slowly on hands and knees or near the ground » *The ladybug crawled through the grass.*
creep, drag, edge, inch, slither, on hands and knees

crawl [2]
verb to be full of » *The branch was crawling with red ants.*
be alive with, be full of, be overrun (slang), **swarm, teem**

*The branch was **crawling** with red ants.*

craze
noun a brief enthusiasm for something » *Yoga is Jasmine's latest fitness craze.*
fad, fashion, trend, vogue

crazy [1]
adjective (informal) very strange or foolish » *People thought our plans were crazy.*
foolish, insane, mad, nuts, ridiculous, wild, zany
antonym: **sensible**

crazy [2]
adjective (informal) excited about something » *Gavin's crazy about soccer.*
fanatical, obsessed, passionate, smitten, wild, enamored, zealous

create [1]
verb to make something happen » *The band coming on stage created a buzz of excitement around the room.*
bring about, cause, lead to, occasion

create [2]
verb to invent something » *He created a new type of kite.*
coin, compose, devise, formulate, invent, originate

creative
adjective able to invent » *Jess is so creative—she's writing and illustrating a graphic novel in her spare time.*
fertile, imaginative, inspired, inventive

credit
noun praise for something » *Luca took all the credit for my great idea.*
commendation, glory, praise, recognition, thanks, acclaim, Brownie points, kudos
antonym: **disgrace**

creepy
adjective (informal) strange and frightening » *The old house is really creepy at night.*
disturbing, eerie, macabre, scary (informal), **sinister, spooky, unnatural**

crime
noun an act that breaks the law » *Shoplifting is a crime.*
misdemeanor, offense, violation, wrong, felony, malfeasance, misdeed, transgression

criminal [1]
noun someone who has committed a crime » *The criminal spent 10 years in prison.*
crook (informal), **culprit, delinquent, offender, villain, evildoer, felon, lawbreaker, malefactor**

criminal 2

adjective involving crime
» *Stealing a car is a serious criminal offense.*
corrupt, crooked, illegal, illicit, unlawful, culpable, felonious, indictable, iniquitous, nefarious
antonym: **legal**

cripple 1

verb to injure severely
» *He was crippled for months after the accident.*
disable, lame, maim, paralyze

cripple 2

verb to prevent from working
» *Snow crippled the bus network so we got the day off.*
bring to a standstill, impair, put out of action

critical 1

adjective very important
» *It is critical to add the ingredients in the right order.*
crucial, deciding, decisive, momentous, pivotal, vital
antonym: **unimportant**

critical 2

adjective very serious
» *Her car was in critical need of a new battery.*
grave, precarious, serious

critical 3

adjective finding fault with something or someone
» *The boy thought his teacher was too critical and had given him an unfair grade.*
carping, derogatory, disapproving, disparaging, scathing, captious, cavilling, censorious, fault-finding
antonym: **complimentary**

criticism

noun expression of disapproval
» *His criticism of the play was harsh.*
censure, disapproval, disparagement, fault-finding, flak (informal), **panning** (informal), denigration, stricture
antonym: **praise**

criticize

verb to find fault » *The bus driver was criticized for not being on time.*
censure, condemn, find fault with, knock (informal), **pan** (informal), **put down,** disparage, excoriate, lambast, lambaste
antonym: **praise**

crook

noun (informal) a criminal
» *The man is a crook and a liar.*
cheat, rogue, scoundrel (old-fashioned), **shark, swindler, thief, villain**

crooked 1

adjective bent or twisted
» *The nails were crooked after Dad's attempts to hammer them into the hard wall.*
bent, deformed, distorted, irregular, out of shape, twisted, warped
antonym: **straight**

crooked 2

adjective dishonest or illegal
» *My parents hoped the salesman wasn't crooked.*
corrupt, criminal, dishonest, fraudulent, illegal, shady (informal), dishonorable, nefarious, unprincipled
antonym: **honest**

cross 1

verb to go across
» *The bridge crosses the river.*
ford, go across, span, traverse

*The bridge **crosses** the river.*

cross 2

verb to meet and go across
» *The bus stop is near the traffic lights where the roads cross.*
crisscross, intersect

cross 3

noun a mixture of two things
» *The dog was a cross between a collie and a retriever.*
blend, combination, mixture

cross 4

adjective (Britain) angry
» *I'm very cross with him.*
angry, annoyed, fractious, fretful, grumpy, in a bad mood, irritable, irascible, peevish, testy, tetchy

crouch

verb to squat down
» *We all crouched in the grass.*
bend down, squat

*We all **crouched** in the grass.*

crowd 1

noun a large group of people
» *A huge crowd gathered in the square.*
horde, host, mass, mob, multitude, swarm, throng

crowd 2

verb to gather close together
» *Hundreds of fans crowded into the hall.*
congregate, gather, swarm, throng

crowded

adjective full of people
» *It was a crowded room.*
congested, full, overflowing, packed

crucial

adjective very important
» *He kept his nerve at the crucial moment and won the game.*
central, critical, decisive, momentous, pivotal, vital

*The monkey used the stone as a **crude** tool to open the nuts.*

crude 1

adjective rough and simple
» *The monkey used the stone as a crude tool to open the nuts.*
primitive, rough, rudimentary, simple

crude 2

adjective rude and offensive
» *He had a crude and embarrassing sense of humor.*
coarse, tasteless, vulgar, boorish, crass
antonym: **refined**

cruel

adjective deliberately causing hurt » *Her words were cruel.*
barbarous, brutal, callous, cold-blooded, heartless, inhumane, sadistic, savage, vicious
antonyms: **compassionate, kind**

cruelty

noun cruel behavior
» *Leaving Maz out of the final match was an act of cruelty.*
barbarity, brutality, callousness, inhumanity, savagery, viciousness
antonyms: **compassion, kindness**

crumple

verb to squash and wrinkle
» *She crumpled the paper in her hand.*
crease, crush, screw up, wrinkle

a b c d e f g h i j k l m n o p q r s t u v w x y z

*My little brother loves to **crush** the garlic.*

crush ①
verb to destroy the shape of by squeezing » *My little brother loves to crush the garlic.*
crumble, crumple, mash, squash

crush ②
verb to defeat completely » *His soccer team was crushed with a 6–0 defeat.*
overcome, put down, quell, stamp out, vanquish

cry ①
verb to have tears coming from your eyes » *The movie made her cry.*
bawl, blubber, howl, sob, weep, whimper, wail

cry ②
verb to call out loudly » *"See you soon!" they cried.*
call, exclaim, shout, yell

cry ③
noun a loud or high shout » *The fans in the stadium gave a cry of disappointment when the player missed the basket.*
call, exclamation, shout, yell

cunning ①
adjective smart and deceitful » *The boy had a cunning plan.*
artful, crafty, devious, scheming, sly, wily, foxy
antonym: **open**

cunning ②
noun intelligence and deceit » *The goats showed cunning in finding food.*
deviousness, guile

curb ①
verb to keep something within limits » *Owen must learn to curb his temper.*
check, contain, control, limit, restrain, suppress

curb ②
noun an attempt to keep something within limits » *Parents called for stricter curbs on who could be invited to the school party.*
brake, control, limit, limitation, restraint

cure ①
verb to make well » *The ointment cured the rash.*
heal, remedy

cure ②
noun something that makes an illness better » *The medicine was a cure for his infection.*
medicine, remedy, treatment

curiosity ①
noun the desire to know » *The man showed curiosity in his family tree.*
inquisitiveness, interest

curiosity ②
noun something unusual » *The museum was full of relics and curiosities.*
freak, marvel, novelty, oddity, rarity

*The museum was full of relics and **curiosities**.*

curious ①
adjective wanting to know » *He was curious about the new neighbors.*
inquiring, inquisitive, interested, nosy (informal)
antonym: **incurious**

curious ②
adjective strange and unusual » *The store was full of curious trinkets.*
bizarre, extraordinary, odd, peculiar, singular, strange, unusual
antonym: **ordinary**

current ①
noun a strong continuous movement of water » *She was almost swept away by the fast current of the river.*
flow, tide, undertow

current ②
adjective happening, being done, or being used now » *His current car goes much faster than his last one.*
contemporary, fashionable, ongoing, present, present-day, today's, up-to-the-minute
antonym: **past**

curve ①
noun a bending line » *There was a curve in the road.*
arc, bend, trajectory, turn
related word: *adjective* **sinuous**

curve ②
verb to move in a curve » *The road curved sharply to the left.*
arc, arch, bend, swerve

custom ①
noun a traditional activity » *The tea-drinking ceremony is an ancient Chinese custom.*
convention, practice, ritual, tradition

custom ②
noun something a person always does » *It was her custom to get up at 7 o'clock every morning.*
habit, practice, routine, wont

customer
noun someone who buys something » *The new toy store was filled with customers.*
buyer, client, consumer, patron, purchaser, shopper

*The tailor **cut** the cloth with a sharp pair of scissors.*

cut ①
verb to mark, injure, or remove part of (something or someone) with something sharp » *The tailor cut the cloth with a sharp pair of scissors.*
chop, clip, nick, score, slice, slit, trim

cut ②
verb to reduce something » *Dad cut the amount of TV we watched.*
cut back, decrease, lower, reduce, slash, abridge, downsize, rationalize
antonym: **increase**

cut ③
noun a mark or injury made by cutting » *Sofia had a cut on her finger.*
gash, incision, slash, slit

cut ④
noun a reduction in something » *There was a cut in the number of books in the library.*
cutback, decrease, lowering, reduction, saving
antonym: **increase**

cute
adjective pretty or attractive » *You were such a cute baby!*
adorable, appealing, attractive, charming, dear, good-looking, gorgeous, pretty
antonym: **ugly**

cynical
adjective always thinking the worst of people » *Alex had a cynical attitude towards life that made him seem world-weary.*
distrustful, sceptical

Dd

Hail **damaged** the corn crop.

daft

adjective (Britain) extremely silly » *Wearing shorts in snowy weather is a daft idea.*
crazy, foolish, ludicrous, preposterous, ridiculous, silly, stupid
antonym: **sensible**

damage 1

verb to cause harm to something » *Hail damaged the corn crop.*
harm, hurt, injure

damage 2

noun harm that is done to something » *The tornado caused damage to the town, destroying several houses.*
harm, injury

damages

plural noun money asked for or paid for injury or damage » *The company was forced to pay damages for the dangerous cars they built.*
award, penalty

damp 1

adjective slightly wet » *The towel was damp once he had used it after swimming.*
clammy, dank, humid, moist, sodden, soggy, wet

danger

noun the possibility of harm » *A stampeding hippo is a great danger in Africa.*
hazard, jeopardy, menace, peril, risk, threat
antonym: **safety**

The ocean can be **dangerous** during a storm.

dangerous

adjective likely to cause harm » *The ocean can be dangerous during a storm.*
hazardous, perilous, risky, treacherous
antonym: **safe**

dare 1

verb to challenge someone to do something » *I dare you to jump off the top diving board.*
challenge, defy, throw down the gauntlet

dare 2

verb to have the courage to do something » *Nobody dared to complain to the angry man.*
risk, venture

daring 1

adjective willing to take risks » *They made a daring escape by helicopter.*
adventurous, audacious, bold, brave, fearless, intrepid, valiant
antonym: **cautious**

daring 2

noun the courage to take risks » *Ben showed his daring when he spoke in class for five minutes without notes.*
audacity, boldness, bravery, courage, guts (informal)**, nerve** (informal)**, fearlessness, intrepidity, temerity**
antonym: **caution**

dark 1

adjective lacking light » *It was too dark to see what was happening.*
black, cloudy, dim, dingy, murky, overcast, shadowy, swarthy
antonym: **light**

dark 2

noun lack of light » *It is difficult to see in the dark.*
▼ SEE BELOW

dash 1

verb to rush somewhere » *Madison dashed toward the finish line.*
bolt, fly, race, run, rush, sprint, tear, make haste, hasten

dash 2

verb to throw or be thrown violently against something » *The huge waves dashed against the rocks.*
break, crash, hurl, slam, smash

dark

2 *noun* lack of light » *It is difficult to see in the dark.*

dim
I'm squinting to adjust to the dim.

darkness
The room was plunged into darkness.

gloom
Can you see in the gloom?

murk
I can't make much out in this murk.

dusk
It's only 6 o'clock. It's dusk— it's not pitch-black yet.

antonym: **light**
The light helps me see.

a b c **d** e f g h i j k l m n o p q r s t u v w x y z

A B C D E F G H I J K L M N O P Q R S T U V W X Y Z

dash [3]

verb to ruin or frustrate someone's hopes or ambitions » *The children's hopes of a picnic were dashed by the rain.*
crush, destroy, disappoint, foil, frustrate, shatter, thwart, confound, quash

dash [4]

noun a sudden movement or rush » *Theo made a dash for the door.*
bolt, race, run, rush, sprint, stampede

dash [5]

noun a small quantity of something » *He added a dash of salt to his meal.*
drop, pinch, splash, sprinkling

daydream [1]

noun a series of pleasant thoughts » *His mind often drifted into a daydream.*
dream, fantasy, pipe dream, reverie

*His mind often drifted into a **daydream**.*

daydream [2]

verb to think about pleasant things » *Noah daydreams of being famous.*
dream, fantasize

dazed

adjective unable to think clearly » *At the end of the interview I felt dazed and exhausted.*
bewildered, confused, dizzy, light-headed, numbed, stunned, disorientated, punch-drunk, stupefied

dead [1]

adjective no longer alive » *He found a dead jellyfish washed up on the beach.*
deceased, departed, extinct, late
antonym: **alive**

dead [2]

adjective no longer functioning » *The radio is dead.*
defunct, not working

deadly

adjective causing death » *The Brazilian wandering spider is the world's most deadly arachnid.*
destructive, fatal, lethal, mortal

deal

verb to cope successfully with something » *Ethan deals with stress by doing yoga.*
attend to, cope with, handle, manage, see to, take care of

dear [1]

noun a person for whom you have affection » *Happy Valentine's Day, dear.*
angel, beloved (old-fashioned), darling, love, sweetheart, treasure (informal)

*Happy Valentine's Day, **dear**.*

dear [2]

adjective much loved » *He was a dear friend of mine and I miss him.*
beloved, cherished, darling, esteemed, precious, prized, treasured

*She didn't buy the handbag because it was too **dear**.*

dear [3]

adjective (Britain) costing a lot » *She didn't buy the handbag because it was too dear.*
costly, expensive, pricey (informal)

deceive

verb to make someone believe something that is untrue » *The ad deceived the public by claiming the product would make them look younger.*
con (informal), double cross, dupe, fool, mislead, take in, trick, bamboozle, beguile, hoodwink

decent [1]

adjective of an acceptable standard » *The pay was decent although not generous.*
adequate, passable, reasonable, respectable, satisfactory, tolerable

decent [2]

adjective correct and respectable » *She was a decent person who always tried to do the right thing.*
proper, respectable
antonym: **improper**

deceptive

adjective likely to make people believe something untrue » *The deceptive raccoon looks cute, but it can be vicious when cornered.*
false, fraudulent, illusory, misleading, unreliable, delusive, specious

decide

verb to choose to do something » *She decided to sign up for swimming lessons.*
choose, come to a decision, determine (formal), elect (formal), make up your mind, reach a decision, resolve (formal)

decision

noun a judgment about something » *The judges came to a decision about who the winner was in the race.*
conclusion, finding, judgment, resolution, ruling, verdict

declaration

noun a forceful or official announcement » *She made her declaration in public for all to hear.*
affirmation, protestation (formal), statement, testimony, assertion, avowal

*She made her **declaration** in public for all to hear.*

declare

verb to state something forcefully or officially » *Sundeep declared that he was going to sail around the world.*
affirm, announce, assert, certify, proclaim, profess (formal), pronounce, state, attest, aver, avow

decline [1]

verb to become smaller or weaker » *The plants in the garden declined during winter.*
decrease, diminish, drop, fall, go down, plummet, reduce, dwindle, wane
antonym: **increase**

decline 2

verb to refuse politely to accept or do something
» *He declined their invitation as he didn't want to go out.*
abstain, excuse yourself, refuse, turn down
antonym: **accept**

decline 3

noun a gradual weakening or decrease » *There was a decline in the number of bees visiting the hive this year.*
decrease, downturn, drop, fall, recession, shrinkage, slump
antonym: **increase**

decorate 1

verb to make more attractive
» *She decorated her room with posters and pictures.*
adorn, deck, ornament, beautify, bedeck, embellish, festoon

*She **decorated** her room with posters and pictures.*

decorate 2

verb to put paint or wallpaper on » *They decided to decorate the house and paint her bedroom walls yellow.*
do up (informal),
renovate

decrease 1

verb to become or make less
» *The dentist said we should decrease the amount of sugar we eat.*
cut down, decline, diminish, drop, dwindle, lessen, lower, reduce, shrink, abate, curtail, subside, wane
antonym: **increase**

*The sudden **decrease** in sales was a shock.*

decrease 2

noun a lessening in the amount of something » *The sudden decrease in sales was a shock.*
decline, drop, lessening, reduction, abatement, curtailment, cutback, diminution
antonym: **increase**

deep 1

adjective having a long way to the bottom » *The rabbit dug a deep hole.*
bottomless, yawning
antonym: **shallow**

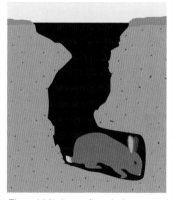

*The rabbit dug a **deep** hole.*

deep 2

adjective great or intense
» *Joe had a deep love of sports and played on many teams.*
extreme, grave, great, intense, profound, serious

deep 3

adjective low in sound
» *The man had a deep voice and sang bass in the choir.*
bass, low, resonant, sonorous
antonym: **high**

defeat 1

verb to win a victory over someone » *I defeated last year's arm-wrestling champion.*
beat, conquer, crush, rout, trounce, vanquish (formal)

defeat 2

noun a failure to win
» *His basketball team suffered a crushing defeat.*
conquest, debacle (formal), **rout, trouncing**
antonym: **victory**

defect

noun a fault or flaw
» *A software defect made the phone unusable.*
deficiency, failing, fault, flaw, imperfection, shortcoming, weakness

defend 1

verb to protect from harm
» *The cat defended her kittens from the dog next door.*
cover, guard, protect, safeguard, shelter, shield

defend 2

verb to argue in support of
» *I defended his silence, explaining that he was shy, not rude.*
endorse, justify, stick up for (informal), **support, uphold**

defender

noun a person who argues in support of something
» *The man was a committed defender of human rights.*
advocate, champion, supporter

defense 1

noun action to protect something » *Many plant-eating dinosaurs had spikes and weapons on their tails as a form of defense.*
cover, protection, resistance, safeguard, security

defense 2

noun an argument in support of something » *Jason's only defense for taking the chocolate without asking was that he was hungry.*
argument, excuse, explanation, justification, plea

deficiency

noun a lack of something
» *The disease scurvy is caused by a deficiency of vitamin C.*
deficit, deprivation, inadequacy, lack, want (formal)
antonym: **abundance**

deficient

adjective lacking in something
» *The patchy, muddy lawn was deficient in grass.*
inadequate, lacking, poor, short, wanting

definite 1

adjective unlikely to be changed » *Dad set a definite limit to my vacation money.*
assured, certain, decided, fixed, guaranteed, settled

definite 2

adjective certainly true
» *Hot cocoa was a definite help in getting to sleep.*
clear, positive, black-and-white, clear-cut, cut-and-dried

deformed

adjective abnormally shaped
» *The deformed carrot looked as if it had two legs.*
disfigured, distorted

*The **deformed** carrot looked as if it had two legs.*

a b c d e f g h i j k l m n o p q r s t u v w x y z

A
B
C
D
E
F
G
H
I
J
K
L
M
N
O
P
Q
R
S
T
U
V
W
X
Y
Z

degrade

verb to humiliate someone
» *Ava was sorry that her mean remark had degraded her friend.*
demean, humiliate

delay ①

verb to put something off until later » *Lunch was delayed by an hour because our guests were late.*
defer, postpone, put off, shelve, suspend

delay ②

verb to slow or hinder something » *Fallen trees on the road delayed her trip home.*
hinder, impede, obstruct, set back, hold up, retard

delay ③

noun a time when something is delayed » *The fog grounded planes, causing flight delays.*
interruption, obstruction, setback

delete

verb to remove something written » *She deleted the final paragraph because it repeated an earlier one.*
cross out, erase, rub out, blue-pencil, edit out, strike out

deliberate ①

adjective done on purpose » *When I found the textbook under Doug's desk, I realized it was part of a deliberate attempt to cheat on the exam.*
calculated, conscious, intentional, premeditated, studied
antonym: **accidental**

deliberate ②

adjective careful and not hurried » *The vet's movements were gentle and deliberate as he felt the cat's leg for bruising.*
careful, cautious, measured, methodical
antonym: **casual**

*The girl **deliberated** over what to eat.*

deliberate ③

verb to think carefully about a choice » *The girl deliberated over what to eat.*
debate, meditate, mull over, ponder, reflect

delicious

adjective tasting very good
▶▶ SEE RIGHT

delight ①

noun great pleasure or joy » *It gives me great delight to welcome you to our new home.*
glee, happiness, joy, pleasure, rapture, satisfaction

delight ②

verb to give someone great pleasure » *The squeaky toy delighted the baby.*
amuse, captivate, charm, enchant, please, thrill

demand

verb to need or require something » *Running the obstacle course demanded strength and coordination.*
involve, need, require, take, want, call for, entail, necessitate

deny ①

verb to say that something is untrue » *He denied he broke the ornament on purpose.*
contradict, refute, abjure, disavow, disclaim, gainsay, rebut, repudiate
antonym: **admit**

deny ②

verb to refuse to believe something » *She denied the existence of ghosts.*
reject, renounce

deny ③

verb to refuse to give something » *Pamela's mom denied her any more snacks before dinner.*
refuse, withhold

department

noun a section of an organization » *The store's sock department was always busier than swimwear in winter.*
division, office, section, unit

depend on ①

verb to rely on
» *You can depend on me to help you in an emergency.*
bank on, count on, rely on, trust

depend on ②

verb to be affected by
» *The taste depends on the quality of the ingredients.*
be determined by, hinge on, be subject to, hang on, rest on

deposit

verb to put down or leave somewhere » *She deposited the coin in the piggy bank.*
drop, lay, leave, place, put down

*She **deposited** the coin in the piggy bank.*

*No one knew who owned the **derelict** house with the broken window.*

derelict

adjective abandoned and in poor condition » *No one knew who owned the derelict house with the broken window.*
abandoned, dilapidated, neglected, ruined

descend

verb to move downward
» *We descended the stairs.*
dip, dive, fall, go down, plummet, sink
antonym: **ascend**

describe

verb to give an account of something » *The teacher asked Amy to describe what she did in her spare time.*
define, depict, portray, characterize, detail

deserve

verb to have a right to something » *Mom works hard, so she deserves a rest.*
be entitled to, be worthy of, earn, justify, merit, warrant

design ①

verb to make a plan of something » *She couldn't wait to design her new bedroom herself.*
draft, draw up, plan

design ②

noun a plan or drawing
» *Brad showed us his design for a vegetable garden.*
model, plan, blueprint, schema

design ③

noun the shape or style of something » *Mel had a funky new design of clock.*
form, pattern, shape, style

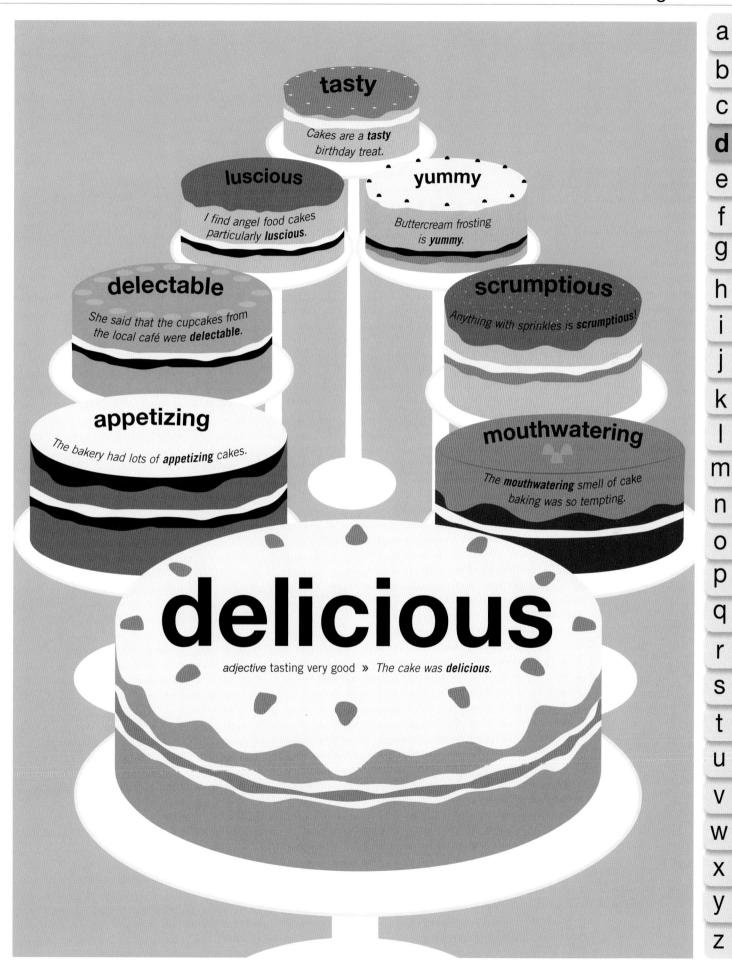

tasty

Cakes are a **tasty** birthday treat.

luscious

I find angel food cakes particularly **luscious**.

yummy

Buttercream frosting is **yummy**.

delectable

She said that the cupcakes from the local café were **delectable**.

scrumptious

Anything with sprinkles is **scrumptious**!

appetizing

The bakery had lots of **appetizing** cakes.

mouthwatering

The **mouthwatering** smell of cake baking was so tempting.

delicious

adjective tasting very good » The cake was **delicious**.

a b c **d** e f g h i j k l m n o p q r s t u v w x y z

A
B
C
D
E
F
G
H
I
J
K
L
M
N
O
P
Q
R
S
T
U
V
W
X
Y
Z

desire ①

verb to want something
» *We can stay longer at the fair if you desire.*
crave, fancy (Britain)**, long for, want, wish, yearn,** ache for, covet

desire ②

noun a feeling of wanting something » *I have a strong desire to help people.*
appetite, craving, hankering, longing, wish, yearning, yen (informal)

despair ①

noun a loss of hope
» *Emma felt despair at the thought of another long car trip.*
dejection, despondency, gloom, hopelessness

despair ②

verb to lose hope » *The people despaired over the death of their beloved leader.*
feel dejected, feel despondent, lose heart, lose hope

despite

preposition in spite of
» *He gave a great talk despite his fear of public speaking.*
in spite of, notwithstanding (formal)**, regardless of**

destroy

verb to ruin something completely » *The fire destroyed the building.*
annihilate, demolish, devastate, obliterate, raze, ruin, wreck

*The fire **destroyed** the building.*

*The **destruction** of the rain forest left many animals homeless.*

destruction

noun the act of destroying something » *The destruction of the rain forest left many animals homeless.*
annihilation, demolition, devastation, obliteration

detail

noun an individual feature of something » *We discussed every detail of the play.*
aspect, element, particular, point, respect, fine point, nicety

determination

noun a firm decision to do something » *Adam showed determination in his training for the Olympics.*
perseverance, persistence, resolution, resolve (formal)**, tenacity,** doggedness, single-mindedness, steadfastness, willpower

determine ①

verb to cause or control a situation or result » *The size of the chicken determines the cooking time.*
control, decide, dictate, govern, shape

determine ②

verb to decide or settle something firmly
» *The date of the game had not yet been determined.*
arrange, choose, decide, fix, resolve, settle

determine ③

verb to find out the facts about something » *The X-ray will determine if there are any broken bones.*
ascertain (formal)**, confirm, discover, establish, find out, verify**

determined

adjective firmly decided » *Mia was determined to finish the race, however long it took her.*
bent on, dogged, intent on, persistent, purposeful, resolute (formal)**, single-minded, tenacious,** steadfast, unflinching, unwavering

develop ①

verb to grow or become more advanced » *The seedling developed new leaves.*
advance, evolve, grow, mature, progress, result, spring

*The seedling **developed** new leaves.*

develop ②

verb to become affected by an illness or fault » *He developed pneumonia.*
catch, contract (formal)**, fall ill, get, go down with, pick up, succumb**

devious

adjective achieving your goal by sly methods » *He got another turn by being devious, claiming he'd missed out last time.*
calculating, scheming, underhand, wily

devoted

adjective very loving and loyal
» *He was a devoted father.*
constant, dedicated, doting, faithful, loving, loyal, true

die ①

verb to stop living » *The flowers had drooped and died.*
check out, croak (slang)**, expire** (formal)**, pass away, pass on, perish** (formal)

die ②

verb to fade away » *Trang reassured her that the worry she felt would soon die.*
fade away, fade out, peter out

die out

verb to cease to exist » *Many ancient customs have died out.*
disappear, fade, vanish

difference ①

noun a lack of similarity between things » *There is a huge difference between the size of a Yorkshire Terrier and a Great Dane.*
contrast, discrepancy, disparity, distinction, divergence, variation
antonym: **similarity**

*There is a huge **difference** between the size of a Yorkshire Terrier and a Great Dane.*

difference ②

noun the amount by which two quantities differ
» *The difference between 17 and 19 is two.*
balance, remainder

difficult

1 *adjective* not easy to do or solve
» *The puzzle was **difficult** to finish.*

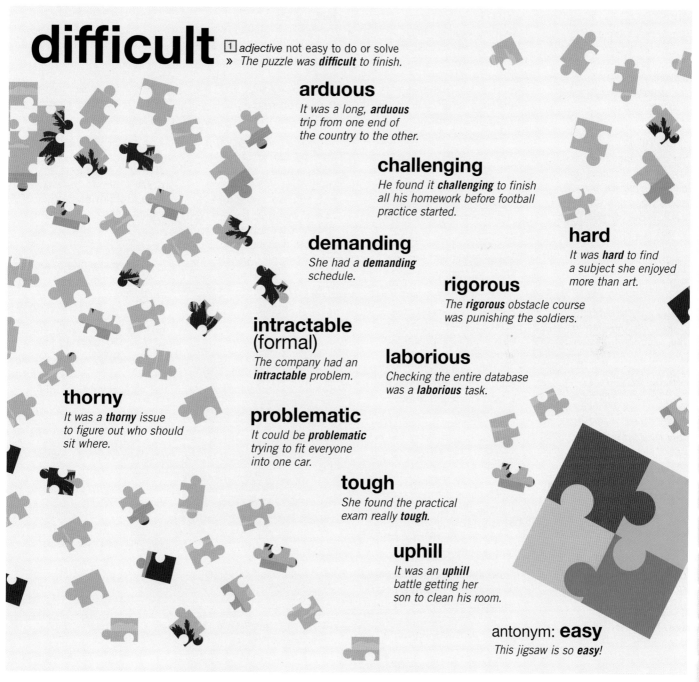

arduous
*It was a long, **arduous** trip from one end of the country to the other.*

challenging
*He found it **challenging** to finish all his homework before football practice started.*

hard
*It was **hard** to find a subject she enjoyed more than art.*

demanding
*She had a **demanding** schedule.*

rigorous
*The **rigorous** obstacle course was punishing the soldiers.*

intractable (formal)
*The company had an **intractable** problem.*

laborious
*Checking the entire database was a **laborious** task.*

thorny
*It was a **thorny** issue to figure out who should sit where.*

problematic
*It could be **problematic** trying to fit everyone into one car.*

tough
*She found the practical exam really **tough**.*

uphill
*It was an **uphill** battle getting her son to clean his room.*

antonym: **easy**
*This jigsaw is so **easy**!*

---

different 1
adjective unlike something else » *His shiny green shoes were different from everyone else's.*
contrasting, disparate (formal), **dissimilar, opposed, unlike, at odds, at variance, divergent** (formal)
antonym: **similar**

different 2
adjective unusual and out of the ordinary » *Jane's hairstyle was different, shaved at the front and long at the back.*
special, unique

different 3
adjective distinct and separate » *The school supports a different charity every year.*
another, discrete (formal), **distinct, individual, separate**

difficult 1
adjective not easy to do or solve
▲ SEE ABOVE

difficult 2
adjective not easy to deal with » *He was difficult to deal with because of his mood swings.*
demanding, troublesome, trying, obstreperous, refractory, unmanageable

difficulty 1
noun a problem » *The main difficulty was that her car wouldn't start.*
complication, hassle (informal), **hurdle, obstacle, pitfall, problem, snag, trouble, impediment, stumbling block**

difficulty 2
noun the quality of being difficult » *Getting on and off the bus on crutches was a difficulty she had to overcome.*
hardship, strain, tribulation (formal), **arduousness, laboriousness**

dig 1
verb to break up soil or sand » *The dog used its front paws to dig a hole in the ground.*
burrow, excavate, gouge, hollow out, quarry, till, tunnel

a b c d e f g h i j k l m n o p q r s t u v w x y z

dig [2]
verb to push something in
» *She could feel the tight bracelet digging into her arm.*
jab, poke, thrust

dig [3]
noun a push or poke
» *Daisy silenced Minh with a dig in the arm.*
jab, poke, prod, thrust

Daisy silenced Minh with a dig in the arm.

dim [1]
adjective not bright or well-lit
» *The light from the lamp was dim, and he couldn't see well enough to read his book.*
dark, dull, gray, murky, poorly lit, shadowy

dim [2]
adjective vague or unclear
» *She had a dim memory of seeing the girl somewhere before.*
faint, hazy, indistinct, obscure, shadowy, vague, fuzzy, ill-defined, indistinguishable
antonym: **clear**

dim [3]
adjective (informal) slow to understand » *He is rather dim, but don't offend him by saying so!*
dumb (informal), obtuse, slow, stupid, thick (informal)
antonym: **bright**

diminish
verb to reduce or become reduced » *The cookie stash diminished throughout the day.*
contract, decrease, lessen, lower, reduce, shrink, weaken

direct [1]
adjective in a straight line or with nothing in between
» *Dad took the most direct route to the airport.*
immediate, personal, straight, uninterrupted
antonym: **indirect**

direct [2]
adjective clear and honest
» *He gave a direct answer to her rambling question: "No."*
blunt, candid, forthright, frank, straight, straightforward
antonym: **devious**

direct [3]
verb to control and guide something » *Christopher is captain and directs the team on the field.*
control, guide, lead, manage, oversee, run, supervise

direction [1]
noun the line in which something is moving
» *He walked for an hour in the wrong direction.*
course, path, route, way

He walked for an hour in the wrong direction.

direction [2]
noun control and guidance of something » *He chopped vegetables under the chef's direction.*
charge, command, control, guidance, leadership, management

dirt [1]
noun dust or mud
» *The bike was covered in dirt.*
dust, filth, grime, muck, mud

dirt [2]
noun earth or soil » *He drew a circle in the dirt with a stick.*
earth, soil

dirty [1]
adjective marked with dirt
▼ SEE BELOW

dirty [2]
adjective unfair or dishonest
» *It was a dirty deal that tricked Joe into doing his brother's chores as well as his own.*
corrupt, crooked
antonym: **honest**

dirty

[1] *adjective* marked with dirt
» *He was always getting his clothes dirty.*

filthy
What a filthy T-shirt!

grimy
Her boots were grimy from the grass and mud.

mucky
Don't put your mucky clothes on the carpet.

grubby
The team was told to wash their grubby hands before eating.

disable
verb to stop something from working » *You need to disable the alarm before you enter the house.*
deactivate, defuse, immobilize

disadvantage
noun an unfavorable circumstance » *They considered the advantages and disadvantages of moving to a new house.*
drawback, handicap, minus, weakness, downside, hindrance
antonym: **advantage**

disagree ①
verb to have a different opinion » *She disagreed with everything he said.*
differ, dispute, dissent
antonym: **agree**

*She **disagreed** with everything he said.*

disagree ②
verb to think that something is wrong » *I disagree with your statement that cats are boring because they sleep all the time.*
object, oppose, take issue with

disagreeable
adjective unpleasant in some way » *The smell of old cabbage was disagreeable.*
horrible, horrid, nasty, objectionable, obnoxious, unfriendly, unpleasant
antonym: **agreeable**

disagreement ①
noun a dispute about something » *My friend and I had a disagreement about which pop group was the best.*
altercation (formal), argument, difference, dispute, quarrel, squabble, tiff
antonym: **agreement**

disagreement ②
noun an objection to something » *There was disagreement over the manager insisting we wear formal clothes to work.*
dissent, objection, opposition

disappear ①
verb to go out of sight » *The aircraft disappeared off the radar.*
be lost to view, drop out of sight, fade, recede, vanish
antonym: **appear**

disappear ②
verb to stop existing » *The snow disappeared when the sun came out.*
cease (formal), die out, go away, melt away, pass, vanish

disappointed
adjective sad because hopes have not been fulfilled » *I was disappointed that we didn't go swimming.*
dejected, despondent, disenchanted, disillusioned, downcast, saddened, disheartened, let down
antonym: **satisfied**

disappointment ①
noun sadness because hopes have not been fulfilled » *Book early to avoid disappointment.*
dejection, despondency, regret, disenchantment, disillusionment

disappointment ②
noun something that does not meet your expectations » *The film was a disappointment; it was really boring.*
blow, setback

disapproval
noun the belief that something is wrong » *John's mom expressed disapproval when he wore ripped jeans to school.*
censure, condemnation, criticism
antonym: **approval**

disapprove
verb to think that something is wrong » *Everyone disapproved of the stickers all over Maria's precious violin.*
condemn, deplore (formal), dislike, find unacceptable, take a dim view of, frown on, take exception to
antonym: **approve**

disaster
noun a very bad accident » *The flood was a disaster.*
calamity (formal), catastrophe, misfortune, tragedy

discard
verb to get rid of something » *She discarded the piece of paper with her old notes on it.*
cast aside, dispose of, dump (informal), jettison, shed, throw away, throw out

*She **discarded** the piece of paper with her old notes on it.*

discern
verb (formal) to notice or understand something with difficulty » *Abby discerned someone walking toward her through the mist.*
detect, make out, notice, observe, perceive, see, spot

discharge ①
verb to send something out » *The cleaned water will be discharged into the sea.*
emit, empty, expel, flush, give off, release

discharge ②
verb to allow someone to leave prison or a hospital » *He had surgery, but was discharged from the hospital yesterday.*
free, let go, liberate, release, set free

discharge ③
verb to dismiss someone from a job » *He was discharged for shouting at his boss.*
dismiss, eject, fire (informal), sack (informal)

stained
*His shorts were **stained** from the grass.*

unclean
*The **unclean** uniform will go straight into the washing machine.*

antonym: **clean**
*The substitute didn't play and so his uniform remained **clean**.*

A
B
C
D
E
F
G
H
I
J
K
L
M
N
O
P
Q
R
S
T
U
V
W
X
Y
Z

discover

verb to find something or find out about something
» She **discovered** a shell in the rock pool.

come across
The children **came across** the pool when exploring the beach.

unearth
He **unearthed** a shell hidden in the mud.

find
She didn't know what she would **find** in the water.

find out
He wanted to **find out** more about hermit crabs.

learn
He went to the library to **learn** about rock pools.

stumble on or **stumble across**
Stumbling across the rock pool was the highlight of their day at the beach.

realize
They **realized** that the tide was coming in.

discharge [4]

noun a sending away from a job or institution
» *A broken leg led to her discharge from the team for the rest of the season.*
dismissal, ejection, expulsion,
the sack (Britain, informal)

discourage

verb to make someone lose enthusiasm » *Don't let these problems discourage you.*
daunt, deter, dissuade, put off, demoralize, dishearten
antonym: **encourage**

discover

verb to find something or find out about something
◀◀ SEE LEFT

discuss

verb to talk about something » *We discussed what we should do tomorrow.*
debate, exchange views on, go into, talk about

discussion

noun a talk about something » *The teachers sat in another room to have a discussion.*
consultation, conversation, debate, dialogue, discourse, talk

The teachers sat in another room to have a discussion.

disgrace [1]

noun loss of respect because of a dishonorable action
» *By refusing to shake hands after the game, he has brought disgrace upon the whole team.*
scandal, shame, discredit, dishonor
antonym: **credit**

disgrace [2]

verb to bring shame upon
» *The dog disgraced itself by ripping the cushions.*
discredit, shame

disgraceful

adjective deserving of shame » *Grace had wasted a disgraceful amount of paper while trying to write the letter.*
scandalous, shameful, shocking, discreditable, dishonorable

disgust [1]

noun a strong feeling of dislike » *Leah felt disgust at the thought of eating a worm.*
nausea, repulsion, revulsion

Leah felt disgust at the thought of eating a worm.

disgust [2]

verb to cause someone to feel disgust » *The foul smell disgusted him.*
repel, revolt, sicken, nauseate, turn your stomach

disgusting

adjective very unpleasant or unacceptable » *That garbage dump is one of the most disgusting things I've ever seen.*
foul, gross, obnoxious, repellent, revolting, sickening, vile, nauseating, repugnant

dishonest

adjective not truthful » *It is dishonest to mislead people.*
corrupt, crooked, deceitful, fraudulent, lying, mendacious, untruthful
antonym: **honest**

dishonesty

noun dishonest behavior
» *Her lies and dishonesty had annoyed people.*
cheating, corruption, deceit, trickery, duplicity, fraudulence, mendacity
antonym: **honesty**

disintegrate

verb to break into many pieces » *The sandcastle disintegrated when the tide came in.*
break up, crumble, fall apart, fall to pieces, fragment

The sandcastle disintegrated when the tide came in.

dislike [1]

verb to consider something unpleasant » *We don't always have liver on the menu because lots of people dislike it.*
abhor (formal), **be averse to, detest, hate, loathe, not be able to abide, not be able to bear, not be able to stand**
antonym: **like**

dislike [2]

noun a feeling of not liking something » *Mom looked at the weeds in the garden with dislike.*
animosity, antipathy, aversion, distaste, hatred, hostility, loathing
antonym: **liking**

disobey

verb to deliberately refuse to follow instructions » *He was forever disobeying rules.*
break, defy, flout, infringe, violate, contravene (formal), **transgress**
antonym: **obey**

Her drawer was in disorder, and it was impossible to find an eraser.

disorder [1]

noun a state of untidiness
» *Her drawer was in disorder, and it was impossible to find an eraser.*
clutter, disarray, muddle
antonym: **order**

disorder [2]

noun a lack of organization
» *The play ended in disorder when they all forgot their lines and walked off the stage.*
chaos, confusion, disarray, turmoil

disorder [3]

noun a disease or illness
» *She had a rare nerve disorder.*
affliction, complaint, condition, disease, illness

dispose of

verb to get rid of something
» *Tie the bag and dispose of it.*
discard, dispense with, dump, get rid of, throw away

disprove

verb to show that something is not true » *The science experiment will either prove or disprove the theory.*
discredit, give the lie to, invalidate, prove false, refute
antonym: **prove**

dispute [1]

noun an argument
» *The dispute between them is now settled.*
argument, clash, conflict, disagreement, feud, row, wrangle

a b c d e f g h i j k l m n o p q r s t u v w x y z

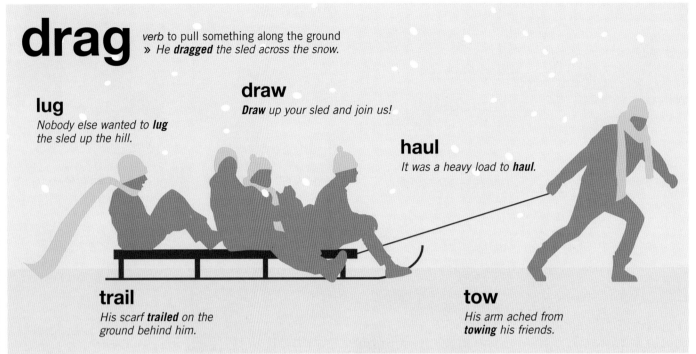

drag

verb to pull something along the ground
» He **dragged** the sled across the snow.

lug
Nobody else wanted to **lug** the sled up the hill.

draw
Draw up your sled and join us!

haul
It was a heavy load to **haul**.

trail
His scarf **trailed** on the ground behind him.

tow
His arm ached from **towing** his friends.

---

dispute ②
verb to question something's truth or wisdom
» Tim disputed the claim that he hadn't even tried to win.
challenge, contest, contradict, deny, query, question
antonym: **accept**

distant ①
adjective far away in space or time » A distant ship appeared on the horizon.
far, outlying, out-of-the-way, remote, faraway, far-flung, far-off
antonym: **close**

A **distant** ship appeared on the horizon.

distant ②
adjective cold and unfriendly
» He is polite but distant.
aloof, detached, reserved, withdrawn, standoffish, unapproachable
antonym: **friendly**

distinguish ①
verb to see the difference between things » A pet can't distinguish right from wrong.
differentiate, discriminate, tell, tell apart, tell the difference

distinguish ②
verb to just recognize something » I heard shouting but was unable to distinguish the words.
discern, make out, pick out, recognize

distract
verb to stop someone from concentrating » Playing computer games distracted Felipe from his homework.
divert, draw away, sidetrack, turn aside

distress ①
noun great suffering » The pain from her broken arm was causing her distress.
heartache, pain, sorrow, suffering

distress ②
noun the state of needing help » The ship sent out a signal that it was in distress.
difficulty, need, straits, trouble

distress ③
verb to cause someone unhappiness » It distressed Gran that the cousins left without saying goodbye.
bother, disturb, grieve, pain, sadden, trouble, upset, worry

distribute ①
verb to hand something out
» The teacher distributed the prizes to the winners.
circulate, hand out, pass around

distribute ②
verb to spread something through an area
» Distribute the sprinkles evenly over the cupcake.
diffuse, disperse, scatter, spread

Distribute the sprinkles evenly over the cupcake.

distribute ③
verb to divide and share something » Chores were evenly distributed among all family members.
allocate, allot, dispense (formal), **divide, dole out, share out,** apportion, mete out

disturb ①
verb to intrude on someone's peace » She crept past her sleeping father so as not to disturb him.
bother, disrupt, intrude on

disturb ②
verb to upset or worry someone » The scenes on the news disturbed him.
agitate, distress, shake, trouble, unsettle, upset, worry

dive
verb to go head first into water » Sharon dived into the pool.
jump, leap, submerge

divide ①
verb to split something up » He divided the can of food between the two cats.
cut up, partition, segregate, separate, split, split up
antonym: **join**

*A fence **divides** the field between the sheep and the cows.*

divide ②
verb to form a barrier between things » *A fence divides the field between the sheep and the cows.*
bisect, separate

divide ③
verb to cause people to disagree » *My parents were divided over politics.*
come between, set against one another, split

division ①
noun separation into parts » *The city's division into two parts was caused by the railroad that ran through its center.*
partition, separation

division ②
noun a disagreement » *There were divisions in the community over where the carnival should be held.*
breach, difference of opinion, rupture, split

division ③
noun a section of something » *The costume division was easier to find than the props.*
department, section, sector

dizzy
adjective about to lose your balance » *Manuel had a dizzy spell and almost fell over.*
giddy, light-headed

do ①
verb to carry out a task » *He just didn't want to do any work.*
carry out, execute (formal), **perform, undertake**

do ②
verb to be sufficient » *It is best to send a birthday card, but an email will do.*
be adequate, be sufficient, suffice (formal)

do ③
verb to perform at a certain level » *Connie did well at tap.*
fare, get on, manage

dodge ①
verb to move out of the way » *The player in white dodged the tackle.*
duck, swerve

*The player in white **dodged** the tackle.*

dodge ②
verb to avoid doing something » *He dodged the question by talking about something else.*
avoid, elude, evade, get out of, shirk, sidestep

dog
noun an animal often kept as a pet » *The dog is a loyal pet.*
canine, mongrel, mutt (slang), **pooch** (slang)
related words:
adjective **canine**; *female* **bitch**; *young* **pup, puppy**

doomed
adjective certain to fail » *It was a doomed attempt to retrieve the ball—they would never be able to reach it up in the tree.*
condemned, hopeless, ill-fated

double ①
adjective twice the usual size » *Bad traffic meant it took twice as long to get home.*
twice, twofold

double ②
adjective consisting of two parts » *A double stroller was needed for the twin babies.*
dual, twin, twofold

doubt ①
noun a feeling of uncertainty » *She had doubts about traveling in rainy weather.*
misgiving, qualm, scepticism, uncertainty
antonym: **certainty**

doubt ②
verb to feel uncertain about something » *Sam doubted his ability to play a concerto.*
be dubious, be sceptical, query, question
antonym: **believe**

doubtful
adjective unlikely or uncertain » *It's doubtful he'll do another tour as he wants a change.*
debatable, dubious, questionable, uncertain
antonym: **certain**

down ①
adverb toward the ground, or in a lower place » *He walked down the stairs.*
downward, downstairs
antonym: **up**

*He walked **down** the stairs.*

down ②
adjective depressed » *He felt down when his team lost.*
dejected, depressed, dispirited, fed up (informal), **glum, melancholy, miserable, sad, despondent, morose, pessimistic**

downfall
noun the failure of a person or thing » *The king's greed had been his downfall.*
collapse, fall, ruin

drab
adjective dull and lacking brightness » *The army truck was painted in drab colors.*
dingy, dismal, dreary, dull, gloomy, grey/gray, somber, cheerless, lackluster
antonym: **bright**

*The army truck was painted in **drab** colors.*

drag
verb to pull something along the ground
◄◄ SEE LEFT

drain ①
verb to cause a liquid to flow somewhere » *Kevin pulled out the plug to drain water from the bathtub.*
draw off, pump

drain ②
verb to flow somewhere » *Some rivers drain into lakes.*
discharge, empty, flow, seep

drain ③
verb to use something up » *The long day of traveling drained her of energy.*
consume, exhaust, sap, tax, use up

drastic
adjective severe and urgent » *Now is the time for drastic action if we are going to save the company.*
extreme, harsh, radical, severe

a b c d e f g h i j k l m n o p q r s t u v w x y z

A B C D E F G H I J K L M N O P Q R S T U V W X Y Z

draw [1]
verb to make a picture
» *Lucas decided to draw the view through the window.*
paint, sketch, trace

draw [2]
verb to move somewhere
» *The car drew away from the curb.*
move, pull

draw [3]
verb to pull something » *Max drew his chair closer to the fire.*
drag, haul, pull

drawback
noun a problem that makes something less than perfect
» *The only drawback was that the apartment was too small.*
difficulty, hitch, problem, snag, trouble

dreadful
adjective extremely bad
» *She thought the play was dreadful, with bad acting and no plot.*
appalling, atrocious, awful, frightful, ghastly, horrendous, terrible
antonym: **wonderful**

dream [1]
noun mental pictures while sleeping » *Ahmed had a dream that his rabbit could fly.*
hallucination, trance, vision, delusion, reverie

dream [2]
noun something that you want very much » *His dream was to be promoted to manager.*
ambition, aspiration, daydream, fantasy, Holy Grail, pipe dream

*His **dream** was to be promoted to manager.*

dreary
adjective dull or boring
» *It was a dreary, rainy day.*
drab, dull, humdrum, monotonous, tedious

dress [1]
noun a piece of clothing
» *It was a hot day, so she wore a summer dress.*
frock, gown, robe

*It was a hot day, so she wore a summer **dress**.*

dress [2]
noun clothing in general » *The invitation said "casual dress."*
attire (formal), **clothes, clothing, costume, garb** (formal), **apparel, raiment**

dress [3]
verb to put on clothes
» *The little boy had dressed himself and put his pants on back to front.*
attire (formal), **clothe, garb** (formal)
antonym: **undress**

drink
verb to swallow liquid
▶▶ SEE RIGHT

drip [1]
verb to fall in small drops
» *Rain dripped from the brim of his cap.*
dribble, splash, trickle

drip [2]
noun a small amount of a liquid » *There were drips of paint on the carpet when Dad finished painting the wall.*
bead, drop, droplet, dribble, globule

drive [1]
verb to operate or power a machine or vehicle » *He liked to drive the car on empty roads.*
operate, pilot, power, propel, run, steer, work

drive [2]
verb to force someone to do something » *Ambition drove Jim to work harder.*
compel, force, lead, motivate, prompt, push, spur

drive [3]
verb to force something pointed into a surface » *Rick used a sledgehammer to drive the pegs into the ground.*
hammer, knock, ram, sink, thrust

*Rick used a sledgehammer to **drive** the pegs into the ground.*

drive [4]
noun a trip in a vehicle
» *We decided to go for a drive in the car.*
excursion, jaunt, journey (Britain), **ride, run, spin, trip**

drive [5]
noun energy and determination » *Justin had the drive to succeed against all odds.*
ambition, determination, energy, enterprise, initiative, motivation, vigor

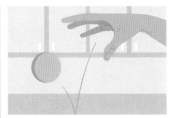

*The ball **dropped** and bounced on the ground.*

drop [1]
verb to fall downward
» *The ball dropped and bounced on the ground.*
descend, fall, plummet, sink, tumble

drop [2]
verb to become less
» *Temperatures can drop to freezing at night.*
decline, decrease, fall, plummet, sink, slump, tumble
antonym: **rise**

drop [3]
noun a small amount of a liquid » *A drop of ink splashed from the end of the pen.*
bead, drip, droplet, dribble, globule

drowsy
adjective tired and sleepy
» *It had been an exhausting day and he felt drowsy.*
lethargic, sluggish

drug [1]
noun a treatment for disease
» *The drug was a type of antibiotic.*
medication, medicine

dry [1]
adjective without any liquid
» *The path was dry after several days of sunshine.*
arid, dried-up, parched
antonym: **wet**

dry [2]
verb to remove liquid from something » *You do the dishes and I'll dry them.*
drain, dehumidify, dehydrate, desiccate
antonym: **moisten**

dubious [1]

adjective not entirely honest or reliable » *Rachel didn't believe his dubious answer that his bus had broken down.*
crooked, dishonest, questionable, suspect, suspicious, unreliable

dubious [2]

adjective doubtful about something » *My parents were dubious about the number of friends I'd invited for a sleepover.*
doubtful, nervous, sceptical, suspicious, unconvinced, undecided, unsure

dull [1]

adjective not interesting » *I found the chess game dull because Millie took so long between moves.*
boring, drab, humdrum, monotonous, tedious, uninteresting
antonym: **interesting**

dull [2]

adjective not bright or clear » *Brown is a dull color, unlike bright, cheerful yellow.*
drab, gloomy, muted, somber, subdued
antonym: **bright**

dull [3]

adjective covered with clouds » *The weather is always dull and foggy.*
cloudy, leaden, murky, overcast
antonym: **bright**

dumb [1]

adjective unable to speak » *We were all struck dumb with surprise.*
mute, silent, speechless

dumb [2]

adjective (informal) slow to understand » *She called him dumb for not understanding what the teacher said, and the teacher told her off for being mean.*
dim, obtuse (formal), stupid, thick (Britain, informal)
antonym: **smart**

They **dumped** the extra sand back at the quarry.

dump [1]

verb to get rid of something » *They dumped the extra sand back at the quarry.*
discharge, dispose of, get rid of, jettison, throw away, throw out

dump [2]

verb (informal) to put something down » *We dumped our coats and ran off.*
deposit, drop

dupe

verb to trick someone » *She realized he'd duped her when he pulled a rabbit from her hat.*
cheat, con (informal), deceive, delude, fool, play a trick on, trick

duty [1]

noun something that you ought to do » *We have a duty to look after the environment.*
obligation, responsibility

duty [2]

noun a task associated with a job » *My main duty as a chauffeur is to drive people from one place to another.*
assignment, job, responsibility, role

duty [3]

noun tax paid to the government » *There's no duty to pay on perfume at the airport.*
excise, levy (formal), tariff, tax

dying: be dying for

verb to want something very much » *I'm dying for a pizza.*
ache for, hunger for, long for, pine for, yearn for

a b c d e f g h i j k l m n o p q r s t u v w x y z

gulp

Gulping the water gave him hiccups.

imbibe

The bride's father **imbibed** too much alcohol at the wedding.

quaff

He **quaffed** huge cups of water after the race.

guzzle

Don't **guzzle** all the juice!

sup

She **supped** her soup straight from the mug.

swig

He **swigged** the lemonade straight from the bottle.

sip

She **sipped** tea from a china cup.

drink

verb to swallow liquid » *He **drank** hot chocolate from his favorite mug.*

Ee

eager
adjective wanting very much to do or have something
» *Robert was eager to earn some extra money and took on a paper round.*
anxious, ardent, avid, enthusiastic, keen, raring to go (informal), fervent, hungry, zealous

early [1]
adjective before the arranged or expected time
» *Kate was early; none of her friends had arrived yet.*
advance, premature, untimely
antonym: **late**

early [2]
adjective near the beginning of a period of time
» *World War I took place in the early 20th century.*
primeval, primitive

early [3]
adverb before the arranged or expected time
» *We arrived early at the movie theater so that we wouldn't have to wait in line.*
ahead of time, beforehand, in advance, in good time, prematurely

earn [1]
verb to get money in return for doing work
» *John earns a good salary.*
bring in, draw, get, make, obtain, net, procure, reap

earn [2]
verb to receive something that you deserve » *Tina earned her scholarship through hard work and determination.*
acquire, attain (formal), **win**

Earth [1]
noun the planet on which we live » *Most of Earth's surface is covered with water.*
globe, planet, world
related word:
adjective **terrestrial**

Most of **Earth's** surface is covered with water.

Jo planted the flower and filled the pot with **earth**.

earth [2]
noun (Britain) soil from the ground » *Jo planted the flower and filled the pot with earth.*
clay, dirt, ground, soil, loam, topsoil, turf

ease [1]
noun lack of difficulty or worry
» *After weeks of practice, Len passed his test with ease.*
leisure, relaxation, simplicity

ease [2]
verb to make or become less severe or intense
» *The doctor gave him some medicine to ease the pain.*
abate, calm, relax, relieve, slacken, allay, alleviate, assuage

eat
[1] *verb* to chew and swallow food
» *There's never any food left when the dogs have finished eating.*

munch

chew

gobble

chomp

snack

gulp

ease [3]

verb to move slowly or carefully
» *He eased open the heavy door and peered outside.*
creep, edge, guide, inch, lower, maneuver, squeeze

easy [1]

adjective able to be done without difficulty » *This is an easy puzzle with lots of clues.*
light, painless, simple, smooth, straightforward
antonym: **hard**

easy [2]

adjective comfortable and without worries » *We had an easy, relaxed day at the beach.*
carefree, comfortable, leisurely, quiet, relaxed

eat [1]

verb to chew and swallow food
▼ SEE BELOW

eat [2]

verb to have a meal
» *We like to eat dinner early.*
breakfast (formal), **dine, feed, have a meal, lunch** (formal), **picnic**

*The body of the van had been **eaten away** by rust.*

eat away

verb to destroy something slowly » *The body of the van had been eaten away by rust.*
corrode, destroy, dissolve, erode, rot, wear away

eccentric [1]

adjective regarded as odd or peculiar » *Joe wears eccentric hats with bells on them.*
bizarre, outlandish, quirky, strange, weird, whimsical

eccentric [2]

noun someone who is regarded as odd or peculiar » *Molly is a bit of an eccentric with her strange views on life.*
character, oddball

economic [1]

adjective concerning the way money is managed » *It is hard to start a business when the economic situation is bad.*
budgetary, commercial, financial, fiscal, monetary

economic [2]

adjective making a profit » *Bananas are an economic crop to grow.*
productive, profitable, viable, moneymaking, profitmaking, remunerative

economical [1]

adjective cheap to use and saving you money » *Our car may not be fast, but it's very economical to run.*
cheap, cost-effective, economic, inexpensive

economical [2]

adjective careful and sensible with money or materials » *It is more economical for us to make hot chocolate at home than to buy it from the café.*
careful, frugal, prudent, thrifty

economy

noun the careful use of things to save money » *Ben always spent too much; he needed to start shopping with economy.*
frugality (formal), **prudence, restraint, thrift**

ecstasy

noun extreme happiness » *Winning the gold medal was total ecstasy!*
bliss, delight, elation, euphoria, exaltation, joy, rapture

*Winning the gold medal was total **ecstasy**!*

devour

swallow

feeds (on)

scarf

nibble

wolf down

consume

a b c d e f g h i j k l m n o p q r s t u v w x y z

A B C D E F G H I J K L M N O P Q R S T U V W X Y Z

*Don't go near the **edge** of the cliff!*

edge 1

noun the place where something ends or meets something else » *Don't go near the edge of the cliff!*
border, boundary, brim, fringe, lip, margin, rim, perimeter, periphery
antonym: **center**

edge 2

verb to move somewhere slowly » *The cat edged toward the mouse, but it saw him and scampered away.*
creep, inch, sidle

educated

adjective having a high standard of learning » *Our teacher is an educated and wise lady.*
cultivated, cultured, intellectual, learned, erudite, well-educated

education

noun the process of learning or teaching » *A good education is essential for success in life.*
coaching, e-learning, instruction, schooling, training, tuition

effect

noun a direct result of something » *Regular piano practice had a real effect on my playing.*
consequence, end result, fruit, result, upshot

efficient

adjective able to work well without wasting time or energy » *Katie's an efficient worker who helps us get things done quickly.*
businesslike, competent, economic, effective, organized, productive
antonym: **inefficient**

effort 1

noun physical or mental energy » *It took a lot of effort to move the heavy box.*
application, energy, exertion, trouble, work

effort 2

noun an attempt or struggle » *Mom's cakemaking efforts are greatly appreciated by her hungry family.*
attempt, bid, stab (informal), **struggle**

elaborate 1

adjective having many different parts » *She threw an elaborate party with lots of entertainment and music, and huge amounts of food.*
complex, complicated, detailed, intricate, involved
antonym: **simple**

elaborate 2

adjective highly decorated » *The wooden box had elaborate carvings.*
fancy, fussy, ornate

*The wooden box had **elaborate** carvings.*

elaborate 3

verb to add more information about something » *He promised to elaborate on the plan by giving more details.*
develop, enlarge, expand

eliminate 1

verb to get rid of someone or something » *My lactose-intolerant friend has to eliminate dairy foods from her diet.*
cut out, do away with, eradicate, get rid of, remove, stamp out

eliminate 2

verb to beat someone in a competition » *Dan's team was eliminated in the first round.*
knock out, put out

embarrass

verb to make someone feel ashamed or awkward » *My dad likes to embarrass me in front of my friends!*
disconcert, fluster, humiliate, shame, discomfit, faze, mortify

embarrassed

adjective ashamed and awkward » *She was easily embarrassed and turned red when anyone looked at her.*
ashamed, awkward, humiliated, red-faced, self-conscious, sheepish, abashed, bashful, discomfited, mortified

embarrassment

noun shame and awkwardness » *I laughed loudly to cover my embarrassment at falling over.*
awkwardness, bashfulness, humiliation, self-consciousness, shame, chagrin, discomfiture, mortification

emergency

noun an unexpected and difficult situation » *It was an emergency—she was lost and couldn't find her way home.*
crisis, crunch, pinch

emit

verb to give out or release something » *The alarm emitted a loud, shrill ring.*
exude, give off, give out, release, send out, utter, produce, radiate, send forth

emphasis

noun special or extra importance » *The book placed more emphasis on the characters than the plot.*
accent, importance, prominence, weight

emphasize

verb to make something seem especially important or obvious » *He emphasized the need for everyone to stay quiet while they visited the reptile house.*
accent, accentuate, highlight, play up, stress, underline, foreground, prioritize, underscore

employ 1

verb to pay someone to work for you » *The family next door employs me to babysit.*
appoint, commission, engage (formal), **hire, take on**

employ 2

verb to use something » *When his parents said no, Kieran employed a new strategy to get what he wanted.*
bring to bear, make use of, use, utilize

employee

noun someone who is paid to work for someone else » *Hannah was one of eight employees on the farm.*
hand, worker, workman

employer

noun someone that other people work for » *The new office assistant thanked her employer for giving her the job.*
boss, gaffer (informal)

employment

noun giving someone paid work or having paid work » *Will you stay in education or look for employment?*
engagement, enlistment, hiring, recruitment
►► SEE RIGHT

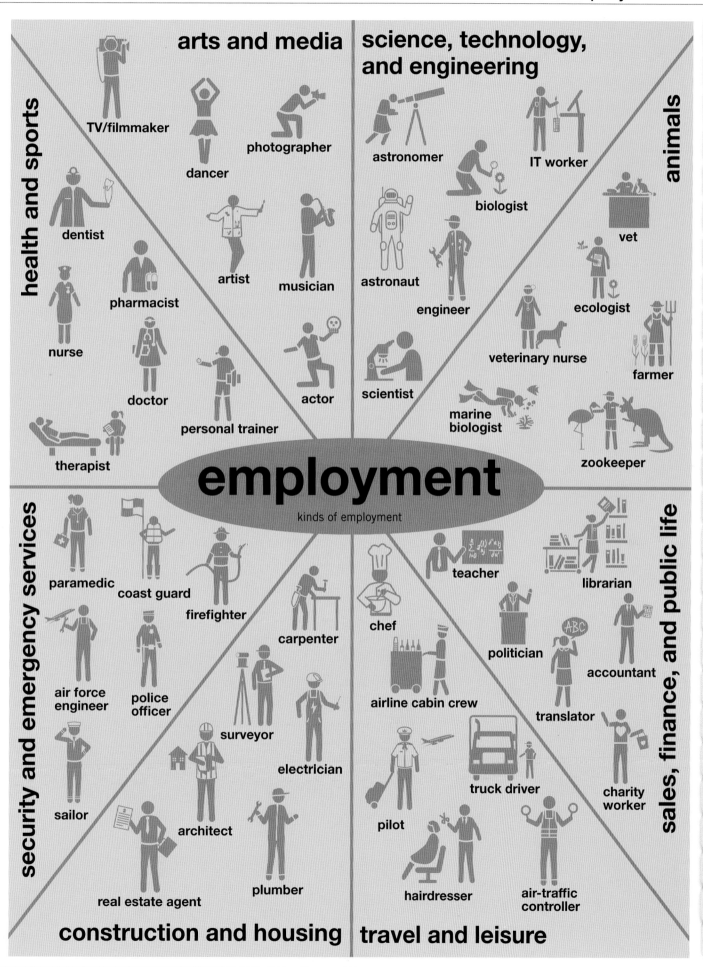

arts and media

science, technology, and engineering

health and sports

animals

TV/filmmaker

photographer

dancer

dentist

artist

musician

pharmacist

nurse

doctor

actor

scientist

personal trainer

therapist

astronomer

IT worker

biologist

vet

astronaut

engineer

ecologist

veterinary nurse

farmer

marine biologist

zookeeper

employment

kinds of employment

security and emergency services

sales, finance, and public life

paramedic

coast guard

firefighter

carpenter

teacher

librarian

chef

politician

air force engineer

police officer

airline cabin crew

accountant

surveyor

translator

sailor

electrician

truck driver

charity worker

architect

pilot

real estate agent

plumber

hairdresser

air-traffic controller

construction and housing

travel and leisure

close
climax
ending
finish
conclusion
culmination

end

1 noun the last part of a period or event » *The curtains closed at the **end** of the play.*

antonym:
beginning
*The curtains will open at the **beginning** of tomorrow's performance.*

empty 1
adjective having no people or things in it » *There was no food in the house; the cupboards were empty.*
bare, blank, clear, deserted, unfurnished, uninhabited, vacant
antonym: **full**

empty 2
adjective boring or without value or meaning » *The offer to go on vacation together was an empty promise.*
inane, meaningless, worthless

empty 3
verb to remove people or things » *Danny sat down and emptied the water that had gotten into his boots.*
clear, drain, evacuate, unload
antonym: **fill**

*Danny sat down and **emptied** the water that had gotten into his boots.*

enclose
verb to surround a thing or place completely » *The book arrived enclosed in a protective plastic bag.*
encircle, fence off, hem in, surround, wrap

encourage 1
verb to give someone confidence » *She was encouraged by the teacher's praise for her essay.*
cheer, hearten, reassure
antonym: **discourage**

encourage 2
verb to support a person or activity » *Her family's cheers encouraged Zoe to run faster.*
aid, boost, favor, help, incite, support, foster, further, promote, strengthen

end 1
noun the last part of a period or event
◀◀ **SEE LEFT**

end 2
noun the furthest point of something » *I was staying in a room at the end of the hallway.*
boundary, bounds, edge, extremity, limits, margin

end 3
noun the purpose for which something is done » *By studying for our exams, we're all working toward the same end, which is to pass!*
aim, goal, intention, object, objective, purpose, reason

end 4
verb to come or bring to a finish » *Jim waited for the movie to end before going home.*
bring to an end, cease, conclude, finish, stop, terminate
antonym: **begin**

endanger
verb to put someone or something in danger » *The lack of rain has endangered the plants in my garden*
compromise, jeopardize, put at risk, risk, threaten

endure 1
verb to experience something difficult » *The students endured a three-hour exam.*
cope with, experience, go through, stand, suffer

endure 2
verb to continue to exist » *Phil's jeans endured despite years of wear and tear.*
last, live on, remain, survive

A B C D **E** F G H I J K L M N O P Q R S T U V W X Y Z

enemy

noun someone who is against you » *The knight fought a duel against his enemy.*
adversary, antagonist, foe, opponent
antonym: **friend**

energetic

adjective full of energy » *The energetic kitten climbed the curtains.*
animated, dynamic, indefatigable, spirited, tireless, vigorous

energy

noun the ability and strength to do things » *I don't have the energy to go swimming.*
drive, life, spirit, strength, vigor, vitality, élan, verve, zeal, zest

enjoy

verb to find pleasure in something » *I haven't enjoyed a movie that much in ages!*
appreciate, delight in, like, love, relish, revel in, take pleasure from, take pleasure in

enlarge

verb to make something larger » *The team became so successful that they had to enlarge the stadium.*
add to, expand, extend, increase, magnify, augment, broaden, distend, elongate, lengthen, widen

enlarge on

verb to give more information about something » *The teacher told Paul to enlarge on his answers to get more points on the test.*
develop, elaborate on, expand on

enormous

adjective very large in size or amount » *The enormous monument dominated the skyline.*
colossal, gigantic, huge, immense, massive, tremendous, vast
antonym: **tiny**

ensure

verb to make sure about something » *Eric tried the door again to ensure that it was securely locked.*
guarantee, make certain, make sure

enterprise 1

noun a business or company » *The grocery store was a small family enterprise.*
business, company, concern, establishment, firm, operation

enterprise 2

noun a project or task » *Lara's latest enterprise was to learn how to drive.*
effort, endeavor, operation, project, undertaking, venture

*Lara's latest **enterprise** was to learn how to drive.*

entertain

verb to keep someone amused or interested » *The puppy entertained the whole family.*
amuse, charm, delight, enthral, please

entertainment

noun enjoyable activities » *The television provided the entertainment for the evening.*
amusement, enjoyment, fun, pleasure, recreation

enthusiasm

noun eagerness and enjoyment in something » *Alice showed great enthusiasm for the piano and practiced daily.*
eagerness, excitement, interest, keenness, warmth, ardor, fervor, relish, zeal

*Some of the volunteers were more **enthusiastic** than others.*

enthusiastic

adjective showing great excitement and eagerness for something » *Some of the volunteers were more enthusiastic than others.*
ardent, avid, devoted, eager, excited, keen, passionate, fervent, wholehearted, zealous
antonym: **apathetic**

entrance 1

noun the way into a particular place » *I met Barry at the entrance to the station.*
door, doorway, entry, gate, way in

entrance 2

noun a person's arrival somewhere » *The celebrity made a dramatic entrance.*
appearance, arrival, entry

entrance 3

noun the right to enter somewhere » *If you buy a special pass, you can gain early entrance to the theme park.*
access, admission, entry

entrance 4

verb to amaze and delight someone » *The audience was entranced by the singer's voice.*
bewitch, captivate, charm, delight, enthral, fascinate, enchant, enrapture, spellbind

entry 1

noun a person's arrival somewhere » *The audience fell silent when the hero made his entry onto the stage.*
appearance, arrival, entrance

entry 2

noun the way into a particular place » *The main entry to the house is around the side.*
door, doorway, entrance, gate, way in

entry 3

noun something that has been written down » *Writing about the flight home was Liz's final entry in her travel journal.*
item, note, record

envy 1

noun a feeling of resentment about what someone else has » *He felt envy at the sight of his friend's large back yard.*
jealousy, resentment

envy 2

verb to want something that someone else has » *Jimmy envied Jose's new bike.*
be envious, begrudge, be jealous, covet, resent

*Jimmy **envied** Jose's new bike.*

equal 1

adjective the same in size, amount, or value » *Everyone at the party had an equal number of jelly beans.*
equivalent, identical, the same

equal 2 : equal to

adjective having the necessary ability for something » *Greg was equal to the task and could do it with ease.*
capable of, up to

A B C D **E** F G H I J K L M N O P Q R S T U V W X Y Z

equal ③
verb to be as good as something else » *Mike's swim time equaled his previous best.*
be equal to, match

equip
verb to supply someone with something » *The orienteering teams were equipped with a compass and map.*
arm, endow, fit out, provide, supply

equipment
noun the things you need for a particular job
▶▶ **SEE RIGHT**

erode
verb to wear something away and destroy it » *The cliffs were being eroded by the constant pounding of the sea.*
corrode, destroy, deteriorate, disintegrate

*The cliffs were being **eroded** by the constant pounding of the sea.*

err
verb to make a mistake » *Sophie had erred in her timings and arrived far too late.*
blunder, go wrong, make a mistake, miscalculate

error
noun a mistake » *The error was easy to fix.*
blunder, fault, lapse, mistake, slip

escape ①
verb to manage to get away » *The dog escaped from the back yard.*
break free, break out, get away, make your escape, run away, run off, abscond, bolt

escape ②
verb to manage to avoid something » *Sid was lucky to escape injury when he fell over.*
avoid, dodge, duck, elude, evade

escape ③
noun something that distracts you from something unpleasant » *Listening to music provided Kate with an escape from her hard day.*
distraction, diversion, relief

*Listening to music provided Kate with an **escape** from her hard day.*

essence ①
noun the most basic and important part of something » *The essence of the story could be summed up in a few words.*
core, heart, nature, soul, spirit, crux, kernel, substance

essence ②
noun a concentrated liquid » *Sheryl added a teaspoon of vanilla essence to the chocolate brownies.*
concentrate, extract

essential ①
adjective extremely important » *A battery is essential for making a phone work.*
crucial, indispensable, vital

essential ②
adjective basic and important » *Flour is an essential ingredient for any baker.*
basic, cardinal, fundamental, key, main, principal

essentials
plural noun the things that are most important » *We had enough money to buy only the essentials.*
basics, fundamentals, necessities, prerequisites, rudiments

esteem
noun admiration and respect for another person » *Our teacher is popular and held in high esteem by the rest of the staff.*
admiration, estimation, regard, respect, reverence, honor, veneration (formal)

estimate
noun a guess at an amount, quantity, or outcome » *The final fee was five times higher than the original estimate.*
appraisal, assessment, estimation, guess, quote, reckoning, valuation

eternal
adjective lasting forever » *The baddie in the movie was seeking the secret to eternal life.*
everlasting, immortal, unchanging

even ①
adjective flat and level » *Dad used a spirit level to make sure the shelf was even.*
flat, horizontal, level, smooth
antonym: **uneven**

*Dad used a spirit level to make sure the shelf was **even**.*

even ②
adjective without changing or varying » *The dam let through an even flow of water.*
constant, regular, smooth, steady, uniform

even ③
adjective the same » *At half-time, the scores were even.*
equal, identical, level, neck and neck

event ①
noun something that happens » *He was still amazed by the events of last week.*
affair, business, circumstance, episode, experience, incident, matter

event ②
noun a competition » *The next event is the long jump.*
bout, competition, contest

everyday
adjective usual or ordinary » *Getting up early was part of Linda's everyday life.*
common, daily, day-to-day, mundane, ordinary, routine, banal, unexceptional

evident
adjective easily noticed or understood » *Claire's happiness was evident from the smile on her face.*
apparent, clear, noticeable, obvious, palpable, plain, visible, conspicuous, manifest, patent

evil ①
noun the force that causes bad things to happen » *Most movie plots are based around the conflict between good and evil.*
badness, immorality, sin, vice, wickedness, baseness, depravity, sinfulness
antonym: **good**

evil ②
noun something unpleasant or harmful » *The dentist lectured the class on the evils of sugary foods.*
affliction, ill, misery, sorrow

evil [3]
adjective morally wrong or bad
» *The evil deeds of the superhero's enemy are too many to count.*
bad, depraved, malevolent, sinful, vile, wicked
antonym: **good**

exact [1]
adjective correct in every detail
» *Alf built an exact replica of the first steam engine.*
accurate, authentic, faithful, faultless, precise, true
antonym: **approximate**

exact [2]
verb (formal) to demand and obtain something
» *Vicky wanted to exact a positive response from the school for her statement on recycling.*
command, extract, impose, insist on, insist upon, wring

exactly [1]
adverb with complete accuracy and precision » *The train arrived exactly at five o'clock.*
accurately, faithfully, just, on the dot, precisely, quite
antonym: **approximately**

exactly [2]
interjection an expression implying total agreement
» *"We'll never know the answer." "Exactly! So let's stop guessing."*
absolutely, indeed, precisely, quite

exaggerate
verb to suggest something is more, better, or worse than it really is » *Helen exaggerated the size of the hens she claimed to keep in her yard.*
overdo, overestimate, overstate

exam
noun a test to find out how much you know » *The math exam was three hours long.*
examination, oral, test

examination [1]
noun a careful inspection of something » *The divers carried out an examination of the shipwreck to find out where the ship had come from.*
analysis, inspection, study

a b c d e f g h i j k l m n o p q r s t u v w x y z

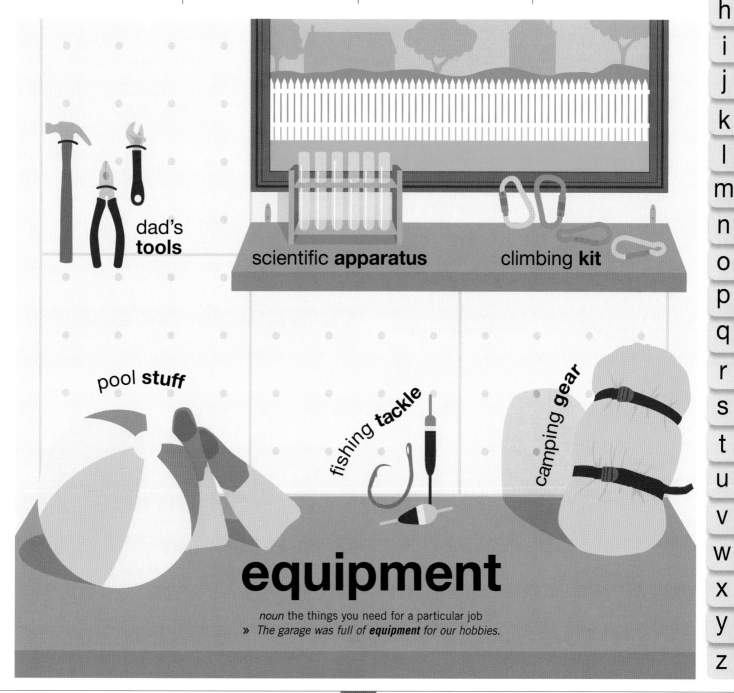

dad's **tools**

scientific **apparatus**

climbing **kit**

pool **stuff**

fishing **tackle**

camping *gear*

equipment
noun the things you need for a particular job
» *The garage was full of **equipment** for our hobbies.*

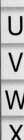

*The doctor did an **examination** of the patient's chest.*

examination 2

noun a check carried out on someone by a doctor » *The doctor did an examination of the patient's chest.*
check, checkup, medical

examine 1

verb to look at something very carefully » *Experts examined the frozen remains of a woolly mammoth.*
analyze, go over, go through, inspect, look over, study, peruse, scrutinize

examine 2

verb to give someone a medical examination » *The patient was examined by several specialists.*
check, inspect, look at, test

example 1

noun something that represents a group of things » *The museum held several examples of Roman swords.*
illustration, sample, specimen

example 2

noun something that people can imitate » *The respect that Grandma showed people is an example to us all.*
ideal, model, paragon, prototype, archetype, exemplar, paradigm

excellent

adjective extremely good » *It's an excellent book, one of my favorites.*
awesome (informal)**, banner, brilliant, cracking** (Britain; informal)**, fantastic, fine, first-class, great, outstanding, superb**
antonym: **terrible**

except

preposition apart from » *Chris always gets the 8:10 train, except when he's running late.*
apart from, but, other than, save (formal)**, with the exception of**

exceptional 1

adjective unusually excellent, talented, or smart » *Lee's piano playing is exceptional, he should be on the stage.*
excellent, extraordinary, outstanding, phenomenal, remarkable, talented
antonym: **mediocre**

exceptional 2

adjective unusual and likely to happen very rarely » *Having two people win first place was an exceptional event in sports history and had never happened before.*
isolated, out of the ordinary, rare, special, unheard-of, unusual, unprecedented (formal)
antonym: **common**

excess 1

noun behavior that goes beyond what is acceptable » *Stacie shopped to excess and regretted her purchases.*
extravagance, indulgence, intemperance, overindulgence

*Stacie shopped to **excess** and regretted her purchases.*

excess 2

noun a larger amount than necessary » *An excess of houseplants made the room look like a jungle.*
glut, overdose, surfeit, surplus, overabundance, plethora, superfluity
antonym: **shortage**

excess 3

adjective more than is needed » *The airline charged us an additional fee for our excess baggage.*
extra, superfluous, surplus

excessive

adjective too great » *We never travel first class because the cost is excessive.*
enormous, exaggerated, needless, undue, unreasonable, disproportionate, exorbitant, extravagant, immoderate, inordinate

exchange 1

verb to give something in return for something else » *We exchanged phone numbers.*
barter, change, swap, switch, trade

*We **exchanged** phone numbers.*

exchange 2

noun the act of giving something for something else » *There was a useful exchange of ideas in the classroom.*
interchange, swap, switch, trade

excite 1

verb to make someone feel enthusiastic or nervous » *Zara was extremely excited about her upcoming vacation.*
agitate, animate, thrill, titillate

excite 2

verb to cause a particular feeling or reaction » *The dull movie failed to excite anyone.*
arouse, elicit, evoke, incite, inspire, provoke, stir up, fire, foment, inflame, kindle, rouse

*The children were very **excited** to get a dog.*

excited

adjective happy and enthusiastic » *The children were very excited to get a dog.*
agitated, enthusiastic, feverish, high (informal)**, thrilled**
antonym: **bored**

excitement

noun interest and enthusiasm » *The release of his latest song has caused great excitement.*
activity, adventure, agitation, commotion, enthusiasm, thrill, animation, elation, furore, tumult

exciting

adjective making you feel happy and enthusiastic » *It was the most exciting race I'd ever seen, no one could predict who would win.*
dramatic, electrifying, exhilarating, rousing, stimulating, thrilling, intoxicating, sensational, stirring
antonym: **boring**

exclude 1

verb to decide not to include something » *The teacher excluded the easy words from the spelling test.*
eliminate, ignore, leave out, omit, rule out
antonym: **include**

exclude 2

verb to stop someone going somewhere or doing something » *The cat was excluded from the living room to stop it from scratching the furniture.*
ban, bar, forbid, keep out, blackball, debar

exclusive

adjective available only to a few rich people » *The restaurant was so exclusive, you could only get in by invitation.*
chic, classy, posh (informal), **select, upmarket**

excuse [1]

noun a reason or explanation » *Stop making excuses and get on with your work!*
explanation, justification, pretext, reason

excuse [2]

verb to forgive someone or someone's behavior » *Please excuse my late arrival.*
forgive, overlook, pardon, turn a blind eye to

exempt

adjective excused from a duty or rule » *Ann was exempt from singing in the choir due to her sore throat.*
excused, immune, not liable

exercise

noun activity that keeps you fit » *Half an hour of exercise is the best way to start the day.*
activity, exertion, training, work, workout

*Half an hour of **exercise** is the best way to start the day.*

exhaust [1]

verb to make very tired » *The marathon exhausted her and she felt ready to go to bed.*
drain, fatigue, tire out, wear out

exhaust [2]

verb to use something up completely » *Stuart drank so much coffee, he exhausted the supply of coffee beans.*
consume, deplete, run through, use up

expand

verb to make or become larger » *The balloon expanded when it was filled with air.*
develop, enlarge, extend, fill out, grow, increase, swell
antonym: **contract**

*The balloon **expanded** when it was filled with air.*

expand on

verb to give more information about something » *Please expand on your story, I want to hear more details.*
develop, elaborate on, enlarge on

expect [1]

verb to believe that something is going to happen » *The vet expects the baby elephant will be born in the next 12 hours.*
anticipate, assume, believe, imagine, presume, reckon, think, envisage, forecast, foresee, predict

expect [2]

verb to believe that something is your right » *I expect to be given a raise.*
demand, rely on, require

expensive

adjective costing a lot of money » *The shoes were very expensive, and it took Charlie a long time to save up for them.*
costly, dear, pricey, exorbitant, overpriced
antonym: **cheap**

*We chose the dancers with the most **experience** to take on the leading roles in the ballet.*

experience [1]

noun knowledge or skill in a particular activity » *We chose the dancers with the most experience to take on the leading roles in the ballet.*
expertise, know-how, knowledge, training, understanding

experience [2]

noun something that happens to you » *Mark's around-the-world trip was an experience that he'd never forget.*
adventure, affair, encounter, episode, incident, ordeal

experience [3]

verb to have something happen to you » *We're experiencing a few technical problems.*
encounter, have, meet, undergo

experienced

adjective very skilful as a result of practice » *After 20 dives, Naomi considered herself an experienced diver.*
expert, knowledgeable, practiced, seasoned, well-versed
antonym: **inexperienced**

expert [1]

noun a skilled or knowledgeable person » *Nick is an expert on cheetahs.*
ace (informal), **authority, buff** (informal), **geek, guru, master, professional, specialist, wizard**
antonym: **novice**

expert [2]

adjective skilled and knowledgeable » *Becky's expert performance on the guitar impressed everyone.*
able, adept, experienced, knowledgeable, proficient, skillful, skilled, adroit, dexterous, masterly, practiced

explain

verb to make clear by providing extra information » *The teacher explained how the machine worked.*
define, describe, illustrate, elucidate, expound

explanation

noun a helpful or clear description » *The principal wanted an explanation for why the children were late to class.*
clarification, definition, description, exposition

explode [1]

verb to burst or cause to burst loudly » *The party balloons exploded and made them all jump.*
blow up, burst, detonate, go off, set off

explode [2]

verb to become angry suddenly » *I asked him if he'd move up a seat and he just exploded.*
blow up, erupt, go berserk, go crazy

explode [3]

verb to increase suddenly and rapidly » *Sales of computer games have exploded in recent years.*
rocket, shoot up, soar

*Sales of computer games have **exploded** in recent years.*

a b c d e f g h i j k l m n o p q r s t u v w x y z

explosion
noun a violent burst of energy
» *There was an explosion as the fireworks lit up the sky.*
bang, blast

expose 1
verb to make something visible
» *The dog's digging exposed the buried treasure.*
reveal, show, uncover

expose 2
verb to tell the truth about someone or something
» *Sonny's real reason for wanting his allowance early was exposed when he appeared wearing a brand new jacket.*
bring to light, reveal, show up, uncover, unearth

express 1
verb to say what you think
» *Sonia expressed a desire to take part in a foreign language exchange group.*
communicate, phrase, put, put across, utter, voice, articulate, couch, enunciate, verbalize

express 2
adjective very fast
» *The express train was the quickest way to get to the city.*
direct, fast, high-speed, nonstop

*The **express** train was the quickest way to get to the city.*

expression 1
noun a look that shows your feelings » *The expression on Dad's face was one of relief when we told him he hadn't missed Mom's birthday.*
countenance, face, aspect, mien

expression 2
noun a word or phrase used to communicate » *Helen hadn't heard that particular expression before, but she understood its meaning.*
idiom, phrase, remark, term

extend 1
verb to have a particular size or position » *The caves extend for miles beneath the hills.*
continue, hang, reach, stretch

extend 2
verb to stick out » *A large rock extended from the cliffs.*
jut out, project, protrude (formal)**, stick out**

*A large rock **extended** from the cliffs.*

extend 3
verb to make something larger » *Mom wants to extend the house and build a conservatory.*
add to, develop, enlarge, expand, widen, augment, broaden, supplement

extensive 1
adjective covering a large area » *It took several hours to cross the extensive forest.*
broad, expansive, large, spacious, sweeping, vast, wide

extensive 2
adjective very great in effect » *The flood caused extensive damage across the whole area.*
comprehensive, considerable, far-reaching, great, pervasive, untold, widespread

*The giraffe stretched its neck to its full **extent** to reach the leaves.*

extent
noun the length, area, or size of something » *The giraffe stretched its neck to its full extent to reach the leaves.*
degree, level, measure, scale, size, expanse, magnitude

extra 1
adjective more than is usual or expected » *Neha placed an extra blanket on the bed because it was very cold that night.*
added, additional, excess, further, more, new, spare, ancillary, auxiliary, supplementary

extra 2
noun something that is not included with other things » *The parents had to pay extra for private riding lessons.*
addition, bonus

extract 1
verb to take or get something out of somewhere » *Citric acid can be extracted from orange juice.*
draw, mine, obtain, pull out, remove, take out

extract 2
verb to get information from someone » *The police interviewed the suspect in an attempt to extract information from him.*
draw, elicit (formal)**, get, glean, obtain**

extract 3
noun a small section of music or writing » *Joanne read an extract from her story.*
excerpt, passage, reading, section, snatch, snippet

extraordinary
adjective unusual or surprising » *Seeing a shooting star is an extraordinary experience.*
amazing, bizarre, odd, singular, strange, surprising, unusual
antonym: **ordinary**

extreme 1
adjective very great in degree or intensity » *He felt extreme pain in his knee while jogging.*
acute, deep, dire, great, intense, profound, severe

*He felt **extreme** pain in his knee while jogging.*

extreme 2
adjective unusual or unreasonable » *Flora's angry reaction was extreme and she regretted it once she'd calmed down.*
drastic, exceptional, excessive, extravagant, radical, unreasonable

extreme 3
noun the highest, lowest, or furthest degree or point » *We ran right the length of the park, from one extreme to the other.*
boundary, depth, end, height, limit, ultimate, acme, apex, nadir, pinnacle, zenith

A B C D E F G H I J K L M N O P Q R S T U V W X Y Z

Ff

face [1]
noun the front part of the head » *A strong wind was blowing in my face, making my eyes water.*
countenance, features, mug (slang), **physiognomy**

face [2]
verb to look toward something or someone » *Her room faced onto the street.*
be across from, be opposite from, look at, overlook

face [3]
noun a surface or side of something » *The explorers approached the mountain's summit via its north face.*
aspect, exterior, front, side, surface

The explorers approached the mountain's summit via its north face.

fact
noun a piece of information that is true » *The fact is that only male lions have manes.*
certainty, reality, truth
antonym: **lie**

factor
noun something that helps to cause a result » *A key factor in ice-skating is good balance.*
aspect, cause, component, consideration, element, influence, part, circumstance, determinant

factory
noun a building where goods are made » *The workers made desks in the furniture factory.*
mill, plant, works

The workers made desks in the furniture factory.

fade
verb to make or become less intense » *The fabric had faded in the bright sunlight.*
die away, dim, discolor, dull, wash out

fail [1]
verb to be unsuccessful » *Claire tried to fix her bike but failed, so she had to walk.*
be defeated, be in vain, be unsuccessful, come to grief, fall through, flunk (informal)
antonym: **succeed**

fail [2]
verb to omit to do something » *Jamie failed to call, even though he said he would.*
neglect, omit

fail [3]
verb to become less effective » *When Dad's eyesight began to fail, he went for an eye test.*
cease, decline, give out, stop working, crash, sink

failure [1]
noun a lack of success » *She tried her best, but it ended in failure.*
breakdown, defeat, downfall, fiasco, miscarriage
antonym: **success**

failure [2]
noun an unsuccessful person or thing » *The storm made the barbecue a complete failure.*
disappointment, flop (informal), **loser, incompetent**

failure [3]
noun a weakness in something » *A failure in the electrical system stopped the doorbell from working.*
deficiency, shortcoming

faint [1]
adjective lacking in intensity » *Rick tried to rub out the picture, but it left a faint outline behind.*
dim, faded, indistinct, low, muted, vague
antonym: **strong**

Rick tried to rub out the picture, but it left a faint outline behind.

faint [2]
adjective feeling dizzy and unsteady » *Mira felt a bit faint after rushing around so much.*
dizzy, giddy, light-headed, enervated, vertiginous

faint [3]
verb to lose consciousness temporarily » *The soldiers had to stand for hours in the heat and one fainted.*
black out, collapse, pass out, swoon (literary)

fair [1]
adjective reasonable and just » *To keep things fair, they all took turns on the zip wire.*
equal, equitable, impartial, legitimate, proper, upright, disinterested, dispassionate, unbiased
antonym: **unfair**

fair [2]
adjective having light-colored hair or pale skin » *She had long, fair hair.*
blonde or **blond, light**
antonym: **dark**

She had long, fair hair.

fair [3]
noun an outdoor entertainment » *Tom had made cakes for the school fair.*
bazaar, carnival, exhibition, festival, show

faith [1]
noun trust in a thing or a person » *I have faith in you to succeed in whatever you do.*
confidence, trust

faith [2]
noun a person's or community's religion » *Charlie followed the Christian faith.*
belief, creed, persuasion, religion

faithful [1]
adjective loyal to someone or something » *The dog was my uncle's faithful companion.*
devoted, loyal, staunch, true, steadfast, unwavering
antonym: **unfaithful**

faithful [2]
adjective accurate and truthful » *The movie was faithful to the novel.*
accurate, exact, strict, true

fake [1]
noun a deceitful imitation of a thing or person » *These paintings are fakes.*
copy, forgery, fraud, imitation, reproduction, sham

fake [2]
adjective imitation and not genuine » *Alice wore a fake mustache as part of her costume.*
artificial, counterfeit, false, imitation, phoney or **phony** (informal), **assumed**
antonym: **real**
related word: *prefix* **pseudo-**

*Alice wore a **fake** mustache as part of her costume.*

fake [3]
verb to pretend to experience something » *She faked a stomachache so she wouldn't have to eat the school lunch.*
feign, pretend, simulate

*Nicky **fell** from his bike onto the path.*

fall [1]
verb to descend toward the ground » *Nicky fell from his bike onto the path.*
collapse, drop, plunge, topple, trip
antonym: **rise**

fall [2]
verb to become lower or less » *The number of fish in the sea has fallen due to overfishing.*
decline, decrease, diminish, dwindle, plummet, subside, abate, depreciate, ebb
antonym: **increase**

fall [3]
noun a reduction in amount » *There has been a fall in ice cream sales now that summer is over.*
decline, decrease, drop, reduction, slump
antonym: **rise**

false [1]
adjective not true or correct » *Ellen was accused of spreading false rumors.*
erroneous, fictitious, incorrect, mistaken, untrue
antonym: **true**

false [2]
adjective not genuine but intended to seem so » *The woman was wearing false eyelashes.*
artificial, bogus, dummy, fake, faux, forged, man-made, simulated, spurious
antonym: **genuine**
related word: *prefix* **pseudo-**

false [3]
adjective unfaithful and deceitful » *Ivy was a false friend, betraying Belinda to their teacher.*
deceitful, disloyal, insincere, unfaithful, duplicitous, perfidious

fame
noun the state of being very well-known » *The movie brought him international fame.*
eminence, glory, prominence, renown, reputation

familiar
adjective knowing something well » *Most children are familiar with nursery rhymes.*
acquainted with, aware of, knowledgeable about, versed in
antonym: **unfamiliar**

family [1]
noun a group of relatives » *My family always gets together for dinner.*
descendants, relations, relatives
related word: *adjective* **familial**

*My **family** always gets together for dinner.*

family [2]
noun a group of related species » *Tigers are members of the cat family.*
class, classification, kind

famous
adjective very well-known » *The chef's TV show made him famous.*
celebrated, distinguished, illustrious, legendary, noted, renowned, lionized
antonym: **unknown**

fan
noun an enthusiast about something or someone » *George was the band's biggest fan.*
addict, adherent, admirer, buff, devotee, geek (slang), **lover, supporter, zealot,** aficionado, enthusiast

*Joao and Carla were soccer **fanatics** and went to every game.*

fanatic
noun someone who is extremely enthusiastic about something » *Joao and Carla were soccer fanatics and went to every game.*
activist, devotee, extremist, militant, zealot

fanatical
adjective showing extreme support for something » *Lisa was fanatical about animal conservation.*
fervent, obsessive, passionate, rabid, wild, immoderate, zealous

fancy [1]
verb (Britain) to want to have or do something » *Liam fancied having some pizza.*
be attracted to, hanker after, have a yen for, would like

fancy [2]
adjective special and elaborate » *She was wearing a fancy hat, full of feathers.*
decorated, elaborate, extravagant, intricate, ornate, baroque, embellished, ornamented
antonym: **plain**

far [1]
adverb at a great distance from something » *The top of the mountain was far above us.*
afar, a great distance, a long way, deep, miles

far [2]
adverb to a great extent or degree » *The computer he bought was far better than the other options.*
considerably, incomparably, much, very much

far ③

adjective very distant

▶▶ SEE RIGHT

fascinate

verb to be of intense interest to someone » *He was fascinated by the fossil collection.*

absorb, bewitch, captivate, enthral, intrigue, beguile, **enchant, spellbind, transfix**

fashion ①

noun a popular style of dress or behavior » *Diana dressed according to the latest fashion.*

buzz, craze, fad, flavor, rage, style, trend, vogue

fashion ②

noun a manner or way of doing something » *Paul thanked my mother for the ride in his usual polite fashion.*

manner, method, mode, style, tone, way

fashion ③

verb to make and shape something » *The child fashioned a figure from some playdough.*

construct, create, make, mould, shape, work

*The child **fashioned** a figure from some playdough.*

fashionable

adjective very popular » *The fashionable restaurant was a favorite of the rich and famous.*

cool, current, hip, in (informal), **latest, popular, prevailing,** chic, in vogue, trendsetting, trendy
antonym: **old-fashioned**

fast ①

adjective moving at great speed » *The fast train sped along the tracks.*

accelerated, breakneck, hurried, quick, rapid, speedy, swift, fleet
antonym: **slow**

fast ②

adverb quickly and without delay » *You'll have to get there fast to make the start of the movie.*

hastily, hurriedly, quickly, rapidly, swiftly
antonym: **slowly**

fast ③

adverb firmly and strongly » *Alex held fast to the swing.*

firmly, securely, tightly

*Alex held **fast** to the swing.*

fasten

verb to close or attach something » *Fasten your seat belts.*

attach, fix, join, lock, secure, tie

fat

adjective weighing too much » *The dog had become a bit fat in his old age.*

chubby, fleshy, gross, obese, overweight, plump, roly-poly (informal), **rotund, tubby** (informal), **stout**
antonym: **thin**

fatal ①

adjective causing death » *A bite from a funnel web spider can be fatal to humans.*

deadly, incurable, lethal, mortal, terminal

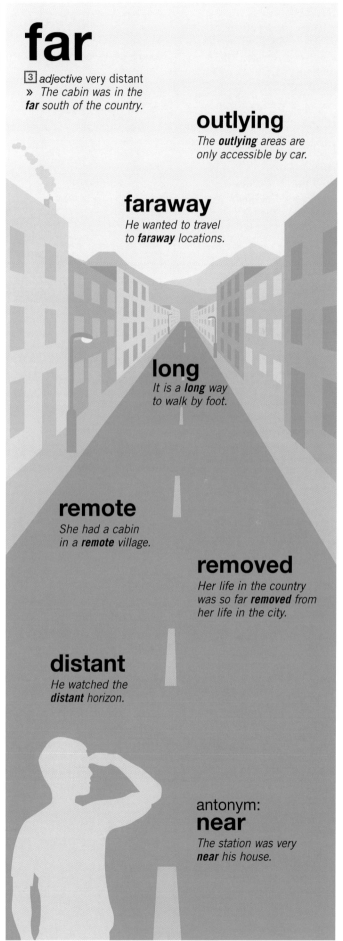

far

③ *adjective* very distant
» *The cabin was in the **far** south of the country.*

outlying
The **outlying** areas are only accessible by car.

faraway
He wanted to travel to **faraway** locations.

long
It is a **long** way to walk by foot.

remote
She had a cabin in a **remote** village.

removed
Her life in the country was so far **removed** from her life in the city.

distant
He watched the **distant** horizon.

antonym:
near
The station was very **near** his house.

fatal [2]
adjective having an undesirable effect » *There was a fatal flaw in the plan and the plot failed.*
calamitous, catastrophic, disastrous, lethal

fate
noun a power believed to control events » *Fate would decide who won the lottery.*
chance, circumstance, destiny, fortune, providence, kismet, predestination

fault [1]
noun something for which someone is responsible » *It was Edie's fault that the man had fallen over—she'd left her bag in his way.*
blame, liability, responsibility

fault [2]
noun a defective quality in something » *There was a fault with the vending machine and no drinks would come out.*
blemish, defect, deficiency, drawback, failing, flaw, imperfection, weakness
antonym: **strength**

fault [3]
verb to find reasons to be critical of someone » *Lydia's conduct cannot be faulted—she behaves beautifully all the time.*
blame, censure, criticize

faulty
adjective containing flaws or errors » *The sound system was faulty and kept making ear-piercing noises.*
defective, flawed, imperfect, invalid, unsound, fallacious, imprecise, malfunctioning

favor [1]
noun a liking or approval of something » *Everyone was in favor of the new plans—no one argued against them.*
approval, esteem, grace, support
antonym: **disapproval**

favor [2]
noun a kind and helpful action » *Can you do me a favor?*
courtesy, good turn, kindness, service
antonym: **wrong**

favor [3]
verb to prefer something or someone » *Jim favored the brown boots over the black.*
prefer, single out

*Jim **favored** the brown boots over the black.*

favorable [1]
adjective of advantage to someone » *The wind was favorable for sailing and we set out to sea.*
advantageous, beneficial, good, opportune, suitable, auspicious, propitious, timely
antonym: **unfavorable**

favorable [2]
adjective positive and expressing approval » *Jake received a favorable review, which really boosted his confidence.*
affirmative, amicable, approving, friendly, positive, sympathetic, welcoming
antonym: **unfavorable**

favorite [1]
adjective being someone's best-liked person or thing » *Mia's favorite food is toast.*
best-loved, dearest, favored, preferred

favorite [2]
noun the thing or person someone likes best » *Tracy was the teacher's favorite and was always asked to hand out the books.*
darling, idol, pet, pick

favoritism
noun unfair favor shown to a person or group » *The team captain showed favoritism in picking his friend for the team.*
bias, one-sidedness, nepotism, partiality, partisanship
antonym: **impartiality**

fear [1]
noun an unpleasant feeling of danger » *Julie suffered from a fear of heights.*
alarm, awe, dread, fright, panic, terror, apprehensiveness, cravenness, trepidation

fear [2]
verb to feel frightened of something » *There is no need to fear my dog—she won't bite.*
be afraid, be frightened, be scared, dread, take fright

feature [1]
noun a particular characteristic of something » *The fireplace was an original feature of the old house.*
aspect, attribute, characteristic, mark, property, quality

feature [2]
noun a special article or program » *The magazine included a feature on the season's latest trends.*
article, column, item, piece, report, story

*The magazine included a **feature** on the season's latest trends.*

feature [3]
verb to include and draw attention to something » *The TV program featured an interview with the movie's star.*
emphasize, give prominence to, spotlight, star

*Elsa was **feeling** left out.*

feel [1]
verb to experience emotionally » *Elsa was feeling left out.*
experience, suffer, undergo

feel [2]
verb to believe that something is the case » *Grace felt that telling the teacher was the right thing to do.*
believe, consider, deem, judge, think

feel [3]
verb to touch something physically » *Daisy felt the rabbit's soft fur.*
finger, fondle, stroke, touch

feeling [1]
noun the experiencing of an emotion » *Max couldn't hide his feelings of jealousy.*
emotion, fervor, heat, passion, sentiment

feeling [2]
noun a physical sensation » *Zoe had an uneasy feeling and the hair stood up on the back of her neck.*
sensation, sense

feeling [3]
noun an opinion on something » *Brett had strong feelings about global warming and its effects on the environment.*
inclination, opinion, point of view, view

fellowship [1]
noun a feeling of friendliness within a group » *Lydia felt a sense of fellowship with the new people she'd met in her class.*
brotherhood, camaraderie, companionship

fellowship [2]

noun a group of people with a common interest
» *The fellowship of writers met once a month.*
association, brotherhood, club, league, society

female [1]

noun a person or animal that can have babies » *The baby chimpanzees were cared for by the females in the group.*
girl, lady, woman
antonym: **male**

female [2]

adjective relating to females
» *She was the world's fastest female distance runner.*
feminine, girlish, womanly
antonym: **male**

fertile

adjective capable of producing plants or offspring
» *The fertile soil produced healthy plants with lots of fruit.*
fruitful, productive, prolific, rich, fecund
antonym: **barren**

fervent

adjective showing sincere and enthusiastic feeling
» *Mom is a fervent admirer of this artist and buys his paintings whenever she can.*
ardent, committed, devout, enthusiastic, impassioned, passionate, zealous

festival [1]

noun a time of religious celebration » *Easter, Passover, and Holi are springtime festivals in different religions.*
anniversary, holiday

*The music **festival** was lively.*

festival [2]

noun an organized series of events » *The music festival was lively.*
carnival, entertainment, fair, gala

few

adjective small in number
» *There were few seats left on the bus so we had to stand.*
infrequent, meager, not many, scanty, scarce, sparse
antonym: **many**

fidget

verb to move and change position restlessly » *Stop fidgeting and sit still!*
fiddle (informal), jiggle, squirm, twitch

field [1]

noun an area of farmland
» *The field was full of sheep.*
green, meadow, pasture

field [2]

noun a particular subject or interest » *The discovery was a breakthrough in the field of physics.*
area, arena, department, domain, province, specialty, discipline

fierce [1]

adjective wild and aggressive
» *The fierce lion chased the antelope.*
aggressive, dangerous, ferocious, murderous, barbarous, fell, feral
antonym: **gentle**

fierce [2]

adjective very intense
» *There was a fierce contest between the two teams.*
ferocious, intense, keen, relentless, strong

fight [1]

verb to take part in a battle or contest » *The boxer fought hard to win the final round.*
battle, brawl, grapple, struggle

fight [2]

noun an aggressive struggle
» *The kittens would have play fights.*
action, battle, bout, combat, duel, skirmish

*The kittens would have play **fights**.*

fight [3]

noun an angry disagreement
» *Steve felt bad after his fight with Aaron, so he went back to apologize.*
argument, dispute, row, squabble

fighter

noun someone who physically fights another person
» *Soldiers are trained fighters.*
soldier, warrior

figure [1]

noun a number, or an amount represented by a number
» *Jim was happy with the figure he paid for the new car.*
amount, digit, number, numeral, statistic, total

figure [2]

noun a shape, or the shape of someone's body » *The ballerina has an elegant figure.*
body, build, form, physique, shape, silhouette

*The ballerina has an elegant **figure**.*

figure [3]

noun a person » *Gandhi was an inspirational figure for so many people.*
character, dignitary, person, personality, player

figure [4]

verb (informal) to guess or conclude something » *I figure I'll get it right eventually if I try enough times.*
expect, guess, suppose

fill

verb to make something full
▼ SEE BELOW

---

fill

verb to make something full
» *The hamster **filled** its cheek pouches with food.*

gorge

He **gorges** on food until there's no room for any more.

pack

All hamsters **pack** food into their cheeks.

cram

His cheeks were **crammed** with sunflower seeds.

stuff

Can he **stuff** any more in there?

stock

We **stock** the pantry with plenty of pet food.

antonym: **empty**

The hamster completely **emptied** the food bowl.

a b c d e f g h i j k l m n o p q r s t u v w x y z

final ①
adjective being the last one in a series **»** *Tonight is the final episode of my most favorite TV show of all time.*
closing, concluding, eventual, last, ultimate
antonym: **first**

final ②
adjective unable to be changed or questioned **»** *The umpire's decision is final.*
absolute, conclusive, definite, definitive

finally ①
adverb happening after a long time **»** *After waiting a week, the package finally arrived.*
at last, at the last moment, eventually, in the end, in the long run

finally ②
adverb in conclusion of something **»** *And finally, before I finish, I'd like to talk to you about my favorite book.*
in conclusion, in summary, lastly

finance ①
verb to provide the money for something **»** *The school fair raised enough money to finance the new science labs.*
back, fund, pay for, support

finance ②
noun the managing of money and investments **»** *Banks play a leading role in the world of finance.*
banking, budgeting, commerce, economics, investment

financial
adjective relating to money **»** *Sam solved his financial problems by dogsitting to supplement his allowance.*
economic, fiscal, money, budgetary, monetary, pecuniary

find ①
verb to discover something **»** *I can't find my notes.*
come across, detect, discover, locate, track down, turn up, unearth, descry, espy, ferret out
antonym: **lose**

find ②
verb to realize or learn something **»** *We found that we got along quite well.*
become aware, detect, discover, learn, realize

fine ①
adjective good and admirable **»** *Lindsey wears fine clothes—unlike my shabby outfits.*
admirable, beautiful, excellent, magnificent, outstanding, splendid

fine ②
adjective small in size or thickness **»** *A spider's web is made up of fine threads of silk.*
delicate, lightweight, powdery, sheer, small, diaphanous, gauzy, gossamer

A spider's web is made up of fine threads of silk.

fine ③
adjective subtle and precise **»** *We had a general plan, but needed to sort out the fine details.*
fastidious, keen, precise, refined, sensitive, subtle

finish ①
verb to complete something **»** *Tom finished his homework in time to watch TV before bed.*
close, complete, conclude, end, finalize
antonym: **start**

finish ②
noun the last part of something **»** *Naomi tried to stay awake to see the movie through to the finish.*
close, completion, conclusion, end, ending, finale, culmination, consummation, termination
antonym: **start**

finish ③
noun the surface appearance of something **»** *Would you like a matte or gloss finish on your photos?*
grain, luster, polish, shine, surface, texture

fire ①
noun the flames produced when something burns **»** *A fire flickered in the fireplace.*
blaze, combustion, flames, inferno

A fire flickered in the fireplace.

fire ②
verb to shoot or detonate something **»** *Jerry fired the pistol to start the race.*
detonate, explode, launch, set off, shoot

fire ③
verb (informal) to dismiss someone from a job **»** *She was fired from her job.*
ax, discharge, dismiss, sack (Britain; informal)

firm ①
adjective solid and not soft **»** *Put the gelatin in the fridge until it is completely firm.*
compressed, congealed, hard, rigid, set, solid, stiff
antonym: **soft**

firm ②
adjective resolute and determined **»** *The teacher was firm in her decision to keep the class after the bell.*
adamant, decisive, determined, inflexible, resolute, staunch, unshakable, steadfast, unwavering

firm ③
noun a commercial organization **»** *We employed a local firm to decorate the house.*
business, company, corporation, enterprise, organization

first ①
adjective done or in existence before anything else **»** *Neil Armstrong was the first human to set foot on the Moon.*
earliest, inaugural, initial, opening, original, pioneer
antonym: **last**

first ②
adverb done or occurring before anything else **»** *First wash your hands, then you can eat.*
beforehand, earlier, initially, to begin with

first ③
adjective more important than anything else **»** *Your safety is our first priority.*
chief, foremost, leading, prime, principal

first-rate
adjective excellent **»** *Ely was a first-rate cellist.*
excellent, exceptional, first-class, marvelous, outstanding, splendid, superb, superlative (formal), unparalleled

fissure
noun a deep crack in rock or the ground **»** *There was a deep fissure in the rock that was too dangerous for the climbers to cross.*
cleft, crack, crevice, fault, rift, split

*The plug **fits** the socket exactly.*

fit ①

verb to be the right shape or size » *The plug fits the socket exactly.*
belong, correspond, dovetail, go with, match

fit ②

verb to place something in position » *Chris fitted the new stereo into the car.*
adapt, arrange, place, position

fit ③

adjective in good physical condition » *The doctor said I was fit and healthy.*
healthy, in good condition, robust, trim, well
antonym: **unfit**

fitting ①

adjective appropriate and suitable for something » *The fireworks were a fitting end to a great day.*
appropriate, apt, correct, proper, right, suitable, decorous, deserved, seemly

fix ①

verb to attach or secure something » *Mom fixed the shelves to the wall.*
adhere, affix, attach, bind, fasten, hang, latch, secure, stick

fix ②

verb to repair something broken » *Dad fixed the leaky faucet.*
correct, doctor, mend, patch up, rebuild, refurbish, renovate, repair, revamp

fix ③

noun (informal) a difficult situation » *He was in a fix and wasn't sure what to do.*
difficulty, mess, predicament, quandary

fixtures

noun parts attached to something else » *The bathroom fixtures were chrome.*
accessory, attachment, component, part, unit

flabby

adjective fat and with loose flesh » *Doing sit-ups can help tone a flabby stomach.*
sagging, slack, flaccid, pendulous
antonym: **taut**

flash ①

noun a sudden short burst of light » *There was a flash of lightning.*
burst, flare, sparkle

flash ②

verb to shine briefly and often repeatedly
▶▶ SEE RIGHT

flashy

adjective showy in a vulgar way » *Ricky wore flashy clothes.*
flamboyant, garish, showy, tacky (informal), tasteless
antonym: **modest**

*Ricky wore **flashy** clothes.*

flat ①

noun a number not going up or down » *Sales of the dolls have been flat for two years.*
even, near, round

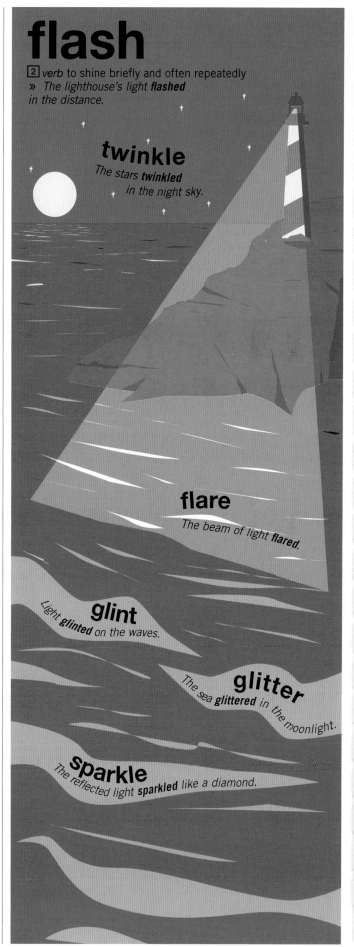

flash

② *verb* to shine briefly and often repeatedly » *The lighthouse's light **flashed** in the distance.*

twinkle
The stars **twinkled** in the night sky.

flare
The beam of light **flared**.

glint
Light **glinted** on the waves.

glitter
The sea **glittered** in the moonlight.

sparkle
The reflected light **sparkled** like a diamond.

a b c d e f g h i j k l m n o p q r s t u v w x y z

*Lisa and Jude upgraded their TV to one with a **flat** screen.*

flat ②

adjective level and smooth
» *Lisa and Jude upgraded their TV to one with a flat screen.*
horizontal, level, leveled, smooth, unbroken
antonym: **uneven**

flat ③

adjective without emotion or interest » *The disappointing musical performance left the audience feeling flat.*
boring, dull, insipid, monotonous, weak

flatter ①

verb to praise someone, often insincerely
» *Nick flattered Steven about his violin playing, but secretly thought some of the notes were wrong.*
compliment, fawn

flatter ②

verb to make more attractive
» *Those clothes really flatter your figure.*
enhance, set off, suit

flattery

noun flattering words and behavior » *Vicky was suspicious of Dan's flattery— what did he want from her?*
adulation, fawning, sweet talk, blandishment, compliments, endearments

flaw

noun an imperfection in something » *There was a crucial flaw in their plan.*
blemish, defect, fault, imperfection

flee

verb to run away from something » *The boys fled the park pursued by a dog.*
bolt, escape, fly, leave, run away, take flight

*The boys **fled** the park pursued by a dog.*

*Ben practiced yoga and had a **flexible** body.*

flexible ①

adjective able to bend or be bent easily » *Ben practiced yoga and had a flexible body.*
elastic, lithe, pliable, supple, ductile, lissom, lissome, pliant

flexible ②

adjective able to adapt or change » *My time is flexible, so let's meet whenever is best for you.*
adaptable, discretionary, open

flinch

verb to move suddenly with fear or pain » *A sharp pain in her knee made Laura flinch.*
cringe, shrink, start, wince

float ①

verb to be supported by water or air
▼ SEE BELOW

float ②

verb to be carried on the air
» *The smell of freshly baked bread floated past my window.*
drift, glide, hang, hover

flood ①

noun a large amount of water coming suddenly » *Many houses and cars were damaged in the flood.*
deluge, downpour, spate, torrent

*Many houses and cars were damaged in the **flood**.*

flood ②

noun a sudden large amount of something » *A flood of people entered the store all at once.*
rush, stream, torrent

float

① *verb* to be supported by water or air
» *Many boats were **floating** on the water.*

be on the surface

lie on the surface

drift

stay afloat

bob

flood ③
verb to overflow with water
» *The river flooded its banks.*
deluge, drown, overflow, submerge, swamp

flourish ①
verb to develop or function successfully or healthily
» *The strawberries were flourishing in the garden.*
bloom, boom, come on, do well, prosper, succeed, thrive
antonym: **fail**

flourish ②
verb to wave or display something » *The conductor flourished his baton wildly, lost in the music.*
brandish (literary), **display, hold aloft, wave**

flourish ③
noun a bold sweeping or waving movement » *Linda gave a flourish as she tried on the coat.*
flick, sweep, wave

*Linda gave a **flourish** as she tried on the coat.*

*The waterfall **flowed** down the steep drop.*

flow ①
verb to move or happen in a continuous stream
» *The waterfall flowed down the steep drop.*
circulate, glide, roll, run, slide

flow ②
noun a continuous movement of something » *The flow of busy traffic prevented him from crossing the road.*
current, drift, flood, stream, tide

fluent
adjective expressing yourself easily and without hesitation
» *The girl was fluent in three languages.*
articulate, easy, effortless, flowing, ready
antonym: **hesitant**

fly ①
verb to move through the air
» *The child chased the birds, and they flew high out of reach.*
flit, flutter, sail, soar

fly ②
verb to move very quickly
» *Debbie flew down the stairs because she was very late.*
dart, dash, hurry, race, rush, speed, tear

foam ①
verb to swell and form bubbles
» *The soap foamed as I washed my hands.*
bubble, fizz, froth

*The soap **foamed** as I washed my hands.*

foam ②
noun a mass of tiny bubbles
» *There was a lot of foam on top of my hot chocolate.*
bubbles, froth, head, lather

focus ①
verb to concentrate your vision on something » *The optician told Ron to focus on the red dot on the screen.*
aim, concentrate, direct, fix

focus ②
noun the center of attention
» *The celebrity guest was the main focus of the gala dinner.*
center, focal point, hub, target

foil ①
verb to prevent something from happening » *"Foiled again!" the bad guy exclaimed as the sheriff arrested him.*
check, counter, defeat, frustrate, thwart, circumvent, nullify

foil ②
noun a contrast to something
» *Luke is very serious and made the perfect foil for the comedian's jokes.*
antithesis, background, complement, contrast

fold ①
verb to bend something
» *To make an origami boat, fold the paper as shown.*
bend, crease, crumple, tuck, turn under

*To make an origami boat, **fold** the paper as shown.*

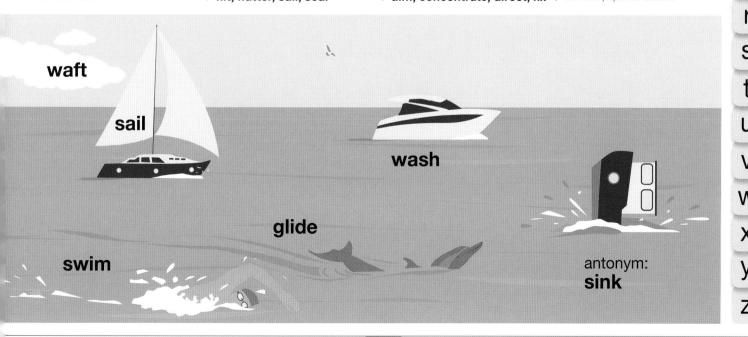

waft
sail
wash
glide
swim
antonym: **sink**

a b c d e f g h i j k l m n o p q r s t u v w x y z

A B C D E F G H I J K L M N O P Q R S T U V W X Y Z

coppice
*The oaks in the **coppice** were cut back to encourage growth.*

copse
*The **copse** behind the house was too small to shade the yard.*

grove
*There was no undergrowth in the olive **grove**.*

jungle
*The **jungle** was dense and swampy.*

forest
noun a wooded area of trees and dense vegetation
» *Harry spotted a deer in the **forest**.*

backwoods
*Growing up hunting and tracking in the **backwoods** made it hard for Jeff to live in a big city.*

rain forest
*The **rain forest** was hot and steamy.*

thicket
*The **thicket** was thick with brambles.*

woods
*Tina and Hugh walked slowly through the cool and shady **woods**.*

woodland
*Tom left the **woodland** and walked across a field.*

fold ②

noun a crease in something
» *The fabric of Martha's dress hung in folds.*
bend, crease, pleat, wrinkle

follow ①

verb to come after someone or something
» *Night follows day.*
come after, succeed, supersede
antonym: **precede**

follow ②

verb to pursue someone » *The goslings followed their mother.*
hound, pursue, stalk, track

*The goslings **followed** their mother.*

follow ③

verb to act in accordance with something » *Follow the instructions carefully.*
comply, conform, obey, observe

follower

noun a supporter of a person or belief » *Steve's blog had thousands of followers.*
believer, disciple, fan, henchman, supporter, adherent, protagonist
antonym: **leader**

fond ①

adjective feeling affection or liking » *My sister had become very fond of her new hamster.*
adoring, affectionate, devoted, doting, having a liking for, loving

fond ②

adjective (Britain) unlikely to happen or be fulfilled » *Amy had fond hopes of becoming an actress one day.*
deluded, empty, foolish, naive, vain, delusory, overoptimistic

*The refrigerator was full of **food** for the week ahead.*

food

noun things eaten to provide nourishment » *The refrigerator was full of food for the week ahead.*
chow, diet, fare, foodstuffs, grub, nourishment, provisions, refreshment, subsistence, victuals
related word:
noun **gastronomy**

fool ①

noun an unintelligent person » *Ben is smart, but he likes to play the fool.*
dope (informal), dunce, idiot, ignoramus

fool ②

verb to trick someone » *Don't let Gus fool you with his charm.*
con (informal), deceive, dupe, mislead, trick, bamboozle, hoodwink

foolish

adjective silly and unwise » *Emma felt foolish when she wore her shirt inside out.*
inane, nonsensical, senseless, silly, unintelligent, unwise
antonym: **wise**

forbid

verb to order someone not to do something » *Mary was forbidden from watching TV after 9pm.*
ban, exclude, outlaw, prohibit, veto
antonym: **allow**

force ①

verb to compel someone to do something » *The snow forced us to abandon the car and walk.*
compel, drive, make, oblige, pressurize, coerce, impel, obligate

force ②

noun a pressure to do something » *The rebels took the building by force.*
compulsion, duress, pressure

force ③

noun the strength of something » *The force of gravity is what causes an apple to fall to the ground.*
impact, might, power, pressure, strength

foreign

adjective relating to other countries » *Jack's passport contained stamps from all the foreign countries he'd visited.*
distant, exotic, overseas

foremost

adjective most important or best » *Nadia is the school's foremost soccer player.*
best, chief, first, greatest, leading, most important, prime, principal, top

*Nadia is the school's **foremost** soccer player.*

forest

noun a wooded area of trees and dense vegetation
◀◀ SEE LEFT

forget

verb to fail to remember something » *I forgot my keys and now I'm locked out.*
fail to remember, omit, overlook
antonym: **remember**

forgive

verb to stop blaming someone for something » *Will you ever forgive me for forgetting your birthday?*
absolve, condone, excuse, pardon
antonym: **blame**

forgiveness

noun the act of forgiving
» *I ask for your forgiveness.*
acquittal, mercy, pardon, remission, absolution, exoneration

form ①

noun a type or kind
» *Sam spoke a form of Chinese that Anna couldn't understand.*
class, kind, sort, type, variant, variety

form ②

noun the shape or pattern of something » *The 3D jigsaw had the form of a globe.*
contours, layout, outline, shape, structure

form ③

verb to be the elements that something consists of
» *Rachel's childhood formed the basis of her novel.*
compose, constitute, make up, serve as

form ④

verb to organize, create, or come into existence » *Paul formed a bowl from clay.*
assemble, create, develop, draw up, establish, fashion, make

*Paul **formed** a bowl from clay.*

a b c d e f g h i j k l m n o p q r s t u v w x y z

A
B
C
D
E
F
G
H
I
J
K
L
M
N
O
P
Q
R
S
T
U
V
W
X
Y
Z

confidant
Dan is Pete's **confidant**—he tells him everything.

crew
Tony was surrounded by his football **crew**.

companion
Ruby and Lily were constant **companions**.

ally
Sam was Ben's **ally** whenever there was an argument.

squad (slang)
Sharon goes out with her **squad** on weekends.

friend

noun a person you know and like
» *Tim sat with his **friends** most lunch hours.*

soul mate
Jen and Sally are **soul mates** and know what each other is thinking.

pal
Sam and Dan are great **pals**.

sidekick
Ben's **sidekick** feeds him lines so he can tell his jokes.

formal 1

adjective in accordance with convention
» *We attended a formal dinner at the hotel.*
conventional, correct, precise, stiff
antonym: **informal**

formal 2

adjective official and publicly recognized » *No formal announcement has been made.*
approved, legal, official, prescribed, regular

former

adjective existing in the past
» *The former Olympic champion congratulated this year's winners.*
ancient, bygone, old, past

formidable

adjective difficult to overcome
» *Climbing the cliff was going to be a formidable challenge.*
challenging, daunting, difficult, intimidating, mammoth, onerous

*Climbing the cliff was going to be a **formidable** challenge.*

*The old **fort** was built to defend the harbor from attack.*

fort

noun a building for defense and shelter » *The old fort was built to defend the harbor from attack.*
castle, citadel, fortification, fortress

fragile

adjective easily broken or damaged » *The antique china plate was extremely fragile.*
breakable, dainty, delicate, flimsy, frail, frangible, infirm
antonym: **tough**

fragrance

noun a pleasant smell
» *The flowers had a sweet fragrance.*
aroma, perfume, scent, smell

*The flowers had a sweet **fragrance**.*

fragrant
adjective having a pleasant smell » *The lemongrass and ginger made the curry wonderfully fragrant.*
aromatic, perfumed, sweet-smelling

frank
adjective open and straightforward » *Ryan and his mom had a frank discussion about his poor exam results.*
blunt, candid, honest, open, plain, straightforward

fraud ☐1
noun the act of deceiving someone » *Susan committed fraud by taking on someone else's identity.*
deceit, deception, guile, hoax, trickery, chicanery, duplicity, spuriousness

fraud ☐2
noun someone or something that deceives you » *Don't believe what that man says—he's a fraud.*
charlatan, cheat, fake, forgery, imposter, quack

free ☐1
adjective not being held prisoner » *The chicks escaped from their cage and were found running free in the back yard.*
at large, at liberty, liberated, loose
antonym: **captive**

The chicks escaped from their cage and were found running free in the back yard.

free ☐2
adjective available without payment » *Tom was giving away free magazines at the local store.*
complimentary, gratis, unpaid, without charge

free ☐3
verb to release from captivity » *Nathan's friends helped him to free his foot from beneath the rock.*
discharge, liberate, release, set at liberty, set loose, emancipate, unfetter
antonym: **imprison**

freedom ☐1
noun the ability to choose » *Sara had the freedom to decide for herself what to wear.*
discretion, latitude, leeway, license, scope

freedom ☐2
noun the state of being free or being set free » *Lydia felt an amazing sense of freedom now that summer vacation was here.*
emancipation, liberty, release, deliverance
antonym: **captivity**

freedom ☐3: freedom from
noun the absence of something unpleasant » *She enjoyed freedom from pain for the first time that day when she took off her tight shoes.*
exemption, immunity

frenzy
noun wild and uncontrolled behavior » *The fish darted around in a feeding frenzy.*
agitation, fury, hysteria, madness, rage, delirium, paroxysm

frequent ☐1
adjective happening often » *Alex walked the dog on a frequent basis.*
common, continual, everyday, habitual, recurrent, repeated
antonym: **rare**

frequent ☐2
verb to go somewhere often » *When they had nothing else to do, the boys frequented the local park.*
attend, haunt, patronize, visit
antonym: **avoid**

friend
noun a person you know and like
◄◄ SEE LEFT

friendly
adjective kind and pleasant » *Peter had a friendly relationship with his neighbor.*
affectionate, amiable, close, cordial, genial, welcoming, companionable, comradely, convivial
antonym: **unfriendly**

*Peter had a **friendly** relationship with his neighbor.*

friendship
noun a state of being friendly with someone » *Their friendship was important to him.*
affection, attachment, closeness, goodwill
antonym: **hostility**

frighten
verb to make someone afraid » *The dog tried to frighten the others away by barking fiercely.*
alarm, intimidate, scare, startle, terrify, terrorize, unnerve

frightened
adjective having feelings of fear about something » *The cat was frightened by the noise of the fireworks.*
afraid, alarmed, petrified, scared, startled, terrified, cowed, panicky, terror-stricken

frightening
adjective causing someone to feel fear » *Thunder and lightning can be quite frightening.*
alarming, hair-raising, intimidating, menacing, terrifying

frivolous
adjective not serious or sensible » *She knew buying another party dress was frivolous.*
flippant, foolish, juvenile, puerile, silly
antonym: **serious**

front ☐1
noun the part that faces forward » *The front wall of the house was painted blue.*
face, frontage
antonym: **back**

front ☐2
noun the outward appearance of something » *Despite feeling nervous, Jo put on a brave front.*
appearance, exterior, face, show

front ☐3: in front
preposition further forward » *The car in front stopped suddenly so Mom slammed on the brakes.*
ahead, before, leading

frown
verb to draw the eyebrows together » *Ann frowned at the naughty child.*
glare, glower, knit your brows, scowl

frozen
adjective extremely cold » *Neil felt frozen, despite his big winter jacket.*
arctic, chilled, frigid, icy, numb

*Neil felt **frozen**, despite his big winter jacket.*

frustrate
verb to prevent something from happening » *Charlie's efforts to start a fire were frustrated by the rain.*
block, check, foil, thwart, forestall, nullify

a b c d e f g h i j k l m n o p q r s t u v w x y z

A B C D E F G H I J K L M N O P Q R S T U V W X Y Z

fulfill

verb to carry out or achieve something » *Sam knew he would fulfill his dream and travel the world one day.*
accomplish, achieve, carry out, perform, realize, satisfy

full ①

adjective filled with something » *The suitcase was so full of clothes, we couldn't close it.*
filled, loaded, packed, saturated
antonym: **empty**

*The suitcase was so **full** of clothes, we couldn't close it.*

full ②

adjective leaving nothing out » *I want to hear the full story of what happened.*
comprehensive, detailed, exhaustive, extensive, maximum, thorough

full ③

adjective loose-fitting » *Her full skirt was made of a lot of material.*
baggy, loose, voluminous

fun ①

noun an enjoyable activity
▶▶ SEE RIGHT

fun ② : make fun of

verb to tease someone » *Don't make fun of him.*
deride, laugh at, mock, ridicule, taunt, lampoon, rib, satirize

function ①

noun the useful thing that something or someone does » *The function of an oven is to heat food.*
duty, job, purpose, remit, responsibility, role

function ②

noun a large formal dinner, reception, or party » *Her parents were going to a function in the city.*
dinner, gathering, party, reception

function ③

verb to operate or work » *The heater was not functioning properly— it was stone cold.*
go, operate, perform, run, work

fund ①

noun an amount of money » *Ali needed to find a way to add to his savings fund.*
capital, foundation, pool, reserve, supply

fund ②

noun a large amount of something » *She had a fund of knowledge about dinosaurs.*
hoard, mine, reserve, reservoir, store

fund ③

verb to provide the money for something » *Helen was raising money to fund a local charity.*
finance, pay for, subsidize, support

funny ①

adjective being strange or odd » *Chris heard a funny noise.*
mysterious, odd, peculiar, puzzling, strange, unusual

funny ②

adjective causing amusement » *Jessica laughed at her sister's funny story.*
amusing, comic, comical, hilarious, humorous, witty, droll, jocular, risible
antonym: **serious**

*Jessica laughed at her sister's **funny** story.*

furious ①

adjective extremely angry » *The man was furious that my ball had broken his window.*
enraged, fuming, infuriated, livid, mad, raging, frenzied, incensed, tumultuous

furious ②

adjective involving great energy, effort, or speed » *There was a furious contest between the two race car drivers.*
breakneck, fierce, frantic, frenzied, intense, manic, frenetic

fuss ①

noun anxious or excited behavior » *What's all the fuss about?*
agitation, bother, commotion, confusion, stir, to-do, ado, fluster, palaver

fuss ②

verb to behave in a nervous or restless way » *Waiters fussed around the table.*
bustle, fidget, fret

fussy

adjective difficult to please » *The toddler was a fussy eater and refused to eat pasta.*
choosy (informal), discriminating, exacting, fastidious, particular, finicky, persnickety

futile

adjective having no chance of success » *Kelly made a futile effort to catch the fish, but it slipped through her fingers.*
abortive, forlorn, unsuccessful, useless, vain
antonym: **successful**

future

adjective relating to a time after the present » *Future generations may one day live on the Moon.*
approaching, coming, forthcoming, impending, later, prospective
antonym: **past**

fun

① *noun* an enjoyable activity » *The theme park was so much **fun**.*

amusement

enjoyment

entertainment

pleasure

recreation

Gg

gadget

noun a small machine or tool » *The kitchen was full of gadgets to make cooking easier.*
appliance, device, machine, tool, implement, instrument, utensil

The kitchen was full of gadgets to make cooking easier.

gain 1

verb to get something gradually » *The motorcycle gained speed.*
achieve, acquire, earn, obtain, secure, win, attain, capture, reap

gain 2

verb to obtain an advantage » *I did my training in an office to gain work experience.*
benefit, profit

gain 3

noun an increase or improvement in something » *Jeff's financial gains were down to good work and determination.*
advance, growth, improvement, increase, rise

gamble 1

verb to bet money on something » *Louis gambled on the lottery once a year, on his birthday.*
back, bet, wager

gamble 2

verb to take a risk » *He had gambled on it being a hot day and wore his shorts.*
chance, risk, stake, hazard, take a chance, venture

He had gambled on it being a hot day and wore his shorts.

gamble 3

noun a risk that someone takes » *We are taking a gamble on a young player.*
chance, lottery, risk

The atmosphere was great for the first game of the season.

game

noun an occasion on which people compete » *The atmosphere was great for the first game of the season.*
clash, contest, match

gap 1

noun a space or a hole in something
▼ **SEE BELOW**

gap 2

noun a period of time » *After a two-year gap, the fair came back to town.*
hiatus (formal), **interlude, interval, lull, pause**

gap

1 *noun* a space or a hole in something » *I found a gap big enough to stick my hand through.*

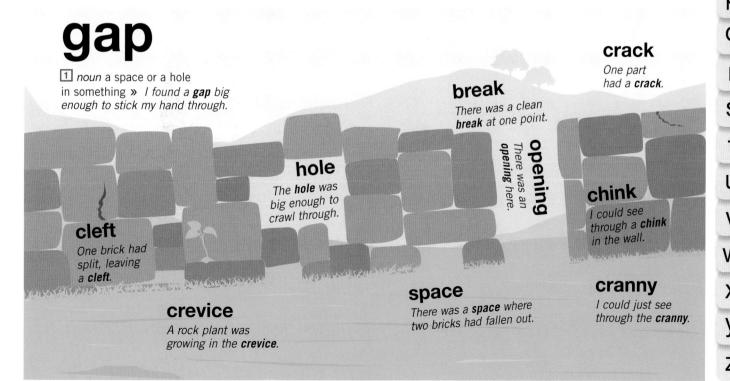

cleft
One brick had split, leaving a **cleft**.

crevice
A rock plant was growing in the **crevice**.

hole
The **hole** was big enough to crawl through.

break
There was a clean **break** at one point.

opening
There was an **opening** here.

space
There was a **space** where two bricks had fallen out.

crack
One part had a **crack**.

chink
I could see through a **chink** in the wall.

cranny
I could just see through the **cranny**.

a b c d e f g h i j k l m n o p q r s t u v w x y z

gap 3

noun a difference between people or things
» *There was a gap between what they hoped for, and what they got.*
difference, disparity (formal), **inconsistency**

garbage 1

noun things that people do not want » *Garbage was piled on the street, ready to be collected.*
debris, junk (informal), **litter, refuse** (formal), **rubbish** (Britain), **trash, waste**

garbage 2

noun (informal) ideas and opinions that are untrue or unimportant » *I personally think that this is garbage.*
drivel, gibberish, nonsense, rubbish

garbled

adjective confused or incorrect » *Anita couldn't understand the garbled voicemail message.*
confused, distorted, incomprehensible, jumbled, unintelligible

gasp 1

verb to breathe in quickly through your mouth
» *Beth gasped for air after running so fast.*
choke, gulp, pant, puff, catch your breath, fight for breath

*Beth **gasped** for air after running so fast.*

gasp 2

noun a short quick breath of air
» *The audience gave a gasp as the actor walked on stage.*
gulp, pant, puff

gather 1

verb to come together in a group
▶▶ SEE RIGHT

gather 2

verb to bring things together » *The squirrel gathered the nuts into a pile.*
accumulate, amass, collect, hoard, stockpile

*The squirrel **gathered** the nuts into a pile.*

gather 3

verb to learn or believe something » *Listening to the headlines, I gathered that the band had fallen out over money problems.*
assume, conclude, hear, learn, understand

gathering

noun a meeting with a purpose » *Lucas had been nervous about the hockey team gathering, but it had ended up being fun.*
assembly, congregation, get-together (informal), **meeting, rally, conference, congress, convention**

gaudy

adjective colorful in a vulgar way » *The fake gems in the jewelry were gaudy.*
bright, flashy, garish, loud, showy, tacky (informal), **vulgar, jazzy, ostentatious, tasteless, tawdry**

general 1

adjective relating to the whole of something » *There was a general increase in student numbers across all majors.*
broad, comprehensive, overall, generic, indiscriminate, panoramic, sweeping
antonym: **specific**

general 2

adjective widely true, suitable or relevant » *The campaign should raise general awareness about bullying.*
broad, common, universal, widespread, accepted
antonym: **special**

generosity

noun willingness to give money, time, or help » *Elsa is well known for her generosity about sharing her candy.*
benevolence, charity, kindness, bounty, liberality, munificence, open-handedness
antonym: **cheapness**

generous 1

adjective very large » *Amir donated a generous amount of clothes to charity.*
abundant, ample, plentiful
antonym: **meager**

*Amir donated a **generous** amount of clothes to charity.*

generous 2

adjective willing to give money, time, or help » *The offer to make all the invitations was very generous.*
charitable, hospitable, kind, lavish, liberal, munificent, open-handed, prodigal, unstinting
antonym: **cheap**

genius 1

noun a very intelligent or talented person » *Lena was a mathematical genius.*
brain, master, mastermind, virtuoso

genius 2

noun extraordinary ability or talent » *Bradley is a mathematician of pure genius.*
brains, brilliance, intellect

*Bradley is a mathematician of pure **genius**.*

gentle

adjective not violent or rough » *The mother reminded her children to be gentle with the toys.*
benign, kind, kindly, meek, mild, placid, soft, tender, compassionate, humane, lenient, sweet-tempered
antonym: **cruel**

genuine

adjective not fake or pretend » *Experts are convinced that the painting is a genuine work by the artist Monet.*
authentic, bona fide, certified, echt (informal), **honest, real, true**
antonym: **fake**

A B C D E F G H I J K L M N O P Q R S T U V W X Y Z

get [1]
verb to obtain or receive something » *I'll get us some drinks for the picnic.*
acquire, fetch (Britain), **obtain, procure** (formal), **receive, secure** (formal)

get [2]
verb to change from one state to another » *Once it gets dark, people close the curtains and put on the lights.*
become, grow, turn

get along
verb to enjoy someone's company » *The two friends always did get along very well.*
be compatible, hit it off (informal)

ghost
noun the spirit of a dead person » *Lots of children dressed up as ghosts on Halloween.*
apparition, phantom, specter, spirit
related word:
adjective **spectral**

*Ann bought the **gift** for her friend.*

gift [1]
noun something you give someone » *Ann bought the gift for her friend.*
bequest (formal), **contribution, donation, legacy, present**

gift [2]
noun a natural skill or ability » *Huan had a gift for music.*
ability, aptitude, flair, talent

give [1]
verb to provide someone with something » *I gave her a glass of orange juice.*
award, deliver, donate, grant, hand, present, provide, supply, accord, administer, bestow, confer
antonym: **take**

give [2]
verb to collapse or break under pressure » *The bookcase was likely to give if any more books were placed on it.*
buckle, cave in, collapse, give way, yield

give in
verb to admit that you are defeated » *The kids kept whining until their dad gave in and took them to the park.*
capitulate, concede, submit, succumb, surrender, yield

glad
adjective happy about something » *I'm so glad you could make it, I haven't seen you for such a long time!*
delighted, happy, joyful, overjoyed, pleased
antonym: **sorry**

glance [1]
noun a brief look at something » *They exchanged glances when the teacher's back was turned, as they knew they were about to get homework.*
glimpse, look, peek, peep

glance [2]
verb to look at something quickly » *Wyatt glanced quickly at his watch so the teacher wouldn't notice.*
glimpse, look, peek, peep, scan

glance [3]
verb to hit something quickly and bounce away » *The ball glanced off the goal post.*
bounce, brush, skim,

glare [1]
verb to look angrily at someone » *Joe glared at his sister.*
frown, glower, scowl

*Joe **glared** at his sister.*

glare [2]
noun an angry look » *When the teacher gave them a glare, the class calmed down.*
frown, scowl

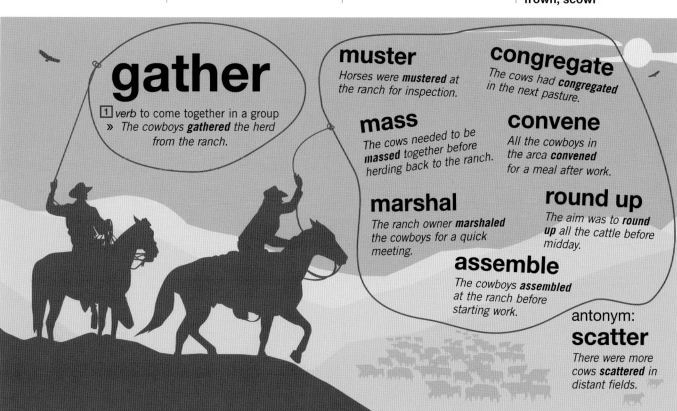

gather
[1] *verb* to come together in a group » *The cowboys **gathered** the herd from the ranch.*

muster
*Horses were **mustered** at the ranch for inspection.*

congregate
*The cows had **congregated** in the next pasture.*

mass
*The cows needed to be **massed** together before herding back to the ranch.*

convene
*All the cowboys in the area **convened** for a meal after work.*

marshal
*The ranch owner **marshaled** the cowboys for a quick meeting.*

round up
*The aim was to **round up** all the cattle before midday.*

assemble
*The cowboys **assembled** at the ranch before starting work.*

antonym:
scatter
*There were more cows **scattered** in distant fields.*

a b c d e f g h i j k l m n o p q r s t u v w x y z

good

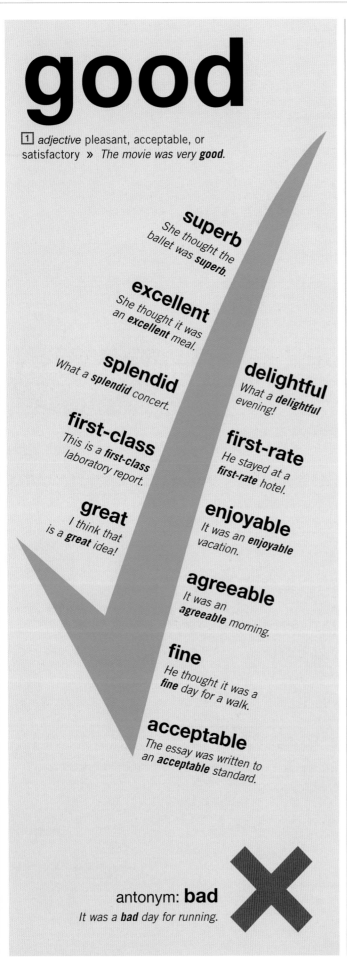

[1] *adjective* pleasant, acceptable, or satisfactory » *The movie was very **good**.*

superb
She thought the ballet was **superb**.

excellent
She thought it was an **excellent** meal.

splendid
What a **splendid** concert.

first-class
This is a **first-class** laboratory report.

great
I think that is a **great** idea!

delightful
What a **delightful** evening!

first-rate
He stayed at a **first-rate** hotel.

enjoyable
It was an **enjoyable** vacation.

agreeable
It was an **agreeable** morning.

fine
He thought it was a **fine** day for a walk.

acceptable
The essay was written to an **acceptable** standard.

antonym: **bad**
It was a **bad** day for running.

glare [3]
noun very bright light
» *Vicky tilted her rearview mirror to avoid the glare of the headlights from the car behind.*
blaze, glow

gloomy [1]
adjective feeling very sad
» *Carla felt gloomy at the prospect of leaving her old house.*
dejected, down, glum, miserable, sad, blue, despondent, downhearted
antonym: **cheerful**

gloomy [2]
adjective dark and depressing
» *The room was gloomy with all the curtains closed.*
dark, dismal, dreary, dull
antonym: **sunny**

The room was **gloomy** with all the curtains closed.

glory [1]
noun fame and admiration that someone gets
» *Winning the competition was her moment of glory.*
fame, honor, immortality, praise, prestige, acclaim, eminence, renown
antonym: **disgrace**

glory [2]
noun something impressive or beautiful » *Spring arrived in all its glory.*
grandeur, magnificence, majesty, splendor

glory [3]
noun to be extremely happy
» *Whenever she was on stage singing, she was in her glory .*
in her element

*Use polish to give your shoes a **gloss**.*

gloss
noun a bright shine on a surface » *Use polish to give your shoes a gloss.*
brilliance, gleam, polish, sheen, shine

glossy
adjective smooth and shiny
» *The leaves were dark and glossy.*
bright, brilliant, polished, shiny, sleek

glow [1]
noun a steady light
» *Madison felt soothed by the glow of the fireplace.*
gleam, glimmer, light

glow [2]
verb to shine with a dull steady light » *The sun glowed through the trees.*
gleam, glimmer, shine, smolder

glue
verb to stick things together
» *Glue the two halves together.*
fix, paste, seal, stick

go [1]
verb to move or travel somewhere » *I usually go into town on the weekends.*
advance, drive, fly, journey (formal), leave, proceed (formal), set off, travel

go [2]
verb to work correctly
» *The car won't go.*
function, work

go ③
noun an attempt to do something » *I always wanted to have a go at waterskiing.*
attempt, shot (informal), **stab** (informal), **try**

goal
noun something that a person hopes to achieve » *The goal is to finish the race as fast as you can without dropping the egg from the spoon.*
aim, end, intention, object, objective, purpose, target

gobble up
verb to eat food very quickly » *Pete gobbled up the pasta as if he hadn't eaten for days.*
bolt, devour, wolf down

*Pete **gobbled up** the pasta as if he hadn't eaten for days.*

good ①
adjective pleasant, acceptable, or satisfactory
◄◄ SEE LEFT

good ②
adjective skillful or successful » *Miguel was really good at art.*
accomplished, adept, clever, competent, proficient, skilled, talented
antonym: **incompetent**

good ③
adjective kind, thoughtful, and loving » *You are so good to me, bringing me flowers.*
benevolent, considerate, generous, kindhearted, obliging, thoughtful

*As the service was unusually slow, the waiter gave her a free drink as a gesture of **goodwill**.*

goodwill
noun kindness and helpfulness toward other people
» *As the service was unusually slow, the waiter gave her a free drink as a gesture of goodwill.*
benevolence, favor, friendliness, friendship

gossip
noun informal conversation about other people » *The friends met once a week for a coffee and gossip.*
dirt, hearsay, chitchat, prattle, scandal, tittle-tattle

go through
verb to experience an unpleasant event » *I was going through a very difficult time at school.*
endure, experience, undergo

grab
verb to take hold of something roughly » *He grabbed her hand to stop her from falling.*
clutch, grasp, seize, snatch

*He **grabbed** her hand to stop her from falling.*

grace
noun an elegant way of moving » *The swans on the river swim with such grace.*
elegance, poise
antonym: **clumsiness**

grade
verb to arrange things according to quality » *Chilies are graded according to how hot they taste.*
class, classify, group, rate, sort, evaluate, sequence

gradual
adjective happening or changing slowly » *There was a gradual introduction of new school rules.*
continuous, progressive, slow, steady
antonym: **sudden**

grand ①
adjective very impressive in size or appearance
» *The grand building in the center of the city is the palace.*
imposing, impressive, magnificent, majestic, monumental, splendid, glorious, grandiose, palatial

*The **grand** building in the center of the city is the palace.*

grandiose
adjective very large in size, effect, or cost » *The governor's grandiose house and party made people wonder about his spending habits.*
massive, overblown, palatial, pompous, regal, royal

grant ①
noun a money award given for a particular purpose
» *My application for a music grant has been accepted.*
allocation, allowance, award, handout, subsidy

grant ②
verb to allow someone to have something » *Chloe was granted access to the backstage area.*
allocate, allow, award, give, permit, accord, bestow
antonym: **deny**

*Chloe was **granted** access to the backstage area.*

grant ③
verb (Britain) to admit that something is true » *I grant that the chair was wobbly before you broke it.*
accept, acknowledge, admit, allow, concede
antonym: **deny**

grasp ①
verb to hold something firmly » *Chen grasped the branch to steady himself.*
clutch, grab, grip, hold, seize, snatch

grasp ②
verb to understand an idea » *She failed to grasp the urgency of the situation.*
absorb, appreciate, assimilate, realize, take in, understand

grasp ③
noun a firm hold » *Logan loosened his grasp on the jar.*
clasp, embrace, grip, hold

a b c d e f g h i j k l m n o p q r s t u v w x y z

green

environmentally friendly
There are **environmentally friendly** solar panels on the roof.

ozone-friendly
We burn **ozone-friendly** smokeless fuel.

green

1 *adjective* concerned with environmental issues » *We've done all we can to be green.*

eco-friendly
The **eco-friendly** walls are insulated.

nonpolluting
The wind turbine is a **nonpolluting** energy source.

ecological
Everyone is interested in **ecological** issues such as global warming.

conservationist
Conservationist groups are pleased with our efforts.

grasp 4
noun a person's understanding of something » *My brother has a good grasp of foreign languages.*
awareness, comprehension (formal), **grip, knowledge, understanding**

grateful
adjective pleased and wanting to thank someone » *Grace was grateful for the wonderful birthday party.*
appreciative, indebted, thankful
antonym: **ungrateful**

*Grace was **grateful** for the wonderful birthday party.*

gratitude
noun the feeling of being grateful » *After the walk, the dog wagged its tail in gratitude.*
appreciation, recognition, thanks
antonym: **ingratitude**

grave 1
noun a place where someone is buried when they die » *They visited her grave twice a year.*
mausoleum, pit, sepulchre, tomb, burial chamber, catacomb

grave 2
adjective (formal) very serious » *The students looked grave as they filed into the hall for the assembly.*
acute, critical, heavy (informal), **serious, sober, solemn, somber**

graze 1
verb to slightly injure your skin » *Anton fell over and grazed his left arm.*
scrape, scratch, skin

graze 2
noun a slight injury to your skin » *Oscar just has a graze, not a major cut.*
abrasion (formal), **scrape, scratch**

great 1
adjective very large in size » *There are great glaciers in the Arctic Ocean.*
big, colossal, huge, large, enormous, extensive, gigantic, immense, stupendous, tremendous, vast
antonym: **small**

*There are **great** glaciers in the Arctic Ocean.*

*They erected a statue to honor the **great** leader.*

great 2
adjective important or famous » *They erected a statue to honor the great leader.*
celebrated, chief, distinguished, eminent, famed, famous, illustrious, important, main, major, momentous, notable, principal, prominent, renowned, serious, significant

great [3]

adjective (informal) very good
» *Frances thought the surprise birthday party was a great idea and joined in with the planning.*
excellent, fantastic (informal), **fine, first-rate, marvelous** (informal), **outstanding, superb, terrific** (informal), **tremendous** (informal), **wonderful**
antonym: **terrible**

greedy

adjective wanting more than you need
» *The greedy cat ate more than it needed.*
materialistic, acquisitive, avaricious, grasping, ravenous, voracious

*The **greedy** cat ate more than it needed.*

green [1]

adjective concerned with environmental issues
◄◄ SEE LEFT

green [2]

noun or adjective
Shades of green:
apple green, avocado, bottle green, chartreuse, emerald, forest green, grass green, jade, khaki, lime, olive, pea green, pistachio, sage, sea green, turquoise
related word:
adjective **verdant**

*The president was **greeted** by local political leaders.*

greet

verb to say hello to someone when they arrive » *The president was greeted by local political leaders.*
meet, receive (formal), **welcome,** hail, salute

grey/gray [1]

adjective being dull and dismal » *The rush hour crowds looked fed-up and grey.*
colorless, dull, nondescript, unremarkable

grey/gray [2]

noun or adjective
Shades of grey:
ash, charcoal, gunmetal, hoary, leaden, pewter, platinum, silver, silvery, slate, steel grey, stone, taupe, whitish

grief

noun a feeling of extreme sadness » *She felt a sense of grief when her best friend moved abroad.*
agony, blues (informal), **distress, heartache, misery, sadness, sorrow, unhappiness,** anguish, dejection, heartbreak, woe
antonym: **happiness**

grieve [1]

verb to feel extremely sad
» *The nation grieved for the loss of their much-loved president at the state funeral.*
agonize, anguish, hurt, lament, languish, mourn, suffer, pine for

grieve [2]

verb (Britain) to make someone feel extremely sad » *It grieved Elaine to be away from her pets when she was on vacation.*
distress, pain, sadden, upset
antonym: **cheer**

grim

adjective looking very serious » *Her face was grim upon hearing the bad news.*
grave, severe, solemn, stern

grip [1]

noun a firm hold on something » *Aiden's grip on the bag was strong and fast.*
clasp, grasp, hold

grip [2]

noun someone's control over something » *The principal kept a tight grip on the school budget.*
clutches, control, influence, power

grip [3]

verb to hold something firmly » *The girl gripped the rope and began to climb.*
clutch, grasp, hold

*The girl **gripped** the rope and began to climb.*

ground

noun the surface of the Earth » *We sat on the ground and had a picnic.*
dirt, earth, land, soil, terrain

*The school's **grounds** were used for sports and other activities.*

grounds [1]

plural noun the land surrounding a building » *The school's grounds were used for sports and other activities.*
estate, fields, land

grounds [2]

plural noun the reason for doing or thinking something » *Owen was against buying a new car on the grounds of expense.*
basis, cause, excuse, justification, reason, foundation, pretext, rationale

group [1]

noun a number of people or things » *The group of soccer fans sang in unison.*
band, bunch, collection, crowd, gang, pack, party, set, aggregation, assemblage, coterie

group [2]

verb to link people or things together » *The students were grouped into four teams.*
arrange, class, classify, organize, sort, assort, marshal

grow [1]

verb to increase in size or amount » *The girl's hair grew very long.*
develop, expand, increase, multiply
antonym: **shrink**

grow [2]

verb to pass gradually into a particular state » *I grew more tired as the day went on.*
become, get, turn

a b c d e f g h i j k l m n o p q r s t u v w x y z

A
B
C
D
E
F
G
H
I
J
K
L
M
N
O
P
Q
R
S
T
U
V
W
X
Y
Z

grow ③

verb to be alive or exist
▼ **SEE BELOW**

growth

noun the act of getting bigger
» *The doctor measured the child's growth.*
development, enlargement, expansion, increase

The doctor measured the child's growth.

grumble ①

verb to complain in a bad-tempered way » *"This is very inconvenient," he grumbled.*
carp, complain, groan, moan, mutter, whine, whinge (Britain; informal)

grumble ②

noun a bad-tempered complaint » *I didn't hear any grumbles when we were first planning what food should be served at the party.*
complaint, moan, murmur, objection, protest, whinge (Britain; informal)

grumpy

adjective bad-tempered and annoyed » *Alex was grumpy because he had forgotten his homework.*
crabby (informal), **grouchy** (informal), **irritable, sulky, sullen, surly, bad-tempered, cantankerous**

guarantee ①

noun something that makes another thing certain » *The digital radio came with a guarantee that it would be replaced or fixed if anything was wrong with it.*
assurance, pledge, promise, undertaking, word

guarantee ②

verb to make it certain that something will happen » *The free cupcakes were guaranteed to attract customers to the food stall.*
ensure, pledge, promise

guard ①

verb to protect someone or something » *The dog guarded the house by barking at any intruders.*
defend, protect, safeguard, shelter, shield, watch over

guard ②

verb to stop someone making trouble or escaping » *Police guarded the angry crowds as they marched through the town.*
patrol, police, supervise

The security guard kept watch over the parking ramps.

guard ③

noun someone who guards people or places
» *The security guard kept watch over the parking ramps.*
sentry, warden, sentinel, warder, watchman

guess ①

verb to form an idea or opinion about something
» *I guess I'll have the cake for dessert.*
estimate, imagine, reckon (Britain), **speculate, suppose, suspect, think, conjecture, hazard, surmise**

guess ②

noun an attempt to give the right answer » *Stefan made a guess that the time was three o'clock.*
feeling, reckoning, shot, speculation, hypothesis

guide ①

verb to lead someone somewhere » *Ella took Elliott by the arm and guided him out.*
accompany, direct, escort, lead, conduct, convoy, shepherd, usher

guide ②

verb to influence someone
» *Guided by her father's advice, Paloma bought the red bicycle.*
counsel (formal), **govern, influence**

guilty ①

adjective having done something wrong
» *The dog was guilty of eating all the dog treats.*
convicted, criminal, blameworthy, culpable, felonious
antonym: **innocent**

guilty ②

adjective unhappy because you have done something bad » *Sadie felt guilty for spilling coffee on the carpet.*
ashamed, regretful, remorseful (formal), **sorry, conscience-stricken, contrite, shamefaced**

gullible

adjective easily tricked
» *Ivan was very gullible and believed everything the other boy said.*
naive, trusting, credulous, unsuspecting
antonym: **suspicious**

gush

verb to flow in large quantities
» *Water gushed from the tap.*
flow, pour, spurt, stream, cascade, issue, jet

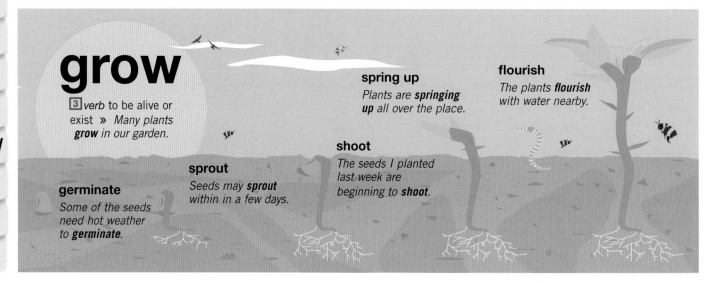

grow

③ *verb* to be alive or exist » *Many plants grow in our garden.*

germinate
Some of the seeds need hot weather to germinate.

sprout
Seeds may sprout within in a few days.

shoot
The seeds I planted last week are beginning to shoot.

spring up
Plants are springing up all over the place.

flourish
The plants flourish with water nearby.

Hh

habit ①

noun something that is done regularly » *Jonathan has an annoying habit of leaving the top off the toothpaste.*
convention, custom, practice, routine, tradition

habit ②

noun an addiction to something » *Jess has a bad chocolate habit—she eats one chocolate bar every day.*
addiction, dependence

habitat

noun the natural home of a plant or animal » *Crocodiles live in tropical habitats.*
environment, territory
▼ SEE BELOW

hackneyed

adjective used too often to be meaningful » *Diego could only find hackneyed postcards of palm trees and alligators when he went to Florida.*
banal, clichéd, stale, tired, trite, run-of-the-mill, threadbare, timeworn
antonym: **original**

hail

verb to attract someone's attention » *Fatima hailed me from across the street.*
call, signal to, wave down

halt ①

verb to bring something to an end » *The barbecue was finally halted by a rainstorm.*
cease, check, curb, cut short, end, terminate
antonym: **begin**

halt ②

verb to come or bring to a stop » *She held her hand out and halted the cars.*
draw up, pull up, stop

*She held her hand out and **halted** the cars.*

halt ③

noun an interruption or end to something » *When the bell rang for lunch, she brought the class to a halt.*
close, end, pause, standstill, stop, stoppage, impasse, termination

hamper

verb to make movement or progress difficult for someone » *I was hampered by a lack of information.*
frustrate, hinder, impede, obstruct, restrict, encumber, fetter

hand down

verb to pass from one generation to another » *Recipes are handed down from parents to their children.*
bequeath (formal), give, leave, pass down, pass on, bestow, will

---

forest
Forests *are found in cooler, wetter areas where there is enough rain for trees to grow.*

desert
With little annual rainfall, ***deserts*** *are the driest places on Earth.*

polar regions
The icy Arctic and Antarctic are ***polar regions.***

habitat
types of habitat

Mediterranean
The ***Mediterranean*** *can be very hot and humid.*

grasslands
Grasslands *are usually very dry and home to many grazing animals.*

rain forest
More species of wildlife are found in ***rain forests,*** *or jungles, than anywhere else in the world.*

a b c d e f g h i j k l m n o p q r s t u v w x y z

A B C D E F G H I J K L M N O P Q R S T U V W X Y Z

happy

[1] *adjective* feeling or causing joy
» *The children were so **happy** when dessert arrived.*

glad

pleased

joyful

delighted

jubilant

elated

handicap [1]
noun something that makes progress difficult
» *Not speaking the same language was a real handicap.*
barrier, disadvantage, drawback, hindrance, impediment, obstacle

handicap [2]
verb to make something difficult for someone » *Lack of proper tools handicapped my father's attempt to build a dresser.*
burden, hamper, hinder, impede, restrict

handle [1]
noun the part of an object by which it is held » *The broom handle suddenly broke.*
grip, hilt

*The broom **handle** suddenly broke.*

handle [2]
verb to hold or move with the hands » *Please remember to wear gloves when handling cleaning products.*
feel, finger, grasp, hold, touch

handle [3]
verb to deal with or control something
» *Thalia handled the travel arrangements.*
administer, conduct, deal with, manage, supervise, take care of

handsome [1]
adjective very attractive in appearance » *The main actor was talented and very handsome.*
attractive, good-looking
antonym: **ugly**

handsome [2]
adjective large and generous
» *They made a handsome profit from the bake sale.*
ample, considerable, generous, liberal, plentiful, sizable or sizeable
antonym: **small**

*Keep a pencil and paper **handy** so you can take notes during the telephone call.*

handy [1]
adjective conveniently near
» *Keep a pencil and paper handy so you can take notes during the telephone call.*
at hand, at your fingertips, close, convenient, nearby, on hand

handy [2]
adjective easy to handle or use » *Paul gave me some handy hints on how to care for houseplants.*
convenient, easy to use, helpful, neat, practical, useful, user-friendly

hang [1]
verb to be attached at the top with the lower part free
» *Miguel's jacket hung from a hook behind the door.*
dangle, droop

hang [2]
verb to fasten something to another thing at the top
» *Sarah hung clothes on the line.*
attach, drape, fasten, fix, suspend

*Sarah **hung** clothes on the line.*

happen
verb to take place
» *Laura and Claire happened to be in the same store, at the same time.*
come about, follow, occur, result, take place, ensue, materialize

thrilled

over the moon

overjoyed

ecstatic

euphoric

happiness
noun a feeling of great pleasure » *Freya was overwhelmed with happiness.*
delight, ecstasy, elation, joy, pleasure, satisfaction, exuberance, felicity, merriment
antonym: **sadness**

happy ①
adjective feeling or causing joy
▲ SEE ABOVE

happy ②
adjective fortunate or lucky » *By happy coincidence, Jody bumped into an old friend on the train.*
auspicious, convenient, favorable, fortunate, lucky, opportune, timely
antonym: **unlucky**

hard ①
adjective firm, solid, or rigid » *The cheese was so hard he struggled to cut it.*
firm, rigid, solid, stiff, strong, tough
antonym: **soft**

hard ②
adjective requiring a lot of effort » *Clearing out the garage was hard work, so he always put it at the bottom of his to-do list.*
arduous, exhausting, laborious, rigorous, strenuous, tough
antonym: **easy**

hard ③
adjective difficult to understand » *Eve found her algebra homework very hard.*
baffling, complex, complicated, difficult, puzzling
antonym: **simple**

*Eve found her algebra homework very **hard**.*

harden
verb to make or become stiff or firm » *Kat put the frosting in the fridge to harden it.*
bake, cake, freeze, set, solidify, stiffen
antonym: **soften**

hardly
adverb almost not or not quite » *There is hardly any water left in the bottle.*
barely, just, only just, scarcely

*There is **hardly** any water left in the bottle.*

hardship
noun difficult circumstances » *There are many countries suffering financial hardship.*
adversity, destitution, difficulty, misfortune, want, oppression, privation, tribulation

harm ①
verb to injure someone or damage something » *The bear ate our supplies, but didn't harm anyone.*
abuse, damage, hurt, ill-treat, ruin, wound

harm ②
noun injury or damage » *She accidentally stepped on his toe, but didn't mean to cause him harm.*
abuse, damage, hurt, injury

harmful
adjective having a bad effect on something » *Eating chocolate is harmful to dogs.*
damaging, destructive, detrimental, hurtful, pernicious, baleful, baneful, deleterious, injurious
antonym: **harmless**

a b c d e f g h i j k l m n o p q r s t u v w x y z

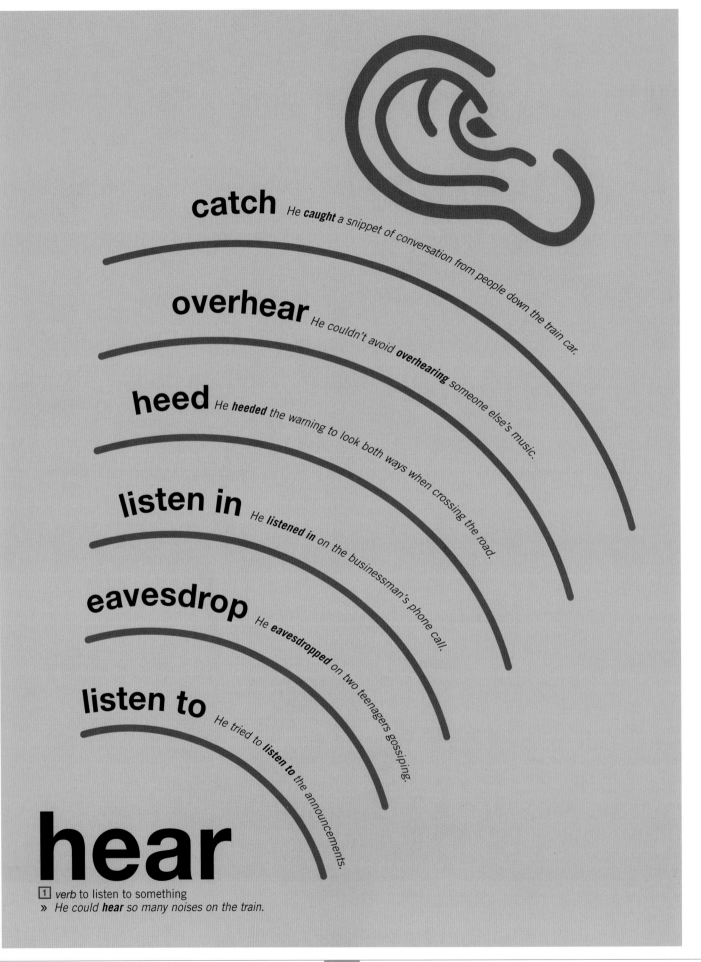

catch — He **caught** a snippet of conversation from people down the train car.

overhear — He couldn't avoid **overhearing** someone else's music.

heed — He **heeded** the warning to look both ways when crossing the road.

listen in — He **listened in** on the businessman's phone call.

eavesdrop — He **eavesdropped** on two teenagers gossiping.

listen to — He tried to **listen to** the announcements.

hear

1 *verb* to listen to something
» *He could **hear** so many noises on the train.*

harmless

adjective safe to use
or be near **»** *This experiment
is harmless to plants.*
**innocuous, nontoxic,
not dangerous, safe**
antonym: **harmful**

harsh

adjective severe, difficult,
and unpleasant **»** *The
weather conditions were
harsh in the mountains.*
**austere, cruel, hard,
ruthless, severe, stern,**
draconian, spartan
antonym: **mild**

*The weather conditions were
harsh in the mountains.*

hassle 1

noun (informal) something that
is difficult or causes trouble
» *Traveling into downtown
Chicago, with all the traffic
and crowds, is such a hassle.*
**bother, effort,
inconvenience,
trouble, upheaval**

hassle 2

verb (informal) to annoy
someone by nagging or making
demands **»** *My sister started
hassling me to go to the movies
with her.*
**badger, bother, go on at,
harass, nag, pester**

hasty

adjective done or happening
suddenly and quickly
» *Sandy made a hasty exit just
before the train door closed.*
**brisk, hurried, prompt,
rapid, swift**

hate 1

verb to have a strong dislike
for something or someone
» *I really hate mustard.*
**abhor, be sick of, despise,
detest, dislike, loathe**
antonym: **love**

hate 2

noun a strong dislike **»** *Bullies
are people who are full of hate.*
**animosity, aversion, dislike,
hatred, hostility, loathing,**
animus, detestation,
enmity, odium
antonym: **love**

hateful

adjective extremely unpleasant
» *It was a hateful thing to say.*
**abhorrent, despicable,
horrible, loathsome,
obnoxious, offensive**

hatred

noun an extremely strong
feeling of dislike **»** *The bully
made her feel full of hatred.*
**animosity, antipathy,
aversion, dislike,
hate, revulsion**
antonym: **love**

haughty

adjective showing excessive
pride **»** *Ben was very
arrogant and spoke
to them in a haughty tone.*
**arrogant, conceited,
disdainful, proud,
snobbish, stuck-up**
(informal)
antonym: **humble**

have 1

verb to own something **»** *Riley
has two tickets for the concert.*
hold, keep, own, possess

*Riley **has** two tickets
for the concert.*

have 2

verb to experience something
» *Alex had a marvelous time.*
**endure, enjoy, experience,
feel, sustain, undergo**

head 1

noun a person's mind and
mental abilities **»** *I don't
have a head for languages.*
**aptitude, brain, common
sense, intelligence, mind,
wits,** intellect, rationality

head 2

noun the top, front, or start of
something **»** *We finally
reached the head of the line.*
**beginning, front, source,
start, top**
antonym: **tail**

head 3

noun the person in charge
of something **»** *The school
has a new head of the
music program.*
**boss, chief, director, leader,
manager, president,
principal**

head 4

verb to be in charge
of something **»** *Our teacher
heads the English department.*
**be in charge of, control,
direct, lead, manage, run**

health 1

noun the condition of your
body **»** *Exercise is good
for your health.*
**condition, constitution,
shape**

health 2

noun a state in which a person
is feeling well **»** *In the hospital,
they nursed me back to health.*
**fitness, good condition,
wellbeing**
antonym: **illness**

healthy 1

adjective having good health
» *Zoe was a very healthy child.*
**active, fit,
in good shape** (informal),
robust, strong, well
antonym: **sick**

*I always eat a **healthy** breakfast.*

healthy 2

adjective producing good health
» *I always eat a healthy
breakfast.*
**beneficial, bracing,
good for you, nourishing,
nutritious, wholesome,**
invigorating, salubrious,
salutary
antonym: **unhealthy**

heap 1

noun a pile of things
» *As the bulldozers worked,
the heap of rubble grew.*
**hoard, mass, mound,
pile, stack**

heap 2

verb to pile things up
» *Cora heaped potatoes
onto Tom's plate.*
pile, stack

heaps

plural noun (informal) plenty
of something **»** *Ahmed
always seems to have heaps
of cash.*
loads (informal), **lots**
(informal), **plenty, stacks,
tons** (informal)

hear 1

verb to listen to something
◀◀ SEE LEFT

hear 2

verb to learn about something
» *I heard that they didn't
enjoy their vacation, which
is a shame.*
**ascertain, discover,
find out, gather,
learn, understand**

a b c d e f g h i j k l m n o p q r s t u v w x y z

A B C D E F G H I J K L M N O P Q R S T U V W X Y Z

heat [1]

noun the quality of being warm or hot » *The heat of the midday sun was intense.*
high temperature, warmth
antonym: **cold**
related word: *adjective* **thermal**

heat [2]

noun a state of strong emotion » *In the heat of the argument, he said things he didn't mean.*
excitement, fervor, intensity, passion, vehemence

heat [3]

verb to raise the temperature of something » *Heat the oil in a frying pan.*
reheat, warm up
antonym: **cool**

Heat the oil in a frying pan.

heaven [1]

noun the place where good people are believed to go when they die » *She told them that he was now in heaven.*
hearafter, next world, paradise, promised land, Zion, Elysium (Greek), happy hunting ground (Native American), nirvana (Buddhism and Hinduism), Valhalla (Norse) antonym: **hell**

heaven [2]

noun a place or situation liked very much » *Martin was in kid heaven as he walked around the candy store.*
bliss, ecstasy, paradise, rapture

*The strawberry birthday cake was **heavenly**.*

heavenly

adjective delightful or blissful » *The strawberry birthday cake was heavenly.*
beautiful, blissful, delightful, excellent, glorious, superb

heavy [1]

adjective great in weight or force » *The bag was very heavy, I had to carry it using both hands.*
bulky, massive
antonym: **light**

heavy [2]

adjective serious or important » *The mood was heavy following the sad news.*
deep, grave, profound, serious, solemn, weighty
antonym: **trivial**

heed [1]

verb to pay attention to someone's advice » *No one heeded my warning about the spicy food.*
follow, listen to, pay attention to, take notice of

heed [2]

noun careful attention » *He pays too much heed to her.*
attention, notice

hell [1]

noun the place where souls of evil people are believed to go after death » *Some people believe that hell is where the devil lives.*
abyss, inferno, fire and brimstone, Hades (Greek), hellfire, underworld
antonym: **heaven**

hell [2]

noun (informal) an unpleasant situation or place » *Canceled trains can make your commute hell.*
agony, anguish, misery, nightmare, ordeal

hello

interjection a greeting » *I stopped by to say hello.*
g'day or **gidday** (Australia and New Zealand),
good afternoon (formal),
good evening (formal),
good morning (formal),
hi (informal),
how do you do? (formal)
antonym: **goodbye**

help [1]

verb to make something easier or better for someone » *Dan began to help with the chores.*
aid, assist, lend a hand, support

*Dan began to **help** with the chores.*

help [2]

noun assistance or support » *The books she had borrowed were not much help for her exams.*
advice, aid, assistance, guidance, helping hand, support

helper

noun a person who gives assistance » *There is one adult helper for every two children on the field trip.*
aide, assistant, deputy, right-hand man, supporter, henchman

helpful [1]

adjective giving assistance or advice » *The staff in the office are very helpful.*
accommodating, cooperative, kind, supportive
antonym: **unhelpful**

helpful [2]

adjective making a situation better » *Having the right equipment is always helpful.*
advantageous, beneficial, constructive, profitable, useful

helpless

adjective weak or unable to cope » *The newborn kittens were helpless.*
defenseless, powerless, unprotected, vulnerable, weak

hesitant

adjective uncertain about something » *At first Isaac was hesitant to accept the role.*
diffident, doubtful, reluctant, unsure, wavering, irresolute, vacillating

hesitate

verb to pause or show uncertainty » *Sue hesitated before replying to the question.*
dither, pause, waver

hide [1]

verb to put something where it cannot be seen » *The kitten hid under the basket.*
cache, conceal, secrete, stash (informal)

*The kitten **hid** under the basket.*

hide ②

noun the skin of a large animal
» *They wrapped themselves in animal hides to keep warm.*
pelt, skin

high ①

adjective tall or a long way above the ground » *The Burj Khalifa is so high it towers over neighboring buildings.*
elevated, lofty, soaring, steep, tall, towering
antonym: **low**

*The Burj Khalifa is so **high** it towers over neighboring buildings.*

high ②

adjective great in degree, quantity, or intensity » *There is a high risk of sunstroke on beach vacations.*
acute, excessive, extraordinary, extreme, great, severe
antonym: **low**

hill

noun an area of high ground » *There is a large hill behind our house.*
brae (Scotland), down, dune, elevation, fell, foothill, height, hillock, hummock, hump, knoll, mound, prominence, tor

hinder

verb to get in the way of someone or something » *A thigh injury hindered her ability to run.*
block, check, delay, frustrate, hamper, impede, encumber, stymie

hint ①

noun an indirect suggestion
» *Victor gave a strong hint that we might go out to eat later.*
clue, indication, intimation, suggestion

hint ②

noun a helpful piece of advice
» *I hope my cousin will give me some fashion hints.*
advice, pointer, suggestion, tip

hint ③

verb to suggest something indirectly » *My mother hinted at her disapproval of the TV program.*
imply, indicate, insinuate, intimate, suggest

hire ①

verb to employ the services of someone » *They are hiring staff to work in the store on Saturdays.*
appoint, commission, employ, engage, sign up

hire ②

verb to pay money to use something » *She hired the witch costume for the party.*
charter, lease, rent

For Hire

*She **hired** the witch costume for the party.*

hit ①

verb to strike someone or something forcefully
▶▶ SEE RIGHT

hit

① *verb* to strike someone or something forcefully
» *He **hit** the machine with a big mallet.*

hammer
batter
pound
wallop
belt
beat
strike
whack
bash
punch
thump
smack
slap
bang
knock
swat
rap
tap
pat

a b c d e f g h i j k l m n o p q r s t u v w x y z

A B C D E F G H I J K L M N O P Q R S T U V W X Y Z

°C °F

scalding

Be careful, the water in the pot is scalding.

boiling

It's boiling in here; let's open a window.

scorching

I like to go swimming on a scorching day.

hot

1 *adjective* having a high temperature » *The pan was too hot to touch.*

warm

The water in the bath is warm.

heated

The heated swimming pool was perfect after being outside.

antonym:
cold
It's so cold where I live.

---

hit 2

verb to collide with something » *The car hit a traffic sign.*
bang into, bump, collide with, meet head-on, run into, smash into

hit 3

noun the action of hitting something » *Give it a good hard hit with a hammer.*
blow, knock, rap, slap, smack, stroke

hoard 1

verb to store for future use » *People began to hoard cans of food after the flood warning.*
save, stockpile, store

People began to hoard cans of food after the flood warning.

hoard 2

noun a store of things » *Mia found a hoard of Roman silver buried in the field.*
cache, fund, reserve, stockpile, store, supply

hoarse

adjective rough and unclear » *Nick's voice was hoarse from screaming.*
croaky, gruff, husky, rasping
antonym: **clear**

hobby

noun an enjoyable activity pursued in your spare time » *My hobbies are music and photography.*
diversion, leisure activity, leisure pursuit, pastime

*Ellie **held** her bag up so her friend could see what she had bought.*

hold 1

verb to carry or support something » *Ellie held her bag up so her friend could see what she had bought.*
carry, clasp, clutch, embrace, grasp, grip

hold 2

noun power or control over someone or something » *The teacher has a considerable hold over her pupils.*
control, dominance, sway

hold 3

noun the act or a way of holding something » *Ethan tightened his hold on the rope so he didn't fall.*
grasp, grip

hole 1

noun an opening or hollow in something » *The contractors cut holes into the stone.*
gap, hollow, opening, pit, split, tear

hole 2

noun a weakness in a idea or argument » *There are some holes in that idea.*
defect, error, fault, flaw, loophole

hole 3

noun (informal) a difficult situation » *Due to the crisis, he admitted the government was in a hole.*
fix (informal), **hot water** (informal), **mess, predicament, tight spot**

holiday
noun time spent away from school, work, or home for rest or enjoyment » *Ed couldn't wait for the Labor Day holiday.*
break, leave, recess, time off, vacation

holy ①
adjective relating to God or a particular religion » *The Bible is a holy book for Christians.*
blessed, consecrated, hallowed, sacred, sacrosanct, venerated

holy ②
adjective religious and leading a good life » *Monks are holy men.*
devout, pious, religious, saintly, virtuous, God-fearing, godly
antonym: **wicked**

home ①
noun the building in which someone lives » *Her parents stayed at home to watch a movie.*
abode, dwelling, house, residence

home ②
adjective involving your own home or region » *The home team won the game easily.*
domestic, internal, local, national, native
antonym: **foreign**

homely
adjective simple, ordinary, and comfortable » *The room was small and homely.*
comfortable, cosy, modest, simple, welcoming
antonym: **grand**

honest
adjective truthful and trustworthy » *He is a very honest, decent man.*
law-abiding, reputable, trustworthy, truthful, virtuous
antonym: **dishonest**

honor ①
noun personal integrity » *It was an honor to be part of a team that worked so hard.*
decency, goodness, honesty, integrity
antonym: **dishonor**

honor ②
noun an award or mark of respect » *The star was showered with honors, including the top trophy.*
accolade, commendation, homage, praise, recognition, tribute, acclaim, kudos

*The star was showered with **honors**, including the top trophy.*

honor ③
verb to give someone special praise » *The soloist was honored by the conductor.*
commemorate, commend, decorate, glorify, praise

hooligan
noun a destructive and violent young person » *The hooligans damaged two buses.*
delinquent, gangster, hood, lout, thug, tough, vandal, yob (Britain; slang)

hope
noun a wish or feeling of desire and expectation » *Sam had high hopes that the weather would improve before his camping trip.*
ambition, dream, expectation

hopeless ①
adjective certain to fail or be unsuccessful » *Marooned on the desert island, our situation seemed hopeless.*
forlorn, futile, impossible, pointless, useless, vain

hopeless ②
adjective bad or inadequate » *The buses in the morning are hopeless, so it is difficult to get to work.*
inadequate, pathetic, poor, useless (informal)

horrible ①
adjective disagreeable or unpleasant » *The burger from the cafeteria was horrible.*
awful, disagreeable, horrid, mean, nasty, unpleasant

horrible ②
adjective causing shock, fear, or disgust » *A horrible crime was committed last night.*
appalling, dreadful, grim, gruesome, terrifying

horrify
verb to cause to feel horror or shock » *This latest robbery will horrify homeowners.*
appall, disgust, dismay, outrage, shock, sicken

horror ①
noun a strong feeling of alarm or disgust » *Mila gazed in horror at the mess the dog had made in the kitchen.*
alarm, dread, fear, fright, panic, terror

horror ②
noun a strong fear of something » *Felix had a horror of deep water and avoided it whenever he could.*
abhorrence, aversion, disgust, hatred, loathing, revulsion, abomination, odium, repugnance

horse
noun an animal domesticated for riding » *Maria rode her horse daily so that she was ready for the competition.*
bronco, equine, nag (informal), **pony, mount, steed**
related words:
adjectives **equestrian, equine, horsey;** *noun* **equitation;** *male* **stallion;** *female* **mare;** *young* **colt, filly, foal**

hostile
adjective unfriendly, aggressive, and unpleasant » *His suggestion received a hostile response.*
antagonistic, belligerent, malevolent, unkind
antonym: **friendly**

*His suggestion received a **hostile** response.*

hostility
noun aggressive or unfriendly behavior toward someone or something » *The fans showed hostility to the visiting team.*
animosity, antagonism, hatred, ill will, malice, resentment, animus, detestation, enmity
antonym: **friendship**

hot ①
adjective having a high temperature
◄◄ **SEE LEFT**

a b c d e f g h i j k l m n o p q r s t u v w x y z

hot ②
adjective very spicy
» *The curry was so hot, it stung his mouth.*
peppery, spicy
antonym: **bland**

house
noun a building in which people live » *They live in a large house with eight rooms.*
abode, building, dwelling, home, residence

hug ①
verb to hold someone close to you » *Lynn and I hugged each other.*
clasp, cuddle, embrace, squeeze

*Lynn and I **hugged** each other.*

hug ②
noun the act of holding someone close to you » *Deeksha gave him a hug.*
clasp, embrace

huge
adjective extremely large in amount, size, or degree » *A huge crowd gathered to watch the match.*
colossal, enormous, giant, immense, massive, vast, gargantuan, prodigious
antonym: **tiny**

humane
adjective showing kindness and sympathy toward others » *They hoped to create a fairer, more humane society.*
benevolent, caring, charitable, compassionate, kind, merciful, thoughtful, altruistic, humanitarian

humble ①
adjective not vain or boastful » *The musician gave a great performance, but he was humble and wouldn't accept the praise.*
meek, modest, unassuming
antonym: **haughty**

humble ②
adjective ordinary or unimportant » *A few herbs will transform a humble stew into a dish fit for a king.*
lowly, modest, ordinary, simple

humble ③
verb to make someone feel humiliated » *The young chess player humbled his experienced opponent.*
chasten, deflate, disgrace, humiliate

humid
adjective damp and hot » *It was hot and humid in the jungle, making the trip hard.*
clammy, muggy, steamy, sticky

*It was hot and **humid** in the jungle, making the trip hard.*

humiliate
verb to hurt someone's pride » *I was upset that he humiliated me in front of all my friends.*
disgrace, embarrass, humble, put down, shame

humor ①
noun something that is thought to be funny » *The movie's humor contains a serious message.*
comedy, wit, drollery, jocularity

*John agreed to wear the blue top, but with bad **humor**.*

humor ②
noun (Britain) the mood someone is in » *John agreed to wear the blue top, but with bad humor.*
frame of mind, mood, spirits, temper

humor ③
verb to please someone so that they will not become upset » *As he ranted, she nodded, partly to humor him.*
flatter, indulge, mollify, pander to

hungry
adjective wanting to eat » *I didn't have any lunch, so I'm really hungry.*
famished, ravenous, starving

hurry ①
verb to move or do something as quickly as possible » *Emma hurried through the train station to get to her platform on time.*
dash, fly, get a move on (informal), rush, scurry

hurry ②
verb to make something happen more quickly » *Nina tried to hurry Jaime, so they wouldn't miss the bus.*
accelerate, hasten, quicken, speed up
antonym: **slow down**

hurt ①
verb to cause someone to feel pain » *I didn't mean to hurt her, but she fell over when I gave her a playful push.*
harm, injure, wound

hurt ②
verb to upset someone or something » *That lie you told really hurt me.*
distress, sadden, upset, wound

hurt ③
adjective upset or offended » *He felt hurt by all the lies.*
aggrieved, offended, upset, wounded, piqued, rueful

hygiene
noun the principles and practice of health and cleanliness » *Kristina cared about her personal hygiene, so she showered every day.*
cleanliness, sanitation

hypnotize
verb to put someone into a state in which they seem to be asleep but can respond to suggestions » *He will hypnotize you and stop you from biting your nails.*
put in a trance, put to sleep, entrance, mesmerize

hysterical ①
adjective in a state of uncontrolled excitement or panic » *Calm down. Don't get hysterical.*
frantic, frenzied, overwrought, raving

hysterical ②
adjective (informal) extremely funny » *We loved listening to his stand-up routine, it was always hysterical.*
comical, hilarious

*We loved listening to his stand-up routine, it was always **hysterical**.*

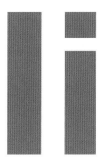

icon
noun a picture that represents a person or thing » *The tablet screen is full of app icons.*
avatar, representation, thumbnail

The tablet screen is full of app icons.

idea ①
noun what you know about something » *I think we're lost—I have no idea where we are.*
clue, guess, hint, inkling, notion, suspicion

idea ②
noun an opinion or belief about something » *My grandmother has old-fashioned ideas about clothes and refuses to leave the house without her hat.*
belief, conviction, impression, notion, opinion, view

idea ③
noun a plan or suggestion for something
▼ SEE BELOW

ideal ①
noun a principle or idea you try to achieve » *My dad has high ideals and always tries to live up to them.*
principle, standard, value

ideal ②
noun the best example of something » *She's my ideal of what a best friend should be.*
epitome, example, model, paragon, prototype, standard, archetype, criterion, paradigm

ideal ③
adjective being the best example of something » *He was the ideal person for the Saturday job since he already had lots of experience.*
classic, complete, consummate, model, perfect, supreme

identify ①
verb to recognize or name someone or something » *Joe tried to identify the handwriting on the letter because the sender hadn't signed their name.*
diagnose, label, name, pinpoint, place, recognize

identify ②:
identify with
verb to understand someone's feelings » *I can't identify with the book's main character.*
associate with, empathize with, feel for, relate to, respond to

idiot
noun a stupid person » *You're an idiot for carrying too much at once!*
fool, imbecile, nitwit, oaf, twit (informal)

idiotic
adjective extremely foolish or silly » *Sending the letter to the wrong person was an idiotic thing to do.*
daft (informal), **dumb** (informal), **foolish, senseless, silly, stupid, foolhardy, insane**

idle
adjective doing nothing » *I was idle on that vacation, and just read books and relaxed.*
jobless, redundant, unemployed, unproductive, inactive, stationary
antonym: **busy**

I was idle on that vacation, and just read books and relaxed.

plan
He had a cunning **plan** to take over the market.

recommendation
The producer gave **recommendations** for improvements.

scheme
She asked if he had a **scheme** for the game.

idea
③ *noun* a plan or suggestion for something
» *He had a great idea for a new game.*

solution
He came up with a **solution** to the problem.

suggestion
People had lots of **suggestions** for what to call the game.

theory
He had a **theory** that there was a gap in the market for the new game.

A B C D E F G H I J K L M N O P Q R S T U V W X Y Z

imaginary

adjective existing in your mind, but not in real life
» *Kevin's little sister, Karina, had an* **imaginary** *friend.*

Kevin's little sister, Karina, had an **imaginary** friend who lived in a **fictional** place called Wonderland and had the **fictitious** name of Elsanna. They rode on **mythical** unicorns and acted out all sorts of **hypothetical** scenarios. In an **ideal** world, they would be best friends forever. Karina knew her friend was **illusory**, but still liked to play her **invented** games.

fictional

fictitious

mythical

hypothetical

ideal

illusory

invented

antonym: **real**

*In the **real** world, Karina's brother could be grumpy.*

ignorant ①

adjective not knowing about something » *He was ignorant of the rules so didn't have a tie on the first day of work.*
inexperienced, innocent, oblivious, unaware, unconscious

ignorant ②

adjective not knowledgeable about things » *Elijah was determined not to be ignorant, so he read the news every day.*
green, naive, unaware, uneducated, unlearned, untutored

ignore

verb to take no notice of someone or something » *Julia ignored Huan when he came into the room.*
blank (slang)**, discount, disregard, neglect, overlook**

ill

adjective unhealthy or sick » *Patricia was ill with the flu.*
ailing, poorly (Britain; informal)**, queasy, sick, unhealthy, unwell,** indisposed, infirm, under the weather
antonym: **healthy**

Patricia was ill with the flu.

illegal

adjective forbidden by the law » *Shoplifting is an illegal activity.*
banned, criminal, illicit, outlawed, prohibited, unlawful, proscribed, unauthorized, wrongful
antonym: **legal**

illness

noun a particular disease » *His illness was a mystery— no one knew what was wrong.*
affliction, ailment, bug (informal)**, complaint, disease, disorder, lurgy** (Britain; informal)**, malady, sickness**

illusion ①

noun a false belief » *Pedro is under the illusion that he is very important.*
delusion, fallacy, fancy, misconception

illusion ②

noun a thing that you think you can see » *Seeing its reflection gave the fox the illusion of another fox.*
hallucination, mirage, semblance, chimera, phantasm

Seeing its reflection gave the fox the illusion of another fox.

imaginary

adjective existing in your mind, but not in real life
◀◀ SEE LEFT

imagination

noun the ability to form new ideas » *Harry is smart, but lacks imagination, and just copied the project.*
creativity, ingenuity, inventiveness, originality, vision

imagine ①

verb to have an idea of something » *Clara could not imagine a more peaceful scene.*
conceive, envisage, fantasize, picture, visualize

imagine ②

verb to believe that something is the case » *I imagine you're talking about my brother.*
assume, believe, gather, guess (informal)**, suppose, suspect,** surmise

imitate

verb to copy someone or something » *My son imitates everything I do.*
ape, copy, emulate, impersonate, mimic, simulate, mirror, mock, parody

My son imitates everything I do.

immediate ①

adjective happening or done without delay » *Mia's immediate reaction was to laugh.*
instant, instantaneous

immediate ②

adjective most closely connected to you » *I live with my immediate family.*
close, direct, near

immediately ①

adverb right away » *Logan replied to my message immediately.*
at once, directly, instantly, now, promptly, right away, straight away (Britain)**,** forthwith, posthaste

immediately ②

adverb very near in time or position » *The football field was immediately behind the school.*
closely, directly, right

An immense cloud turned the sky black.

immense

adjective very large or huge » *An immense cloud turned the sky black.*
colossal, enormous, giant, gigantic, huge, massive, vast
antonym: **tiny**

imminent

adjective going to happen very soon » *I was excited about my sister's imminent arrival.*
close, coming, forthcoming, impending, looming, near

immune

adjective not subject to or affected by something » *He seems immune to the cold.*
exempt, free, protected, resistant, safe, unaffected, insusceptible, invulnerable

impatient ①

adjective easily annoyed » *You are too impatient with others.*
brusque, curt, irritable, intolerant, snappy
antonym: **patient**

impatient ②

adjective eager to do something » *Maya was impatient to leave.*
eager, restless

impede

verb to make someone's or something's progress difficult » *Fallen trees impeded our walk to school this morning.*
block, delay, disrupt, get in the way, hamper, hinder, obstruct

a b c d e f g h i j k l m n o p q r s t u v w x y z

A B C D E F G H I J K L M N O P Q R S T U V W X Y Z

imperfect
adjective having faults or problems » *We live in an imperfect world.*
broken, damaged, defective, faulty, flawed, deficient, impaired, rudimentary
antonym: **perfect**

impersonal
adjective not concerned with people and their feelings » *She found him strangely distant and impersonal.*
aloof, cold, detached, formal, neutral, remote, bureaucratic, businesslike, dispassionate

implore
verb to beg someone to do something » *"Tell me what to do!" Stefan implored Sara.*
beg, beseech (literary), **plead with**

important 1
adjective necessary or significant » *Her friends are the most important people in her life.*
momentous, serious, significant, weighty, salient, seminal
antonym: **unimportant**

important 2
adjective having great influence or power » *The principal is the most important person in the school.*
eminent, foremost, influential, leading, notable, powerful, preeminent, prominent

impose 1
verb to force something on someone » *Fines were imposed on the culprits.*
dictate, enforce, inflict, levy, ordain

impose 2 : impose on
verb to take advantage of someone » *I should stop imposing on your hospitality.*
abuse, take advantage of, use

impossible
adjective unable to happen or be believed » *Finishing the race seemed impossible.*
absurd, hopeless, inconceivable, ludicrous, out of the question, unthinkable, outrageous, unattainable, unworkable
antonym: **possible**

impression 1
noun the way someone or something seems to you » *Conor's first impressions of the hotel were good.*
feeling, hunch, idea, notion, sense

impression 2 : make an impression
verb to have a strong effect on people » *He certainly made a good impression on his teachers, as he presented his work perfectly.*
cause a stir, influence, make an impact

impressionable
adjective easy to influence » *Parents were worried about the effect the movie might have on impressionable teenagers.*
gullible, open, receptive, sensitive, susceptible, vulnerable, ingenuous, suggestible

impressive
adjective tending to impress » *Winning so many medals was an impressive achievement.*
awesome, exciting, grand, powerful, stirring, striking, dramatic, moving

*Winning so many medals was an **impressive** achievement.*

*He was **imprisoned** for fraud.*

imprison
verb to lock someone up » *He was imprisoned for fraud.*
confine, detain, incarcerate, jail, lock up, send to prison, constrain, immure, intern
antonym: **free**

improbable
adjective unlikely or unbelievable » *Helen told an improbable story about the dog eating her homework.*
doubtful, dubious, far-fetched, implausible, unbelievable, unlikely
antonym: **probable**

improve
verb to get or make better » *My grades have definitely improved since the summer.*
advance, better, enhance, look up (informal), **progress, upgrade,** ameliorate, develop, reform
antonym: **worsen**

improvement
noun the fact or process of getting better » *There was a dramatic improvement in the food since he'd been in the cooking class.*
advance, development, enhancement, progress, upturn

impudence
noun disrespectful talk or behavior toward someone » *Have you ever heard such impudence?*
audacity, boldness, cheek (Britain; informal), **chutzpah** (informal), **gall, impertinence, insolence, nerve**

inability
noun a lack of ability to do something » *Kylie's inability to run was due to her injured left knee.*
impotence, inadequacy, incompetence, ineptitude
antonym: **ability**

inadequate 1
adjective not enough in quantity » *Our supplies of popcorn were inadequate for the long movie.*
insufficient, lacking, poor, scarce, short
antonym: **adequate**

inadequate 2
adjective not good enough » *He had no idea what he was supposed to be doing and felt inadequate for the task.*
deficient, incapable, incompetent, inept, pathetic, useless

*He had no idea what he was supposed to be doing and felt **inadequate** for the task.*

inappropriate
adjective not suitable for a purpose or occasion » *Running around is inappropriate behavior for the classroom.*
improper, incongruous, unfit, unseemly, unsuitable, untimely, wrong
antonym: **appropriate**

incentive
noun something that encourages you to do something » *Luca had an incentive to study now that the vacation was booked.*
bait, encouragement, inducement, motivation, stimulus, lure, motive, spur

incident
noun an event » *This morning's incident of calling the teacher "Dad" was so embarrassing.*
circumstance, episode, event, happening, occasion, occurrence

incite
verb to excite someone into doing something » *The campaigners incited a protest.*
agitate for, goad, instigate, provoke, whip up

include
verb to have as a part » *A cake recipe usually includes eggs, flour, and sugar.*
contain, cover, embrace, encompass, incorporate, involve
antonym: **exclude**

income
noun the money someone or something earns » *Jake was thrilled—he had an income at last.*
earnings, pay, profits, salary, takings, wages, proceeds, receipts, revenue

*Jake was thrilled—he had an **income** at last.*

incomparable
adjective too good to be compared with anything else » *The view from the peak was one of incomparable beauty.*
inimitable, peerless (literary), superlative, supreme, unparalleled, unrivaled, matchless, unequaled

*John was an **incompetent** carpenter.*

incompetent
adjective lacking the ability to do something correctly » *John was an incompetent carpenter.*
bungling, incapable, inept, unable, unfit, useless, ineffectual, inexpert, unskilful
antonym: **competent**

incomplete
adjective not finished or whole » *An incomplete letter lay on the desk.*
deficient, fragmental, halfway, insufficient, partial, imperfect, undeveloped, unfinished
antonym: **complete**

increase 1
verb to make or become larger in amount » *The population continues to increase.*
amplify, build up, enlarge, expand, extend, grow, multiply, swell, augment, escalate
antonym: **decrease**

increase 2
noun a rise in the amount of something » *Valeria asked for an increase in pay.*
gain, growth, increment, rise, upsurge
antonym: **decrease**

incredible 1
adjective totally amazing
▶▶ SEE RIGHT

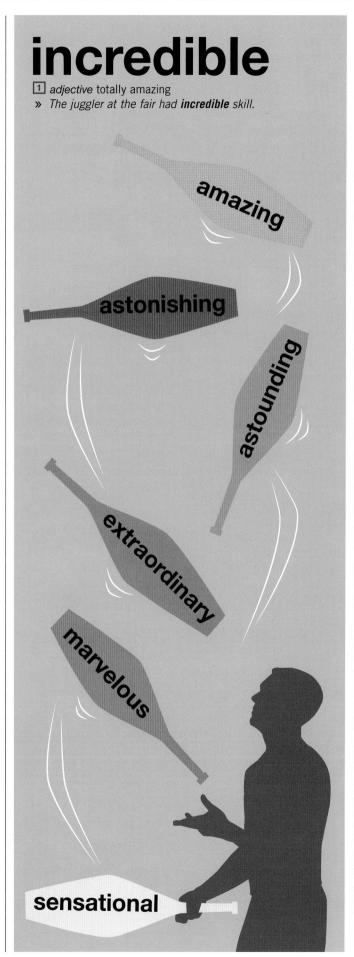

incredible
1 *adjective* totally amazing
» *The juggler at the fair had **incredible** skill.*

amazing · astonishing · astounding · extraordinary · marvelous · sensational

A B C D E F G H I J K L M N O P Q R S T U V W X Y Z

incredible 2
adjective impossible to believe
» *Sofia told an incredible story about a dragon trapped in a mountain cave.*
absurd, far-fetched, improbable, unbelievable, unimaginable, unthinkable, implausible, inconceivable, preposterous

indecent
adjective shocking or rude
» *Carter refused to play the song because its lyrics were indecent.*
crude, improper, rude, vulgar

independent 1
adjective separate from other people or things » *Each hiker had their independent tent in the clearing.*
autonomous, free, separate, unrelated

*Each hiker had their **independent** tent in the clearing.*

independent 2
adjective not needing other people's help » *Zoe is a fiercely independent child.*
individualistic, liberated, self-sufficient, unaided

indicate
verb to show something » *He smiled to indicate his relief.*
denote, reveal, show, signal, signify, imply, manifest, point to

indication
noun a sign of something
» *Roger gave no indication that he had heard me.*
clue, hint, sign, signal, suggestion, warning, intimation

indirect
adjective not done or going directly, but by another way
» *We took an indirect route to avoid the traffic jam.*
meandering, oblique, rambling, roundabout, tortuous, wandering
antonym: **direct**

individual 1
adjective relating to separate people or things
» *Maria made individual chocolate cakes for the twins' birthday celebration.*
discrete (formal), independent, separate, single

individual 2
adjective different and unusual
» *I have developed my own individual writing style.*
characteristic, distinctive, idiosyncratic, original, personal, special, unique

individual 3
noun a person, different from any other person
» *Tim took part in the competition as an individual.*
character, party, person, soul, personage

industrious
adjective tending to work hard
» *The industrious bees were making honey in their hive.*
busy, conscientious, diligent, hardworking, tireless
antonym: **lazy**

*The **industrious** bees were making honey in their hive.*

inefficient
adjective badly organized and slow » *We live in the countryside and have an inefficient bus service.*
disorganized, incapable, incompetent, inept, sloppy, ineffectual, inexpert, slipshod
antonym: **efficient**

inexperienced
adjective lacking experience of a situation or activity
» *Inexperienced drivers should avoid roads in big cities.*
green (informal), naive, new, raw, unaccustomed
antonym: **experienced**

infect
verb to cause disease in something » *One mosquito can infect many people.*
affect, blight, contaminate, taint

infectious
adjective spreading from one person to another » *My cold was infectious—my whole family caught it.*
catching, contagious, spreading, communicable, virulent

*My cold was **infectious**—my whole family caught it.*

inferior 1
adjective having a lower position than something or someone else » *The status of a prince is inferior to that of a king.*
lesser, lower, minor, secondary, second-class, subordinate
antonym: **superior**

inferior 2
adjective of low quality
» *Ruben gave an inferior performance because he was feeling unwell.*
mediocre, poor, second-class, second-rate, shoddy
antonym: **superior**

inferior 3
noun a person in a lower position than another
» *You must be polite to your inferiors.*
junior, menial, subordinate, underling
antonym: **superior**

infinite
adjective without any limit or end » *The start of summer vacation presented an infinite number of possibilities.*
boundless, eternal, everlasting, inexhaustible, perpetual, untold, bottomless, interminable, limitless

influence 1
noun power over other people
» *Ethan has a lot of influence over his classmates.*
authority, control, importance, power, sway, ascendancy, domination

influence 2
noun an effect that someone or something has » *Lily stayed up late, under the influence of her friend.*
effect, hold, magnetism, spell, weight

influence 3
verb to have an effect on someone or something
» *Older siblings can influence their younger siblings.*
affect, control, direct, guide, manipulate, sway

inform
verb to tell someone about something » *Please inform me of any delays.*
advise (formal), brief, enlighten, notify, tell, apprise, communicate

*The party was **informal**, so they wore shorts.*

informal
adjective relaxed and casual
» *The party was informal, so they wore shorts.*
casual, colloquial, easy, familiar, natural, relaxed
antonym: **formal**

information
noun the details you know about something
» *Our teacher would not give us any information about the test questions.*
data, facts, findings, info, intelligence, knowledge, material, news, notice, word

inform
verb to tell the police about someone who has committed a crime » *Jay informed the police who broke into the bank.*
betray, denounce, narc on (slang), **snitch on** (slang), **tell on** (informal)

ingredient
noun a thing that something is made from » *Lisa bought the necessary ingredients to bake banana bread.*
component, constituent, element

*Lisa bought the necessary **ingredients** to bake banana bread.*

inhabit
verb to live in a place
» *The people who inhabit these islands are used to the cold.*
dwell, live, lodge, occupy, populate, reside (formal)

inhabitant
noun someone who lives in a place » *I am an inhabitant of Norway.*
citizen, inmate, native, occupant, resident

inheritance
noun something that is passed on » *The house will be his son's inheritance.*
bequest, heritage, legacy

injure
verb to damage part of someone's body
» *The dog had injured her leg.*
harm, hurt, maim, wound

*The dog had **injured** her leg.*

injury
noun damage to part of the body » *Although the cat fell from quite high up, it had suffered no injuries.*
damage, harm, wound

injustice
noun unfairness and lack of justice » *The players complained about the injustice of the referee.*
bias, discrimination, inequality, inequity, prejudice, raw deal (informal), **unfairness, unjustness, wrong**
antonym: **justice**

innocence
noun inexperience of evil or unpleasant things
» *The baby's face was a picture of innocence.*
gullibility, inexperience, naivety, simplicity, artlessness, ingenuousness, unworldliness

innocent ①
adjective not guilty of a crime
» *The man had an alibi and was clearly innocent.*
blameless, clear, not guilty
antonym: **guilty**

innocent ②
adjective without experience of evil or unpleasant things
» *They were so young and innocent.*
childlike, guileless, naive, pure, spotless, artless, ingenuous, unworldly

insane
adjective mad » *I would go insane if I stayed indoors every day.*
crazy, deranged, mad (Britain), **mentally ill, out of your mind, unhinged**

insert
verb to put something into something else » *Emil inserted the key into the lock.*
enter, implant, introduce, place, put, set

*Emil **inserted** the key into the lock.*

inside
adjective surrounded by the main part and often hidden
» *On the ship we had an inside cabin with no window.*
inner, innermost, interior, internal
antonym: **outside**

insides
plural noun (informal) the parts inside your body » *My insides ached from eating too much.*
entrails, guts, innards, internal organs, viscera, vitals

*My **insides** ached from eating too much.*

insignificant
adjective small and unimportant » *I grew up in a small, insignificant town.*
irrelevant, little, minor, petty, trifling, trivial, unimportant, inconsequential
antonym: **significant**

insincere
adjective saying things you do not mean » *Eric told Eva what she wanted to hear, but his words were insincere.*
deceitful, dishonest, false, two-faced
antonym: **sincere**

insist
verb to demand something forcefully » *My mother always insists that I eat everything on my plate.*
demand, press, urge

inspect
verb to examine something carefully » *Alice inspected her salad for caterpillars.*
check, examine, eye, investigate, scan, survey, audit, scrutinize, vet

A B C D E F G H I J K L M N O P Q R S T U V W X Y Z

instant 1
noun a short period of time
» *The rain stopped in an instant.*
flash, minute, moment, second, split second

instant 2
adjective immediate and without delay » *He took an instant liking to her.*
immediate, instantaneous, prompt

instinct
noun a natural tendency to do something » *My dog has a strong instinct to chase rabbits.*
feeling, impulse, intuition, sixth sense, urge

instruct 1
verb to tell someone to do something » *The teacher instructed the class to be quiet.*
command, direct, order, tell
antonym: **forbid**

instruct 2
verb to teach someone about a subject or skill » *Larry instructs budding sailors on how to raise the sail.*
coach, educate, school, teach, train, tutor

*Larry **instructs** budding sailors on how to raise the sail.*

insufficient
adjective not enough for a particular purpose » *There were insufficient refreshments for the hungry players.*
deficient, inadequate, lacking, scant, short
antonym: **sufficient**

insult 1
verb to offend someone by being rude to them » *I did not mean to insult you.*
abuse, affront, offend, put down, slander, slight, snub
antonym: **compliment**

insult 2
noun a rude remark that offends someone » *The two men exchanged insults.*
abuse, affront, offense, put-down, slight, snub
antonym: **compliment**

*The two men exchanged **insults**.*

intelligence
noun the ability to understand and learn things » *The tricky quiz really tested the teams' intelligence.*
cleverness, comprehension, intellect, perception, sense, understanding, wit, acumen, capacity, nous

intelligent
adjective able to understand and learn things » *Dolphins are an intelligent species.*
acute, brainy (informal), bright, clever, quick, sharp, smart
antonym: **stupid**

intend 1
verb to decide or plan to do something » *Harper intended to stay for lunch.*
aim, be determined, mean, plan, propose, resolve

intend 2
verb to mean for a certain use » *This book is intended for younger children.*
aim, design, earmark, mean

*Michaela watched the screen with **intense** concentration.*

intense 1
adjective very great in strength or amount » *Michaela watched the screen with intense concentration.*
acute, deep, extreme, fierce, great, powerful, profound, severe

intense 2
adjective tending to have strong feelings » *The actor's intense performance was gripping.*
ardent, earnest, fervent, fierce, impassioned, passionate, vehement

intention
noun a plan to do something » *Layla announced her intention of going to the party.*
aim, goal, idea, object, objective, purpose

interest 1
noun a feeling of wanting to know about something » *I have a great interest in that period of history.*
attention, concern, curiosity, fascination

interest 2
noun a hobby » *Of her many interests, Nora enjoyed knitting the most.*
activity, hobby, pastime, pursuit

*Of her many **interests**, Nora enjoyed knitting the most.*

interest 3
verb to attract someone's attention and curiosity » *This picture interests me most, I love the colors.*
appeal, captivate, fascinate, intrigue, stimulate
antonym: **bore**

interesting
adjective making you want to know, learn, or hear more » *We had an interesting conversation about bats in the car this morning.*
absorbing, compelling, entertaining, gripping, intriguing, stimulating
antonym: **boring**

interfere 1
verb to try to influence a situation » *Stop interfering and leave her alone.*
butt in, intervene, intrude, meddle, tamper

interfere 2
verb to have a damaging effect on a situation » *The loud music interfered with her sleep.*
conflict, disrupt

internet
noun a worldwide network of computers » *Hazel used the internet to book her vacation.*
blogosphere, cloud, cyberspace, net, web, world wide web

*Hazel used the **internet** to book her vacation.*

interrogate
verb to question someone thoroughly » *I interrogated everyone involved.*
examine, grill (informal), question, quiz, cross-examine, cross-question

interrupt [1]
verb to start talking when someone else is talking
» *He tried to speak, but she interrupted him.*
butt in, heckle

interrupt [2]
verb to stop a process or activity for a time » *The match was interrupted by rain.*
break, discontinue, suspend

interval
noun a period of time between two moments or dates
» *The football players practiced in intervals of intense sprints and short rest periods.*
break, gap, hiatus, interlude, intermission, pause

*Piper had agreed to **intervene** when things got heated.*

intervene
verb to step in to prevent conflict » *Piper had agreed to intervene when things got heated.*
arbitrate, mediate

introduction [1]
noun the act of presenting someone or something new
» *The introduction of a new uniform was discussed.*
establishment, inauguration, initiation, institution, launch

introduction [2]
noun a piece of writing at the beginning of a book
» *The book contains a new introduction by the author.*
foreword, preface, prologue

intrude
verb to disturb someone or something » *I don't want to intrude on your privacy.*
butt in, encroach, infringe, interrupt, trespass, violate

invade
verb to enter a country by force » *The Vikings invaded much of Europe.*
attack, enter, occupy, violate

invent [1]
verb to be the first person to think of a device or idea
▼ SEE BELOW

invent [2]
verb to make up a story or excuse » *I tried to invent a plausible excuse for why I was late.*
concoct, construct, cook up, devise, fabricate, make up, manufacture

investigate
verb to find out all the facts about something » *Police are still investigating the incident.*
examine, explore, probe, research, sift, study

a b c d e f g h i j k l m n o p q r s t u v w x y z

invent

[1] *verb* to be the first person to think of a device or idea » *The busy professor **invented** a Walkomatic robot to walk his dog for him.*

 conceive
*The professor **conceived** the idea when his dog whined for a walk.*

 coin
*He **coined** the name "Walkomatic."*

 come up with
*He was the first person to **come up with** the idea of a dog-walking robot.*

 design
*The professor **designed** several models.*

formulate
*He **formulated** plans to make the robot move.*

 improvise
*He **improvised** by using empty cans to make the robot's body.*

 originate
*He wanted to be famous for being the person who **originated** the Walkomatic.*

A B C D E F G H I J K L M N O P Q R S T U V W X Y Z

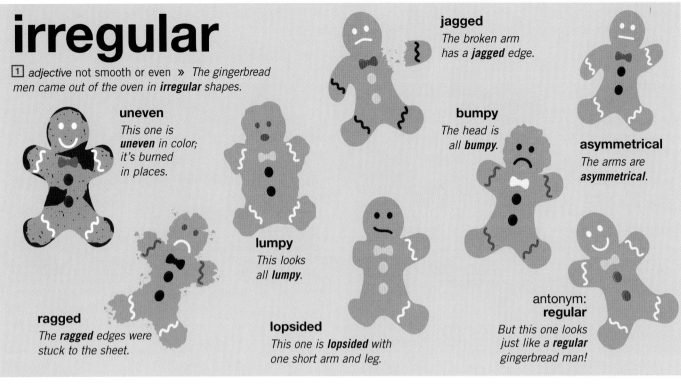

irregular

1 *adjective* not smooth or even » *The gingerbread men came out of the oven in* **irregular** *shapes.*

uneven
This one is **uneven** *in color; it's burned in places.*

lumpy
This looks all **lumpy**.

ragged
The **ragged** *edges were stuck to the sheet.*

lopsided
This one is **lopsided** *with one short arm and leg.*

jagged
The broken arm has a **jagged** *edge.*

bumpy
The head is all **bumpy**.

asymmetrical
The arms are **asymmetrical**.

antonym:
regular
But this one looks just like a **regular** *gingerbread man!*

invincible
adjective unable to be defeated » *When the defending champion is playing well, he is invincible.*
impregnable, indomitable, unbeatable, indestructible, insurmountable, unassailable

invisible
adjective unable to be seen » *Hugo's face was invisible beneath his hat.*
concealed, disguised, hidden, inconspicuous, unseen, imperceptible, indiscernible
antonym: **visible**

involve
verb to have as a necessary part » *Preparing for an exam involves a great deal of discipline.*
incorporate, require, take, take in, entail, necessitate

irrational
adjective not based on logical reasons » *Her fear of ghosts is irrational—they don't exist.*
absurd, crazy, illogical, nonsensical, unsound, silly, unreasonable

irregular 1
adjective not smooth or even
▲ SEE ABOVE

irregular 2
adjective not forming a regular pattern » *Stephen worked irregular hours.*
erratic, haphazard, occasional, patchy, random, variable, fitful, sporadic
antonym: **regular**

irresponsible
adjective not concerned with the consequences of your actions » *His irresponsible attitude often got him into trouble with his parents.*
careless, reckless, thoughtless, wild
antonym: **responsible**

irritable
adjective easily annoyed » *My mom had slept badly and was tense and irritable.*
bad-tempered, cantankerous, crabby (informal), grouchy, petulant, ratty (Britain; informal), touchy, irascible, tetchy

irritate
verb to annoy someone » *Nathan's tuneless whistling always irritates me.*
anger, annoy, bother, exasperate, irk, needle (informal), ruffle, wind up (informal), gall, provoke

issue 1
noun a subject that people are talking about » *There were several issues to be discussed at the teacher-parent meeting.*
concern, matter, problem, question, subject, topic

issue 2
noun a particular edition of a newspaper or magazine » *Jade bought the latest issue of her favorite magazine.*
copy, edition, instalment

Jade bought the latest **issue** *of her favorite magazine.*

issue 3
verb to make a formal statement » *They have issued a statement explaining what really happened.*
deliver, give, make, pronounce, read out, release
antonym: **withdraw**

issue 4
verb to give something officially » *Teachers will be issued with passes to get into the staff room.*
equip, furnish (formal), give out, provide, supply

item 1
noun one of a collection or list of things » *When Chloe opened her suitcase, several items were missing.*
article, matter, point, thing

item 2
noun a newspaper or magazine article » *There was an item in the paper about his daring rescue of the cat.*
article, feature, notice, piece, report

jagged
adjective sharp and spiky
» *The waves broke against the jagged rocks.*
barbed, craggy, rough, serrated, sharp
antonym: **smooth**

jail [1]
noun a place where prisoners are held » *Chris was sentenced to 18 months in jail.*
clink (slang), **nick** (Britain, Australia, and New Zealand; slang), **prison, lockup, penal institution, penitentiary**

jail [2]
verb to put in prison
» *He was jailed for 20 years.*
detain, imprison, incarcerate

jam [1]
noun a crowded mass of people or things » *Nora was late because she was stuck in a traffic jam.*
crowd, crush, mass, mob, multitude, throng

*Nora was late because she was stuck in a traffic **jam**.*

jam [2]
noun a difficult situation
» *We're in a real jam now.*
bind, dilemma, fix (informal), **hole** (slang), **hot water** (informal), **pickle** (informal), **plight, predicament, quandary, trouble**

jam [3]
verb to push something somewhere roughly
» *Martin jammed his hat on to his head.*
cram, force, ram, stuff

jam [4]
verb to become stuck
» *She tried to leave the room, but the door jammed.*
stall, stick

jealous
adjective wanting to have something that someone else has » *I was jealous of my friend's new shoes.*
envious, resentful, covetous

job [1]
noun the work someone does to earn money » *I'm looking for a job on a farm.*
employment, occupation, position, post, profession, trade

job [2]
noun a duty or responsibility
» *It's your job to do the dishes tonight.*
concern, duty, function, responsibility, role, task

join [1]
verb to become a member of something » *Adam joined a band as the lead singer.*
enlist, enrol, sign up
antonym: **resign**

join [2]
verb to fasten two things together
▶▶ **SEE RIGHT**

join
[2] *verb* to fasten two things together » *The paper dolls were **joined** at their hands and feet.*

attach
*She **attached** a strap to her bag.*

connect
*The two rooms were **connected** by a passage.*

couple
*An engine is **coupled** with a transmission.*

fasten
*The bench was **fastened** to the floor.*

link
*He **linked** a clip to the chain.*

splice
*The ropes were **spliced** together.*

tie
*He **tied** the dog to the post with her leash.*

antonym:
separate
*Grace **separated** a doll from the chain to give to her friend.*

a
b
c
d
e
f
g
h
i
j
k
l
m
n
o
p
q
r
s
t
u
v
w
x
y
z

That joke was so funny.

joke ①

noun something that makes people laugh » *That joke was so funny.*
gag (informal), **jest, lark, prank, quip, wisecrack** (informal), **witticism,** jape

joke ②

verb to say something funny » *Alex was always joking about her appearance.*
banter, chaff, jest, kid (informal), **quip, tease**

journey ①

noun the act of traveling a long distance from one place to another » *We took a train journey through the mountains.*
excursion, expedition, passage, tour, trek, trip, voyage

We took a train journey through the mountains.

journey ②

verb (Britain) to travel from one place to another » *We journeyed through France.*
go, proceed, tour, travel, trek, voyage

joy

noun great happiness
» *Her face glowed with joy.*
bliss, delight, ecstasy, elation, rapture, exaltation, exultation, **felicity**
antonym: **misery**

joyful

adjective extremely happy
» *My father gave a joyful smile when he saw me.*
delighted, elated, jubilant, over the Moon (informal), **enraptured**

judge ①

noun the person in charge of a law court » *The judge called for order in the court.*
adjudicator, beak (Britain; slang), **justice, magistrate**
related word: *adjective* **judicial**

The judge called for order in the court.

judge ②

noun someone who picks the winner or keeps control of a competition » *The judges inspected each dog carefully before selecting the finalists.*
adjudicator, referee, umpire

judge ③

verb to form an opinion about someone or something
» *Don't judge me for having another slice of pizza.*
appraise, assess, consider, estimate, evaluate, rate

judge ④

verb to pick the winner or keep control in a competition
» *Entrants will be judged in two age categories.*
decide, referee, umpire, adjudge, adjudicate

judgment

noun an opinion or decision based on evidence » *It's hard to form a judgment without all the facts.*
appraisal, assessment, conclusion, opinion, ruling, verdict, view

jump ①

verb to leap up or over something » *I jumped over the fence.*
bound, clear, hurdle, leap, spring, vault

I jumped over the fence.

jump ②

verb to increase suddenly
» *Sales of coats jumped when the temperature dropped below zero.*
escalate, increase, rise, surge

jump ③

noun a leap into the air
» *Ryan misjudged his jump and landed in the stream.*
bound, leap, vault

junior

adjective having a relatively low position compared to others
» *I started as a junior waitress, but now I run the restaurant.*
inferior, lesser, lower, subordinate
antonym: **senior**

What are you going to do with all that junk?

junk

noun old articles that people usually throw away » *What are you going to do with all that junk?*
clutter, odds and ends, refuse, rubbish (Britain), **scrap, trash**

justice ①

noun fairness in the way that people are treated
» *He had been treated unfairly and wanted justice.*
equity, fair shake (informal), **fairness, impartiality, right**
antonym: **injustice**

justice ②

noun the person in charge of a law court
» *Oliver was sworn in as a Justice of the state's Supreme Court.*
judge, jurist, magistrate

justify

verb to show that something is reasonable or necessary
» *Tina justified eating a large lunch by going for a long walk afterward.*
defend, excuse, explain, vindicate, warrant

Kk

*Hugo was a **keen** amateur wildlife photographer.*

keen 1
adjective (Britain) showing eagerness and enthusiasm for something » *Hugo was a keen amateur wildlife photographer.*
ardent, avid, eager, enthusiastic, fond of, into (informal)

keen 2
adjective quick to notice or understand things » *She has a keen eye for a bargain.*
astute, brilliant, perceptive, quick, shrewd

keep 1
verb to have and take care of something » *His father keeps sheep and pigs.*
care for, maintain, preserve

keep 2
verb to store something » *Zoe kept her toys in a box.*
deposit, hold, store

keep 3
verb to do what you said you would do » *I always keep my promises.*
carry out, fulfill, honor

kidnap
verb to take someone away by force » *Lisa's brother kidnapped her teddy bear.*
abduct, capture, seize

kill
verb to make someone or something die » *The dog killed a rat.*
assassinate, destroy, execute, exterminate, massacre, murder, slaughter, slay, annihilate, dispatch

kin
plural noun the people who are related to you » *She has gone to live near her husband's kin.*
family, kindred, people, relations, relatives

kind 1
noun a particular type of person or thing » *That's my favorite kind of cheese.*
brand, breed, category, class, classification, genre, grade, sort, species, type, variety

kind 2
adjective considerate toward other people » *Thank you for being so kind to me.*
benevolent, benign, charitable, compassionate, considerate, good, humane, kind-hearted, kindly, thoughtful, unselfish, lenient, philanthropic
antonym: **cruel**

*Thank you for being so **kind** to me.*

kindness
noun the quality of being considerate toward other people » *Everyone has treated me with great kindness.*
benevolence, charity, compassion, gentleness, humanity, kindliness, magnanimity, philanthropy, tenderness
antonym: **cruelty**

*He wore a crown and robe to play the **king** in the school show.*

king
noun a man who is the head of a royal family » *He wore a crown and robe to play the king in the school show.*
monarch, sovereign
related words: *adjectives* **royal, regal, monarchical**

know 1
verb to understand or be aware of something » *I don't know anything about cars.*
apprehend, be aware of, comprehend, perceive, see, understand

know 2
verb to be familiar with a person or thing » *I believe you two already know each other.*
be acquainted with, be familiar with, recognize

knowledge
noun all you know about something
▼ SEE BELOW

knowledge
noun all you know about something
» *She had no **knowledge** of French.*

command
comprehension
education
grasp
learning
scholarship
understanding
wisdom

a b c d e f g h i j k l m n o p q r s t u v w x y z

Ll

*She couldn't buy new clothes due to a **lack** of money.*

label [1]
noun a piece of paper or plastic attached to something for information » *The label said the shirt was made of cotton.*
sticker, tag, ticket

*The **label** said the shirt was made of cotton.*

label [2]
verb to put a label on something » *The toy was labeled "Made in China."*
flag, sticker, tag

labor [1]
noun very hard work » *Fred soon discovered that weeding and digging the garden was hard labor.*
effort, exertion, industry, toil, work

labor [2]
noun the workforce of a country or industry » *Some businesses take on extra labor to help at busy times.*
employees, workers, workforce

labor [3]
verb to work very hard » *The farm workers labored all night to finish the harvest.*
slave, toil, work
antonym: **relax**

lack [1]
noun the shortage or absence of something that is needed » *She couldn't buy new clothes due to a lack of money.*
absence, deficiency, scarcity, shortage, want, dearth, insufficiency
antonym: **abundance**

lack [2]
verb to be without something that is needed » *Katie was a good baker, but didn't enter any competitions because she lacked confidence.*
be deficient in, be short of, miss

lag
verb to make slower progress than other people or things » *The runner-up is lagging 10 points behind the champion.*
fall behind, trail

lake
noun a large area of water surrounded by land » *Jay went for a swim in the lake.*
lagoon, loch (Scotland), mere, reservoir, tarn

lame [1]
adjective unable to walk properly because of an injured leg » *The old soldier was lame in one leg.*
hobbling, limping

lame [2]
adjective weak or unconvincing » *No one believed Sam's lame excuse for arriving late.*
feeble, flimsy, pathetic, poor, unconvincing, weak

lament [1]
verb to express sorrow or regret over something » *Freya lamented the loss of her favorite sweater.*
grieve, mourn, wail, weep, bemoan, bewail, whine

lament [2]
noun something you say to express sorrow or regret » *The old man sang a lament for his lost youth.*
moan, wail, gripe, lamentation, plaint

laugh

[1] *verb* to make a noise that shows you are amused or happy » *The comedian told such a funny joke that we all **laughed**.*

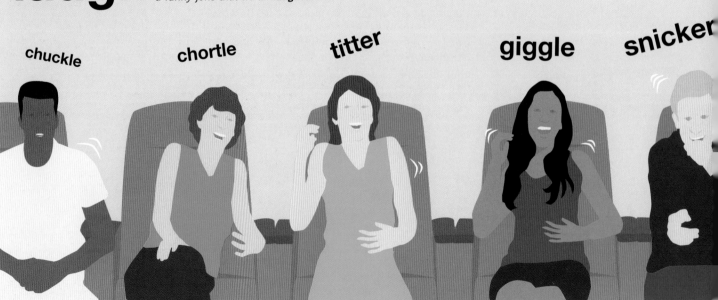

chuckle   **chortle**   **titter**   **giggle**   **snicker**

land [1]
noun an area of ground that someone owns » *My parents keep horses on their land.*
estate, grounds, property

land [2]
noun a region or country » *The US is known as the land of opportunity.*
country, nation, province, region, territory

land [3]
verb to arrive on the ground after flying or sailing » *The plane landed in New York at noon.*
alight, dock, touch down

*The plane **landed** in New York at noon.*

language [1]
noun the system of words people use to communicate » *She speaks four languages.*
dialect, idiom, jargon, lingo (informal), tongue, vernacular, vocabulary, argot, cant, lingua franca, patois

language [2]
noun the style in which you speak or write » *The poem was written in flowery language.*
lingo (informal), phrasing, style, wording, phraseology, terminology

large
adjective of a greater size or amount than usual » *We have a large kitchen with lots of cupboards.*
big, colossal, enormous, giant, gigantic, great, huge, immense, massive, vast, gargantuan, sizable or sizeable
antonym: **small**

last [1]
adjective the most recent » *Our last vacation was a year ago.*
latest, most recent, preceding, previous
antonym: **first**

last [2]
adjective happening or remaining after all the others of its kind » *She read the last page and closed the book.*
closing, concluding, final, ultimate
antonym: **first**

last [3]
verb to continue to exist or happen » *The movie lasted for two and a half hours.*
carry on, continue, endure, persist, remain, survive

late [1]
adjective after the expected time » *The train was nearly an hour late.*
behind, behind time, belated, delayed, last-minute, overdue, tardy, unpunctual
antonym: **early**

late [2]
adjective dead, especially recently » *My late husband would have loved this place.*
dead, deceased, departed, defunct, perished

laugh [1]
verb to make a noise that shows you are amused or happy
▼ SEE BELOW

laugh [2]
noun the noise you make when amused or happy » *He let out a loud laugh at the joke.*
chortle, chuckle, giggle, guffaw, snigger, titter

law [1]
noun a country's system of rules » *Vandalism is against the law.*
charter, code, constitution
related words: *adjectives* **legal, judicial**

law [2]
noun one of the rules of a country » *The government introduced a new law to help reduce crime rates.*
act, code, decree, regulation, rule, statute, edict, ordinance

lawyer
noun someone who advises people about the law » *The lawyer spoke in court.*
advocate, attorney, counsel, solicitor

*The **lawyer** spoke in court.*

cackle **guffaw** **howl** **roar**

A B C D E F G H I J K L M N O P Q R S T U V W X Y Z

lay [1]

verb to put something somewhere » *Lay a sheet of newspaper on the floor.*
place, put, set, set down, settle, spread

lay [2]

verb to arrange or set something out » *A man came to lay the carpet.*
arrange, set out

layer

noun something that covers a surface or comes between two other things » *A fresh layer of snow covered the street.*
blanket, coat, coating, covering, film, sheet, stratum

layout

noun the way in which something is arranged » *The hotel layout was so confusing, it was hard to find our rooms.*
arrangement, design, format, plan

laze

verb to relax and do no work » *Tanya spent a few days lazing on the beach.*
idle, loaf, lounge
antonym: **work**

Tanya spent a few days lazing on the beach.

lazy

adjective not willing to work or move » *Our lazy dog refused to come out for a walk.*
idle, slack, good-for-nothing, indolent, shiftless, slothful, torpid, workshy
antonym: **industrious**

lead [1]

verb to guide or take someone somewhere » *She led him toward the door.*
conduct, escort, guide, steer, usher

lead [2]

verb to be in charge of » *The captain led his team to a convincing victory.*
command, direct, govern, head, manage, supervise

The captain led his team to a convincing victory.

lead [3]

noun a clue that may help solve a crime » *The police are following up several leads.*
clue, indication, trace

leader

noun the person in charge of something » *Sophie was the expedition leader.*
boss (informal), **captain, chief, commander, director, head, principal, ringleader**
antonym: **follower**

leading

adjective particularly important, respected, or advanced » *He was a leading authority on modern art.*
chief, eminent, key, main, major, principal, prominent, top, foremost, preeminent

lead to

verb to cause something to happen » *Regular exercise leads to a healthier life.*
cause, contribute to, produce, bring on, conduce to, result in

The hotel lobby had leaflets of nearby tourist attractions.

leaflet

noun a piece of paper with information about a subject » *The hotel lobby had leaflets of nearby tourist attractions.*
booklet, brochure, circular, pamphlet, handbill, mailshot

leak [1]

verb to escape from a container or other object » *The bottle of lemonade had leaked all over the sandwiches.*
escape, ooze, seep, spill

leak [2]

noun a hole that lets gas or liquid escape » *The plumber plugged the leaks in the pipe.*
chink, crack, fissure, hole, puncture

leap [1]

verb to jump a great distance or height » *The deer leaped into the air.*
bounce, bound, jump, spring, vault

leap [2]

noun a jump of great distance or height » *He made a huge leap right over the river.*
bound, jump, spring

learn [1]

verb to gain knowledge by studying or training » *I am trying to learn French because I'm going to France next year.*
grasp, master, pick up

learn [2]

verb to find out about something » *On learning who she was, I asked to meet her.*
ascertain, determine, discover, find out, gather, hear, understand

learned

adjective having gained a lot of knowledge by studying » *My father is a very learned man in the field of history.*
academic, erudite, intellectual, literate, scholarly, lettered, well-read

least

adjective as small or few as possible » *Which cheese contains the least fat?*
fewest, lowest, minimum, slightest, smallest
antonym: **most**

leave [1]

verb to go away from a person or place
▶▶ SEE RIGHT

leave [2]

noun a period of time off work » *Why don't you take a few days' leave?*
time off, vacation, furlough, sabbatical

lecture [1]

noun a formal talk about a particular subject » *The professor gave a lecture on the basics of chemistry.*
address, discourse, presentation, sermon, speech, talk, exposition, oration

The professor gave a lecture on the basics of chemistry.

abandon
*The late passenger **abandoned** his coffee to rush for the train.*

decamp
*A person **decamped** quickly after realizing they were on the wrong train!*

depart
*The crowd cheered as the train **departed**.*

desert
*The crowd **deserted** the platform after the train had gone.*

leave

1 *verb* to go away from a person or place » *The train **left** the platform on time.*

ditch
*The man **ditched** the seat when he saw the conductor.*

dump
*He decided to **dump** his luggage at the end of the train car.*

go
*There was an announcement that the train was about to **go**.*

quit
*Tom decided to **quit** his job as a train conductor.*

withdraw
*The crowd **withdrew** from the platform edge as the train moved away.*

lecture 2
noun a talk intended to tell someone off » *The police gave us a stern lecture on personal safety.*
reprimand, scolding, telling-off, ticking-off (Britain; informal), **warning**

lecture 3
verb to teach by giving formal talks to audiences » *The eminent scientist lectures all over the world.*
give a talk, speak, talk, teach

left-wing
adjective believing in reforming, socialist policies » *People said Mary had left-wing views.*
leftist, liberal, radical, socialist

legacy
noun objects or money someone leaves you when he or she dies » *The singer left his sons a generous legacy.*
bequest, estate, heirloom, inheritance

legal 1
adjective relating to the law » *Each country has its own legal system.*
forensic, judicial, judiciary

legal 2
adjective allowed by the law » *My parents are the legal owners of our house.*
authorized, lawful, legitimate, permissible, rightful, valid, constitutional, sanctioned
antonym: **illegal**

leisure
noun time when you can relax » *A long vacation meant plenty of time for leisure.*
free time, recreation, relaxation, time off
antonym: **work**

*A long vacation meant plenty of time for **leisure**.*

leisurely
adjective unhurried or calm » *We enjoyed a leisurely walk along the beach.*
comfortable, easy, gentle, relaxed, unhurried
antonym: **hasty**

length 1
noun the distance from one end of something to the other » *The fish was about three feet in length.*
distance, extent, span

length 2
noun the amount of time something lasts for » *The movie is two hours in length.*
duration, period, space, span, term

a b c d e f g h i j k l m n o p q r s t u v w x y z

like

2 *verb* to find someone or something pleasant
» *I really like this music.*

adore
She adored her pug.

appreciate
I appreciate good food.

be fond of
Are you fond of him?

be into (informal)
He was really into the band's latest song.

be partial to
I am partial to action movies.

enjoy
She enjoyed swimming in the ocean.

go for
What kind of music do you go for?

have a soft spot for
I have a soft spot for people with red hair.

have a weakness for
He had a weakness for chocolate.

love
She loved getting presents.

relish
He relished the idea of celebrating his birthday.

antonym: **dislike**
I dislike playing hockey.

lengthen
verb to make something longer
» *My pants had to be lengthened because I'd grown.*
extend, make longer, prolong, stretch, elongate, protract
antonym: **shorten**

lessen
verb to decrease in size or amount » *Andy put on an extra sweater to lessen the risk of getting cold.*
abate, decrease, diminish, dwindle, lower, minimize, reduce, shrink, de-escalate, downsize
antonym: **increase**

lesson
noun a period of time for being taught » *Johanna took piano lessons once a week.*
class, coaching, lecture, period, tutoring

let
verb to allow someone to do something » *Leah's parents wouldn't let her go to the party.*
allow, give permission, permit, sanction
antonym: **forbid**

let down
verb to disappoint » *I don't know why I believed my brother when he said he'd help me—he always lets me down.*
disappoint, fail

level 1
adjective completely flat » *An ice rink should have a perfectly level surface.*
flat, horizontal
antonym: **uneven**

level 2
verb to make something flat » *We leveled the ground.*
flatten, plane, smooth

level 3
noun a point on a scale that measures something » *Crime levels have started to decline.*
grade, rank, stage, standard, status

lie 1
verb to rest somewhere horizontally » *He was lying on his back, reading a book.*
loll, lounge, recline, sprawl, be prostrate, be recumbent, be supine, repose

lie 2
verb to say something that is not true » *The actor lied about his age and told the reporter he was much younger.*
be dishonest, fib, perjure yourself, tell a lie, forswear yourself

lie 3
noun something you say that is not true » *His whole story was a lie, none of it was true.*
deceit, fabrication, falsehood, fib, fiction

life
noun the time during which you are alive » *My grandmother has had a long and active life.*
existence, life span, lifetime, time
related words:
adjectives **animate, vital**

lift 1
verb to move something to a higher position » *Ria strained to lift the heavy pile of books.*
elevate, hoist, pick up, raise
antonym: **lower**

lift 2
verb to remove something such as a ban or law » *They wore earrings to school when the ban on jewelry was lifted.*
cancel, end, relax, remove, rescind, revoke

light 1
noun brightness that enables you to see things » *The sun's light filtered through the shutters.*
brightness, brilliance, glare, glow, illumination, radiance, incandescence, luminescence, luminosity, phosphorescence
antonym: **dark**
related word: *prefix* **photo-**

light [2]
adjective pale in color
» *Steve wore a light blue shirt.*
bleached, fair, pale, pastel,
blond or **blonde**
antonym: **dark**

light [3]
adjective not weighing much
» *Now that it was empty,*
the cardboard box was light.
flimsy, lightweight,
portable, slight
antonym: **heavy**

light [4]
adjective to make a place bright
» *The dining room was lit*
by a single candle.
brighten, illuminate, light up
antonym: **darken**

light [5]
verb to make a fire start
burning » *It's time*
to light the barbecue.
ignite, kindle
antonym: **extinguish**

like [1]
preposition similar to
» *He looks just like*
his father.
akin, analogous,
parallel, similar
antonym: **unlike**

like [2]
verb to find someone
or something pleasant
◄◄ SEE LEFT

likely
adjective having a good chance
of happening » *It's likely my*
brother will have a mushroom
pizza as usual.
anticipated, expected,
liable, possible, probable
antonym: **unlikely**

limit [1]
noun a point beyond which
something cannot go
» *My mom never drives*
above the speed limit.
bounds, deadline,
maximum, ultimate,
utmost

limit [2]
verb to prevent something from
going any further » *Don't limit*
yourself to one activity.
confine, curb, fix, ration,
restrict, circumscribe,
delimit, demarcate

limp
adjective not stiff or firm
» *The week-old lettuce*
had limp leaves.
drooping, flabby, floppy,
slack, soft, flaccid, pliable
antonym: **stiff**

line [1]
noun a long thin mark on
something » *Use a ruler*
to draw a line down the
center of the page.
rule, score, streak, stripe

line [2]
noun a row of people or things
» *A long line of fans waited*
to get a glimpse of the singer.
column, file, queue,
rank, row

line [3]
noun the route along which
something moves » *The golfer*
studied the ball's line of flight.
course, path, route,
track, trajectory

The golfer studied the ball's
line of flight.

link [1]
noun a connection between
two things » *The wedding*
guest had links to both the
bride's and groom's families.
affiliation, association,
attachment, bond,
connection, relationship,
tie, affinity, liaison

The friends linked hands as they
ran across the field.

link [2]
verb to connect two things
» *The friends linked hands*
as they ran across the field.
attach, connect, couple,
fasten, join, tie
antonym: **separate**

liquid [1]
noun a substance that is not
solid and can be poured
» *Make sure you drink enough*
liquids, particularly water.
fluid, liquor, solution

liquid [2]
adjective in the form of a liquid
» *Liquid detergent comes in a*
bottle, not a box.
fluid, molten, runny

list [1]
noun a set of things written
down one below the other
» *There were six names*
on the list.
catalog, directory,
index, inventory, listing,
record, register

list [2]
verb to put things on a list
» *The cookies' ingredients are*
listed on the package.
catalog, index, record,
register, enumerate,
itemize, tabulate

listen
verb to hear and pay attention
to something » *I'll repeat*
that for those of you who
weren't listening.
attend, hark, hear,
pay attention

little [1]
adjective small in size or
amount » *The girl was too*
little to ride on the rollercoaster.
dainty, dwarf, mini,
miniature, minute, pygmy,
small, tiny, wee (Scotland)
antonym: **large**

little [2]
noun a small amount or degree
» *We offered her plenty*
to eat, but she would only
take a little.
hardly any, meager, measly,
not much, paltry, scant

live [1]
verb to have your home
somewhere » *Carrie has*
lived in Boston for 20 years.
dwell, frequent, inhabit,
occupy, reside,

live [2]
verb to be alive » *The tortoise*
has lived for over 100 years.
be alive, exist

live [3]
adjective not dead or artificial
» *I was horrified to find a live*
mouse sitting in my shoe.
alive, animate, living

lively
adjective full of life and
enthusiasm » *My sister*
has a lively personality.
active, animated, energetic,
perky, sparkling, sprightly,
vivacious
antonym: **dull**

load [1]
noun something being carried
» *The crane can lift huge,*
heavy loads.
cargo, consignment,
freight, shipment

The crane can lift huge,
heavy loads.

a b c d e f g h i j k l m n o p q r s t u v w x y z

A B C D E F G H I J K L M N O P Q R S T U V W X Y Z

load [2]
verb to put a lot of things on or into » *We loaded the car with supplies for the camping trip.*
fill, pack, pile, stack

loan [1]
noun a sum of money that you borrow » *He asked his father for a loan so he could buy a new bicycle.*
advance, credit, mortgage

loan [2]
verb to lend something to someone » *She loaned me her best coat to wear to the party.*
advance, lend

local [1]
adjective belonging to the area where you live » *The local store is on the corner of the next road.*
community, district, neighborhood, parish, regional

local [2]
noun a person who lives in a particular area » *Every week, the locals met at the café at the end of the street.*
inhabitant, native, resident

locate
verb to find out where someone or something is » *We located our missing friend in the café.*
find, pinpoint, track down

We located our missing friend in the café.

locate: be located
verb being in a particular place » *The restaurant is located near the movie theater.*
be placed, be sited, be situated

The castle has a beautiful hilltop location.

location
noun a place or position » *The castle has a beautiful hilltop location.*
place, point, position, site, situation, spot, whereabouts, locale, locus

lock [1]
verb to close and fasten something with a key » *Lock the door when you leave the house.*
latch, padlock
antonym: **unlock**

lock [2]
noun a device used to fasten something » *No one could open the door because the lock was stiff.*
latch, padlock

logical [1]
adjective using logic to figure something out » *His argument was logical and made sense.*
consistent, rational, reasoned, sound, valid, cogent, coherent
antonym: **illogical**

logical [2]
adjective sensible in the circumstances » *There has to be a logical explanation for the mysterious noise we heard.*
judicious, obvious, plausible, reasonable, sensible, wise
antonym: **illogical**

lonely [1]
adjective unhappy because of being alone » *The old lady was lonely and wished she had visitors.*
alone, forlorn, forsaken, lonesome

lonely [2]
adjective isolated and not visited by many people » *A lonely tree blew in the wind on the bleak hillside.*
deserted, desolate, isolated, remote, secluded, uninhabited, godforsaken, out-of-the-way, unfrequented

long [1]
adjective continuing for a great amount of time » *A long and awkward silence followed her shocking announcement.*
extended, interminable, lengthy, lingering, long-drawn-out, prolonged, protracted, slow, sustained
antonym: **short**

long [2]
adjective great in length or distance » *There was a long line to enter the building.*
elongated, extensive, lengthy
antonym: **short**

There was a long line to enter the building.

long [3]
verb to want something very much » *He longed for a relaxing vacation.*
ache, covet, crave, hunger, lust, pine, yearn

longing
noun a strong wish for something » *She had a real longing for a hot drink.*
craving, desire, hankering, hunger, thirst, yearning

look [1]
verb to turn your eyes toward something and see it
▶▶ SEE RIGHT

lonely [2]
adjective isolated and not visited by many people » *A lonely tree blew in the wind on the bleak hillside.*

look [2]
verb to appear or seem to be » *He looked younger than his age.*
appear, look like, seem, seem to be

look [3]
noun the action of turning your eyes toward something » *Lucy took a look at her reflection in the mirror.*
gaze, glance, glimpse, peek

look [4]
noun the way someone or something appears » *He had the look of a happy man.*
air, appearance, bearing, expression, face, semblance

look after
verb to take care of someone or something » *Will you look after my cats next week?*
care for, mind, nurse, take care of, tend, watch

look-alike
noun a person who looks like someone else » *He makes a living as an Elvis look-alike.*
dead ringer (informal), **double, spitting image** (informal)

look for
verb to try to find a person or thing » *I'm looking for my bag, have you seen it?*
forage, hunt, search, seek

loose [1]
adjective not firmly held or fixed » *The little girl had a loose tooth.*
free, unsecured, wobbly
antonym: **secure**

The little girl had a loose tooth.

*Chris wore his shirt **loose** to cool off.*

loose ②

adjective not fitting closely
» *Chris wore his shirt loose to cool off.*
baggy, slack, sloppy
antonym: **tight**

loosen

verb to make something looser
» *Harry loosened the knot in his tie.*
slacken, undo, untie
antonym: **tighten**

loot ①

verb to steal from a place during a riot or battle
» *Gangs began breaking windows and looting stores.*
pillage, plunder, raid, ransack

loot ②

noun stolen or illegal money or goods » *Sadly, the loot was never recovered.*
booty, haul, plunder, spoils, swag (slang)

lose ①

verb to be unable to find
» *I've lost my keys.*
drop, mislay, misplace
antonym: **find**

lose ②

verb to be beaten
» *We lost the game.*
be beaten, be defeated
antonym: **win**

lost ①

adjective not knowing where you are » *I think we're lost.*
adrift, astray, off course

lost ②

adjective unable to be found » *She missed her lost toy.*
mislaid, misplaced, missing, vanished

lot ① : a lot or lots

noun a large amount of something » *Remember to drink lots of water.*
abundance, a great deal, masses (informal),
piles (informal), **plenty, quantities, scores**

lot ②

noun an amount or number
» *He fired the whole lot of them for being late.*
batch, bunch (informal),
crowd, group, quantity, set

loud ①

adjective having a high level of sound » *We heard a loud bang from downstairs.*
blaring, deafening, noisy, resounding, strident, thunderous, clamorous, sonorous, stentorian
antonym: **quiet**

loud ②

adjective too brightly colored
» *He wore a loud tie to the fancy dress party.*
flamboyant, flashy, garish, gaudy, lurid
antonym: **dull**

lovable

adjective easy to love
» *I find puppies cute and lovable, but my friend doesn't like them nipping at her ankles.*
adorable, charming, enchanting, endearing, sweet, captivating, engaging, winsome
antonym: **hateful**

love ①

verb to feel strong affection for someone » *I love my family so much.*
adore, cherish, worship, be in love with, dote on, hold dear, idolize
antonym: **hate**

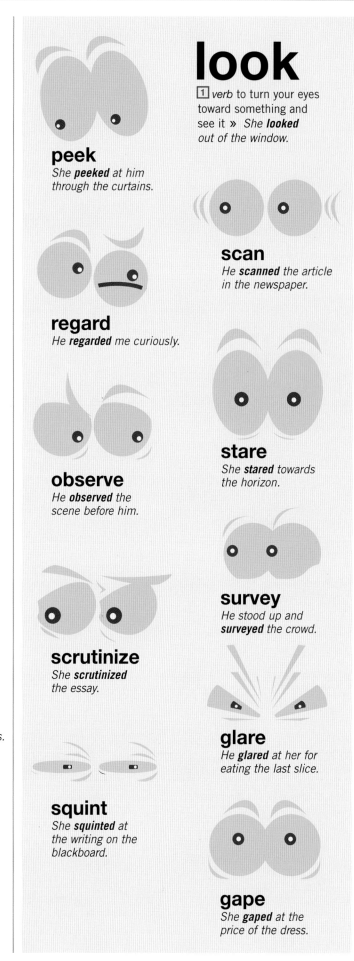

look

① *verb* to turn your eyes toward something and see it » *She **looked** out of the window.*

peek
*She **peeked** at him through the curtains.*

regard
*He **regarded** me curiously.*

observe
*He **observed** the scene before him.*

scrutinize
*She **scrutinized** the essay.*

squint
*She **squinted** at the writing on the blackboard.*

scan
*He **scanned** the article in the newspaper.*

stare
*She **stared** towards the horizon.*

survey
*He stood up and **surveyed** the crowd.*

glare
*He **glared** at her for eating the last slice.*

gape
*She **gaped** at the price of the dress.*

a b c d e f g h i j k l m n o p q r s t u v w x y z

love [2]
verb to like something very much » *We both love fishing and go every weekend.*
appreciate, enjoy, like, relish, delight in, have a weakness for, take pleasure in
antonym: **hate**

love [3]
noun a strong feeling of affection » *There is nothing like a mother's love for her children.*
adoration, affection, ardor, devotion, infatuation, passion
antonym: **hatred**

There is nothing like a mother's **love** *for her children.*

love [4]
noun a strong liking for something » *Her love of animals has inspired her to become a vet.*
devotion, fondness, liking, weakness, partiality, penchant
antonym: **hatred**

lovely
adjective very attractive and pleasant » *You look lovely in that outfit.*
attractive, beautiful, delightful, enjoyable, pleasant, pretty
antonym: **horrible**

loving
adjective feeling or showing love » *He is a loving husband and father.*
affectionate, devoted, doting, fond, tender, warm, demonstrative, solicitous, warm-hearted
antonym: **cold**

low [1]
adjective short or not far above the ground » *The sun was low in the sky.*
little, short, small, squat, stunted, sunken
antonym: **high**

low [2]
adjective small in degree or quantity » *The prices were low so we bought more clothes.*
minimal, modest, poor, reduced, scant, small
antonym: **high**

lower [1]
verb to move something downward » *Sara lowered herself into the bathtub.*
drop, let down, take down
antonym: **raise**

lower [2]
verb to make something less in amount » *The government promised to lower taxes.*
cut, decrease, diminish, lessen, minimize, reduce, slash
antonym: **increase**

loyal
adjective firm in your friendship or support » *Kim was a loyal friend, visiting Ted every day while he was recovering.*
constant, dependable, faithful, staunch, true, trusty, steadfast, true-hearted, unswerving, unwavering
antonym: **treacherous**

Kim was a **loyal** *friend, visiting Ted every day while he was recovering.*

luck
noun something that happens by chance » *It was just luck that we happened to meet.*
accident, chance, destiny, fate, fortune, fortuity, predestination

lucky [1]
adjective having a lot of good luck » *Colin has always been lucky at games, winning every time.*
blessed, charmed, fortunate
antonym: **unlucky**

lucky [2]
adjective happening by chance with good consequences » *Suhel was lucky to be dealt such a good hand of cards that he easily won the game.*
fortuitous, fortunate, opportune, timely, adventitious, propitious, providential
antonym: **unlucky**

lump [1]
noun a solid piece of something » *Jane kneaded the big lump of dough.*
ball, cake, chunk, hunk, piece, wedge

Jane kneaded the big **lump** *of dough.*

lump [2]
noun a bump on the surface of something » *I've got a big lump on my head from when I walked into the shelf.*
bulge, bump, hump, swelling, protrusion, protuberance

lure [1]
verb to attract someone somewhere or into doing something » *We lured the ducks out of the water with bread crumbs.*
attract, beckon, draw, entice, tempt

lure [2]
noun something that you find very attractive » *It was a hot day, and the lure of the swimming pool was strong.*
attraction, bait, magnet, pull, temptation

lurk
verb to wait hidden for someone or something » *He thought he saw someone lurking in the doorway.*
lie in wait, loiter, skulk

luxurious
adjective expensive and full of luxury » *We stayed in a luxurious hotel; it had the biggest pool I've ever seen.*
deluxe, lavish, opulent, plush (informal), **posh** (informal), **sumptuous, upscale** (informal)
antonym: **plain**

luxury [1]
noun comfort in expensive surroundings » *We led a life of luxury on vacation and didn't care how much it cost.*
affluence, opulence, sumptuousness

luxury [2]
noun something enjoyable that you do not have often » *Renting a sports car was a real luxury for my dad.*
extra, extravagance, indulgence, treat

lying [1]
noun the action of telling lies » *I've had enough of his lying; why can't he just tell the truth for once?*
deceit, dishonesty, fabrication, fibbing, perjury, dissimulation, duplicity, mendacity

lying [2]
adjective telling lies » *Don't trust him, he is a lying cheat.*
deceitful, dishonest, false, untruthful, dissembling, mendacious
antonym: **honest**

machine

noun a piece of equipment » *Joe used a washing machine to wash his clothes.*
apparatus, appliance, contraption, device, instrument, mechanism

*Joe used a washing **machine** to wash his clothes.*

mad

adjective (informal) angry about something » *My friends got mad at me for interfering.*
angry, enraged, fuming, furious, incensed, infuriated, irate, livid (informal)

magic

noun a special power » *Do you believe in magic?*
sorcery, witchcraft, necromancy, occultism

magical

adjective wonderful and exciting » *I've heard that Paris is a magical city.*
bewitching, enchanting, entrancing, spellbinding

main

adjective most important » *Our main reason for going to Paris is to see the Eiffel Tower.*
cardinal, chief, foremost, leading, major, predominant, primary, prime, principal

mainly

adverb true in most cases » *The kittens were mainly multicolored.*
chiefly, generally, largely, mostly, predominantly, primarily, principally, for the most part, in general, on the whole

*The kittens were **mainly** multicolored.*

major

adjective very important or serious » *There's a major problem with your car's engine—it won't start.*
critical, crucial, leading, outstanding, significant
antonym: **minor**

majority

noun more than half » *The majority of our basketball team are girls.*
best part, better part, bulk, mass, most, lion's share, preponderance

*The **majority** of our basketball team are girls.*

make ①

verb to construct something
▼ SEE BELOW

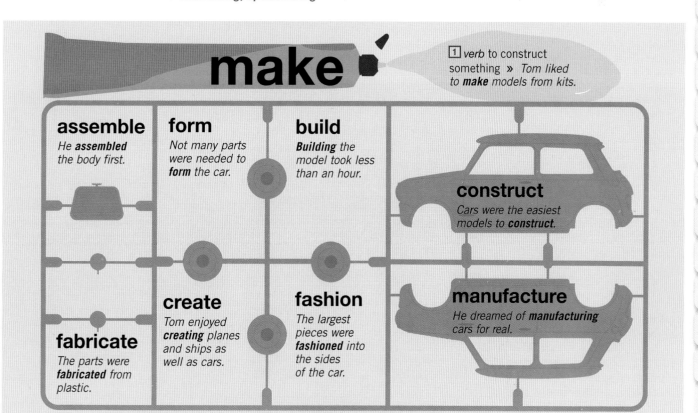

make

① *verb* to construct something » *Tom liked to **make** models from kits.*

assemble
He **assembled** the body first.

form
Not many parts were needed to **form** the car.

build
Building the model took less than an hour.

construct
Cars were the easiest models to **construct**.

fabricate
The parts were **fabricated** from plastic.

create
Tom enjoyed **creating** planes and ships as well as cars.

fashion
The largest pieces were **fashioned** into the sides of the car.

manufacture
He dreamed of **manufacturing** cars for real.

*Her mother **made** her clean up the mess.*

make [2]

verb to force someone to do something » *Her mother made her clean up the mess.*
compel, drive, force, oblige, coerce, impel

make [3]

noun a particular type » *My uncle always wears a certain make of wristwatch.*
brand, model

make up [1]

verb to form the parts of something » *Boys make up more than half of our history class.*
compose, comprise, constitute, form

make up [2]

verb to invent a story » *Tessa made up a story about why she was late—she didn't admit she'd just overslept.*
concoct, fabricate, invent, formulate, manufacture

making [1]

noun the act of creating something » *More than 100 people were involved in the making of this movie.*
assembly, building, construction, creation, fabrication, manufacture, production

making [2]: in the making

adjective about to become something » *The new recruit was a soldier in the making.*
budding, emergent, potential, up-and-coming

male

adjective relating to men » *I knew my father was at the door as soon as I heard the deep male voice.*
manly, masculine
antonym: **female**

malicious

adjective having the intention of hurting someone » *Pete was accused of spreading malicious rumors about Rita.*
cruel, malevolent (formal), **mean, spiteful, vicious, malignant, rancorous** (formal)

man [1]

noun an adult male human being » *Jaime is a charming young man.*
dude (informal), **fellow, gentleman, guy** (informal), **hombre, male**
antonym: **woman**

man [2]

noun people in general » *All men are equal.*
humanity, human race, mankind, Homo sapiens, humankind

manage [1]

verb to succeed in doing something » *The crew managed to stop the fire from spreading any further.*
cope with, succeed in

*The crew **managed** to stop the fire from spreading any further.*

manage [2]

verb to be in charge of something » *Within two years, Joe was managing the store.*
be in charge of, command, control, direct, run

management [1]

noun the act of running an organization » *The zoo needed better management to shorten the entrance lines.*
control, direction, running

management [2]

noun the people who run an organization » *The management is investing more in research.*
administration, board, bosses (informal), **directors, employers**

manager

noun a person in charge of running an organization » *We welcomed our new manager in the morning meeting.*
boss (informal), **director, executive**

*We welcomed our new **manager** in the morning meeting.*

maneuver [1]

verb to move something skilfully » *It took expertise to maneuver the boat.*
guide, navigate, negotiate, steer

maneuver [2]

noun a clever action » *Sam used cunning maneuvers to win.*
dodge, ploy, ruse, tactic, machination, stratagem, subterfuge

manifest

adjective (formal) obvious or easily seen » *His manifest failure to notice the puddle resulted in Len getting wet feet.*
blatant, clear, conspicuous, glaring, obvious, patent, plain

manner [1]

noun the way that you do something » *She smiled again in a friendly manner.*
fashion, mode, style, way

manner [2]

noun the way someone behaves » *Kim's kind manner made her feel at ease.*
bearing, behavior, conduct, demeanor, comportment, deportment

manufacture [1]

verb to make goods in a factory » *Several car models are manufactured at the factory.*
assemble, fabricate, make, mass-produce, process, produce

manufacture [2]

noun the making of goods in a factory » *His job is to supervise the manufacture of cars.*
assembly, fabrication, making, mass production, production

*His job is to supervise the **manufacture** of cars.*

many [1]

adjective a large number » *Sue has many friends.*
countless, innumerable, myriad, numerous, umpteen (informal), **multifarious, multitudinous**
antonym: **few**

many [2] : many of

pronoun a large number of people or things » *I'd read many of my books already, so I went to the library to take out more.*
a lot, a mass, a multitude, large numbers, lots (informal), **plenty, tons**
antonym: **few**

mar

verb a affect something in a negative way » *The president's reputation was marred by many scandals.*
blemish, cloud, color, poison, shame, spoil, tarnish

mark [1]

noun a small stain » *I can't get this mark off the curtain and it's wrecking the pattern.*
blot, line, smudge, spot, stain, streak

mark [2]

verb to stain something » *The pen in Marianna's pocket leaked and marked her pants.*
smudge, stain, streak

market

noun a place to buy or sell things » *We bought fresh fish at the market today.*
bazaar, fair

marriage [1]

noun the formal union of two people who live together » *We have a happy marriage—we've been together for 20 years.*
matrimony (formal),
wedlock (formal)
related words:
adjectives **conjugal, connubial, marital, nuptial**

marriage [2]

noun a union » *The dessert was a perfect marriage of vanilla and chocolate.*
alliance, association, coupling, link, match, merger, union

*Tall grasses grew in the **marsh**.*

marsh

noun an area of low-lying, poorly drained land that is sometimes flooded » *Tall grasses grew in the marsh.*
bog, fen, mire, morass, mudflats, quagmire, quicksands, saltmarsh, slough, swamp, wetland

marvelous

adjective wonderful or excellent » *The couple had a marvelous time at the opera.*
brilliant, excellent, first-rate, magnificent, remarkable, splendid, superb, wonderful
antonym: **terrible**

mass [1]

noun a large number or amount » *Fatima had masses of homework to get through.*
crowd, heap, load, lump, mob, pile, throng

mass [2]

adjective involving a large number of people » *There were mass protests about the tax increases.*
general, popular, universal, widespread

mass [3]

verb to gather together in a large group » *The children massed to watch the relay race.*
assemble, congregate, gather, group

master

verb to learn how to do something » *Eliana found it easy to master the recorder.*
become proficient in, get the hang of (informal), **grasp, learn**

match [1]

noun an organized game » *Ken was looking forward to the tennis match.*
competition, contest, game

match [2]

verb to be similar to » *The shoes matched her dress.*
agree, correspond, fit, go with, suit, tally, accord, harmonize

material [1]

noun any type of cloth » *Sara's skirt was made of thick material.*
cloth, fabric

material [2]

noun a solid substance » *He gathered the materials needed for repairing the wall.*
matter, stuff, substance

*He gathered the **materials** needed for repairing the wall.*

matter [1]

noun something that you have to deal with » *Rachel found business matters very dull.*
affair, business, issue, question, situation, subject

matter [2]

noun any substance » *The atom is the smallest divisible particle of matter.*
material, stuff, substance

matter [3]

verb to be important » *It does not matter what you wear for the party.*
be of consequence, count, make a difference

mature [1]

verb to become fully developed » *Children seem to mature earlier these days.*
come of age, grow up, reach adulthood

mature [2]

adjective fully developed » *He's very mature for his age.*
adult, full-grown, fully fledged, grown, grown-up

maximum [1]

adjective being the most that is possible » *The maximum number of books that will fit on a shelf is 20.*
top, utmost
antonym: **minimum**

maximum [2]

noun the most that is possible » *Matt turned the volume of the radio up to the maximum.*
ceiling, height, most, upper limit, utmost
antonym: **minimum**

*Matt turned the volume of the radio up to the **maximum**.*

maybe

adverb it is possible that » *Maybe it would have been quicker to take the bus.*
conceivably, it could be, perhaps, possibly, perchance

*The restaurant served such **meager** portions we went home hungry.*

meager

adjective very small and inadequate » *The restaurant served such meager portions we went home hungry.*
inadequate, measly (informal)**, paltry, scant, sparse,** exiguous, insubstantial, scanty, skimpy, wimpy

meal

noun an occasion when people eat » *My father cooked a special meal for my birthday.*
banquet, buffet, chow, dinner, feast, supper, repast, smorgasbord, spread

mean ①

verb to convey a message » *A red traffic light means that you have to stop.*
denote, express, imply, indicate, insinuate, intend, signify

mean ②

verb to intend to do something » *I meant to call you, but didn't have time.*
aim, design, dream, intend, plan, propose

meaning

noun the idea expressed by something » *Tom had to look up the meaning of the word in the dictionary.*
drift, gist, message, significance, connotation, import

measure ①

verb to check the size of something » *We measured how tall our little brother was.*
gauge, survey, calibrate, quantify

measure ②

noun an amount of something » *There was a measure of silence after the actor's shocking announcement.*
amount, degree, portion, proportion

measure ③

noun an action to achieve something » *Tough measures are needed to maintain order.*
act, action, deed, expedient, maneuver, means, procedure, step

medicine

noun something you take to make you feel better » *The doctor prescribed some medicine for my infection.*
cure, drug, medication, pill, tablet, remedy

medium ①

adjective average in size » *Ella was of medium height.*
average, common, mean, medium-sized,

*Ella was of **medium** height.*

medium ②

noun a means of communication » *The government released the news through the medium of TV.*
channel, vehicle, agency, instrument

meek

adjective quiet and timid » *Janet was a meek girl, always agreeing with whatever her friends said.*
deferential, docile, mild, submissive, timid, unassuming, acquiescent, compliant, mild-mannered
antonym: **bold**

meet ①

verb to be in the same place as someone » *I met my cousin by chance.*
bump into (informal)**, come across, come upon, encounter, run across, run into**

meet ②

verb to gather in a group » *We meet for lunch at a café once a week.*
assemble, congregate, convene, gather, get together

*We **meet** for lunch at a café once a week.*

meet ③

verb to fulfill a need » *Meals must meet the needs of growing children.*
answer, fulfill, satisfy

meeting ①

noun an event at which people come together for a purpose » *All the parents went to a meeting about the new playground.*
audience, conference, congress, convention, gathering, get-together (informal)**, reunion,** conclave, convocation

meeting ②

noun an occasion when you meet someone » *I had a chance meeting with an old friend while I was shopping.*
assignation (literary)**, encounter, rendezvous, tryst**

melodramatic

adjective behaving in an exaggerated way » *Eva was so melodramatic, leaving the café because she didn't like the table they gave her.*
histrionic, sensational, theatrical

melt ①

verb to become liquid » *The ice cream started melting into a puddle.*
dissolve, thaw, liquefy

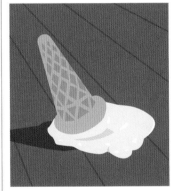

*The ice cream started **melting** into a puddle.*

melt ②

verb to disappear » *Isabella's anger melted when she saw what Leo had brought her.*
disappear, disperse, dissolve, evaporate, vanish

memorable

adjective likely to be remembered » *The cup final was a memorable victory over the league champions.*
catchy, historic, notable, striking, unforgettable

memory

noun the ability to remember » *I have an excellent memory for phone numbers.*
recall, remembrance (formal)**,** recollection, retention

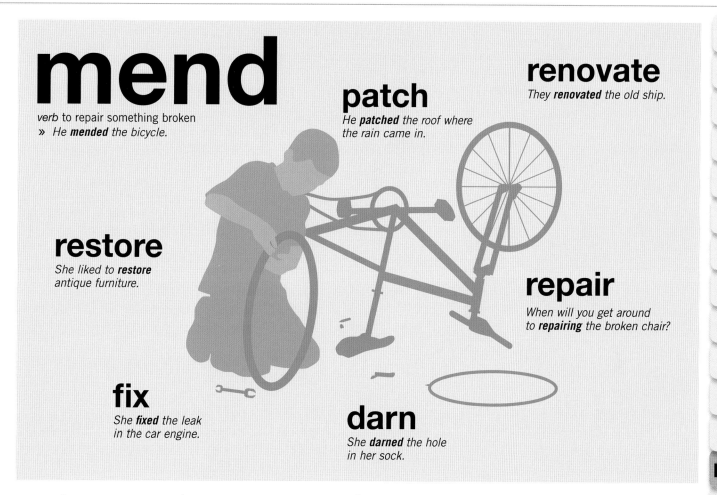

mend
verb to repair something broken
» He **mended** the bicycle.

patch
He **patched** the roof where the rain came in.

renovate
They **renovated** the old ship.

restore
She liked to **restore** antique furniture.

repair
When will you get around to **repairing** the broken chair?

fix
She **fixed** the leak in the car engine.

darn
She **darned** the hole in her sock.

---

a b c d e f g h i j k l m n o p q r s t u v w x y z

---

mend
verb to repair something broken
▲ SEE ABOVE

mention 1
verb to talk about something briefly » *I mentioned the party to Lisa, but I don't know if she'll come.*
allude to, bring up, broach, hint, intimate, refer to, touch on, touch upon

mention 2
noun a brief comment about something » *There was no mention in the program of my role in the play.*
allusion, reference

merciful 1
adjective showing kindness » *The merciful king treated his subjects with kindness.*
compassionate, humane, kind
antonym: **merciless**

merciful 2
adjective showing forgiveness » *The teacher was merciful and gave us no homework over the holidays.*
forgiving, lenient
antonym: **merciless**

merciless
adjective showing no kindness or forgiveness » *The airport staff were merciless when I forgot my passport and wouldn't let me on the plane.*
callous, cruel, heartless, implacable, ruthless, hard-hearted, pitiless, unforgiving
antonym: **merciful**

mercy 1
noun the quality of kindness » *The wrestler showed no mercy to his opponent.*
compassion, kindness, pity, benevolence, charity

mercy 2
noun the quality of forgiveness » *The criminal threw himself upon the mercy of the court.*
forgiveness, leniency, clemency, forbearance

merit 1
noun worth or value » *The movie's producer argued that profits mattered more than artistic merit.*
excellence, value, virtue, worth

merit 2
noun a good quality that something has » *They discussed the merits of the different cakes on offer.*
advantage, asset, strength, strong point, virtue

merit 3
verb to deserve something » *Buying a new camera merits careful consideration.*
be entitled to, be worthy of, deserve, earn, warrant

mess 1
noun a state of untidiness » *The room was a mess after the party.*
chaos, disarray, disorder

*The room was a **mess** after the party.*

mess 2
noun a situation that is full of problems » *How are we going to get out of this mess?*
fix (informal), jam (informal), muddle, turmoil

mess 3: mess up
verb to spoil something » *He messed up his career.*
blow, botch, bungle, foul up, goof, ruin, screw up, spoil

message 1
noun a piece of information for someone
▼ SEE BELOW

message 2
verb to send information to » *Fred messaged his friends to tell them about the game.*
email or e-mail, IM, instant message, text

messenger
noun someone who carries a message » *We will send a messenger to the airport to collect the photographs.*
agent, courier, envoy, page, runner, emissary, go-between

method
noun a way of doing something » *Emily used a traditional method to make jam.*
approach, mode, procedure, technique, way

middle 1
noun the part farthest from the edges » *There was a large table in the middle of the room.*
center, halfway point, midst, midpoint, midsection

middle 2
adjective farthest from the edges » *Carl sat down on the middle seat, between his parents.*
central, halfway, intermediate, median

mild 1
adjective not strong or powerful » *Flo used a mild shampoo to wash her hair.*
insipid, weak
antonym: **strong**

mild 2
adjective gentle and good-tempered » *My uncle is a mild man who is very good with animals.*
affable, gentle, meek, placid, easygoing, equable, pacific, peaceable

mild 3
adjective warmer than usual » *The area is famous for its mild winter climate.*
balmy, temperate

mind 1
noun your ability to think » *Our teacher is really smart and has a sharp mind.*
brain, head, imagination, intellect, psyche

mind 2
verb to be annoyed by something » *I don't mind what you get me for my birthday—it's the thought that counts.*
be bothered, care, object

mind 3
verb to be in charge of something » *I'm minding the store while my boss is at a conference next week.*
attend, keep an eye on, take care of, watch

minimum
adjective being the least possible » *My little sister was just tall enough to be the minimum height for the fairground ride.*
least possible, minimal

minor
adjective less important » *Henry fell off his bike, but sustained only minor injuries.*
lesser, petty, secondary, slight, trifling, trivial
antonym: **major**

message
1 *noun* a piece of information for someone
» *He left a **message** on her voicemail.*

communication
She brought a **communication** from the commander.

dispatch
The **dispatch** came from the Middle East news correspondent.

memorandum
The **memorandum** came from the government.

word
There is no **word** on the reported tiger escape from the zoo.

missive
The editor's **missive** was four pages long.

bulletin
The news **bulletin** was at 6pm.

memo
He sent a **memo** around the office about turning off lights.

note
I'll just leave a **note** for Kate.

communiqué
The **communiqué** from the conference explained their decision.

minute [1]

noun a short period of time
» *I'll be with you in a minute.*
flash, instant, moment, second, trice

minute [2]

adjective extremely small
» *The insect was so minute that Kayla needed a magnifying glass to see it clearly.*
microscopic, negligible, slender, small, tiny, diminutive, minuscule
antonym: **vast**

*The insect was so **minute** that Kayla needed a magnifying glass to see it clearly.*

miracle

noun a surprising and fortunate event » *It was a miracle that everyone escaped unharmed.*
marvel, wonder

miserable [1]

adjective very unhappy » *All this rain makes me miserable.*
dejected, depressed, down, downcast, low, melancholy, mournful, sad, unhappy, wretched, disconsolate, sorrowful
antonym: **cheerful**

miserable [2]

adjective causing unhappiness » *Damp, dark, and poky— it was a miserable apartment.*
gloomy, pathetic, sorry, wretched

misery

noun unhappiness » *He felt such misery when his pet died.*
depression, despair, grief, melancholy, sadness, sorrow, unhappiness, woe
antonym: **joy**

misfortune

noun an unfortunate event
» *I had the misfortune to fall off my bike.*
adversity, bad luck

misrepresent

verb to give a false account of something » *My brother deliberately misrepresented what happened when we argued earlier.*
distort, falsify, twist

miss [1]

verb to fail to notice » *Go to the first floor. You can't miss it.*
fail to notice, mistake, overlook

miss [2]

verb to feel the loss of
» *I miss my family when I'm away at school.*
long for, pine for, yearn for

mistake [1]

noun something that is wrong
» *There were a lot of spelling mistakes in his work.*
blunder, error, gaffe, oversight, slip, inaccuracy, miscalculation

*There were a lot of spelling **mistakes** in his work.*

mistake [2]

verb to think one thing is another thing » *I mistook him for the owner of the house.*
confuse with, misinterpret as, mix up with, take for

mistreat

verb to treat someone badly
» *The dog had been mistreated, so we gave it a new home.*
abuse, ill-treat

mix

verb to combine things » *Mix the ingredients together slowly.*
amalgamate, blend, combine, merge, mingle, intermingle, interweave

mixture

noun a combination of things
» *We used a mixture of flour and water to make dough.*
alloy, amalgamation, blend, combination, compound, fusion, medley, amalgam, composite, conglomeration, mix

*We used a **mixture** of flour and water to make dough.*

mix up

verb to confuse two things
» *People often mix us up because we both wear glasses.*
confuse, muddle

mix-up

noun a mistake in something planned » *There has been a mix-up with the reservations.*
mistake, misunderstanding,

moan [1]

verb to make a low sound
» *Laura moaned when she heard the bad news.*
groan, grunt

moan [2]

verb to complain about something » *Carol is always moaning about her husband.*
complain, groan, grumble, whine

moan [3]

noun a low sound
» *She let out a faint moan.*
groan, grunt

mock [1]

verb to make fun of someone
» *My sister mocked my haircut.*
deride (formal), **laugh at, make fun of, poke fun at, ridicule, scoff at**

mock [2]

adjective not genuine » *The adults showed mock surprise when the children performed the same old magic tricks.*
artificial, bogus, counterfeit, dummy, fake, false, feigned, imitation, phoney or **phony** (informal), **pretended, sham,** ersatz, pseudo

mockery

noun the act of mocking someone » *Was there a glint of mockery in his eyes when he said he liked her new dress?*
derision, jeering, ridicule

model [1]

noun a copy of something
» *We saw a model of what this building used to look like.*
dummy, replica, representation, facsimile, mock-up

model [2]

noun a perfect example of something » *My obedient dog is a model of good behavior.*
epitome, example, ideal, paragon, archetype, exemplar

model [3]

verb to make something into a shape » *Jo modeled the clay into an animal.*
carve, fashion, form, mold, sculpt, shape

*Jo **modeled** the clay into an animal.*

a b c d e f g h i j k l **m** n o p q r s t u v w x y z

moderate [1]
adjective neither too much nor too little » *Moderate exercise is good for the health.*
average, fair, medium, middling, reasonable

moderate [2]
verb to become or make less extreme » *The children persuaded their father to moderate his views on pets in bedrooms.*
abate, curb, ease, relax, soften, temper, tone down

modern [1]
adjective relating to the present time » *The modern world increasingly relies on the Internet.*
contemporary, current, present, present-day, recent

modern [2]
adjective new and involving the latest ideas » *The house was full of modern technology.*
latest, new, up-to-date, up-to-the-minute
antonym: **old-fashioned**

modest [1]
adjective small in size or amount » *Olivia made a modest donation to charity each month.*
limited, middling, moderate, small

modest [2]
adjective not boastful » *The famous athlete was modest about his achievements.*
humble, unassuming, self-effacing, unpretentious
antonym: **conceited**

moment [1]
noun a short period of time » *Ted paused for a moment to get his breath back.*
instant, minute, second, split second, flash, trice

moment [2]
noun a point in time » *The phone rang at the exact moment I stepped into the bath tub.*
instant, point, time

*Sue played at being grown-up and counting the **money** she had earned.*

money
noun coins or banknotes » *Sue played at being grown-up and counting the money she had earned.*
bread, capital, cash, dough (informal), **funds, moola**

mood
noun a state of mind » *Liz has been in a really cheerful mood since getting a kitten.*
frame of mind, humor, spirits, state of mind, temper

moody [1]
adjective depressed or unhappy » *Tony was moody because his mother had woken him up.*
irritable, grumpy, morose, sulky, sullen, huffy, testy, touchy

moody [2]
adjective liable to change your mood » *Joey's big sister got very moody in high school.*
temperamental, volatile, capricious, mercurial

more
adjective greater than something else » *Belle has more books than Peter.*
added, additional, extra, further
antonym: **less**

*Belle has **more** books than Peter.*

move
[1] *verb* to change position » *The race started and the competitors began to **move**.*

1 **wriggle** **creep** **scurry** **inch** slither **crawl** **scuttle** scamper **edge**

2 **run** **bolt** **stampede** **fly** **shoot** **dash** jog **hasten** **gallop** dart **sprint** **rush**

motivate

verb to cause a particular behavior » *The teacher used a sticker chart to motivate the children to work hard.*
drive, inspire, lead, move, prompt, provoke

mountain

noun an area of high ground that is taller and steeper than a hill » *After hours of climbing, we finally reached the top of the mountain.*
alp, elevation, height, mount, peak, pinnacle, precipice, sierra, range, ridge

After hours of climbing, we finally reached the top of the mountain.

move ☐1

verb to change position
▼ SEE BELOW

move ☐2

verb to change residence » *Lori moved from Chicago to London.*
migrate, move house, relocate

move ☐3

verb to cause a deep emotion » *We were moved to tears.*
affect, touch

movement ☐1

noun a change of position » *The cameras monitor the movement of fish in the river.*
flow, motion

movement ☐2

noun a group of people with similar aims » *Vicky joined the peace movement.*
campaign, faction, group, organization

moving

adjective causing deep emotion » *The father of the bride gave a moving speech.*
affecting, emotional, poignant, stirring, touching

muddle ☐1

noun a state of disorder » *The drawer is in a muddle; I can't find what I want.*
chaos, confusion, disarray, disorder, disorganization, jumble, mess, tangle

muddle ☐2

verb to mix things up » *I often muddle my words when I'm nervous.*
confuse, jumble, mix up

multiply

verb to increase in number » *The number of children in the park multiplied in summer.*
increase, proliferate

mumble

verb to speak quietly » *Speak up, don't mumble!*
murmur, mutter

mysterious ☐1

adjective strange and not well understood » *My favorite jacket went missing under mysterious circumstances.*
arcane (formal), **baffling, cryptic, enigmatic, mystifying,** abstruse, obscure, recondite

mysterious ☐2

adjective secretive about something » *Stop being so mysterious and tell me where you've hidden the keys.*
furtive, secretive

mystery

noun something that is not understood » *There is a mystery surrounding our dog's disappearance.*
conundrum, enigma, puzzle, riddle

a b c d e f g h i j k l m n o p q r s t u v w x y z

tear
hurry **race**

Nn

nag
verb to keep complaining about something to someone »» *My dad nagged me to keep the bathroom clean.*
badger, bother, go on at, pester

naked 1
adjective not wearing any clothes »» *Anna's most famous painting was of a naked woman.*
bare, nude, stark-naked, unclothed, undressed
antonym: **clothed**

naked 2
adjective openly displayed or shown »» *His naked ambition was evident in his hard work.*
blatant, evident, manifest, open, unmistakable, overt, patent, stark
antonym: **secret**

name 1
noun a word that identifies a person or thing »» *My name is Joe.*
designation, epithet, nickname, term, title, appellation, denomination, sobriquet
related word:
adjective **nominal**

name 2
noun the opinion people have about someone »» *He lied to protect Janet's good name.*
character, reputation

name 3
verb to give a name to someone »» *She named her daughter Kate, after her grandmother.*
baptize, call, christen, dub, style, term

*We crossed a **narrow** stream.*

narrow
adjective having a small distance from side to side »» *We crossed a narrow stream.*
fine, slender, slim, thin
antonym: **wide**

narrow-minded
adjective unwilling to consider new ideas or other people's opinions »» *My friend is rather narrow-minded and doesn't like exploring new ideas.*
biased, bigoted, insular, opinionated, prejudiced, parochial, reactionary
antonym: **tolerant**

nasty
adjective very unpleasant »» *The rotten apple left a nasty taste in my mouth.*
disagreeable, disgusting, foul, horrible, repellent, unpleasant, vile
antonym: **pleasant**

natural 1
adjective normal and to be expected »» *Her natural reaction was to laugh at jokes.*
common, everyday, normal, ordinary, typical, usual
antonym: **unnatural**

natural 2
adjective not trying to pretend »» *The new babysitter was so natural with the children.*
candid, frank, genuine, real, unaffected, artless, ingenuous
antonym: **false**

natural 3
adjective existing from birth and not learned »» *I'm a terrible dancer—I have no natural rhythm.*
inborn, inherent, innate, instinctive, intuitive, native, immanent, indigenous

nature
noun someone's character »» *It's not in my nature to sit still for long.*
character, make-up, personality

naughty
adjective tending to behave badly »» *The teacher told the children off for being naughty.*
bad, disobedient, impish, mischievous, wayward
antonym: **well-behaved**

navigate
verb to figure out the direction in which a ship, plane, or car should go »» *Sam navigated the plane through the fog.*
guide, pilot, steer

near 1
preposition not far from »» *The cat curled up near the fireplace.*
adjacent to, alongside, close to, next to, not far from

*The cat curled up **near** the fireplace.*

near 2
adjective not far away in distance »» *The restaurant we're going to is near here.*
adjacent, adjoining, close, nearby
antonym: **far**

near 3
adjective not far away in time »» *Our final exams are near.*
approaching, forthcoming, imminent, looming, near at hand, nigh, upcoming

nearly
adverb not completely but almost »» *The beach was nearly empty after the storm.*
almost, as good as, just about, practically, virtually

neat
adjective having everything arranged in an organized way »» *Jo always kept her desk neat.*
orderly, smart, spruce, tidy, trim
antonym: **untidy**

*Jo always kept her desk **neat**.*

necessary 1
adjective needed so that something can happen »» *Juan made the necessary arrangements for his vacation.*
essential, imperative, indispensable, required, vital, de rigueur, requisite
antonym: **unnecessary**

necessary 2
adjective (formal) sure to happen or exist »» *Wrinkles are a necessary result of getting old.*
certain, inevitable, inexorable, unavoidable

need
verb to require something or be required to do something »» *You need a ticket to enter.*
demand, require, want

A B C D E F G H I J K L M N O P Q R S T U V W X Y Z

neglect ①
verb to fail to take care of someone or something
» *My toast burned because I had neglected it.*
ignore, overlook, turn your back on

neglect ②
verb (formal) to fail to do something » *Alex neglected to give me his address, so I don't know where to send the card.*
fail, forget, omit

neglect ③
noun lack of care » *Most of her plants died from neglect.*
disregard, indifference, unconcern

nervous
adjective worried about something
▶▶ **SEE RIGHT**

neutral
adjective not supporting either side » *I stayed neutral during my friends' argument.*
disinterested, dispassionate, impartial, nonaligned, nonpartisan, unbiased, unprejudiced
antonym: **biased**

never
adverb at no time at all
» *I never said I was leaving.*
at no time, not ever

new
adjective recently created or discovered » *A new hotel has opened in our town.*
advanced, current, fresh, groundbreaking, latest, modern, recent, ultramodern, up-to-date, up-to-the-minute
antonym: **old**

news
noun information about things that have happened » *Jackie waited for news of his arrival.*
bulletin, disclosure, dispatch, information, intelligence, latest (informal), **tidings** (formal), **word**

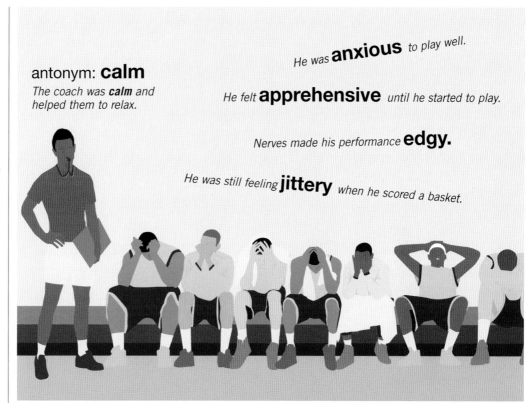

antonym: **calm**
*The coach was **calm** and helped them to relax.*

He was **anxious** to play well.

He felt **apprehensive** until he started to play.

Nerves made his performance **edgy.**

He was still feeling **jittery** when he scored a basket.

The new player was obviously **jumpy.**

He was too **tense** to throw the ball correctly.

He felt **uptight** and uneasy.

He had me **worried** for a moment.

nervous
adjective worried about something
» *He was always **nervous** before a game.*

a b c d e f g h i j k l m n o p q r s t u v w x y z

nice

1 *adjective* attractive or enjoyable

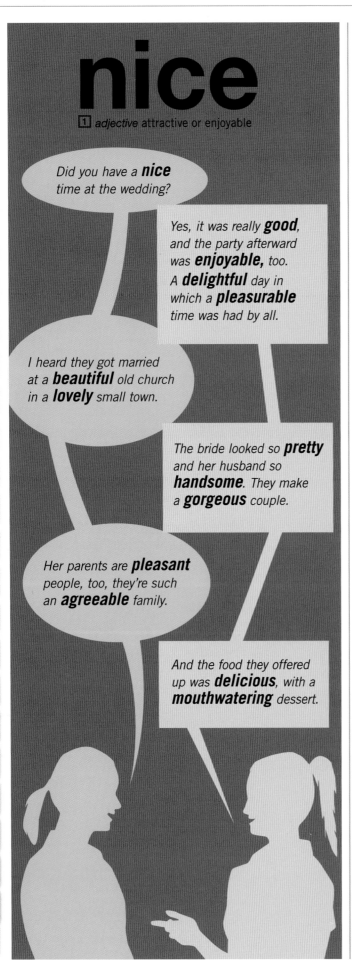

Did you have a **nice** time at the wedding?

Yes, it was really **good**, and the party afterward was **enjoyable,** too. A **delightful** day in which a **pleasurable** time was had by all.

I heard they got married at a **beautiful** old church in a **lovely** small town.

The bride looked so **pretty** and her husband so **handsome**. They make a **gorgeous** couple.

Her parents are **pleasant** people, too, they're such an **agreeable** family.

And the food they offered up was **delicious**, with a **mouthwatering** dessert.

next 1

adjective coming immediately after something else
» *Their next child was a girl.*
ensuing, following, subsequent, succeeding

next 2

adverb coming immediately after something else
» *After Sue and Dan, Steve arrived next at the party.*
afterward, subsequently

next 3

adjective in a position closest to something » *I shut the dog away in the next room.*
adjacent, adjoining, closest, nearest, neighboring

nice 1

adjective attractive or enjoyable
◄◄ SEE LEFT

nice 2

adjective kind or friendly
» *Sending flowers was a nice gesture.*
amiable, charming, considerate, engaging, friendly, good-natured, kind, kindly, likable, thoughtful

nice 3

adjective good or satisfactory
» *The worker did a nice job on the new back yard fence.*
fine, neat, tidy, trim

no

interjection not at all
» *"Any problems?"*
"No, everything is fine, thanks."
absolutely not, certainly not, definitely not, not at all, of course not
antonym: **yes**

noble 1

adjective deserving admiration because of honesty, bravery, and unselfishness » *Giving his prize money away was noble.*
generous, honorable, magnanimous, upright, virtuous, worthy
antonym: **ignoble**

noble 2

noun someone from the highest social rank » *The old castle belonged to a family of nobles.*
aristocrat, lord, nobleman, peer
antonym: **peasant**

noise

noun a loud or unpleasant sound » *Bill wore headphones while using the jackhammer to muffle the noise.*
commotion, din, hubbub, pandemonium, racket, row, uproar, clamor, rumpus, tumult
antonym: **silence**

Bill wore headphones while using the jackhammer to muffle the noise.

noisy

adjective making a lot of noise » *The bus was full of noisy students shrieking with excitement.*
deafening, loud, piercing, strident, tumultuous, vociferous, clamorous, riotous, uproarious
antonym: **quiet**

nominate

verb to suggest someone for a position or role
» *My English teacher nominated me for the award.*
name, propose, recommend, select, submit, suggest

nonsense

noun foolish words or behavior
» *Stop talking such nonsense!*
drivel, garbage (informal), **inanity, rot, rubbish** (Britain), **waffle** (Britain; informal)

normal

adjective usual and ordinary
» *A normal commute to school takes 20 minutes.*
average, conventional, habitual, ordinary, regular, routine, standard, typical, usual
antonym: **unusual**

nosy

adjective trying to find out about other people's business
» *Our nosy neighbor is always watching us through the curtains.*
curious, eavesdropping, inquisitive, prying

note 1

noun a short letter » *I wrote a note asking him to come over.*
communication (formal), **letter, memo, memorandum, message, reminder, epistle, missive** (old-fashioned)

note 2

noun a written record that helps you remember something
» *The secretary made a note of the rescheduled meeting.*
account, jotting, record, register

*The secretary made a **note** of the rescheduled meeting.*

note 3

noun an atmosphere, feeling, or quality » *I detected a note of envy in Reg's voice when he talked about his cousin's designer shoes.*
hint, tone, touch, trace

note 4

verb to become aware of or mention a fact » *Paul noted that the rain had stopped and went outside.*
mention, notice, observe (formal), **perceive, register, remark, see**

notice 1

verb to become aware of something » *I noticed that Billy was the only person who wasn't laughing.*
detect, discern, note, observe, perceive, see, spot

notice 2

noun a written announcement
» *The students looked at the notice on the board.*
advertisement, bill, poster, sign

*The students looked at the **notice** on the board.*

notice 3

noun warning that something is going to happen » *She was transferred to another group without notice.*
advance warning, intimation, notification, warning

noticeable

adjective obvious and easy to see » *There has been a noticeable improvement in Sam's piano playing since he started practicing.*
conspicuous, evident, obvious, perceptible, unmistakable, manifest, salient

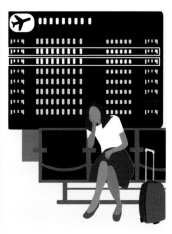

*The airport display board **notified** the passengers of the delay.*

notify

verb to inform someone officially of something
» *The airport display board notified the passengers of the delay.*
advise (formal), **inform, tell, warn**

notorious

adjective well-known for something bad » *The district was notorious for crime.*
disreputable, infamous, scandalous

now

adverb at the present time or moment » *I need to see Gary now, before he leaves.*
at once, currently, immediately, nowadays, pronto (informal), **right away, without delay**

nuisance

noun someone or something that is annoying » *Don was a nuisance, always teasing her.*
annoyance, bother, hassle (informal), **inconvenience, irritation, pain** (informal), **pest, plague, vexation**

*Don was a **nuisance**, always teasing her.*

numb 1

adjective unable to feel anything » *My leg went numb after I sat on it too long.*
dead, frozen, insensitive, paralyzed, benumbed, insensible

numb 2

verb to make you unable to feel anything » *The cold numbed my fingers, and I wished I was wearing gloves.*
dull, freeze, paralyze, stun, benumb, deaden, immobilize

number 1

noun a word or symbol used for counting » *Pick a number between one and ten.*
digit, figure, numeral, character, integer

number 2

noun a quantity of things or people » *A large number of people attended the carnival.*
collection, crowd, horde, multitude

*A large **number** of people attended the carnival.*

numerous

adjective existing or happening in large numbers » *We've met before on numerous occasions.*
countless, lots of, many, multiple, several, untold

Oo

oaf
noun a clumsy or aggressive person » *My brother can be such an oaf, always knocking things over.*
brute, hulk, lout, slouch

oath
noun a formal promise » *When you join the our club, you have to take an oath.*
pledge, promise, vow

obedient
adjective tending to do what you are told » *The horse was calm and obedient—perfect for young riders.*
law-abiding, submissive, subservient, amenable, compliant
antonym: **disobedient**

obey
verb to do what you are told » *Everyone should obey the law.*
abide by, adhere to, comply with, follow, observe
antonym: **disobey**

object ①
noun anything solid and nonliving » *My dog likes to chew on all kinds of objects.*
article, thing

My dog likes to chew on all kinds of objects.

object ②
noun an aim or purpose » *The object of the exercise is to raise money for the charity.*
aim, goal, idea, intention, objective, purpose

object ③
verb to express disapproval » *Al objected to seeing the movie because it was too long.*
oppose, protest, challenge, debate
antonym: **approve**

objection
noun disapproval of something » *Despite objections from her father, Jackie wore shorts and athletic shoes.*
opposition, protest
antonym: **support**

obligatory
adjective required by a rule or law » *He said that attendance was obligatory—no one was allowed to miss the class.*
compulsory, forced, mandatory, required, requisite

obscure ①
verb to make something difficult to see
▶▶ SEE RIGHT

obscure ②
adjective known by only a few people » *We went to an obscure restaurant in a side street, away from the crowds.*
little-known, unknown
antonym: **famous**

obscure ③
adjective difficult to understand » *The author used such obscure language in his book, Ciara needed to look up some of the words in a dictionary to understand them.*
arcane, cryptic, opaque, enigmatic, esoteric
antonym: **simple**

observant
adjective good at noticing things » *The artist was very observant and captured every detail of the flowers in his painting.*
attentive, perceptive, vigilant, watchful, eagle-eyed, sharp-eyed

The artist was very observant and captured every detail of the flowers in his painting.

observe ①
verb to watch something carefully » *The zoologists spent years observing the behavior of chimpanzees.*
monitor, scrutinize, study, survey, view, watch

observe ②
verb to notice something » *The teacher took the class for a walk in the woods and asked them to write down what wildlife they observed.*
discover, note, notice, see, spot, witness

observe ③
verb to make a comment about something » *"You've had your hair cut," Dad observed.*
comment, mention, remark, say, state

obsession
noun a compulsion to think about something » *Wayne had always had an obsession with trains.*
complex, fixation, mania, preoccupation, thing (informal)

obstacle
noun something that makes it difficult to go forward » *The main obstacle to cleaning my bedroom is the broken vacuum cleaner.*
barrier, difficulty, hindrance, hurdle, impediment, obstruction, bar, stumbling block

obstinate
adjective unwilling to change your mind » *He is obstinate and will not give up.*
dogged, headstrong, inflexible, intractable, stubborn, wilful, intransigent, recalcitrant
antonym: **flexible**

obstruct
verb to block a road or path » *The fallen tree obstructed the road.*
bar, block, choke, clog

The fallen tree obstructed the road.

*My older sister **obtained** an award for her ballet performance.*

obtain
verb to get something
» *My older sister obtained an award for her ballet performance.*
acquire, get, get hold of, get your hands on (informal), **procure** (formal), **secure** (formal)

obvious
adjective easy to see or understand » *It was obvious that Jessica was trying to impress the teacher because she was always the first to put up her hand when a volunteer was asked for.*
apparent, blatant, clear, evident, overt, palpable, plain, self-evident, conspicuous, manifest, patent

occasion ①
noun an important event
» *The launch of a ship is a grand occasion.*
affair, event

occasion ②
noun an opportunity to do something
» *The family meal was the perfect occasion for telling everyone about his travel plans.*
chance, opportunity, time

occasional
adjective happening sometimes » *We look forward to our occasional trips to the beach, they are always a lot of fun!*
intermittent, episodic, periodic, sporadic
antonym: **frequent**

occur ①
verb to happen or exist
» *Thunderstorms often occur in late summer.*
appear, arise, be present, exist, happen, take place

occur ②
verb to come into your mind
» *It didn't occur to me to check the calendar and I turned up on the wrong day.*
cross your mind, dawn on, strike

odd
adjective strange or unusual
» *He looked odd, wearing sunglasses at night.*
bizarre, curious, funny, peculiar, offbeat, singular (formal), **strange, weird**
antonym: **ordinary**

offend
verb to upset or embarrass someone » *I didn't mean to offend you when I commented on your hat.*
disrespect, insult, outrage
antonym: **please**

offensive
adjective rude and upsetting
» *Some people found the words of the song offensive.*
abusive, insulting, objectionable

*Catherine **offered** us one of the cupcakes she'd baked.*

offer ①
verb to make something available for someone to take
» *Catherine offered us one of the cupcakes she'd baked.*
give, hold out, make available, propose, put forward, suggest, tender, extend, proffer, submit

offer ②
noun something that someone offers you » *Sue had refused several job offers because they were too far away.*
proposal, proposition

cloud
*The sun was **clouded** with fog.*

conceal
*They heard birds **concealed** in the trees.*

cloak
*The lake was **cloaked** in fog.*

shroud
*The boat was **shrouded** in mist.*

hide
*The lake was partly **hidden** by trees.*

mask
*There were many leaves **masking** the view of the sun.*

screened
*The trees **screened** the lake.*

obscure
① *verb* to make something difficult to see
» *The trees **obscured** their view of the lake.*

a b c d e f g h i j k l m n o p q r s t u v w x y z

151

old

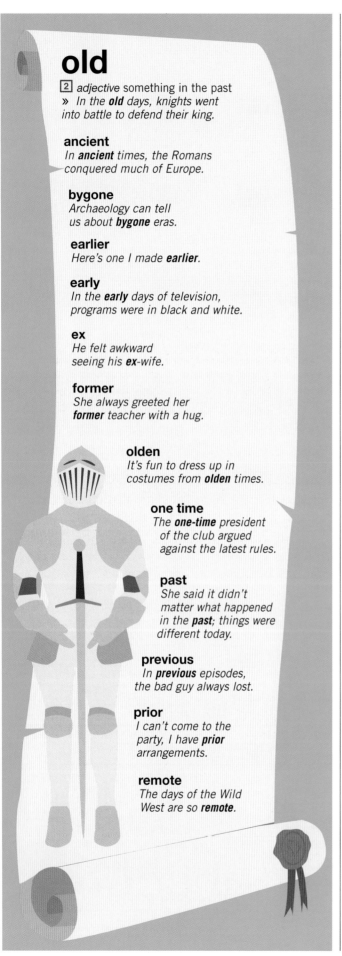

[2] *adjective* something in the past
» *In the* **old** *days, knights went into battle to defend their king.*

ancient
In **ancient** *times, the Romans conquered much of Europe.*

bygone
Archaeology can tell us about **bygone** *eras.*

earlier
Here's one I made **earlier.**

early
In the **early** *days of television, programs were in black and white.*

ex
He felt awkward seeing his **ex**-wife.

former
She always greeted her **former** *teacher with a hug.*

olden
It's fun to dress up in costumes from **olden** *times.*

one time
The **one-time** *president of the club argued against the latest rules.*

past
She said it didn't matter what happened in the **past**; *things were different today.*

previous
In **previous** *episodes, the bad guy always lost.*

prior
I can't come to the party, I have **prior** *arrangements.*

remote
The days of the Wild West are so **remote.**

official [1]
adjective approved by someone in authority » *Official figures show that more people use the pool in summer than winter.*
authorized, certified, formal, licensed
antonym: **unofficial**

official [2]
noun someone in authority » *We asked an official for directions to our seats.*
executive, officer, representative, bureaucrat, functionary

often
adverb happening many times » *My parents often go to Italy on vacation.*
frequently, repeatedly

okay or OK
adjective (informal) acceptable or satisfactory » *Is it okay if I bring a friend to your party?*
acceptable, all right

old [1]
adjective having lived for a long time » *Gareth helped the old lady with her shopping.*
aged, ancient, elderly, senior
antonym: **young**

old [2]
adjective something in the past
◀◀ SEE LEFT

old-fashioned
adjective no longer fashionable » *Grandma has an old-fashioned record player.*
antiquated, archaic, dated, obsolete, outdated, outmoded, out of date, passé, behind the times, old-time, vintage
antonym: **fashionable**

Grandma has an **old-fashioned** *record player.*

omen
noun a sign of what will happen » *There is a proverb that says a black cat crossing your path is an omen of very bad luck.*
sign, warning, auspice, foreboding

ominous
adjective suggesting that something bad will happen » *There was an ominous silence in the store after Tom broke the expensive vase.*
sinister, threatening, inauspicious, menacing, portentous

omit
verb to not include something » *Omit the ham to make the recipe suitable for vegetarians.*
exclude, leave out, overlook, skip

only [1]
adverb involving one person or thing » *Only Keith knows whether or not he'll be well enough to play.*
just, merely, purely, simply, solely

only [2]
adjective having no other examples » *The only tree in the field is an oak.*
one, sole

The **only** *tree in the field is an oak.*

open [1]
verb to cause something not to be closed » *Mom opened the door to let us in.*
uncover, undo, unlock, unfasten, unseal
antonym: **shut**

*I left an **open** box of chocolates on the table and my sister ate them.*

open [2]

adjective not closed » *I left an open box of chocolates on the table and my sister ate them.*
ajar, uncovered, undone, unlocked, unfastened, unsealed
antonym: **shut**

open [3]

adjective not trying to deceive someone » *Arthur had always been open with his mother and had no secrets from her.*
candid, frank, honest

opening [1]

adjective coming first » *We have tickets for the opening game of the season.*
first, inaugural, initial, introductory

opening [2]

noun the first part of something » *Lots of people went to the opening of the store.*
beginning, commencement (formal), **start**
antonym: **conclusion**

*Lots of people went to the **opening** of the store.*

opening [3]

noun a hole or gap » *A fox came into our yard through a narrow opening in the fence.*
chink, cleft, crack, gap, hole, slot, space, vent, aperture, fissure, orifice

opinion

noun a belief or view » *Please tell me what you think about my book, I value your opinion.*
assessment, belief, estimation, judgment, point of view, view, viewpoint

oppose

verb to disagree with something » *The workers opposed the proposed pay cut.*
fight against, resist, speak out against, take a stand against, take issue with
antonym: **support**

*The workers **opposed** the proposed pay cut.*

opposite [1]

adjective completely different from something » *We had opposite views—she wanted to go out and I wanted to stay home.*
conflicting, contrary, contrasting, opposed, reverse, antithetical, diametrically opposed

*Hot is the **opposite** of cold.*

opposite [2]

noun a completely different person or thing » *Hot is the opposite of cold.*
antithesis (formal), **contrary, converse, counter, negative, reverse, counterpoint, inverse**

opposition

noun disagreement about something » *Much of the opposition to the school's plan for a new cafeteria came from the pupils.*
disapproval, hostility, resistance
antonym: **support**

oppressed

adjective treated cruelly or unfairly » *The actor felt oppressed by the film studio's neverending demands.*
abused, downtrodden, enslaved, tyrannized

oppression

noun cruel or unfair treatment » *The people's fight against oppression became a famous story of bravery.*
persecution, tyranny, subjection, subjugation

optimistic

adjective hopeful about the future » *David woke in an optimistic mood—it was going to be a good day.*
buoyant, confident, hopeful, positive, sanguine
antonym: **pessimistic**

oral

adjective spoken rather than written » *Marie did well in her French oral test.*
spoken, verbal

orange

noun or adjective
Shades of orange:
amber, apricot, carrot, ocher, peach, tangerine

ordeal

noun a difficult and unpleasant experience » *Putting up the tent in the rain was an ordeal.*
hardship, nightmare, torture, trial, tribulation (formal)

order [1]

noun a command by someone in authority » *The crew must follow the orders of the captain.*
command, decree, dictate, directive, instruction

order [2]

noun a well-organized situation » *The kitchen was a mess—it took hours to restore order.*
harmony, regularity, symmetry
antonym: **disorder**

order [3]

verb to tell someone to do something » *The policeman ordered the driver to stop.*
command, decree, direct, instruct, ordain
antonym: **forbid**

orderly

adjective well-organized or well-arranged » *The vehicles were parked in orderly rows.*
neat, regular, tidy
antonym: **disorderly**

*The vehicles were parked in **orderly** rows.*

a b c d e f g h i j k l m n o p q r s t u v w x y z

153

A B C D E F G H I J K L M N O P Q R S T U V W X Y Z

ordinary

adjective not special or different » *Fred lived in an ordinary house in the suburbs.*
conventional, normal, regular, routine, standard, usual, run-of-the-mill, unexceptional, unremarkable
antonym: **special**

organization [1]

noun a group or business » *My mother volunteers at many charitable organizations, and is well known in the community.*
association, body, company, confederation, group, institution, outfit (informal)

organization [2]

noun the planning and arranging of something » *Emma was involved in the organization of the party.*
organizing, planning, structuring

organize

verb to plan and arrange something » *Organizing a concert takes a lot of time and effort.*
arrange, establish, plan, set up

origin [1]

noun the beginning or cause of something » *The origins of television date back to the 1920s.*
derivation, root, source, cradle, spring

origin [2]

noun someone's family background » *Elsa was of Swedish origin.*
ancestry, descent, extraction, lineage, stock

original [1]

adjective being the first example of something » *The original owner of our house lived in it all his life.*
first, initial

original [2]

adjective imaginative and smart » *Adam had a wonderfully original idea for the school play—no one had ever seen anything like it before.*
fresh, new, novel, innovative, imaginative
antonym: **unoriginal**

ornament

noun an object that you display » *The shelves were crammed with ornaments.*
adornment, bauble, decoration, knick-knack, trinket

ostentatious

adjective intended to impress people with appearances » *You couldn't miss his ostentatious car—it's large and shiny gold!*
extravagant, flamboyant, flashy, grandiose, pretentious, showy

*You couldn't miss his **ostentatious** car—it's large and shiny gold!*

OUTSTANDING

[1] *adjective* extremely good » *Natalie is an **outstanding** tennis player.*

brilliant · superb · excellent · great · exceptional · first-rate · first-class

outbreak

noun a sudden occurrence of something » *An outbreak of influenza led to the school being closed for a few days.*
eruption, explosion

outdo

verb to do something better than another person » *She was very competitive and always tried to outdo her sister.*
go one better than, outshine, surpass, top, best, eclipse

outline 1

verb to describe something in a general way » *The mayor outlined his plans to clean up the city.*
sketch, summarize, delineate

outline 2

noun a general description of something » *Peter gave an outline of his presentation to the teacher for review.*
rundown (informal), **summary, synopsis,** abstract, brief

outline 3

noun the shape of something » *Helena traced around the outline of the rabbit.*
contours, figure, form, shape, silhouette

Helena traced around the outline of the rabbit.

outlook 1

noun your general attitude toward life » *I adopted a positive outlook on life.*
attitude, perspective, view

outlook 2

noun the future prospects of something » *The weather outlook for our vacation next week looks promising.*
future, prospects

out of date

adjective no longer useful » *The information on last week's chart is out of date.*
antiquated, archaic, obsolete, old-fashioned, outdated, outmoded
antonym: **modern**

outside 1

noun the outer part of something » *She stuck leaves on the outside of the glass to decorate it.*
exterior, facade, face, surface
antonym: **inside**

She stuck leaves on the outside of the glass to decorate it.

outside 2

adjective not inside » *We had to use outside showers at the campsite.*
exterior, external, outdoor, outer, outward, surface
antonym: **inside**

outskirts

plural noun the edges of an area » *We live in the outskirts of the city, far from downtown.*
edge, perimeter, periphery, environs

outstanding 1

adjective extremely good
◀◀ SEE LEFT

outstanding 2

adjective still owed » *I have an outstanding debt to my mom, but I'm paying it off slowly.*
due, overdue, owing, payable, unpaid

over

adjective completely finished » *I am glad my finals are finally over.*
at an end, complete, done, finished, gone, past, up

overcome

verb to manage to deal with something » *Molly had overcome her fear of flying and happily boarded the plane.*
conquer, get the better of, master, surmount, triumph over, vanquish (literary)

overlook

verb to ignore or fail to notice something » *Mom overlooked the road sign and missed the turning.*
disregard, forget, ignore, miss, neglect, turn a blind eye to

overrule

verb to reject a decision officially » *The referee's decision was overruled.*
overturn, reverse, repeal, override

oversee

verb to make sure a job is done correctly » *The teacher oversaw the class experiment.*
be in charge of, coordinate, direct, manage, preside, supervise

The teacher oversaw the class experiment.

overthrow

verb to remove someone from power by force » *The government was overthrown in a military coup.*
bring down, depose, oust, topple

Fred's fast ball easily overturned the pins.

overturn 1

verb to knock something over » *Fred's fast ball easily overturned the pins.*
capsize, knock down, knock over, tip over, topple, upset, upend, upturn

overturn 2

verb to reject a decision officially » *The parent teacher association voted to overturn the principal's decision.*
overrule, reverse, countermand, override

overweight

adjective too fat, and therefore unhealthy » *Being overweight increases your risk of health problems.*
fat, heavy, obese, stout, plump, rotund

own 1

adjective belonging to a particular person or thing » *Use your own pencils and stop taking mine!*
personal, private

own 2

verb to have something that belongs to you » *My aunt owns the local store.*
have, keep, possess

own 3 : on your own

adverb without other people » *I work best on my own with no one to disturb me.*
alone, by yourself, independently, unaided

owner

noun the person to whom something belongs » *I tried to find the owner of the lost dog.*
possessor, proprietor

a b c d e f g h i j k l m n o p q r s t u v w x y z

Pp

pacify
verb to calm down someone who is angry » *She shrieked again, refusing to be pacified.*
appease, calm, mollify, placate, soothe, assuage, propitiate

pain ①
noun an unpleasant feeling of physical hurt » *I felt a sharp pain in my neck.*
ache, discomfort, irritation, soreness, trouble, twinge

*I felt a sharp **pain** in my neck.*

pain ②
noun a feeling of deep unhappiness » *He felt the pain of rejection when he wasn't picked for the team.*
agony, anguish, distress, grief, misery

painful ①
adjective causing emotional pain » *Driving past our old home brings back painful memories.*
distressing, grievous, saddening, unpleasant

painful ②
adjective causing physical pain » *She fell off her bike, taking a painful hit to the knee.*
aching, excruciating, sore, tender

pale
adjective quite white or without much color » *Migrating birds filled the pale, misty sky.*
ashen, colorless, faded, sallow, wan, white

panic ①
noun a very strong feeling of fear or anxiety » *The power cut caused panic among shoppers, who were plunged into darkness.*
alarm, dismay, fear, fright, hysteria, terror

panic ②
verb to become afraid or anxious » *The walkers panicked when the cows began to charge.*
become hysterical, go to pieces, lose your nerve

*The walkers **panicked** when the cows began to charge.*

parade
noun a line of people moving as a display » *A military parade marched through the streets.*
cavalcade, march, pageant, procession, train

paralyze
verb to make someone lose feeling and movement » *She was paralyzed with fear at the sight of the spider.*
cripple, disable

parent
noun your father or your mother » *I told my parents that I was going out.*
father, folks, mother

parody
noun an amusing imitation of someone else's style » *Our new play is a parody of a well-known movie.*
imitation, satire, spoof (informal), **takeoff** (informal), lampoon, skit

part ① : take part in
verb to do something with other people » *Thousands took part in this year's marathon.*
be instrumental in, be involved in, have a hand in, join in, participate in, play a part in

*Thousands **took part in** this year's marathon.*

part ②
noun a person's involvement in something » *He tried to conceal his part in the accident.*
capacity, duty, function, involvement, role

pass
① *verb* to exceed or go past something » *Brandon gave a triumphant wave as he **passed** the finish line.*

go beyond
*Wright's speed that day **went beyond** any of his past records.*

outdo
*Erikson **outdid** Wright.*

part ③
noun a piece or section of something » *I like that part of town.*
bit, fraction, fragment, piece, portion, section

participate
verb to take part in an activity » *Everyone participates in the school quiz.*
be involved in, engage in, enter into, join in, take part

particular ①
adjective relating to only one thing or person » *That particular place is dangerous.*
distinct, exact, express, peculiar, precise, specific

particular ②
adjective especially great or intense » *He took particular care to wash the back of his neck, which was very dirty.*
exceptional, marked, notable, singular, special, uncommon, especial, noteworthy

particular ③
adjective not easily satisfied » *Ted was particular about the colors he used when decorating the room.*
choosy (informal), **exacting, fastidious, fussy, meticulous**

partly
adverb to some extent, but not completely » *This is partly my fault.*
in part (formal), **in some measure** (formal), **partially, to some degree, to some extent**

partner ①
noun either member of a couple in a relationship » *My uncle is very happy with his new partner.*
husband, mate, spouse, wife

partner ②
noun the person someone is doing something with » *I have a new tennis partner.*
companion, teammate

party ①
noun an enjoyable social event » *I like to have a party for my birthday every year.*
bash, celebration, event, function, gathering, get-together (informal), **reception, shindig** (informal)

*I like to have a **party** for my birthday every year.*

party ②
noun an organization for people with the same political beliefs » *Ray joined the party in order to meet like-minded people.*
alliance, clique, coalition, faction, grouping

party ③
noun a group who are doing something together » *The landing party crossed the water to the research station.*
band, crew, gang, squad, team, unit

*The landing **party** crossed the water to the research station.*

pass ①
verb to exceed or go past something
▼ SEE BELOW

pass ②
verb to be successful in a test » *Wendy has just passed her driving proficiency test.*
get through, graduate, qualify, succeed
antonym: **fail**

pass ③
noun a document that allows you to go somewhere » *You'll need your pass to get into the building.*
identification, passport, ticket

passage ①
noun a narrow, empty space that connects places » *He cleared a passage for himself through the crammed streets.*
channel, course, path, road, route, way

passage ②
noun a narrow, built space that connects one place with another » *The passage leads to the courtyard of the old building.*
aisle, corridor, hall, lobby

*The **passage** leads to the courtyard of the old building.*

passage ③
noun a section of a book or piece of music » *My flute teacher makes this difficult passage look easy.*
excerpt, extract, quotation, section

a b c d e f g h i j k l m n o p q r s t u v w x y z

exceed
*Blake came in seventh, **exceeding** his past performance.*

overtake
*Khan **overtook** Blake at the last moment.*

surpass
*Booth **surpassed** his personal best.*

outstrip
*Abraham tried hard to **outstrip** Booth.*

passing
adjective lasting only for a short time » *She hoped her son's pink hair was a passing phase.*
fleeting, momentary, short-lived, transitory

passion
noun any strong emotion » *His voice trembled with passion as he spoke of her.*
emotion, excitement, fire, intensity, warmth, zeal

passionate
adjective expressing very strong feelings about something » *I'm passionate about art— I see every exhibition.*
ardent, emotional, heartfelt, impassioned, intense, strong

passive
adjective submissive or not playing an active part » *His passive attitude made it easier for me to take charge.*
docile, receptive, resigned, submissive, acquiescent, compliant, inactive, quiescent

past ① : the past
noun the period of time before the present » *We would like to put the past behind us.*
antiquity, days gone by, former times, long ago

past ②
adjective happening or existing before the present » *We have wonderful pictures of past generations of our family.*
ancient, bygone, former, olden, previous, erstwhile, onetime
antonym: **future**

*We have wonderful pictures of **past** generations of our family.*

past ③
preposition located on the other side of somewhere » *My house is just past the store on the right.*
beyond, by, over

pastime
noun a hobby or something done for pleasure » *My favorite pastime is reading.*
activity, diversion, hobby, recreation

*My favorite **pastime** is reading.*

path ①
noun a strip of ground for people to walk on » *We followed the path along the clifftops.*
footpath, pathway, towpath, track, trail, way

path ②
noun the space ahead of someone as they move along » *A group of reporters stood in the actor's path.*
course, direction, passage, route, way

pathetic ①
adjective causing someone to feel pity » *The shivering dog looked quite pathetic.*
heartbreaking, sad, pitiable, plaintive

pathetic ②
adjective very poor or unsuccessful » *Her excuse for not coming to the party due to homework was pathetic.*
feeble, lamentable, pitiful, poor, sorry

patience
noun the ability to stay calm in a difficult situation » *Dealing with four tired, hungry children required all his patience.*
calmness, composure, cool (slang), restraint, tolerance, equanimity, forbearance, imperturbability

patient ①
adjective staying calm in a difficult situation » *Please be patient— we are very busy today.*
calm, composed, long-suffering, philosophical, serene
antonym: **impatient**

patient ②
noun a person receiving medical treatment » *She enjoyed the company of other patients during her stay in the hospital.*
case, convalescent, sick person, sufferer

pattern ①
noun a decorative design of repeated shapes » *The cushions have a pattern of colorful stripes.*
design, motif

*The cushions have a **pattern** of colorful stripes.*

pattern ②
noun a diagram or shape used as a guide for making something » *I can knit, but only if I follow a pattern.*
design, diagram, plan, stencil, template

pause ①
verb to stop doing something for a short time » *On leaving, Mel paused at the door to say goodbye again.*
break, delay, halt, rest, take a break, wait

pause ②
noun a short period when activity stops » *There was a pause in conversation while the waiter set down two plates.*
break, gap, halt, interruption, interval, rest, stoppage, hiatus

pay ①
verb to give money to someone to settle a debt » *You can pay with cash or a card.*
compensate, honor, settle, recompense, reimburse, remunerate

*You can **pay** with cash or a card.*

pay ②
verb to give someone a benefit » *It pays to be honest.*
be advantageous, be worthwhile

pay ③
noun money paid to someone for work done » *The factory workers went on strike over pay and conditions.*
earnings, fee, income, payment, salary, wages, emolument, recompense, reimbursement, remuneration, stipend

payment
noun an amount of money that is paid to someone » *Mom made the initial payment for my new computer over the telephone.*
advance, deposit, instalment, premium, remittance

peace [1]
noun a state of undisturbed calm and quiet » *Hanna left me in peace to finish my book.*
calm, quiet, silence, stillness, tranquillity, quietude, repose

peace [2]
noun freedom from war » *The government is trying to establish peace in the region.*
armistice, cessation of hostilities, truce
antonym: **war**

peaceful
adjective quiet and calm » *The house was peaceful once the children had left for school.*
calm, placid, quiet, serene, still, tranquil

peak [1]
noun the point at which something is at its greatest or best » *Madison was at the peak of her career as a golfer when she won the gold medal.*
climax, culmination, high point, zenith, acme, apogee,

peak [2]
noun the pointed top of a mountain » *We flew over snow-covered peaks.*
brow, crest, height, pinnacle, summit, top, apex

*We flew over snow-covered **peaks**.*

peak [3]
verb to reach the highest point or greatest level » *The band's fame peaked some years ago.*
be at its height, climax, come to a head, culminate, reach its highest point

peculiar [1]
adjective strange and perhaps unpleasant » *Lee has a peculiar sense of humor.*
bizarre, curious, funny, odd, strange, unique, weird

peculiar [2]
adjective associated with one particular person or thing » *My uncle has his own peculiar way of doing things.*
distinctive, distinguishing, individual, personal, special, unique, idiosyncratic

peek [1]
verb to have a quick look at something » *The squirrel peeked at me through a hole in the tree trunk.*
catch a glimpse, glance, peep, sneak a look

*The squirrel **peeked** at me through a hole in the tree trunk.*

peek [2]
noun a quick look at something » *John took a peek at the presents hidden in the drawer.*
glance, glimpse, look, peep

pent-up
adjective held back for a long time without release » *She had a lot of pent-up anger, which suddenly erupted.*
inhibited, repressed, suppressed

people [1]
plural noun men, women, and children » *Hundreds of people visit the palace every day.*
folk, human beings, humanity, humans, mankind

people [2]
plural noun all the men, women, and children of a particular place » *It's a triumph for the American people.*
citizens, inhabitants, population, public

perceptive
adjective good at noticing or realizing things » *I was impressed by her perceptive account of the poet's life.*
acute, astute, aware, penetrating, sharp, insightful, percipient, perspicacious

perfect [1]
adjective of the highest standard and without fault » *Paolo's English was perfect.*
expert, faultless, flawless, masterly, polished, skilled
antonym: **imperfect**

perfect [2]
adjective complete or absolute » *You have a perfect right to say so, even though I disagree.*
absolute, complete, consummate, sheer, unmitigated, utter

perfect [3]
verb to make something as good as it can be » *She perfected her back flip before the competition.*
hone, improve, polish, refine

*She **perfected** her back flip before the competition.*

perform [1]
verb to carry out a task or action » *The scouts who had performed acts of bravery were awarded medals.*
carry out, complete, do, execute, fulfill

perform [2]
verb to act, dance, or play music in public » *This year, our students are performing a musical.*
act, do, play, present, put on, stage

*This year, our students are **performing** a musical.*

perhaps
adverb maybe » *Perhaps you're right.*
conceivably, it could be, maybe, possibly

period
noun a particular length of time » *Mary will be away for a period of a few months, so she has a lot to organize.*
interval, spell, stretch, term, time, while

permanent
adjective lasting forever or present all the time » *The farmer built a permanent fence to stop the sheep from escaping.*
abiding, constant, enduring, eternal, lasting, perpetual, immutable, imperishable, steadfast
antonym: **temporary**

permission
noun authorization to do something » *I asked permission to leave the table.*
approval, assent, authorization, consent, go-ahead, license
antonym: **ban**

a b c d e f g h i j k l m n o p q r s t u v w x y z

A B C D E F G H I J K L M N O P Q R S T U V W X Y Z

permit [1]

verb to allow something or make it possible » *The guards permitted me to take photographs in the museum when I explained they were for a school project.*
allow, authorize, enable, give the green light to, grant, sanction
antonym: **ban**

permit [2]

noun an official document allowing someone to do something » *Mom needed a parking permit to use that parking ramp.*
authorization, license, pass, passport, permission, warrant

persecute

verb to treat someone with continual cruelty and unfairness » *As we trudged through the swamp, we were persecuted by mosquitoes.*
hound, ill-treat, oppress, pick on, torment, torture

person

noun a man, woman, or child » *The amount of sleep we need varies from person to person.*
human, human being, individual, living soul, soul

personal

adjective belonging to a particular person or thing » *Jake put his personal belongings into a locker for safekeeping.*
individual, own, particular, peculiar, private, special

personality [1]

noun a person's character and nature » *Shreya has such a kind, friendly personality.*
character, identity, individuality, makeup, nature, psyche

personality [2]

noun a famous person in entertainment or sports » *A well-known television personality came to open our new gymnasium.*
big name, celebrity, famous name, household name, star

persuade

verb to make someone do something by reason or charm » *Cy persuaded his mother to let him stay up late.*
bring around (informal)**, coax, entice, induce, sway, talk into, win over, impel**

persuasive

adjective convincing » *Leah gave a persuasive argument against playing computer games.*
compelling, conclusive, effective, plausible, powerful, winning, cogent, incontrovertible
antonym: **unconvincing**

pessimistic

adjective believing that bad things will happen » *He has a pessimistic view of life.*
despondent, gloomy, glum, hopeless
antonym: **optimistic**

pest [1]

noun an insect or animal that damages crops or livestock » *The farmer was dismayed to see that half of the crop had been lost to pests.*
blight, scourge

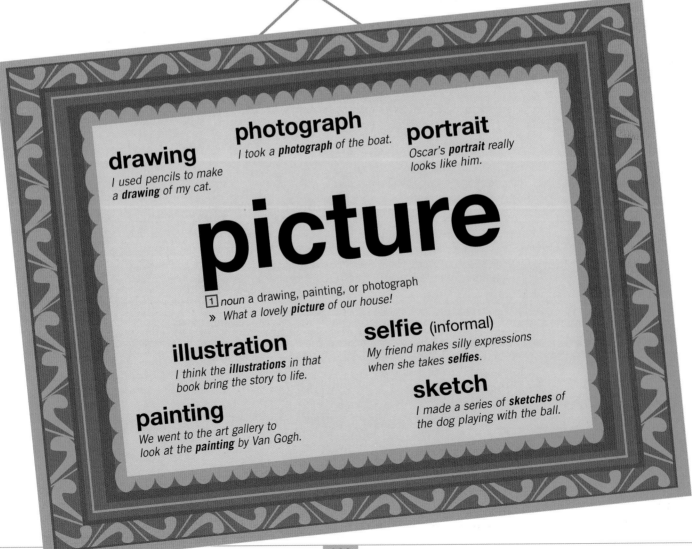

drawing
I used pencils to make a **drawing** of my cat.

photograph
I took a **photograph** of the boat.

portrait
Oscar's **portrait** really looks like him.

picture

[1] *noun* a drawing, painting, or photograph » *What a lovely **picture** of our house!*

illustration
I think the **illustrations** in that book bring the story to life.

selfie (informal)
My friend makes silly expressions when she takes **selfies**.

painting
We went to the art gallery to look at the **painting** by Van Gogh.

sketch
I made a series of **sketches** of the dog playing with the ball.

My friend's little brother is a pest.

pest ②

noun an annoying person
» *My friend's little brother
is a pest.*
**bane, bore, nuisance,
pain** (informal),
pain in the neck (informal)

pester

verb to bother someone
continually » *Our father gets
annoyed when we pester him
for candy.*
**annoy, badger, bother,
bug** (informal)**, drive
someone up the wall** (slang)**,
get on someone's nerves**
(informal)**, bedevil, chivvy**

petty ①

adjective small and
unimportant
» *The competition organizers
have to abide by endless rules
and petty regulations.*
**insignificant,
measly** (informal)**, trifling,
trivial, unimportant**

petty ②

adjective selfish and
small-minded » *I think that
attitude is a bit petty.*
cheap, mean, small-minded

phone ①

noun a device that allows you
to speak to someone in another
place » *Will you please
answer the phone?*
blower (Britain; informal)**,
cellphone, mobile,
mobile phone, smartphone,
telephone**

phone ②

verb to contact a person
by phone » *Phone me when
you get home.*
blow up (slang)**, call,
contact, ring, telephone**

phony

adjective (informal) fake
and intended to deceive
» *We found out later that his
account of events was phony.*
**bogus, counterfeit, fake,
false, forged, sham,
feigned, spurious**
antonym: **genuine**

pick ①

verb to choose something
» *Mom picked the biggest,
juiciest oranges that she
could find.*
**choose, decide upon,
hand-pick, opt for, select,
settle on**

*Mom **picked** the biggest, juiciest
oranges that she could find.*

pick ②

verb to remove a flower or fruit
with your fingers » *Gary
helps his mother pick apples.*
gather, harvest, pluck

pick ③

noun the best » *Only the pick
of the school's athletes are
chosen to go to the national
championships.*
best, elite, flower, pride

pick on

verb to criticize someone
unfairly or treat them unkindly
» *Jason always picks on me if
I answer the question wrong.*
bait, tease, torment

picture ①

noun a drawing, painting,
or photograph
◄◄ **SEE LEFT**

picture ②

verb to imagine something
clearly » *Sam pictured her
with long black hair.*
**conceive of, imagine,
see, visualize, envision,
see in the mind's eye**

piece ①

noun a portion or part of
something » *He helped
himself to the biggest piece
of cake.*
**bit, chunk, fragment, part,
portion, slice**

*He helped himself to the biggest
piece of cake.*

piece ②

noun something that has been
written, created, or composed
» *Our music teacher
composed this piece
for the school choir.*
**article, composition,
creation, study, work**

piece together

verb to assemble things
or parts to make something
complete » *Archaeologists
painstakingly pieced together
the fragments of bone.*
**assemble, join, mend,
patch together, repair,
restore**

pierce

verb to make a hole in
something with a sharp
instrument » *She pierced
the potatoes with a fork so they
wouldn't explode in the oven.*
**bore, drill, lance, penetrate,
puncture**

pig

noun a farm animal kept for
meat » *The pigs wallowed
gleefully in the thick mud.*
hog, piggy (informal)**,
porker, swine**
related words:
adjective **porcine**; *male* **boar**;
female **sow**; *young* **piglet**;
collective noun **litter**;
habitation **sty**

pile ①

noun a quantity of things lying
one on top of another » *Piles
of books covered the floor.*
**heap, hoard, mound,
mountain, stack**

pile ②

noun the raised fibers of a soft
surface » *My feet sank into
the carpet's luxurious pile.*
down, fur, nap

pile ③

verb to put things one on top
of another » *He piled his
plate with sandwiches.*
heap, hoard, stack

*He **piled** his plate
with sandwiches.*

pink

noun or adjective
» *Shades of pink:*
**coral, flesh, fuchsia,
oyster pink, rose, salmon,
shell pink, shocking pink**

a b c d e f g h i j k l m n o p q r s t u v w x y z

A B C D E F G H I J K L M N O P Q R S T U V W X Y Z

*Tim carefully crawled away from the edge of the **pit**.*

pit
noun a large hole in something » *Tim carefully crawled away from the edge of the pit.*
chasm, hole, pothole

pity 1
verb to feel sorry for someone » *I pitied Austin for not being allowed out to the fun fair.*
feel for, feel sorry for, sympathize with

pity 2
noun sympathy for other people's suffering » *She saw no pity in their stony faces.*
charity, compassion, kindness, mercy, sympathy, understanding, clemency, forbearance

pity 3
noun a regrettable fact » *It's a pity we can't all have the same opportunities.*
crying shame, shame

place 1
noun any point or area » *We meet in the same place every week.*
area, location, point, position, site, spot

place 2 : take place
verb to happen » *The meeting took place on Thursday.*
come about, go on, happen, occur

place 3
verb to put something somewhere » *Chairs were placed in rows for the parents.*
deposit, locate, plant, position, put, situate

plain 1
adjective very simple in style with no decoration » *It was a plain, gray stone house.*
austere, bare, spartan, stark
antonym: **fancy**

plain 2
adjective obvious and easy to recognize or understand » *It was plain to me that we were lost.*
clear, comprehensible, distinct, evident, obvious, unmistakable

plain 3
noun a level, often treeless, extent of land » *The plain stretched as far as the horizon.*
flat, flatland, grassland, llano, lowland, mesa, plateau, prairie, savanna, steppe, tableland

*The **plain** stretched as far as the horizon.*

plan 1
noun a way thought out to do something » *We made a plan of what to do on vacation.*
method, proposal, scheme, strategy, system

plan 2
noun a detailed diagram of something » *The receptionist gave us a plan of the hotel.*
blueprint, diagram, layout, scale drawing

plan 3
verb to decide in detail what is to be done » *I always plan my birthday party months in advance.*
arrange, design, devise, draft, formulate

play 1
verb to take part in games or use toys » *Polly was playing with her teddy bear.*
amuse yourself, entertain yourself, frolic, have fun

play 2
verb to take part in a sport or game » *Alan was playing cards with his friends.*
compete, participate, take on, take part, vie with

play 3
noun a piece of drama performed on stage, radio, or television » *The school took us to see a play by Shakespeare.*
comedy, drama, pantomime, show, tragedy

plead
verb to beg someone for something » *She pleaded with her mother to let her go on the ride.*
appeal, ask, beg, beseech (literary), **implore**

pleasant 1
adjective enjoyable or attractive » *We have a pleasant garden full of flowers.*
agreeable, delightful, enjoyable, lovely, nice, pleasurable
antonym: **unpleasant**

*We have a **pleasant** garden full of flowers.*

pleasant 2
adjective friendly or charming » *The hotel staff were pleasant and helpful.*
affable, amiable, charming, friendly, likable or **likeable, nice**
antonym: **unpleasant**

please
verb to give pleasure to » *I cleaned up my bedroom to please my mother.*
amuse, charm, delight, entertain

pleased
adjective happy or satisfied » *I'm pleased my best friend is coming on vacation with us.*
contented, delighted, glad, happy, satisfied

pleasure
noun a feeling of happiness and satisfaction » *The dog takes pleasure in having its chest scratched.*
amusement, enjoyment, happiness, joy, satisfaction

*The dog takes **pleasure** in having its chest scratched.*

plentiful
adjective existing in large amounts » *We have a plentiful supply of food for our expedition.*
abundant, ample, bountiful, copious, infinite, lavish, profuse
antonym: **scarce**

plenty
noun a lot of something » *Our pet hamster has plenty of energy and loves to run in its wheel.*
enough, a great deal, heaps (informal), **lots** (informal), **plethora**

plot 1
noun a secret plan made by a group of people » *The boys made a plot to ambush their little sister.*
conspiracy, intrigue, plan, scheme, cabal, machination, stratagem

polite

1 *adjective* having good manners
» *He is always **polite** and always remembers to say thank you.*

civil
*He is **civil** to his parents except when he's tired and hungry.*

courteous
*He is **courteous** and gives up his seat on the bus.*

respectful
*He is **respectful** of his grandparents' views.*

well behaved
*He is **well behaved** in front of the teachers.*

well mannered
*He is **well mannered** and thinks of other people.*

antonym:
rude
*She is **rude** and always interrupts.*

a b c d e f g h i j k l m n o p q r s t u v w x y z

plot 2
noun the story of a novel or play » *The movie has a ludicrously complicated plot.*
narrative, scenario, story, story line

plot 3
verb to plan something secretly with others » *The students plotted to leave school early so they didn't have to play soccer in the rain.*
conspire, hatch, plan, scheme, cabal, collude, machinate

plug 1
noun a small, round object for blocking a hole
» *She pulled the plug out and the water flowed away.*
bung, cork, stopper

*She pulled the **plug** out and the water flowed away.*

plug 2
verb to block a hole with something » *The plumber worked all night to plug the leak.*
block, fill, seal

plump
adjective a bit fat » *That cat is starting to look plump.*
beefy (informal), burly, chubby, fat, stout, tubby

point 1
noun the purpose or meaning something has » *The point of wearing a coat is to be warm.*
aim, goal, intention, object, purpose

point 2
noun a quality or feature
» *Tact was never her strong point.*
attribute, characteristic, feature, quality, side, trait

point 3
noun the thin sharp end of something » *He pricked his finger on the point of a needle.*
nib, prong, tip

poison
noun a substance that can harm or kill people or animals
» *Mercury is a known poison.*
toxin, venom
related word: *adjective* **toxic**

poisonous
adjective containing something that causes death or illness
» *A few plants are poisonous.*
noxious, toxic, venomous

poke 1
verb to jab or prod someone or something » *She poked a knife into the cake to see if it was cooked.*
dig, elbow, jab, nudge, prod, stab

poke 2
noun a jab or prod » *She gave Richard a playful poke.*
dig, jab, nudge, prod

polish 1
verb to improve a skill or technique » *I need to polish my writing skills.*
brush up, improve, perfect, refine

*Every morning, he **polished** his shoes until they shined.*

polish 2
verb to make smooth and shiny by rubbing » *Every morning, he polished his shoes until they shined.*
buff, shine, wax

polish 3
noun elegance or refinement
» *The lyrics lack the polish of his later songs.*
class (informal), elegance, finesse, grace, refinement, style, politesse, suavity, urbanity

polite 1
adjective having good manners
▲ SEE ABOVE

ponder

verb to think about something deeply
» He **pondered** which course of action to take.

contemplate
He sat and **contemplated** his plans.

consider
He **considered** what was the right thing to do.

think
He **thought** about what to do next.

mull over
He **mulled over** what options to choose.

brood
He **brooded** over the meaning of life.

reflect
He **reflected** on the dream he'd had last night.

polite ☑
adjective cultivated or refined
» *Certain words are not acceptable in polite society.*
cultured, genteel, refined, sophisticated, urbane

politeness
noun the quality of being civil to someone » *She listened to him, but only out of politeness.*
civility, courtesy, decency, etiquette

pollute
verb to contaminate with something harmful
» *Heavy industry pollutes our rivers with nasty chemicals.*
contaminate, infect, poison, taint, adulterate, befoul, smirch

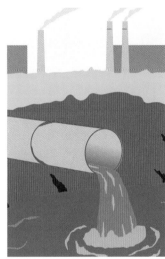

*Heavy industry **pollutes** our rivers with nasty chemicals.*

pompous
adjective behaving in a way that is too serious and self-important » *Nathan is a pompous man with a high opinion of himself.*
arrogant, grandiose, ostentatious, pretentious, puffed up, pontifical, portentous, vainglorious

ponder
verb to think about something deeply
◄◄ SEE LEFT

poor ☐
adjective having little money
» *He was poor until he took a well-paid job.*
broke (informal)**, destitute, hard up** (informal)**, impoverished, penniless, poverty-stricken**
antonym: **rich**

poor ☑
adjective of a low quality or standard » *The lead character was a poor actor.*
feeble, inferior, mediocre, second-rate, shoddy, unsatisfactory

popular ☐
adjective liked or approved of by a lot of people » *These delicious pastries are popular.*
fashionable, favorite, in demand, in favor, sought-after, well-liked
antonym: **unpopular**

popular ☑
adjective involving or intended for ordinary people » *The down-to-earth politician was hoping to win the popular vote.*
common, conventional, general, universal

portion
noun a part or amount of something » *I have spent a large portion of my life here.*
bit, chunk, helping, part, piece, segment, serving

pose ☐
verb to ask a question » *When I finally posed the question "Why?" she merely shrugged.*
ask, put, submit, propound

*When I finally **posed** the question "Why?" she merely shrugged.*

pose ☑
verb to pretend to be someone else » *Gadi posed as a singer to gain backstage access.*
impersonate, masquerade as, pass yourself off as, pretend to be

posh ☐
adjective (informal) formal, fashionable, and expensive
» *We stayed in a posh hotel.*
classy (informal)**, elegant, exclusive, fashionable, smart, stylish, up-market**

posh ☑
adjective upper-class
» *He sounded very posh on the phone.*
aristocratic, genteel, upper-class, blue-blooded, patrician (formal)
antonym: **common**

position ☐
verb to put something somewhere » *Plants were positioned on either side of our front door.*
arrange, lay out, locate, place, put

*Plants were **positioned** on either side of our front door.*

position ☑
noun the place where someone or something is » *The ship's name and position were reported to the coastguard.*
location, place, point, whereabouts

positive ☐
adjective completely sure about something » *I was positive I'd been there before.*
certain, confident, convinced, sure

positive ☑
adjective providing definite proof of the truth or identity of something » *We found positive evidence that the cabinet raider was a mouse.*
clear, clear-cut, conclusive, concrete, firm, incontrovertible, indisputable, unequivocal

positive ☒
adjective tending to emphasize what is good » *I'm hoping for a positive response.*
constructive, helpful
antonym: **negative**

possess ☐
verb to have something as a quality » *The athlete possesses both stamina and great technique.*
be blessed with, be born with, enjoy, have

possess ☑
verb to own something
» *He was said to possess a huge fortune.*
control, hold, occupy, own

possession
noun ownership of something
» *Carl had possession of the ball.*
control, custody, ownership, tenure

*Carl had **possession** of the ball.*

a b c d e f g h i j k l m n o p q r s t u v w x y z

*We packed up our **possessions** ready for moving.*

possessions

plural noun the things owned by someone » *We packed up our possessions ready for moving.*
assets, belongings, effects, estate, property, things

possibility

noun something that might be true or might happen » *Daisy cheered up at the possibility of ice cream.*
chance, hope, likelihood, odds, prospect, risk

possible ①

adjective likely to happen or able to be done » *She was grateful to her music teacher for making the concert possible.*
attainable, feasible, practicable, viable, workable
antonym: **impossible**

possible ②

adjective likely or capable of being true or correct » *It's possible there's an explanation for the delay.*
conceivable, imaginable, likely, potential

postpone

verb to put off to a later time » *The visit has been postponed until tomorrow.*
adjourn, defer, delay, put back, put off, shelve

potential ①

adjective possible but not yet actual » *Sam was looking for potential sponsors for his marathon bid.*
likely, possible, probable

potential ②

noun ability to achieve future success » *The tennis coach recognized the potential of the young player.*
ability, aptitude, capability, capacity, power, wherewithal

pour

verb to flow quickly and in large quantities » *She put her umbrella up because it was pouring.*
course, flow, gush, run, spout, stream

*She put her umbrella up because it was **pouring**.*

poverty

noun the state of being very poor » *I'm raising money for a charity that aims to tackle poverty in developing countries.*
destitution, hardship, insolvency, want, beggary, indigence, penury, privation

power ①

noun control over people and activities » *A president has great power and influence.*
ascendancy, control, dominion, sovereignty, supremacy

power ②

noun authority to do something » *The police have the power to arrest people.*
authority, authorization, licence, privilege, right

power ③

noun physical strength » *Power and bulk are vital to success in rugby.*
brawn, might, strength, vigor

powerful ①

adjective able to control people and events » *The US is one of the world's most powerful countries.*
commanding, dominant, influential

powerful ②

adjective physically strong
▶▶ **SEE RIGHT**

powerful ③

adjective having a strong effect » *It was a powerful argument, but I remained unconvinced.*
compelling, convincing, effective, forceful, persuasive, telling

powerless

adjective unable to control or influence events » *I was powerless to stop her.*
helpless, impotent, incapable

practical ①

adjective involving experience rather than theory » *The book is full of practical suggestions for healthy eating.*
applied, pragmatic, sensible

practical ②

adjective likely to be effective » *The clothes are lightweight and practical for our vacation.*
functional, sensible
antonym: **impractical**

practical ③

adjective able to deal effectively with problems » *She has the practical common sense essential in a team leader.*
accomplished, experienced, proficient, seasoned, skilled, veteran

practice ①

noun something that people do regularly » *We've been getting to know the local practices since moving to the town.*
custom, habit, method, routine, way

practice ②

noun regular training or exercise » *I need more practice to improve my skills.*
drill, exercise, preparation, rehearsal, training

practice ①

verb to do something repeatedly so as to gain skill » *Louis practices cycling for half an hour every day.*
polish, rehearse, train

*Louis **practices** cycling for half an hour every day.*

practice ②

verb to take part in the activities of a religion, craft, or custom » *Acupuncture has been practiced in China for thousands of years.*
do, follow, observe

praise ①

verb to express strong approval of someone » *The teacher praised Rob for his test results.*
admire, applaud, approve, congratulate, pay tribute to, acclaim, eulogize, extol, laud
antonym: **criticize**

praise ②

noun something said or written to show approval » *She is full of praise for her students.*
accolade, approval, commendation, congratulation, tribute, eulogy
antonym: **criticism**

precaution

noun an action intended to prevent something from happening » *When on a boat, wearing a life jacket is an essential precaution.*
insurance, preventative measure, protection, provision, safeguard

powerful

2 *adjective* physically strong

» *The weightlifter had **powerful** muscles.*

mighty

*He was as **mighty** as a giant.*

strapping

*He was a **strapping** young man.*

strong

*He was as **strong** as an ox.*

sturdy

*He had a **sturdy** build.*

vigorous

*He was young and **vigorous**.*

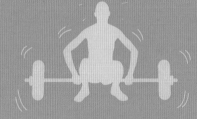

antonym: **weak**

*After his illness, he was too **weak** to lift anything.*

a b c d e f g h i j k l m n o p q r s t u v w x y z

A B C D E F G H I J K L M N O P Q R S T U V W X Y Z

*My mother keeps her **precious** ring in a small case.*

precious

adjective of great value and importance » *My mother keeps her precious ring in a small case.*
expensive, invaluable, priceless, prized, valuable
antonym: **worthless**

precise

adjective exact and accurate » *Millie gave such precise answers that she got full points.*
accurate, actual, correct, exact, particular, specific, very
antonym: **vague**

predicament

noun a difficult situation » *The decision to go will leave my aunt in a predicament.*
fix (informal), **hot water** (informal), **jam** (informal), **scrape** (informal), **tight spot**

predict

verb to say that something will happen in the future » *The judges are predicting a close contest.*
forecast, foresee, foretell, prophesy, forebode, portend, presage, soothsay

prediction

noun something that is forecast in advance » *His prediction that it would rain turned out to be true.*
forecast, prophecy

prefer

verb to like one thing more than another thing » *Does he prefer a particular kind of music?*
be partial to, favor, go for, incline toward, like better

prejudice 1

noun an unreasonable or unfair dislike or preference » *Edie complained that the company had shown prejudice against her because of her age.*
bias, partiality, preconception

prejudice 2

noun intolerance toward certain people or groups » *As outsiders, we experienced some prejudice when we first moved to the area, but that has gone now that people know us.*
bigotry, chauvinism, discrimination, racism, sexism

premonition

noun a feeling that something unpleasant is going to happen » *He had a premonition that there would be an earthquake.*
foreboding, funny feeling (informal), **omen, sign, portent, presage, presentiment**

preoccupied

adjective totally involved with something or deep in thought » *I am preoccupied with the book I'm writing.*
absorbed, engrossed, immersed, oblivious, wrapped up

present 1

adjective being at a place or event » *Dad was present when Sally received her prize.*
at hand, here, in attendance, there, to hand
antonym: **absent**

present 2

noun something given to someone » *Vicky gave me a birthday present.*
donation, gift, offering

present 3

verb to give something to someone » *The mayor presented the prizes.*
award, bestow, donate, give, grant, hand out

press 1

verb to apply force or weight to something » *Press the blue button.*
compress, crush, mash, push, squeeze

press 2

verb to try hard to persuade someone to do something » *My parents are pressing me to invite more people to my birthday party.*
beg, implore, petition, plead, pressurize, urge, entreat, exhort, importune

pretend

verb to claim or give the appearance of something untrue » *Vince pretended to be asleep, but I knew better.*
counterfeit, fake, falsify, feign, pass yourself off as

pretentious

adjective making unjustified claims of importance » *Critics thought her work and ideas were pretentious and empty.*
affected, conceited, ostentatious, pompous, snobbish, bombastic, vainglorious

pretty 1

adjective attractive in a delicate way » *The bouqet of colorful flowers looked pretty.*
attractive, beautiful, cute, lovely

*The bouquet of colorful flowers looked **pretty**.*

pretty 2

adverb (informal) quite or rather » *He spoke English pretty well.*
fairly, kind of (informal), **quite, rather**

prevent

verb to stop something from happening » *Loella was prevented from going on the amusement park ride because she wasn't tall enough.*
avert, foil, hinder, impede, stop, thwart

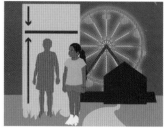

*Loella was **prevented** from going on the amusement park ride because she wasn't tall enough.*

previous

adjective happening or existing before something else » *Zack had won the competition the previous year.*
earlier, former, one-time, past, preceding, prior

price 1

noun the amount of money paid for something » *The price of milk has gone up recently.*
amount, charge, cost, fee, figure, value

price 2

verb to fix the price or value of something » *I don't know why it has been priced so high.*
cost, estimate, put a price on, value

pride 1

noun satisfaction about your achievements » *The chef took pride in the dish he'd made.*
delight, pleasure, satisfaction

pride 2

noun an excessively high opinion of yourself » *His pride made him unpopular.*
arrogance, conceit, egotism, smugness, snobbery, vanity, haughtiness, hauteur, hubris, superciliousness
antonym: **humility**

prim

adjective behaving very correctly and easily shocked by anything rude **»** *My great grandmother's generation were all very prim and proper.*

proper, prudish, puritanical, strait-laced, uptight (informal)

prime ①

adjective main or most important **»** *Our prime reason for wanting to visit Italy is to eat a lot of pasta.*

chief, leading, main, principal

prime ②

adjective of the best quality **»** *He bought a prime cut of meat for the barbecue.*

best, choice, first-rate, select, superior

primitive

adjective very simple or basic **»** *She made a primitive shelter in the back yard.*

crude, rough, rude, rudimentary, simple

*She made a **primitive** shelter in the back yard.*

principal

adjective main or most important **»** *Jay's principal concern is winning the race.*

chief, first, foremost, main, major, primary, prime

principle ①

noun a set of moral rules guiding personal conduct **»** *She resigned from her job out of principle.*

conscience, integrity, morals, scruples, sense of duty

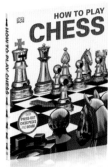

*The book explains the **principles** of chess.*

principle ②

noun a general rule or scientific law **»** *The book explains the principles of chess.*

axiom, canon, doctrine, fundamental, law, dictum, precept, verity

prison

noun a building where criminals are kept in captivity **»** *The prison had high fences and security cameras everywhere.*

can, jail, pen, penal institution, slammer (informal)

prisoner

noun someone kept in prison or captivity **»** *Prisoners are allowed out for an hour of exercise each day.*

captive, convict, hostage

private ①

adjective for few people rather than people in general **»** *We booked a private room for the party.*

exclusive, individual, personal, special

private ②

adjective taking place among a small number of people **»** *They were married in a private ceremony.*

clandestine, confidential, secret
antonym: **public**

prize ①

noun a reward given to the winner of something
▶▶ SEE RIGHT

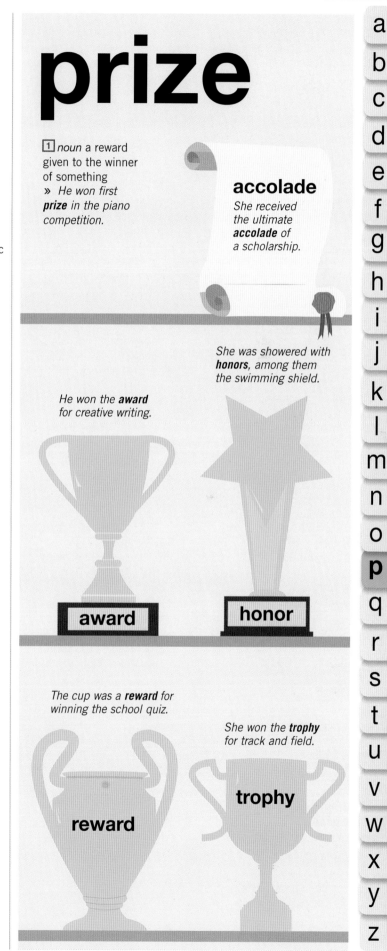

prize

① *noun* a reward given to the winner of something **»** *He won first prize in the piano competition.*

accolade
*She received the ultimate **accolade** of a scholarship.*

*She was showered with **honors**, among them the swimming shield.*

*He won the **award** for creative writing.*

award

honor

*The cup was a **reward** for winning the school quiz.*

*She won the **trophy** for track and field.*

reward

trophy

a b c d e f g h i j k l m n o p q r s t u v w x y z

promise

1 *verb* to say that you will definitely do or not do something
» *I promise I'll come back.*

give your word
I give my word I'll be here.

pledge
I pledge to return.

assure
I assure you I'll return.

vow
I vow that I will be back.

guarantee
I guarantee you'll see me soon.

prize 2
adjective of the highest quality or standard » *The farmer led his prize bull into the ring.*
award-winning, first-rate, outstanding, top

The farmer led his prize bull into the ring.

prize 3
verb to value highly » *These vases are prized by collectors.*
cherish, esteem, treasure, value

probability
noun the likelihood of something happening » *There's a probability that we'll miss the train.*
chances, likelihood, odds, prospect

probable
adjective likely to be true or to happen » *The probable cost of our vacation to the Bahamas will be high.*
apparent, feasible, likely, on the cards, plausible, credible, ostensible
antonym: **improbable**

probably
adverb in all likelihood » *The party is probably going to be in late August.*
doubtless, in all probability, likely, presumably

problem 1
noun an unsatisfactory situation causing difficulties » *The teacher asked the unruly student what the problem was.*
difficulty, predicament, quandary, trouble

Flora worked out the math problem on the board.

problem 2
noun a puzzle that needs to be solved » *Flora worked out the math problem on the board*
conundrum, puzzle, riddle

procedure
noun the correct or usual way of doing something » *He did not follow the correct procedure for booking his ticket.*
method, policy, practice, process, strategy, system

proceed 1
verb to start doing or continue to do something » *I had no idea how to proceed.*
begin, carry on, continue, get under way, go on, start

proceed 2
verb (formal) to move in a particular direction » *She proceeded along the hallway.*
advance, continue, go on, make your way, progress, travel

process 1
noun a method of doing or producing something » *The building process would take three years.*
course of action, means, method, procedure, system

process 2
verb to deal with or treat something » *Your application is being processed.*
deal with, dispose of, handle, take care of

produce 1
verb to make something » *Chocolate is produced from cocoa beans.*
construct, create, invent, make, manufacture

produce [2]
verb to bring out something so it can be seen or discussed » *To rent a car, you must produce a driving license.*
advance, bring forward, bring to light, put forward

product
noun something that is made to be sold » *All of our products are made with natural ingredients.*
commodity, goods, merchandise, produce

productive [1]
adjective producing a large number of things » *Our apple trees are very productive this year.*
fertile, fruitful, prolific, fecund, generative
antonym: **unproductive**

*Our apple trees are very **productive** this year.*

productive [2]
adjective bringing favorable results » *I hope that all this extra work will be productive.*
constructive, useful, valuable, worthwhile
antonym: **unproductive**

profession
noun a job that requires advanced education or training » *Harper was a doctor by profession.*
business, career, occupation

proficient
adjective able to do something well » *Erin is proficient in several languages.*
able, accomplished, adept, capable, competent, efficient, skilful, skilled
antonym: **incompetent**

profit [1]
noun money gained in business or trade » *The new business made a huge profit in its first year.*
earnings, proceeds, revenue, surplus, takings
antonym: **loss**

profit [2]
verb to gain or benefit from something » *We profited from the low turnout—there was a lot of leftover food.*
capitalize on, exploit, make the most of, take advantage of

program
noun a set of instructions that a computer follows to perform a task » *The architect used a computer program to draw up his plans for the house.*
app, application, software

*The architect used a computer **program** to draw up his plans for the house.*

program [1]
verb to make a plan or plot out instructions » *Diana programmed the TV to record the Saturday show.*
compile, formulate, line up, list, map out, set up

program [2]
noun a planned series of events » *The orchestra has a program of 12 concerts over the next few months.*
agenda, schedule, timetable

program [3]
noun a broadcast on radio or television » *He enjoys watching programs about space travel.*
broadcast, show

*He enjoys watching **programs** about space travel.*

progress [1]
noun improvement or development » *Lou is making progress in writing her novel.*
advance, breakthrough, headway, improvement

progress [2]
verb to become more advanced or skilful » *My litttle brother is progressing—he can count to 10 now and he knows colors.*
advance, blossom, develop, improve

prohibit
verb to forbid something or make it illegal » *Dropping litter is prohibited.*
ban, forbid, outlaw, prevent
antonym: **allow**

prominent [1]
adjective important » *A prominent scientist gave us an inspiring lecture.*
eminent, famous, important, notable, noted, renowned, well-known

*The castle stood in a **prominent** position at the top of a steep hill.*

prominent [2]
adjective very noticeable, or sticking out a long way » *The castle stood in a prominent position at the top of a steep hill.*
conspicuous, eye-catching, jutting, noticeable, obvious, pronounced, striking, blatant, salient

promise [1]
verb to say that you will definitely do or not do something
◄◄ SEE LEFT

promise [2]
verb to show signs of » *This promises to be a great book.*
hint at, indicate, show signs of, augur, bespeak, betoken

promise [3]
noun an undertaking to do or not do something » *If you make a promise, you should keep it.*
assurance, guarantee, pledge, undertaking, vow

promising
adjective seeming likely to be good or successful » *He was a promising young athlete.*
gifted, rising, talented, up-and-coming

promote [1]
verb to encourage the progress or success of something » *My parents have always promoted healthy eating.*
back, support

A B C D E F G H I J K L M N O P Q R S T U V W X Y Z

promote 2
verb to encourage the sale of a product by advertising » *She's in Europe promoting her new movie.*
advertise, plug (informal), **publicize**

promote 3
verb to raise someone to a higher rank or position » *Mom has been promoted twice in two years.*
elevate, upgrade

prompt 1
verb to make someone decide to do something » *Rising bus fares have prompted people to walk more.*
cause, induce, inspire, motivate, spur

prompt 2
verb to encourage someone to say something » *"What was that you were saying about a guided tour?" he prompted her.*
coax, remind

prompt 3
adjective done without any delay » *The road needs prompt repairs following the storm.*
immediate, instant, instantaneous, quick, rapid, swift

prompt 4
adverb exactly at the time mentioned » *The invitation specifies eight o'clock prompt.*
exactly, on the dot, precisely, promptly, sharp

Please come to Anna's party on Friday 8pm prompt

The invitation specifies eight o'clock prompt.

prone 1
adjective having a tendency to be affected by or to do something » *Lucy is prone to forgetfulness.*
disposed, given, inclined, liable, susceptible

prone 2
adjective lying flat and face downward » *She lay prone on the grass.*
face down, prostrate

*She lay **prone** on the grass.*

proof
noun evidence that confirms that something is true or exists » *At last, we had proof that rabbits were eating our vegetables.*
confirmation, evidence, testimony, verification, authentication, certification, corroboration, substantiation

proper 1
adjective correct or most suitable » *Mick decided that the proper course of action would be to say nothing.*
appropriate, apt, correct, fitting, right, suitable
antonym: **improper**

proper 2
adjective accepted or conventional » *Jess wanted a proper, white wedding.*
accepted, conventional, orthodox

property 1
noun the things that belong to someone » *Mark was protective of his personal property, and rarely let anyone borrow anything.*
assets, belongings, effects, estate, possessions

property 2
noun a characteristic or quality » *Peppermint leaves have powerful healing properties when drunk as an infusion or eaten as a herb.*
attribute, characteristic, feature, hallmark, quality, trait

proportion
noun part of an amount or group » *A small proportion of the class chose to study a second language.*
percentage, quota, segment, share

prospect
noun expectation or something anticipated » *Mia was excited by the prospect of arriving back home as she had been away for a long time.*
expectation, hope, outlook, promise

protect
verb to prevent someone or something from being harmed » *The traffic cones protected the man while he was repairing the road.*
defend, guard, safeguard, shelter, shield

*The traffic cones **protected** the man while he was repairing the road.*

*He wears plenty of layers for **protection** against the cold.*

protection
noun something that protects » *He wears plenty of layers for protection against the cold.*
barrier, buffer, cover, safeguard, shelter

protest 1
verb to disagree with someone or object to something » *Bethany protested that she was innocent.*
complain, disagree, disapprove, object, oppose, demur, expostulate, remonstrate

protest 2
noun a strong objection » *The teacher ignored their protests and sent them out for a run in the rain.*
complaint, objection, outcry

proud
adjective feeling pleasure or satisfaction » *I was proud of our players today.*
gratified by, honored, pleased

prove
verb to provide evidence that something is definitely true » *This proves that you were right all along.*
ascertain, confirm, demonstrate, establish, verify, authenticate, corroborate, evince, substantiate
antonym: **disprove**

provide

verb to make something available to someone
» *We'll provide refreshments after the game.*
contribute, equip, furnish, outfit, supply

provoke ①

verb to try to make someone angry » *I didn't want to do anything to provoke the bulldog.*
anger, annoy, enrage, goad, insult, irritate, tease

provoke ②

verb to cause an unpleasant reaction » *His sister's teasing finally provoked the little boy to hit her.*
cause, evoke, produce, prompt, rouse, set off, spark off

pry

verb to try to find out about someone else's private business » *Our neighbor is always prying into our business.*
interfere, intrude, poke your nose in (informal), **poke your nose into** (informal), **snoop** (informal)

*Our neighbor is always **prying** into our business.*

public ①

noun people in general
» *Members of the public were picked at random to appear on the TV show.*
masses, nation, people, populace, society

public ②

adjective relating to people in general » *There was a lot of public support for the new sports center.*
civic, general, popular, universal

public ③

adjective provided for everyone to use or open to anyone
» *Public swimming pools can be very busy.*
communal, community, open to the public, universal
antonym: **private**

***Public** swimming pools can be very busy.*

publicity

noun information or advertisements about an item or event » *The actor gave several interviews as part of the publicity campaign for his new movie.*
advertising, plug (informal), **promotion**

publicize

verb to advertise something or make it widely known » *The author appeared on TV to publicize her book.*
advertise, plug (informal), **promote**

publish

verb to make a piece of writing available for reading » *We publish a range of titles.*
bring out, print, put out

*He had been running so hard that he was **puffing**.*

puff

verb to breathe loudly and quickly with your mouth open
» *He had been running so hard that he was puffing.*
breathe heavily, gasp, pant, wheeze

pull ①

verb to draw an object toward you » *We saw the sights of the city from an open carriage pulled by two white horses.*
drag, draw, haul, tow, tug, yank
antonym: **push**

pull ②

noun the attraction or influence of something » *The pull of the bakery was too strong, and she went in and bought fresh bread.*
attraction, lure, magnetism

punctual

adjective arriving or leaving at the correct time » *Our first flight was punctual, so we easily caught our connection.*
in good time, on time, prompt

punish

verb to make someone suffer a penalty for some misbehavior
» *I was punished for being disrespectful, though I didn't mean to sound rude.*
discipline, penalize, rap knuckles, sentence, throw the book at

punishment

noun a penalty for a crime or offense » *The punishment must always fit the crime.*
penalty, retribution, chastening, chastisement, just deserts or **just desserts**

puny

adjective very small and weak
» *The newborn kittens were puny and helpless.*
feeble, frail, sickly, skinny, weak

pupil

noun a student taught at a school » *Our school has 500 pupils.*
scholar (South Africa), **schoolboy, schoolchild, schoolgirl, student**

pure ①

adjective clean and free from harmful substances
» *The water from the spring is pure enough to drink.*
clean, germ-free, pasteurized, spotless, sterilized, unadulterated, unblemished, uncontaminated, unpolluted, untainted
antonym: **impure**

*The water from the spring is **pure** enough to drink.*

pure ②

adjective complete and total
» *Anita won the prize through pure luck.*
absolute, complete, outright, sheer, unmitigated, utter

a b c d e f g h i j k l m n o p q r s t u v w x y z

A
B
C
D
E
F
G
H
I
J
K
L
M
N
O
P
Q
R
S
T
U
V
W
X
Y
Z

push

1 *verb* to apply force to something in order to move it » *He **pushed** his friend on the swing.*

press

*He **pressed** his hands against his friend's back to help her swing.*

ram

*He **rammed** his shoulder against the playground gate to open it.*

shove

*He **shoved** the swing so hard that she almost fell off.*

thrust

*She was **thrust** forward on the swing.*

antonym: **pull**

*She **pulled** her legs back to swing higher.*

purple

noun or *adjective*
Shades of purple:
amethyst, gentian, heather, heliotrope, indigo, lavender, lilac, magenta, mauve, mulberry, plum, puce, royal purple, violet

purpose 1

noun the reason for something » *The purpose of Flora's shopping trip was to buy a new winter coat.*
aim, function, intention, object, point, reason

purpose 2:
on purpose

adverb deliberately
» *Did you do that on purpose?*
by design, deliberately, intentionally, knowingly, purposely

push 1

verb to apply force to something in order to move it
◀◀ **SEE LEFT**

push 2

verb to persuade someone into doing something » *His mother pushed him into auditioning for a part in the play.*
encourage, persuade, press, urge

pushy

adjective (informal) unpleasantly forceful and determined
» *Our new swimming coach can be really pushy.*
aggressive, ambitious, assertive, bossy, forceful, obtrusive

put 1

verb to place something somewhere » *Angela put the photograph on her desk.*
deposit, lay, place, position, rest

put 2

verb to express something
» *I think you put that very well.*
phrase, word

put down 1

verb to criticize someone and make them appear foolish
» *My big sister is always putting me down.*
belittle, criticize, find fault with, humiliate

put down 2

verb to kill an animal that is sick or dangerous » *The dog was so sick that it had to be put down.*
destroy, euthanize, kill, put out of its misery, put to sleep

put off

verb to delay something
» *We have put off making a decision about where to go until next week.*
defer, delay, postpone, put back, put on ice, reschedule

put up with

verb to tolerate something disagreeable » *He put up with his daughter's loud music for an hour before asking her to turn it down.*
abide, bear, stand, stand for, stomach, tolerate, brook, countenance

puzzle 1

verb to perplex and confuse
» *There was something about Renata that puzzled me.*
baffle, bewilder, confuse, mystify, stump, confound, flummox, nonplus, perplex

puzzle 2

noun a game or question that requires a lot of thought to solve » *I enjoy doing crossword puzzles.*
brain-teaser (informal), **poser, problem, riddle**

*I enjoy doing crossword **puzzles**.*

Qq

qualification [1]

noun an officially certified skill » *A person needs many qualifications to become a lawyer.*
ability, accomplishment, achievement, capability

qualification [2]

noun something added to modify, limit, or restrict » *The teachers accepted the principal's changes to the school with a couple of qualifications.*
condition, exception, modification, reservation

qualify

verb to pass the tests necessary for an activity » *My mom qualified as a doctor 30 years ago.*
become licensed, gain qualifications, get certified, graduate

quality [1]

noun the measure of how good something is » *The head chef always makes sure that the food is of the highest quality.*
caliber, distinction, grade, merit, value, worth

*The head chef always makes sure that the food is of the highest **quality**.*

quality [2]

noun a characteristic of something » *His best quality is his kindness.*
aspect, characteristic, feature, mark, property, trait, attribute, peculiarity

quantity [1]

noun an amount you can measure or count » *Petra made a large quantity of cookies for the hockey players.*
amount, number, part, sum, portion, quota

quantity [2]

noun the amount of something that there is » *Our teacher likes to emphasize the importance of quality over quantity when it comes to creative writing.*
extent, measure, size, volume, bulk, expanse, magnitude

quarrel [1]

noun an angry argument » *I had a terrible quarrel with my brother.*
argument, disagreement, dispute, feud, fight, squabble, altercation, fracas, fray

quarrel [2]

verb to have an angry argument
▼ SEE BELOW

queasy

adjective feeling nauseous » *Freya felt queasy so her mom comforted her.*
ill, nauseous, queer, sick, unwell

*Freya felt **queasy** so her mom comforted her.*

query [1]

noun a question » *If you have any queries, please contact us.*
inquiry, question
antonym: **response**

quarrel

[2] *verb* to have an angry argument
» *My sister **quarreled** with my brother.*

!@?#%

%&?£!

argue
She **argued** with her mother about bedtime.

fall out
She **fell out** with her best friend.

bicker
They **bickered** endlessly over whose turn it was to let the dog out.

fight
They often **fought** about who was right.

clash
They had **clashed** before as they just didn't get along.

tiff
She had a **tiff** with her friend, but they made up.

squabble
They **squabbled** over the remote control.

a b c d e f g h i j k l m n o p q r s t u v w x y z

A
B
C
D
E
F
G
H
I
J
K
L
M
N
O
P
Q
R
S
T
U
V
W
X
Y
Z

query 2
verb to question something because it seems wrong » *Gary queried the referee's decision to disallow the goal.*
challenge, dispute, object to, question

question 1
noun a problem that needs to be discussed » *Can we get back to the question of who's organizing the party?*
issue, motion, point, subject, topic

question 2
verb to ask someone questions » *A man is being questioned by the police.*
examine, interrogate, probe, quiz, cross-examine, interview, investigate
antonym: **answer**

question 3
verb to express doubts about something » *I'm fed up with my parents always questioning my decisions.*
challenge, dispute, distrust, doubt, query, suspect

quick 1
adjective moving with great speed » *The students made a quick exit from the classroom when the bell rang.*
brisk, express, hasty, hurtle, fast, rapid, speedy, swift
antonym: **slow**

quick 2
adjective lasting only a short time » *We only had time for a quick chat.*
brief, cursory, hasty, hurried, perfunctory
antonym: **long**

quick 3
adjective happening without any delay » *I received a quick response to my email.*
hasty, prompt, sudden

quickly
adverb with great speed
▶▶ SEE RIGHT

quiet 1
adjective making very little noise » *The radio was so quiet, we couldn't hear it.*
hushed, inaudible, low, silent, soft, noiseless, soundless
antonym: **noisy**

quiet 2
adjective peaceful and calm » *We had a quiet day at home.*
calm, mild, peaceful, restful, serene, tranquil, motionless, placid, untroubled

quiet 3
noun silence or lack of noise » *The teacher asked for quiet.*
calmness, peace, serenity, silence, stillness, tranquillity
antonym: **noise**

*The teacher asked for **quiet**.*

quit
verb to leave a place or stop doing something » *Keira quit her job and went traveling.*
discontinue, give up, leave, resign, retire, stop, abandon, cease

quite 1
adverb fairly but not very » *My uncle is quite old.*
fairly, moderately, rather, reasonably, somewhat

quite 2
adverb completely and totally » *The doctor asked John to lay quite still during the X-ray.*
absolutely, completely, entirely, fully, perfectly, totally, precisely, wholly

quote
verb to repeat the exact words someone has said » *Nadia always quotes from TV shows.*
cite, extract, recite, repeat

fast   hastily
hurriedly   rapidly
speedily   swiftly

quickly

adverb with great speed » *The rocket took off and **quickly** gained height.*

antonym: **slowly**
*The tortoise moves **slowly**.*

Rr

race [1]
noun a group of human beings with shared physical or genetic characteristics » *People of different races live side by side in this city.*
ethnic group, nation, people

race [2]
verb to move very quickly » *Dan raced to catch the bus, but he was too late.*
dash, fly, hurry, run, speed, tear

*Dan **raced** to catch the bus, but he was too late.*

racket
noun a lot of noise » *The workers' drills made such a racket.*
clamor, commotion, din, hubbub, noise, rumpus, cacophony, tumult

rage [1]
noun a feeling of extremely strong anger » *She was trembling with rage.*
anger, frenzy, fury, wrath

*Mariana was **raging** at the fact that she was number 12 in the line.*

rage [2]
verb to be angry or speak angrily » *Mariana was raging at the fact that she was number 12 in the line.*
be furious, fume, lose your temper, rave, storm

rage [3]
verb to continue with great force » *The storm raged all night.*
be at its height, rampage, storm, surge

raid [1]
verb to attack suddenly » *Oliver came home hungry and raided the fridge.*
assault, attack, break into, invade, plunder, pillage, rifle, sack

raid [2]
noun an attack on something » *The street was closed following the bank raid.*
attack, break-in, foray, incursion, sortie

rain [1]
noun water falling from the clouds » *The rain came as a relief after the drought.*
deluge, downpour, drizzle, rainfall, showers

*It **rained** as Caroline was on her way to meet a friend.*

rain [2]
verb to fall from the sky in drops » *It rained as Caroline was on her way to meet a friend.*
drizzle, pour, teem

raise [1]
verb to make something higher » *Flags were raised to signal the start of the national holiday.*
elevate, heave, hoist, lift
antonym: **lower**

raise [2]
verb to take care of children until they are grown up » *Natasha was raised in a large house in the country.*
bring up, nurture, rear

raise [3]
verb to mention or suggest something » *He had raised no objections at the time.*
advance, bring up, broach, introduce, moot, suggest

ramble [1]
verb to go for a long walk » *We rambled across the moors, taking care to avoid any bogs.*
amble, outing, saunter, stroll, walk, wander, perambulate, rove

ramble [2]
verb to talk in a confused way » *Garth started rambling and repeating himself.*
babble, chatter, go on, rattle, run on

rampage [1]
verb to rush around wildly or out of control » *The children rampaged around the yard dressed as cowboys.*
go berserk, rage, run amok, run riot

rampage [2]:
on the rampage
adjective rushing around in a wild and uncontrolled way » *The bull escaped from the field and went on the rampage through the village.*
amok, berserk, wild

random [1]
adjective not based on a definite plan » *Melissa came to the sleepover in a random selection of clothes—a coat, skirt, and pyjamas!*
aimless, arbitrary, haphazard, helter-skelter, indiscriminate, spot, desultory, unpremeditated

*Melissa came to the sleepover in a **random** selection of clothes—a coat, skirt, and pyjamas!*

random [2]: **at random**
adverb without any definite plan » *Children will be chosen at random to represent the school in the parade.*
aimlessly, arbitrarily, haphazardly, indiscriminately, randomly, unsystematically, willy-nilly

range [1]
noun the maximum limits of something » *I tried to call, but was not in range of a signal tower.*
bounds, extent, field, limits, province, scope

a b c d e f g h i j k l m n o p q r s t u v w x y z

range

2 *noun* a number of different things of the same kind
» *The sunglasses are available in a range of colors.*

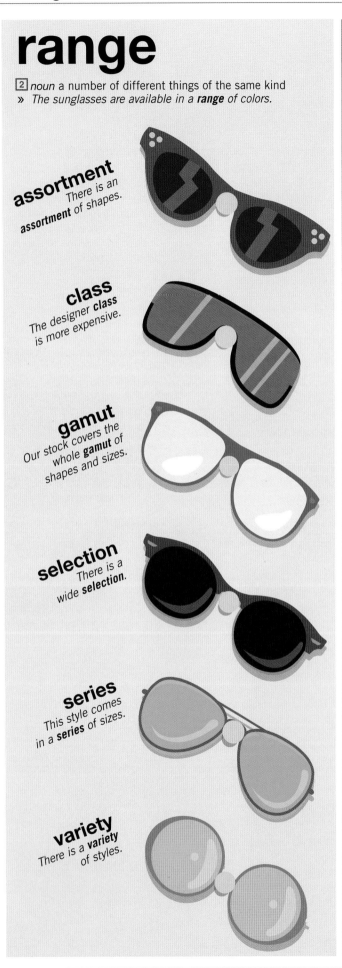

assortment
There is an *assortment* of shapes.

class
The designer *class* is more expensive.

gamut
Our stock covers the whole *gamut* of shapes and sizes.

selection
There is a wide *selection*.

series
This style comes in a *series* of sizes.

variety
There is a *variety* of styles.

range 2
noun a number of different things of the same kind
◀◀ **SEE LEFT**

range 3
verb to vary between two extremes » *The shelves were filled with goods ranging from the everyday to the exotic.*
extend, go, run, stretch, vary

rank 1
noun someone's level in a group » *Franklin rose to the rank of captain.*
class, echelon, grade, level, standing, station, status

rank 2
noun a row of people or things » *Ranks of Mounted Police participated in the parade.*
column, file, line, row

Ranks of Mounted Police participated in the parade.

rank 3
adjective complete and absolute » *Going hiking without a map and compass is rank stupidity.*
absolute, complete, downright, sheer, unmitigated, utter, arrant, egregious

rare
adjective not common or frequent » *We saw a rare species of bird that hardly ever appears in Seattle.*
exceptional, few, scarce, sparse, sporadic, uncommon, unusual
antonym: **common**

rash 1
adjective acting in a hasty and foolish way » *Sven made a rash decision to go swimming in the freezing ocean.*
foolhardy, hasty, impetuous, impulsive, reckless, heedless, injudicious, unthinking

rash 2
noun an irritated area on your skin » *The rash on my leg is really itchy.*
eruption, outbreak

The rash on my leg is really itchy.

rash 3
noun a large number of events happening together » *A rash of bookings followed the television program about the resort.*
epidemic, flood, plague, spate, wave

rate 1
noun the speed or frequency of something » *Our hen lays eggs at the rate of one a day.*
frequency, pace, speed, tempo, velocity

rate 2
noun the cost or charge for something » *We were offered phone calls at cheap rates as part of the package.*
charge, cost, fee, price, tariff

rate 3
verb to give an opinion of someone's or something's qualities » *The app was rated very highly by its users.*
appraise, class, consider, count, rank, regard, adjudge, esteem, evaluate

rather

adverb to a certain extent
» *We got along rather well.*
enough, fairly, pretty, quite, relatively, slightly, somewhat

rational

adjective using reason rather than emotion » *There must be a rational explanation for the lights going out.*
enlightened, logical, reasonable, sensible

rave [1]

verb to talk in an uncontrolled way » *Ed started raving about being treated badly.*
babble, rage, rant

rave [2]

verb (informal) to be enthusiastic about something » *She raved about how good the facilities were at the hotel.*
be wild about (informal), **on about, enthuse, gush**

reach [1]

verb to arrive somewhere » *Len did not stop until he reached the end of the trail.*
arrive at, attain, get as far as, get to, make

reach [2]

verb to extend as far as something » *Annabel used a ladder to reach the book she wanted.*
extend to, go as far as, touch

*Annabel used a ladder to **reach** the book she wanted.*

reach [3]

verb to arrive at a certain stage or level » *Our grades have reached record highs.*
arrive at, attain, climb to, fall to, rise to

reaction [1]

noun a person's response to something » *When she spotted the spider, Louise's reaction was one of horror.*
acknowledgment, answer, feedback, response

*When she spotted the spider, Louise's **reaction** was one of horror.*

reaction [2]

noun a response to something unpopular » *There has been a fierce reaction to the suggestion that the school day be made longer.*
backlash, counterbalance

read [1]

verb to look at and absorb something written » *Nancy read the article with interest.*
glance at, look at, pore over, scan, study

*Nancy **read** the article with interest.*

read [2]

verb to understand the true nature or mood » *Rob wished he could read her thoughts.*
comprehend, decipher, interpret

*We were packed and **ready** to go on vacation.*

ready [1]

adjective prepared for action or use » *We were packed and ready to go on vacation.*
organized, prepared, primed, ripe, set

ready [2]

adjective willing to do something » *Kyle was always ready to help with the dishes.*
agreeable, eager, happy, keen, willing, minded, predisposed

ready [3]

adjective easily produced or obtained » *Lily took a ready meal out of the freezer.*
accessible, available, convenient, handy

real [1]

adjective genuine and not imitation » *The jeweler inspected the gem to see if it was real or a fake.*
authentic, bona fide, genuine, honest, legitimate, rightful, sincere, true, unaffected
antonym: **fake**

*The jeweler inspected the gem to see if it was **real** or a fake.*

real [2]

adjective actually existing and not imagined » *The movie is based on the real story of a famous scientist.*
actual, authentic, concrete, factual, genuine, legitimate, tangible, true
antonym: **imaginary**

realistic [1]

adjective accepting the true situation » *She was realistic that her chances of winning the lottery were virtually zero.*
down-to-earth, level-headed, matter-of-fact, practical, sensible, sober

realistic [2]

adjective true to real life » *My sister's paintings are very realistic.*
authentic, faithful, lifelike, true, naturalistic, representational

*My sister's paintings are very **realistic**.*

reality

noun something that is true and not imagined » *The reality of the situation is that we are lost.*
authenticity, fact, realism, truth

realize

verb to become aware of something » *Nicole hadn't realized how difficult the recipe was.*
appreciate, comprehend, grasp, recognize, understand

a b c d e f g h i j k l m n o p q r s t u v w x y z

really

1 adverb very or certainly
» The friends had a **really** good time at the party.

I'm **absolutely** delighted to see everyone.

I'm **certainly** enjoying myself.

The food is **extremely** tasty.

You must be **terribly** tired after all that dancing.

They organized it in a **remarkably** short time.

I'm having a **truly** wonderful time.

I'm **very** glad I came.

really [1]
adverb very or certainly
◀◀ SEE LEFT

really [2]
adverb in fact
» *Simon really is asleep, he's not pretending.*
actually, in fact, in reality, truly

reason [1]
noun the cause of something that happens » *I had no reason to go out, so I stayed at home.*
cause, grounds, incentive, motive, purpose

reason [2]
noun the ability to think » *Ivy desperately wanted the bag, but reason told her not to buy it because it was too small.*
intellect, judgment, rationality, reasoning, sense

reason [3]
verb to try to persuade someone of something » *I tried to reason with my mother, but she wouldn't listen.*
bring round (informal), persuade, win over

*I tried to **reason** with my mother, but she wouldn't listen.*

reasonable [1]
adjective fair and sensible
» *It was only reasonable to share the chores between us.*
fair, moderate, rational, sane, sensible, sober, steady, wise, judicious, plausible

reasonable [2]
adjective based on good reasoning » *Ali had a reasonable argument based on the facts.*
justifiable, legitimate, logical, sensible, sound, understandable

reasonable [3]
adjective not too expensive
» *The cost of my haircut was reasonable, I'd go there again.*
cheap, competitive, fair, inexpensive, low, modest

reassure
verb to put someone's mind at ease » *Sonia reassured me that everything was fine.*
bolster, cheer up, comfort, encourage, buoy up, hearten, inspirit

rebel
verb to fight against authority and accepted values » *Amy rebelled against school policy and dyed her hair pink.*
defy, mutiny, resist, revolt

*Amy **rebelled** against school policy and dyed her hair pink.*

rebellion
noun an organized opposition to authority » *Fed up with extra work every night, the students staged a rebellion.*
insurrection, mutiny, revolt, revolution, uprising

receive [1]
verb to accept something from someone » *Did you receive my letter?*
accept, be given, get, pick up, take

receive [2]
verb to experience something
» *We received a very warm welcome.*
encounter, suffer, sustain, undergo

receive [3]
verb to welcome visitors
» *Jim and Marie were there to receive the guests when they arrived for the party.*
entertain, greet, meet, take in, welcome

*Jim and Marie were there to **receive** the guests when they arrived for the party.*

recent
adjective happening a short time ago » *Our most recent overseas trip was to Chile.*
current, fresh, new, present-day, up-to-date, contemporary, latter-day

reckon [1]
verb (Britain, informal) to think or believe something is the case » *I reckon they'll be here soon, I told them to come at 3pm.*
assume, believe (formal), consider, judge, suppose, think, deem (formal), hold to be, surmise (formal)

reckon [2]
verb to calculate an amount
» *The figure is now reckoned to be 15 percent.*
calculate, count, estimate, figure out, work out

recognize [1]
verb to know who or what someone or something is
» *I recognized Darren from his red hair.*
identify, know, place, spot

recognize [2]
verb to accept or acknowledge something » *William was recognized as an outstanding pilot by the academy.*
acknowledge, appreciate, honor, salute

reconstruct [1]
verb to rebuild something that has been damaged » *The old cathedral was falling down and has been reconstructed.*
rebuild, recreate, regenerate, renovate, restore, reassemble, remodel

reconstruct [2]
verb to build up from small details » *Archaeologists reconstruct the past from the evidence they find.*
build up, deduce, piece together

record [1]
noun a stored account of something » *The shelves were bulging with medical records.*
account, archives, file, journal, minute, register

record [2]
noun what someone has done in the past » *The interviewer asked for a record of my previous work experience.*
background, career, curriculum vitae, resume track record (informal)

record [3]
verb to note and store information » *Julia records her daily life in her diary.*
blog, document, enter, log, note, register, write down

*Julia **records** her daily life in her diary.*

a b c d e f g h i j k l m n o p q r s t u v w x y z

recover [1]
verb to get better again
» *Pete has still not fully recovered from a nasty cold.*
convalesce, get better, get well, improve, recuperate, revive

recover [2]
verb to get something back again » *Lynn's father managed to recover the lost book from behind the shelves.*
get back, recapture, recoup, regain, retrieve

recovery [1]
noun the act of getting better again » *He made a remarkable recovery after his operation.*
healing, improvement, recuperation, revival, convalescence, rally

recovery [2]
noun the act of getting something back » *The art gallery offered a reward for the recovery of the stolen painting.*
recapture, reclamation, restoration, retrieval

recruit [1]
verb to persuade people to join a group » *Ali helped to recruit volunteers for picking up litter.*
draft, enlist, enrol, muster

recruit [2]
noun someone who has recently joined a group » *The army recruits were given their new uniforms.*
beginner, convert, novice, trainee, tyro

*The army **recruits** were given their new uniforms.*

*I gave my daughter a **red** apple.*

red
noun or adjective
Shades of red:
burgundy, cardinal, carmine, cherry, claret, coral, crimson, flame, maroon, poppy, rose, ruby, scarlet, vermilion, wine
related words:
adjective **rubicund, ruddy**

reduce [1]
verb to make something smaller in size or amount » *Mom reduced her hours at work so she could spend more time at home.*
curtail, cut, cut down, decrease, diminish, lessen, lower, shorten
antonym: **increase**

reduce [2]
verb to bring to a weaker or inferior state » *The village was reduced to rubble in the earthquake.*
degrade, demote, downgrade, drive, force

refer [1]
verb to mention something » *In his speech, Len referred to a recent trip to Canada.*
allude, bring up, cite, mention

refer [2]
verb to look at something to find something out » *We had to refer to the recipe to make the sauce.*
consult, look up

*We had to **refer** to the recipe to make the sauce.*

regular

[1] *adjective* even or equally spaced
» *A clock pendulum has **regular** movement.*

consistent

periodic

constant

rhythmic

even

uniform

*He was a **refined** gentleman with impeccable manners.*

refined 1

adjective well-mannered and polite » *He was a refined gentleman with impeccable manners.*
civilized, genteel, gentlemanly, ladylike, polite
antonym: **common**

refined 2

adjective processed to remove impurities » *White sugar is refined from raw sugar cane.*
distilled, filtered, processed, pure, purified

reform 1

noun a major change or improvement » *The new principal is planning a reform of the school timetable.*
amendment, correction, improvement, rehabilitation, amelioration, betterment, rectification

reform 2

verb to make major changes or improvements to something » *He reformed the athletics program to improve results.*
amend, better, correct, rectify, rehabilitate, ameliorate, emend, revolutionize

refresh

verb to make you feel more energetic » *A glass of fruit juice will refresh you.*
brace, enliven, rejuvenate, revive, stimulate, freshen, invigorate, revitalize, revivify

refuge

noun a place where you go for safety » *We hid from the storm in a tiny mountain refuge.*
asylum, harbor, haven, sanctuary, shelter

refuse 1

verb to say you will not do something » *He refused to talk about the contents of the letter.*
abstain, decline, withhold

refuse 2

verb to say you will not allow or accept something » *I politely refused the offer of a drink as I wasn't thirsty.*
decline, reject, spurn, turn down
antonym: **accept**

refuse 3

noun garbage or waste » *Our household refuse is collected weekly.*
junk (informal)**, litter, rubbish, trash, waste**

regard 1

verb to think of someone or something in a particular way » *I regard Isabella as my best friend.*
consider, judge, look on, see, think of, view

regard 2

verb (literary) to look at someone in a particular way » *Janine regarded the magician's trick with interest.*
contemplate, eye, gaze, look, scrutinize, watch

*Janine **regarded** the magician's trick with interest.*

region

noun a large area of land » *We live in a beautiful mountainous region.*
area, district, land, locality, quarter, sector, territory, tract, zone

regret 1

verb to be sorry something has happened » *Michael regretted forgetting his girlfriend's birthday again.*
be sorry, grieve, lament, mourn, repent, bemoan, bewail, rue

*Michael **regretted** forgetting his girlfriend's birthday again.*

regret 2

noun the feeling of being sorry about something » *He expressed regret that he had caused offense.*
grief, pang of conscience, penitence, remorse, repentance, sorrow, compunction, contrition, ruefulness, self-reproach

regular 1

adjective even or equally spaced
◄◄ **SEE LEFT**

regular 2

adjective usual or normal » *Tom was filling in for the regular sales assistant.*
customary, everyday, habitual, normal, ordinary, routine, typical, usual

reject

verb to refuse to accept or agree to something » *Dad rejected the job offer because the office was too far away.*
decline, deny, rebuff, refuse, renounce, say no to, spurn, turn down, disallow, repudiate
antonym: **accept**

rejoice

verb to be very happy about something » *Today we can rejoice in our success.*
be overjoyed, celebrate, delight, glory, exult, revel

relation 1

noun a connection between two things » *The movie has no relation to the book.*
bearing, bond, connection, correlation, link, relationship

relation 2

noun a member of your family » *I stayed with my relations while I was in Germany.*
kin, kinsman, kinswoman, relative

relationship 1

noun the way people act toward each other » *Valerie has a friendly relationship with her customers.*
affinity, association, bond, connection, rapport

*Valerie has a friendly **relationship** with her customers.*

relationship 2

noun the connection between two things » *There is a clear relationship between happiness and good health.*
connection, correlation, link, parallel

relax

verb to be calm and become less worried » *You can relax during the summer after working hard all year.*
laze, rest, take it easy, unwind

a b c d e f g h i j k l m n o p q r s t u v w x y z

*I spent a **relaxed** evening listening to music.*

relaxed [1]

adjective calm and peaceful
» *I spent a relaxed evening listening to music.*
calm, casual, comfortable, informal, peaceful
antonym: **tense**

relaxed [2]

adjective calm and not worried or tense » *My parents have a relaxed attitude and often let my friends stay over.*
at ease, calm, comfortable, cool, easy, serene, unflustered
antonym: **tense**

relay

verb to give information to someone else » *Ariana relayed your message to me.*
communicate, convey, impart

release [1]

verb to set someone or something free
» *Our teacher finally released us from the lesson.*
deliver, discharge, extricate, free, let go, liberate, set free, emancipate, unfetter

release [2]

verb to make something available » *The new album will be released next week.*
issue, launch, publish, put out

release [3]

noun the setting free of someone or something
» *The charity's aim was the release of animals in captivity back into the wild.*
discharge, emancipation, freedom, liberation, liberty, deliverance

relentless

adjective never stopping or becoming less intense
» *The rain was relentless and did not let up the whole week.*
incessant, nonstop, persistent, sustained, unrelenting, unremitting

relevant

adjective connected with what is being discussed » *Please stick to the point and just talk about what's relevant.*
applicable, apposite, appropriate, apt, pertinent, germane, material
antonym: **irrelevant**

reliable

adjective able to be trusted
» *Mike was reliable and turned up on time every day.*
dependable, faithful, safe, sound, staunch, sure, true, trustworthy
antonym: **unreliable**

religious [1]

adjective connected with religion » *We joined in the religious worship.*
devotional, divine, doctrinal, holy, sacred, scriptural, spiritual, theological

religious [2]

adjective having a strong belief in a god or gods » *Paul is very religious and goes to church every week.*
devout, God-fearing, godly, pious, righteous

reluctant

adjective unwilling to do something » *Dad was reluctant to ask for help.*
averse, disinclined, hesitant, loath, slow, unwilling
antonym: **eager**

remain [1]

verb to stay somewhere
» *My friends went out while I remained at home.*
be left, linger, stay behind, wait

*My friends went out while I **remained** at home.*

remain [2]

verb to stay the same
» *No matter how much she tried to curl her hair, it remained straight.*
continue, endure, go on, last, stay, survive

remember

verb to bring to mind something from the past
» *Remember to feed the cat.*

retain

*I must **retain** all those geography facts.*

recall

*Try to **recall** the words of that poem.*

recognize

*Do you **recognize** this name?*

remainder

noun the part that is left
» *After six weeks of French, we studied Spanish for the remainder of the semester.*
balance, last, others, remains, remnants, rest

remains

plural noun the parts left over
» *We put the remains of lunch in the fridge.*
debris, dregs, leftovers, relics, remnants, residue, scraps, vestiges, detritus, leavings

remark ①

verb to mention or comment on something » *She remarked that my hair was looking nice.*
comment, mention, observe, say, state

remark ②

noun something you say
» *Trudy's remark about my new coat made me happy.*
comment, observation, statement, utterance, word

remember

verb to bring to mind something from the past
▼ **SEE BELOW**

remind

verb to make someone remember something
» *Please remind me to water the plants before we go out.*
bring back to, jog someone's memory, make someone remember, put in mind, refresh someone's memory

remote ①

adjective far off in distance
» *We stayed for a week on a remote farm in the hills.*
distant, far-off, inaccessible, isolated, lonely, outlying

We stayed for a week on a remote farm in the hills.

remote ②

adjective far away in time
» *The days of knights in armor riding into battle are from the remote past.*
distant, far-off

remote ③

adjective not wanting to be friendly » *I tried to talk to her, but she was very remote.*
aloof, cold, detached, distant, reserved, standoffish, withdrawn

remote ④

adjective not very great
» *The chances of us winning the lottery are pretty remote.*
poor, slender, slight, slim, small

remove

verb to take something off or away » *Sue had already bought milk, so she removed it from the shopping list.*
delete, detach, eject, eliminate, erase, extract, get rid of, take away, take off, take out, withdraw, efface, excise, expunge

Sue had already bought milk, so she removed it from the shopping list.

renew

verb to begin something again » *Dawn renewed her subscription to the magazine.*
begin again, recommence, reestablish, reopen, resume

renounce

verb (formal) to reject something or give it up
» *Tina renounced all fast food.*
disown, give up, reject, relinquish, eschew (formal)

*Tina **renounced** all fast food.*

renovate

verb to repair an old building or machine
» *My aunt bought a rundown house and renovated it.*
do up, modernize, recondition, refurbish, repair, restore, revamp

call to mind

*Can you **call to mind** where the keys are?*

reminisce

*We like to **reminisce** with grandpa about the past.*

recollect

*Do you **recollect** what we did last Tuesday?*

antonym: **forget**

*Don't **forget** to do your homework!*

a b c d e f g h i j k l m n o p q r s t u v w x y z

*My dad carried out the **repairs** on the car himself.*

repair [1]
noun something you do to fix something that is damaged » *My dad carried out the repairs on the car himself.*
darn, mend, patch, restoration

repair [2]
verb to fix something that is damaged » *The money will be used to repair the faulty TV.*
fix, mend, patch, patch up, renovate, restore

repay
verb to give back money which is owed » *It will take me years to repay the loan.*
pay back, refund, settle up, make restitution, recompense, reimburse, remunerate, square

repeat
verb to say or write something again » *Since you didn't listen, I'll repeat that.*
echo, reiterate, say again, iterate, recapitulate, restate

repel [1]
verb to horrify and disgust » *The thought of eating snails repels me.*
disgust, offend, revolt, sicken
antonym: **attract**

repel [2]
verb to fight and drive back enemy forces » *Troops positioned along the border are ready to repel an enemy attack.*
drive off, repulse, resist

replace
verb to take the place of something else » *He replaced his car with a bicycle.*
succeed, supersede, supplant, take over from, take the place of

replacement
noun a person or thing that takes the place of another » *Glen has nominated Adam to be his replacement.*
proxy, stand-in, substitute, successor, surrogate

reply [1]
verb to give someone an answer » *She quickly replied to my email.*
answer, counter, respond, retort, return, reciprocate, rejoin, riposte

reply [2]
noun an answer given to someone » *He gave a sharp reply to her endless questions.*
answer, response, retort, rejoinder, riposte

report [1]
verb to tell about or give an official account of something » *Owen reported the theft to the police.*
cover, describe, inform of, notify, state

report [2]
noun an account of an event or situation » *The news report suggested it was a very exciting game.*
account, description, statement

*The news **report** suggested it was a very exciting game.*

represent [1]
verb to stand for something else » *In algebra, letters are used to represent numbers.*
mean, stand for, symbolize, betoken, equate with

represent [2]
verb to describe something in a particular way » *The newspapers represent him as a hero.*
depict, describe, picture, portray, show

representative [1]
noun a person who acts on behalf of another or others » *We elected a school representative.*
agent, delegate, deputy, proxy, spokesman, spokeswoman

representative [2]
adjective typical of the group to which it belongs » *This building is representative of Gaudí's style of architecture.*
characteristic, illustrative, typical, archetypal, emblematic, indicative

*This building is **representative** of Gaudí's style of architecture.*

reputation
noun the opinion that people have of a person or thing » *The school has a reputation for getting good grades.*
character, name, renown, repute, standing, stature

request [1]
verb to ask for something politely or formally » *Alana requested that the door be left open.*
ask, beg, seek, entreat, solicit

request [2]
noun the action of asking for something politely or formally » *The examiner refused the boy's request for more time.*
appeal, application, call, plea, entreaty, petition

require [1]
verb to need something » *A plant requires light, water, and nutrients in order to grow.*
demand, depend on, be in need of, need, want (informal)

require [2]
verb to say that someone must do something » *The rules require employers to provide safety training.*
compel, demand, direct, instruct, oblige, order

requirement
noun something that you must have or do » *There is a legal requirement for children to attend school.*
demand, essential, necessity, need, specification, prerequisite (formal), stipulation (formal)

research [1]
noun the act of studying and finding out about something » *I've been doing some research for my project.*
analysis, examination, exploration, investigation, study

*I've been doing some **research** for my project.*

research [2]
verb to study and find out about something » *She researched good places to visit while they were on vacation.*
analyse, examine, explore, google, investigate, study

resemblance

noun a similarity between two things » *I can see a resemblance between you two.*
analogy, correspondence, likeness, parallel, similarity, comparability, parity, semblance, similitude

resemble

verb to be similar to something else » *Limes resemble green lemons and they both taste sour, too.*
bear a resemblance to, be like, be similar to, look like, parallel, take after

*Limes **resemble** green lemons and they both taste sour, too.*

resent

verb to feel bitter and angry about something » *I resent being treated like an idiot.*
be angry about, be offended by, dislike, object to, take offense at

resentful

adjective bitter about something that has happened » *The boys were resentful that they weren't allowed to go to the park.*
aggrieved, angry, bitter, embittered, huffy, indignant, offended, sore, peeved, piqued

resentment

noun a feeling of anger and bitterness » *Resentment is growing among students at what they claim is unfair treatment by some teachers.*
anger, animosity, bitterness, grudge, huff, indignation, rancor, offense, umbrage

*A table has been **reserved** for us at the restaurant.*

reserve ①

verb to keep for a particular person or purpose » *A table has been reserved for us at the restaurant.*
hoard, hold, keep, put by, save, set aside, stockpile, store

reserve ②

noun a supply kept for future use » *We have plenty of food reserves if we get snowed in.*
cache, fund, hoard, stock, stockpile, store, supply

resign ①

verb to leave a job » *Scott resigned from the company to take another job elsewhere.*
abdicate, hand in your notice, leave, quit, step down (informal)

resign ② :
resign oneself
verb to accept an unpleasant situation » *After playing badly, Samantha had resigned herself to losing her place on the team.*
accept, reconcile yourself, bow

resist

verb to refuse to accept something and try to prevent it » *She resisted her mother's attempts to get her to clean her bedroom.*
defy, fight, oppose, refuse, struggle against
antonym: **accept**

resolve ①

verb to decide firmly to do something » *Miguel resolved to do more exercise.*
decide, determine, intend, make up your mind

resolve ②

verb to find a solution to a problem » *We must find a way to resolve this problem.*
clear up, find a solution to, overcome, solve, sort out, work out

resolve ③

noun absolute determination » *Nothing could weaken Laura's resolve to get fit.*
determination, resolution, tenacity, doggedness, single-mindedness, willpower

*Nothing could weaken Laura's **resolve** to get fit.*

respect ①

verb to have a good opinion of someone » *The new teacher wanted his students to respect him.*
admire, have a good opinion of, have a high opinion of, honor, look up to, think highly of, venerate, esteem, revere, reverence
antonym: **disrespect**

respect ②

noun a good opinion of someone » *The football team had a lot of respect for their old coach.*
admiration, esteem, regard, reverence
antonym: **disrespect**

respectable ①

adjective considered to be acceptable and correct » *Timothy comes from a respectable family.*
decent, good, honorable, proper, reputable, upright, worthy

respectable ②

adjective adequate or reasonable » *His grades were respectable, but not amazing.*
appreciable, considerable, decent, fair, reasonable

responsibility ①

noun the duty to deal with or take care of something » *Mom took care of the house while the vegetable garden was my responsibility.*
duty, obligation, onus

responsibility ②

noun the blame for something that has happened » *We must all accept responsibility for our mistakes.*
blame, fault, guilt, liability, accountability, culpability

responsible ①

adjective being the person in charge of something » *I am responsible for making the sandwiches for the picnic.*
in charge, in control

responsible ②

adjective being to blame for something » *I wonder who is responsible for this mess!*
at fault, guilty, to blame

*I wonder who is **responsible** for this mess!*

responsible ③

adjective sensible and dependable » *Patrick had to show that he would be a responsible pet owner.*
dependable, level-headed, reliable, sensible, sound, trustworthy
antonym: **irresponsible**

a b c d e f g h i j k l m n o p q r s t u v w x y z

A B C D E F G H I J K L M N O P Q R S T U V W X Y Z

*Greg took one slice of cake and left the **rest**.*

rest [1]
noun the remaining parts of something » *Greg took one slice of cake and left the rest.*
balance, others, remainder, surplus

rest [2]
noun a period when you relax and do nothing » *I could do with a rest from all this work.*
break, holiday, leisure, relaxation, respite, vacation

rest [3]
verb to relax and do nothing for a while » *Gary rested on the sofa all night.*
have a break, idle, laze, put your feet up, relax, sit down, take it easy

restless
adjective unable to sit still or relax » *She had been restless and irritable all day.*
edgy, fidgety, fretful, jumpy, on edge, unsettled

restore [1]
verb to cause something to return to its previous state » *The restaurant was anxious to restore its reputation after the poor review.*
reestablish, reinstate, reintroduce, return

restore [2]
verb to clean and repair something » *He specializes in restoring ancient documents.*
fix up, mend, rebuild, reconstruct, refurbish, renovate, repair, recondition, retouch

restrain
verb to hold someone or something back » *Noah had to be restrained by his friends.*
contain, control, curb, hamper, hinder, hold back, inhibit, constrain, rein, straiten

restrict
verb to limit the movement or actions of someone or something » *I restricted the dog to the main floor of the house.*
confine, contain, hamper, handicap, impede, inhibit, limit, restrain, circumscribe, demarcate, straiten

restriction
noun a rule or situation that limits what you can do » *There is a parking restriction outside the hospital entrance.*
constraint, control, curb, limitation, regulation, restraint, stipulation

*There is a parking **restriction** outside the hospital entrance.*

result [1]
noun the situation that is caused by something » *He was eager to hear the result of the game.*
consequence, effect, outcome, product, upshot

result [2]
verb to be caused by something » *Sarah's gold medal resulted from a lot of training and hard work.*
arise, derive, develop, ensue, follow, happen, stem

result in
verb to cause something to happen » *Thorough review results in better exam grades.*
bring about, cause, lead to

retaliate
verb to do something to someone in return for what they did » *Tara retaliated by hiding her sister's favorite book.*
get back at, get even with (informal), get your own back (informal), hit back, pay someone back, take revenge

retreat [1]
verb to move away from someone or something » *The sunbathers on the beach retreated as the tide came in.*
back away, back off, draw back, pull back, withdraw
antonym: **advance**

retreat [2]
noun the action of moving away from someone or something » *We made a hasty retreat when the hotel fire alarm went off.*
departure, evacuation, flight, withdrawal
antonym: **advance**

retreat [3]
noun a quiet place you can go to » *Ben's favorite retreat was his tree house, where he could relax.*
haven, refuge, sanctuary

*Ben's favorite **retreat** was his tree house, where he could relax.*

*Peter called for the dog and she **returned** carrying a stick.*

return [1]
verb to go back to a place » *Peter called for the dog and she returned carrying a stick.*
come back, go back, reappear, turn back

return [2]
verb to give something back » *The company guaranteed to return our money if we didn't like the product.*
give back, pay back, refund, repay, recompense, reimburse

reveal [1]
verb to tell people about something » *The article revealed all the details about the celebrity's life.*
announce, disclose, divulge, get off your chest (informal), let on

reveal [2]
verb to uncover something that is hidden
▶▶ SEE RIGHT

revenge
noun vengeance for wrongs or injury received » *Chris plotted his revenge for the trick his friends had played on him earlier.*
reprisal, retaliation, retribution, vengeance

reverse [1]
verb to change into something different or contrary » *The store won't reverse their decision to increase prices.*
change, invalidate, overrule, overturn, retract, countermand, negate, rescind, revoke

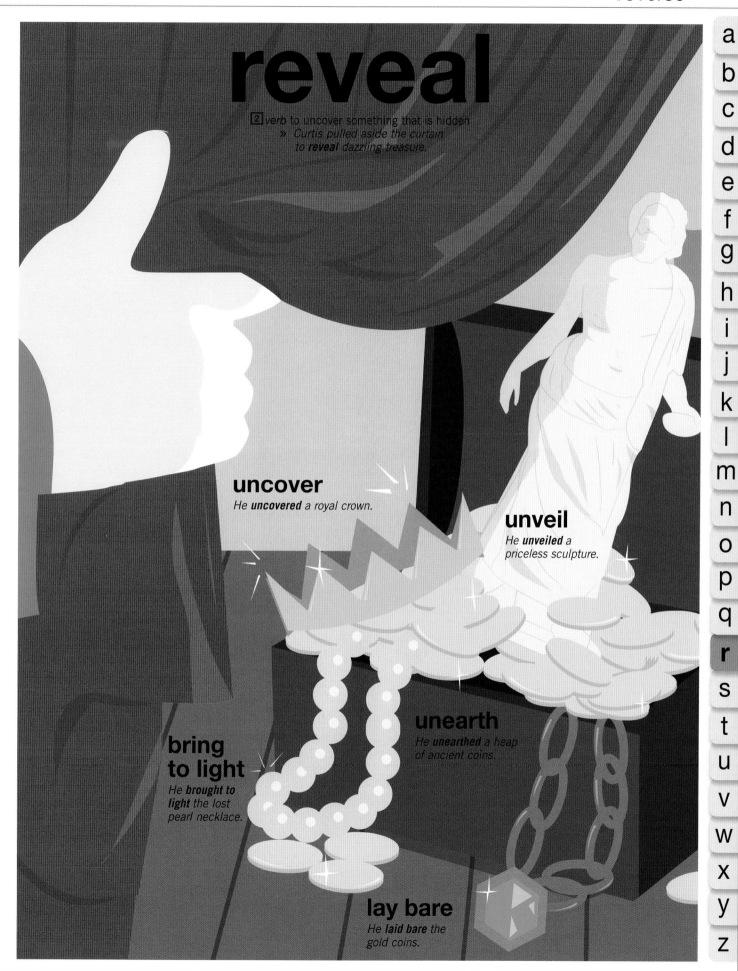

reveal

2 *verb* to uncover something that is hidden.
» *Curtis pulled aside the curtain
to* **reveal** *dazzling treasure.*

uncover
He **uncovered** *a royal crown.*

unveil
He **unveiled** *a
priceless sculpture.*

**bring
to light**
He **brought to
light** *the lost
pearl necklace.*

unearth
He **unearthed** *a heap
of ancient coins.*

lay bare
He **laid bare** *the
gold coins.*

a b c d e f g h i j k l m n o p q r s t u v w x y z

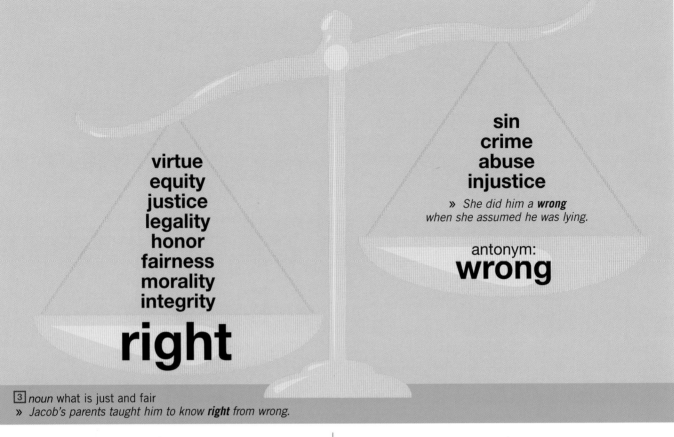

virtue
equity
justice
legality
honor
fairness
morality
integrity

right

sin
crime
abuse
injustice

» *She did him a **wrong**
when she assumed he was lying.*

antonym:
wrong

③ *noun* what is just and fair
» *Jacob's parents taught him to know **right** from wrong.*

---

reverse ②

noun the opposite of what
has just been said or done
» *That's not right—in fact,
the reverse is true.*
**contrary, converse,
opposite**

review ①

noun a critical assessment
of a book or performance
» *The movie got good reviews
in Andy's blog.*
**commentary, criticism,
notice**

*The movie got good **reviews**
in Andy's blog.*

review ②

noun a general survey
or report » *Our class project
was to do a review of pupils'
opinions on school lunches.*
**analysis, examination,
report, study, survey**

revise

verb to alter or correct
something » *Carlos revised
his opinion when he heard
Stefan's point of view.*
**amend, correct, edit,
refresh, revamp, update**

revive

verb to make or become
lively or active again
» *The concert revived
my love of rock music.*
**rally, resuscitate,
invigorate, reanimate,
rekindle, revitalize**

reward

noun something given
in return for a service
» *My mother bought me
a new bike as a reward for
good grades.*
**bonus, bounty, payment,
prize**

rhythm

noun a regular movement or
beat » *The dancers swayed
to the rhythm of the music.*
beat, pulse, tempo, time

rich ①

adjective having a lot of
money and possessions
» *He was a rich young man
with lots of money.*
affluent, loaded (slang),
**opulent, prosperous,
wealthy, well off**
antonym: **poor**

*He was a **rich** young man
with lots of money.*

rich ②

adjective abundant in
something » *Bananas
are rich in vitamin A.*
**abundant, fertile,
plentiful, copious,
fecund, plenteous**

rid: get rid of

verb to remove or destroy
something » *Arnold got rid of
the mouse in the bath tub.*
**dispose of, dump, eject,
jettison, remove, weed out**

ridiculous

adjective very foolish » *Josh
made the ridiculous claim of
having met the queen.*
**absurd, laughable,
ludicrous, preposterous**

right ①

adjective in accordance with
the facts » *She had all the
right answers and got full
points on the test.*
**accurate, correct, exact,
factual, genuine, precise,
strict, true, valid, unerring**
antonym: **wrong**

right ②

adjective most suitable » *The
right time to sleep is at night.*
**acceptable, appropriate,
desirable, done, fit, fitting,
okay** or **OK** (informal),
proper, seemly, suitable

right ③
noun what is just and fair
◀◀ SEE LEFT

right-wing
adjective believing in capitalist and conservative policies
» *Steve agreed with some of the party's right-wing policies, especially lower taxes for the rich.*
conservative, reactionary, Republican, Tory (Britain)

rigid ①
adjective not easy to bend
» *The rigid metal of the chair was uncomfortable to sit on.*
firm, hard, solid, stiff
antonym: **flexible**

rigid ②
adjective unchangeable and often considered severe
» *The school has a rigid schedule that can't be changed.*
fixed, inflexible, set, strict, stringent

ring ①
verb to make a loud clear sound » *Skye heard the school bell ring.*
chime, clang, peal, resonate, toll

ring ②
noun an object or group of things in the shape of a circle
» *My little brother floated on an inflatable rubber ring.*
band, circle, hoop, loop, round

*My little brother floated on an inflatable rubber **ring**.*

ring ③
noun a group of people who help each other, often secretly
» *The twist in the movie's plot was that Jimmy was part of a spy ring.*
band, cell, clique, syndicate

riot ①
noun a disturbance made by an unruly mob » *Large numbers of fans were involved in a riot after the game.*
anarchy, disorder, disturbance, mob violence, strife

riot ②
verb to take part in a riot
» *Some people rioted in protests against the new laws.*
go on the rampage, rampage, run riot, take to the streets

rise ①
verb to move upward » *Smoke rose from the campfire.*
ascend, climb, go up, move up

*Smoke **rose** from the campfire.*

rise ②
verb to increase » *Customers were warned that the prices would rise next year.*
go up, grow, increase, intensify, mount
antonym: **fall**

rise ③
noun an increase in something
» *The glowing review led to a rise in sales of the game.*
improvement, increase, upsurge
antonym: **fall**

risk ①
noun a chance that something unpleasant might happen »
If I go out now, there's a risk I'll miss my package being delivered.
danger, gamble, peril, pitfall

risk ②
verb to do something knowing that something unpleasant might happen » *If he misses this game, he risks losing his place on the team.*
chance, dare, gamble, jeopardize, put in jeopardy

rival ①
noun the person someone is competing with » *The race winner was well ahead of his nearest rival.*
adversary, antagonist, challenger, opponent

rival ②
verb to be the equal or near equal of » *As a vacation destination, South Africa rivals Kenya for weather.*
be a match for, equal, match

river
noun a natural stream of fresh water flowing along a definite course, usually into the ocean
» *A fast-flowing river runs through the national park.*
beck, brook, creek, estuary, rivulet, stream, tributary, watercourse, waterway

*A fast-flowing **river** runs through the national park.*

*There was no traffic at all on the **road** through the mountains.*

road
noun a route used by travelers and vehicles » *There was no traffic at all on the road through the mountains.*
avenue, freeway, highway, route, street, track

rob
verb to take something from a person illegally » *He was robbed of his money.*
burgle, con (informal), **defraud, loot, steal from, swindle**

romantic
adjective connected with love
» *Andy was very romantic and often bought Grace flowers.*
amorous, loving, tender

room ①
noun a separate section in a building » *You can stay in my spare room.*
chamber, office

room ②
noun unoccupied space
» *There wasn't enough room for all his belongings.*
capacity, elbow room, space

rot ①
verb to become rotten
» *The food in the broken fridge started to rot.*
decay, decompose, fester, spoil
related word: *adjective* **putrid**

a b c d e f g h i j k l m n o p q r s t u v w x y z

rot 2

noun the condition that affects things when they rot » *Dad varnished the timber frame to protect against rot.*
decay, deterioration, mould, putrefaction, putrescence

rotten 1

adjective decayed and no longer of use » *The strawberries I bought last week are rotten.*
bad, decayed, decomposed, moldy, sour

The strawberries I bought last week are rotten.

rotten 2

adjective (informal) of very poor quality » *Whose rotten idea was it to go for a picnic in the rain?*
inferior, lousy (slang)**, poor, unsatisfactory**

rough 1

adjective uneven and not smooth » *My bicycle bumped along on the rough ground.*
bumpy, craggy, rocky, rugged, uneven
antonym: **smooth**

rough 2

adjective difficult or unpleasant » *She had a rough time on the ship, feeling seasick all day.*
difficult, hard, tough, unpleasant

rough 3

adjective only approximately correct » *At a rough guess, I'd say there were 1,000 students in my high school.*
approximate, estimated, sketchy, vague, imprecise, inexact

round 1

adjective shaped like a ball or a circle » *Not all balls are round—footballs are oval.*
circular, cylindrical, rounded, spherical

round 2

noun one of a series of events » *After round three, the red team are in the lead by three points to two.*
lap, period, session, stage

Tom couldn't remember the route, so he got out his map.

route

noun a way from one place to another » *Tom couldn't remember the route, so he got out his map.*
channel, course, itinerary, path, road, way

routine 1

adjective ordinary and done regularly » *Dylan underwent a series of routine medical tests.*
everyday, normal, ordinary, regular, standard, typical, usual

routine 2

noun the usual way or order someone does things » *My morning routine is always to shower before breakfast.*
order, pattern, practice, procedure, program, schedule, system

row 1

noun several things arranged in a line » *There were rows of empty seats in the theater.*
bank, column, line, queue (Britain)**, rank**

row 2

noun a serious disagreement » *I had a row with my brother about who broke the laptop.*
altercation, argument, quarrel, squabble

rowdy

adjective rough and noisy » *Nasir complained about being disturbed by his neighbors' rowdy parties.*
boisterous, noisy, unruly, wild, obstreperous, uproarious

royal

adjective concerning a king or a queen or their family » *We saw the royal yacht moored in the harbor.*
imperial, regal, sovereign

rubbish 1

noun (Britain) unwanted things or waste material » *Rubbish was piled up at the side of the road, waiting to be removed.*
garbage, litter, refuse, trash, waste

gallop
The children galloped down the steep hill.

bolt
The cheeky hound bolted after stealing the pie.

dart
The dog darted left and right to avoid capture.

hare
The speedy dog simply hared along!

pound
Tired out, Harry pounded along behind his sister.

jog
The children jogged slowly up the steep inclines.

sprint
Melissa was faster than Harry at sprinting after the dog.

rubbish [2]
noun (Britain) foolish words or speech » *Don't talk rubbish!*
drivel, garbage, hot air (informal), **nonsense**

rude [1]
adjective not polite
» *Ignoring your friends is rude.*
disrespectful, impertinent, impudent, insolent, churlish, discourteous, peremptory
antonym: **polite**

rude [2]
adjective unexpected and unpleasant » *The campers had a rude awakening when a goat ran into their tent.*
abrupt, unpleasant, violent

ruin [1]
verb to destroy or spoil something » *The crops have been ruined by pests.*
break, damage, destroy, devastate, impair, mar, mess up, spoil, undo, wreck

ruin [2]
noun the state of being destroyed or spoiled » *The castle was falling into ruin.*
decay, destruction, devastation, disrepair, downfall, fall

*Sheep grazed near the **ruins** of the ancient temple.*

ruin [3]
noun the remaining parts of a severely damaged thing » *Sheep grazed near the ruins of the ancient temple.*
remains, shell, wreck

rule [1]
noun a statement of what is allowed » *Coming in late was against the rules.*
decree, guideline, law, order, regulation, dictum, ordinance, precept

rule [2] : as a rule
adverb usually or generally » *As a rule, I eat my meals at the kitchen table.*
generally, mainly, normally, on the whole, usually

rule [3]
verb to govern people » *Queen Elizabeth II has ruled the UK longer than any other monarch.*
administer, be in power, govern, lead, reign

ruler
noun a person who rules or commands » *Augustus was a decisive ruler of ancient Rome.*
commander, governor, head of state, leader, monarch, sovereign

rumor
noun a story which may or may not be true » *I heard a rumor that our trip might be canceled.*
gossip, hearsay, whisper, word

run [1]
verb to move on foot at a rapid pace, never having both or all the feet on the ground at the same time
▼ SEE BELOW

run [2]
verb to manage » *Shawn ran a small hotel.*
administer, be in charge of, control, direct, look after, manage, take care of

rush [1]
verb to move fast or do something quickly » *The plumber unblocked the pipe and the water rushed out.*
dash, fly, gush, hasten, hurry, race, run, scurry, shoot

rush [2]
verb to force into immediate action without sufficient preparation » *I don't want to rush you, but I need to know soon if you're coming tonight.*
hurry, hustle, press, pressurize, push

rush [3]
noun a state of hurrying » *Fred was in a rush to catch the last train.*
bustle, dash, hurry, race, scramble, stampede

*Fred was in a **rush** to catch the last train.*

run
[1] *verb* to move on foot at a rapid pace, never having both or all the feet on the ground at the same time
» *The children **ran** down the hill after their dog.*

scurry
The dog **scurried** away when it was chased.

scamper
The dog grabbed the pie from the picnic and **scampered** off.

a b c d e f g h i j k l m n o p q r s t u v w x y z

A B C D E F G H I J K L M N O P Q R S T U V W X Y Z

Ss

sack 1
verb (informal) to dismiss from a job » *Kevin was sacked from his paper round because of his constant lateness.*
ax, discharge, dismiss, fire, terminate

sack 2
verb to hit a quarterback in football before he can throw a pass » *When the quarterback was sacked, he fell to the ground.*
attack, hit, tackle

sacrifice 1
verb to give something up » *Betsy sacrificed her lunch hour to distribute leaflets for charity.*
forego, forfeit, give up,

*Betsy **sacrificed** her lunch hour to distribute leaflets for charity.*

sacrifice 2
noun the action of giving something up » *Louise made many sacrifices in order to save money for her around-the-world trip.*
contribution, donation, offering, renunciation, self-denial

*I'm **sad** because my best friend has moved away.*

sad 1
adjective feeling unhappy about something » *I'm sad because my best friend has moved away.*
blue, dejected, depressed, dismal, down, downcast, forlorn, gloomy, glum, grief-stricken, low, melancholy, mournful, unhappy, wistful,
disconsolate, doleful, heavy-hearted, low-spirited, lugubrious
antonym: **happy**

sad 2
adjective making you feel unhappy » *She sang a sad song of love and loss.*
depressing, dismal, gloomy, heartbreaking, heartrending, mournful, moving, pathetic, poignant, tearful, tragic, upsetting

sadness
noun the feeling of being unhappy » *I said goodbye with a mixture of sadness and joy.*
dejection, depression, desolation, despondency, melancholy, unhappiness,
cheerlessness, dolefulness, sorrowfulness
antonym: **happiness**

safe 1
adjective not causing harm or danger » *The coastguard's green flag showed that the water was safe for swimming.*
harmless, innocuous, wholesome
antonym: **dangerous**

safe 2
adjective not in any danger » *Everyone was safe from the storm in the shelter.*
all right, in safe hands, okay or OK (informal), out of danger, out of harm's way, protected, safe and sound, secure

safeguard 1
verb to protect something » *A plan was in place to safeguard the park from developers who wanted to build on it.*
defend, guard, look after, preserve, protect, save, shield, take care of

safeguard 2
noun something that protects people or things » *The charity puts safeguards in place to protect endangered species.*
barrier, cover, defense, protection, screen, security

safety
noun the state of being safe from harm or danger » *For everyone's safety, the flight attendant ran through the emergency procedure.*
immunity, protection, security
antonym: **danger**

*For everyone's **safety**, the flight attendant ran through the emergency procedure.*

*Mounds of salt were harvested from the **salty** water.*

salty
adjective tasting of or containing salt » *Mounds of salt were harvested from the salty water.*
briny, saline, salted

same
adjective exactly like one another
►► SEE RIGHT

sanction 1
verb to officially approve of or allow something » *The school has sanctioned the selling of baked goods on the premises to raise money for charity.*
allow, approve, authorize, back, endorse, permit, support
antonym: **veto**

sanction 2
noun official approval of something » *The teacher required the sanction of each student's parent for the field trip to go ahead.*
approval, authorization, backing, blessing, permission, support,
assent, mandate, ratification (formal)

sanctions
plural noun penalties for countries that break the law » *Trade sanctions were imposed for four years.*
ban, boycott, embargo, penalties

sane [1]

adjective having a normal, healthy mind » *As the dog ran around in circles, Audrey wondered if it was sane.*
lucid, normal, rational, compos mentis, in your right mind, of sound mind
antonym: **crazy**

sane [2]

adjective showing good sense » *We respected her sane decision to stay at home.*
judicious, levelheaded, rational, reasonable, sensible, sound

sarcastic

adjective saying the opposite of what you mean to make fun of someone » *A sarcastic remark about missing the ball was on the tip of her tongue.*
biting, caustic, cutting, ironic, sardonic, satirical, scathing, snarky, derisive

satisfactory

adjective acceptable or adequate » *The restaurant's food was satisfactory, but nothing special.*
acceptable, adequate, all right, good enough, passable, sufficient
antonym: **unsatisfactory**

satisfied

adjective happy because you have what you want » *The satisfied customers left the sale loaded with bargains.*
content, contented, delighted, happy, pleased
antonym: **disappointed**

satisfy [1]

verb to give someone something they want » *By giving each of the team a particular task, Jason found a solution to satisfy everyone.*
gratify, indulge, please, assuage, pander to, sate, satiate, slake

satisfy [2]

verb to convince of something » *Joe had to satisfy the coach that he was fit enough to play.*
convince, persuade, reassure

satisfy [3]

verb to fulfill a requirement » *Students must satisfy the grade requirements to get in to the college.*
fulfill, meet

savage [1]

noun a violent and uncivilized person or thing » *My mom was angry and accused us of eating like savages.*
barbarian, beast, brute, lout, monster

savage [2]

verb to attack and bite someone or something » *The puppy savaged the toy rattle.*
attack, bite, maul

*The **savage** lion let out an unexpected roar.*

savage [3]

adjective cruel and violent » *The savage lion let out an unexpected roar.*
barbaric, barbarous, brutal, cruel, ferocious, inhuman, vicious, violent

save [1]

verb to rescue someone or something » *Eli saved my life.*
come to someone's rescue, deliver, redeem, rescue, salvage

equal
*They are **equal** in height.*

alike
*The girls are **alike**.*

indistinguishable
*Their hairstyles are **indistinguishable**.*

antonym:
different
*The boys look totally **different** from each other.*

identical
*Their bags are **identical**.*

same
adjective exactly like one another
» *They look the **same**.*

equivalent
*The girls earned **equivalent** grades in school.*

a b c d e f g h i j k l m n o p q r s t u v w x y z

save [2]

verb to keep someone or something safe » *Fences around playgrounds save children from running onto busy roads.*
keep safe, preserve, protect, safeguard

save [3]

verb to keep something for later use » *Chen was saving his allowance to buy a new bike.*
conserve, hoard, keep, put by, reserve, scrape, scrimp, set aside, economize, preserve
antonym: **waste**

*Chen was **saving** his allowance to buy a new bike.*

say [1]

verb to speak words
◀◀ SEE LEFT

say [2]

noun a chance to express your opinion » *Our teacher called a meeting so everyone could have a say.*
voice, vote

saying

noun a well-known sentence or phrase » *"Look before you leap" is a well-known saying.*
adage, axiom, epigram, maxim, proverb, cliche, motto, reflection, truth

scarce

adjective rare or uncommon » *Watermelons are summer fruit, so they are scarce in stores during the winter.*
few, light, meager, scant, sparse, rare, uncommon, unusual
antonym: **common**

scare [1]

verb to frighten someone » *Mike jumped out and scared Clare.*
alarm, frighten, give someone a fright, intimidate, startle, terrify, terrorize, unnerve

scare [2]

noun a short period of feeling very frightened » *Conor gave me a scare when he shrieked.*
fright, shock, start

scare [3]

noun a situation where people worry about something » *The bird flu scare is now over.*
alert, hysteria, panic

scary

adjective (informal) frightening » *We watched a scary movie about ghosts.*
alarming, chilling, creepy (informal)**, eerie, frightening, hair-raising, spooky, terrifying, unnerving**

scatter

verb to throw or drop things all over an area » *The wind scattered the dandelion seeds.*
shower, sow, sprinkle, throw about, broadcast, disseminate, strew
antonym: **gather**

*The wind **scattered** the dandelion seeds.*

scene [1]

noun a picture or view of something » *The scene in the painting was a house on a hill.*
landscape, panorama, view, outlook, vista

*The police were first on the **scene**.*

scene [2]

noun the place where something happens » *The police were first on the scene.*
location, place, setting, site, spot

scene [3]

noun an area of activity » *He is a well-known guitarist on the music scene.*
arena, business, environment, world

scenery

noun the things you see in the countryside » *We drove through the national park, admiring the scenery.*
landscape, panorama, surroundings, terrain, view, outlook, vista

scold

verb to tell someone off » *The teacher scolded the class for being too rowdy.*
ball out, chastise, chew out, chide, lecture, rebuke, reprimand, tell off (informal)**,** admonish, berate

scorn [1]

noun great contempt felt for something » *Tom thought his idea was a good one, and ignored the scorn shown by his friends.*
contempt, derision, disdain, mockery

scorn [2]

verb to treat with great contempt » *Eleanor scorned my offer of help.*
despise, disdain, look down on, slight, contemn, hold in contempt

scornful

adjective showing contempt » *Peter is scornful of his rivals and sure that he will win.*
contemptuous, disdainful, scathing, sneering, supercilious, withering

scrape [1]

verb to rub a rough or sharp object against something » *We had to scrape the frost off the windshield.*
graze, scour, scratch, scuff, skin

*We had to **scrape** the frost off the windshield.*

scrape [2]

verb to make a harsh noise by rubbing » *Sarah scraped her chair across the floor.*
grate, grind, rasp, scratch

scream [1]

verb to shout or cry in a high-pitched voice » *Cameron screamed as his bike sped down the hill.*
cry, howl, screech, shout, shriek, squeal, yell

scream [2]

noun a loud, high-pitched cry » *Heidi let out a scream of joy when she opened her present.*
cry, howl, screech, shriek, squeal, yell

scrounge

verb (informal) to get something by asking rather than working for it » *Harry tried to scrounge a lift.*
beg, bum (informal)**, cadge, freeload** (informal)**, sponge** (informal)

a b c d e f g h i j k l m n o p q r s t u v w x y z

*Sadie and Ryan wore their **scruffy** clothes for painting.*

scruffy

adjective dirty and messy » *Sadie and Ryan wore their scruffy clothes for painting.* **beat up, grungy, ragged, seedy, shabby, tatty, unkempt,** disreputable, ungroomed

scrutinize

verb to examine something very carefully » *Arianna scrutinized the chess board before she made her move.* **examine, inspect, pore over, scan, search, study**

search ①

verb to look for something ►► **SEE RIGHT**

search ②

noun the action of looking for something » *Sam began a search for a different type of skateboard.* **chase, exploration, forage, hunt, probe, pursuit, quest, scout**

secret

adjective known about by only a few people » *The movie stars got married at a secret location on a Pacific island.* **behind-the-scenes, closet** (informal)**, confidential, covert, furtive, hidden, hush-hush, undercover, underground,** cloak-and-dagger, conspiratorial, undisclosed related word: *adjective* **cryptic**

secretive

adjective hiding your feelings and intentions » *Skylar was secretive about wanting to be a singer in case people laughed.* **cagey** (informal)**, reserved, reticent,** tight-lipped, uncommunicative, unforthcoming

section

noun one of the parts into which something is divided » *The dog is allowed only in this section of the house.* **division, instalment, part, piece, portion, segment**

secure ①

verb (formal) to manage to get something » *Julian's good grades helped him to get accepted to a great university.* **acquire, gain, get, obtain, procure** (formal)

secure ②

verb to make something safe » *The mighty stone walls secured the town against attack.* **fortify, make impregnable, make safe, strengthen**

secure ③

verb to fasten or attach something firmly » *The train cars were secured to the engine before it left the station.* **attach, bind, fasten, fix, lock, moor, tie up** antonym: **release**

secure ④

adjective tightly locked or well protected » *The bike was secure, padlocked to the rail.* **fortified, impregnable, protected, safe, shielded**

*The bike was **secure**, padlocked to the rail.*

secure ⑤

adjective firmly fixed in place » *She finally made the child's safety seat secure in the back of the car.* **fastened, firm, fixed, locked, solid, stable, tight**

secure ⑥

adjective feeling safe and happy » *The baby was sound asleep, secure in her mother's arms.* **confident, protected, reassured, relaxed, safe** antonym: **insecure**

*The baby was sound asleep, **secure** in her mother's arms.*

see ①

verb to look at or notice something » *I can see a herd of elephants.* **behold, discern, glimpse, look, notice, observe, perceive, sight, spot,** catch sight of, witness

see ②

verb to realize or understand something » *I see exactly what you mean.* **appreciate, comprehend, follow, get, grasp, realize, understand**

see ③

verb to find something out » *I'll see what's happening outside the gates.* **ascertain, determine, discover, find out**

seek ①

verb to try to find something » *Becky was seeking a book on bonsai trees from her library.* **be after, hunt, look for, search for**

seek ②

verb to try to do something » *I seek to raise as much money as possible for charity.* **aim, aspire to, attempt, endeavor, strive, try**

seem

verb to appear to be » *Lucas seemed shy at first because he was very quiet.* **appear, give the impression of, look, look like**

seize ①

verb to grab something firmly » *Jim seized the phone from my hand.* **grab, grasp, snatch**

seize ②

verb to take control of something » *The knights seized the castle.* **ambush, annex, appropriate, capture, confiscate, hijack, impound, take over,** commandeer, take possession of

select ①

verb to choose something » *The guests each selected a differently decorated cupcake.* **choose, decide on, opt for, pick, settle on, single out, take**

*The guests each **selected** a differently decorated cupcake.*

select ②

adjective of good quality » *The team was a select group of the best players.* **choice, exclusive, first-class, first-rate, hand-picked, prime, special, superior**

selfish

adjective caring only about yourself » *Ella knew it was selfish not to share her candy.*
egoistic or **egoistical**, **egotistic** or **egotistical**, **greedy**, **self-centered**, self-interested, self-seeking, ungenerous

sell ①

verb to let someone have something in return for money » *I decided to sell my bike.*
deal in, **hawk**, **peddle**, **retail**, **trade in**, **vend**
antonym: **buy**

sell ②

verb to have available for people to buy
» *The shop sells doughnuts.*
deal in, **stock**, **trade in**
antonym: **buy**

*The shop **sells** doughnuts.*

send ①

verb to arrange for something to be delivered » *We sent Mom flowers for Mother's Day.*
dispatch, **forward**, **remit**

send ②

verb to transmit a signal or message » *Satellites send and receive signals to and from Earth.*
broadcast, **stream**, **transmit**

senior

adjective the highest and most important in an organization » *The senior officer trained the new recruits.*
best, **better**, **high-ranking**, **superior**
antonym: **junior**

sense ①

noun a feeling you have about something » *Zoe had a sense that everything was going well.*
consciousness, **feeling**, **impression**

sense ②

noun the ability to think and behave sensibly » *Alice had the sense to call me when she got lost.*
brains (informal), **common sense**, **intelligence**, **judgment**, **reason**, **wisdom**, street smarts, wit

sense ③

verb to become aware of something » *Tamika sensed that Jayden wasn't telling her the whole story.*
be aware of, **feel**, **get the impression**, **have a hunch**, **realize**

sensible

adjective showing good sense and judgment » *We panicked when the dog got stuck, but Ted was sensible and calmly freed it.*
down-to-earth, **judicious**, **practical**, **prudent**, **rational**, **sound**, **wise**
antonym: **foolish**

*We panicked when the dog got stuck, but Ted was **sensible** and calmly freed it.*

sensitive

adjective easily upset about something » *The little boy was sensitive about other children playing with his toys.*
delicate, **easily offended**, **easily upset**, **fragile**, **thin-skinned**, **touchy**

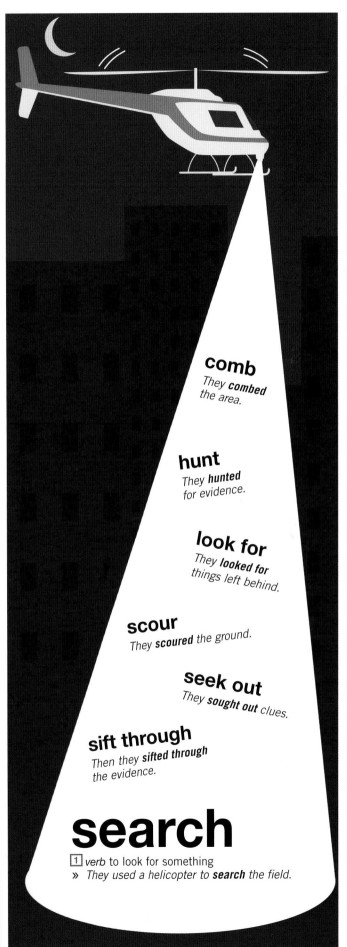

comb
*They **combed** the area.*

hunt
*They **hunted** for evidence.*

look for
*They **looked for** things left behind.*

scour
*They **scoured** the ground.*

seek out
*They **sought out** clues.*

sift through
*Then they **sifted through** the evidence.*

search

① *verb* to look for something » *They used a helicopter to **search** the field.*

a b c d e f g h i j k l m n o p q r s t u v w x y z

A B C D E F G H I J K L M N O P Q R S T U V W X Y Z

*Isabella had a **sentimental** attachment to her old teddy bear.*

sentimental

adjective expressing exaggerated sadness or tenderness » *Isabella had a sentimental attachment to her old teddy bear.*
maudlin, mushy (informal), **nostalgic, sloppy** (informal), **slushy** (informal),
dewy-eyed, mushy, overemotional, soppy

separate ①

adjective not connected to something else » *The house stood in a field, separate from the other houses.*
detached, disconnected, discrete, divorced, isolated, unconnected
antonym: **connected**

separate ②

verb to end a connection between people or things » *The two train cars separated so that they could take the passengers to different destinations.*
detach, disconnect, divide, sunder, uncouple
antonym: **connect**

sequence ①

noun a number of events coming one after another » *The team enjoyed a sequence of wins.*
chain, course, cycle, series, string, succession

sequence ②

noun a particular order in which things are arranged » *The sequence of each day's TV programs is decided in advance.*
arrangement, order, progression, structure

series

noun a number of things coming one after the other » *Logan read a series of books about the same character.*
chain, run, sequence, string, succession

serious ①

adjective very bad and worrying » *Appendicitis is a serious but treatable illness.*
acute, alarming, bad, critical, dangerous, extreme, grave, grievous, grim, intense, precarious, severe, worrying

serious ②

adjective important, deserving careful thought » *Getting a dog is a serious responsibility.*
crucial, deep, difficult, far-reaching, grave, important, momentous, pressing, profound, significant, urgent, weighty
antonym: **funny**

serious ③

adjective sincere about something » *I thought Craig was joking, but he was serious.*
earnest, genuine, heartfelt, honest, in earnest, resolute, resolved, sincere

serious ④

adjective quiet and not laughing » *Keira put on a serious expression for her passport photograph.*
earnest, grave, humorless, pensive, sober, solemn, staid, stern

*Keira put on a **serious** expression for her passport photograph.*

set ①

noun a group of things that belong together » *The set of tools belonged in the garage.*
batch, bunch, bundle, collection, kit, outfit, series, assemblage, compendium, ensemble

set ②

verb to put or place something somewhere » *Eloise set her bag down on the ground.*
deposit, lay, locate, place, position, put, rest, stick

*Eloise **set** her bag down on the ground.*

set ③

adjective fixed and not varying » *We arrived at the set time.*
arranged, established, firm, fixed, predetermined, scheduled

set on

adjective determined to do something » *Josie was set on going to the beach.*
bent on, determined, intent on

settle ①

verb to put an end to an argument or problem » *The dispute was finally settled after a lot of work.*
clear up, decide, dispose of, put an end to, reconcile, resolve, straighten out

settle ②

verb to decide or arrange something » *My friends and I settled on going to the movies.*
agree, arrange, decide on, determine, fix

settle ③

verb to make your home in a place » *We settled in a new part of town.*
make your home, move to, put down roots, take up residence

set up

verb to make arrangements for something » *My sister set up a couple of interviews for part-time jobs.*
arrange, establish, install, institute, organize

sever

verb to cut something off » *The flowers had been severed from their stems during the storm.*
chop off, hack off, lop off

several

adjective indicating a small number » *Clive won several medals in the competition.*
assorted, lots of, some, sundry, various

*Clive won **several** medals in the competition.*

severe ①

adjective extremely bad or unpleasant » *The hurricane caused severe damage.*
acute, critical, dire, extreme, grave, intense, serious, terrible
antonym: **mild**

severe ②

adjective stern and harsh » *Janet gave Lee a severe look when he dropped the vase.*
disapproving, grim, hard, harsh, stern, strict

shabby [1]

adjective ragged and worn in appearance » *Dad's favorite coat was now old and shabby.*
beat up, dilapidated, ragged, scruffy, seedy, tatty, threadbare, worn, down at heel, run-down, worse for wear

shabby [2]

adjective (Britain) behaving meanly and unfairly » *My aunt complained to the manager about the family's shabby treatment by the waiter.*
contemptible, despicable, dirty, mean, rotten (informal), dishonorable, ignoble, scurvy

shake [1]

verb to move something from side to side or up and down » *Shake the bottle before opening it.*
agitate, brandish, jerk, jiggle, sway, vibrate

shake [2]

verb to move from side to side or up and down » *The earthquake caused the ground to shake.*
jolt, quake, quiver, shiver, shudder, tremble, vibrate, joggle, oscillate

shake [3]

verb to shock and upset someone » *The news shook me and I had to lie down.*
distress, disturb, rattle (informal), **shock, unnerve, upset,** discompose, traumatize

shaky

adjective weak and unsteady » *The rope bridge was shaky.*
rickety, tottering, trembling, unstable, unsteady, wobbly

*The rope bridge was **shaky**.*

shame [1]

noun a feeling of guilt or embarrassment » *The shame Ryan felt over his rushed homework made him determined to do well next time.*
embarrassment, humiliation, ignominy, regret, remorse, loss of face, mortification

shame [2]

noun something that makes people lose respect for you » *Bullies bring shame on a school.*
discredit, disgrace, dishonor, scandal

shame [3]

verb to make someone feel ashamed » *My mom was so upset about the state of my bedroom that she shamed me into cleaning it up.*
disgrace, embarrass, humiliate, mortify

shameless

adjective behaving badly without showing any shame » *Greg complimented the teacher in a shameless attempt to get better grades.*
barefaced, brazen, flagrant, unabashed, unashamed

shape [1]

noun the outline of something » *The geometric shapes formed a starlike pattern.*
contours, figure, form, lines, outline

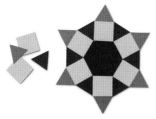

*The geometric **shapes** formed a starlike pattern.*

shape [2]

verb to make something in a particular form » *Shape the dough into a loaf.*
fashion, form, make, model, mold

*The friends **shared** the pizza.*

share [1]

verb to divide something between two or more people » *The friends shared the pizza.*
divide, split

share [2]

noun a portion of something » *I took my share of popcorn.*
allotment, portion, quota, ration

sharp [1]

adjective having a fine cutting edge or point » *Ian used the sharp knife to cut up an apple.*
jagged, keen, pointed, razor-sharp
antonym: **blunt**

sharp [2]

adjective quick to notice or understand things » *The mouse was sharp enough to leave the cheese on the mousetrap.*
alert, astute, bright, clever observant, perceptive, quick, quick-witted

sharp [3]

adjective sudden and significant » *Josie made a sharp turn into the parking lot.*
abrupt, marked, sudden

sheer [1]

adjective complete and total » *The nursery rhyme was sheer nonsense.*
absolute, complete, pure, total, unqualified, utter, unadulterated, unmitigated (formal)

sheer [2]

adjective vertical » *The climbing wall was on the sheer face of a building.*
perpendicular, steep, vertical

sheer [3]

adjective very light and delicate » *Molly wore a sheer black scarf.*
delicate, fine, lightweight, see-through, thin
antonym: **thick**

shelter [1]

noun a place providing protection » *We all met at the bus shelter.*
hostel, refuge, sanctuary

shelter [2]

noun protection from the weather or danger » *The hut provided shelter from the snowy mountainside.*
asylum, cover, harbor, haven, protection, refuge, safety, sanctuary

*The hut provided **shelter** from the snowy mountainside.*

shelter [3]

verb to stay somewhere in order to be safe » *Luca sheltered in the doorway until the rain stopped.*
hide, huddle, take cover

shelter [4]

verb to hide or protect someone or something » *The mother bird sheltered the chicks until they could fly.*
harbor, hide, protect, safeguard, shield

shine
verb to give out a bright light » *The stars shined brightly in the night sky.*
beam, gleam, glow, radiate, shimmer, sparkle

shining
adjective giving out or reflecting light » *Eleanor put sunglasses on to protect her eyes from the shining sunlight.*
bright, brilliant, gleaming, luminous, radiant, shimmering, sparkling, incandescent

shock 1
noun a sudden, upsetting experience » *It was a shock to discover that the screen on her phone had shattered.*
blow, bombshell, distress, trauma

shock 2
verb to make you feel upset » *He was shocked when his exam was canceled at the very last minute.*
numb, paralyze, shake, stagger, stun, traumatize

shock 3
verb to offend because of being rude or immoral » *Nana is easily shocked by my jokes.*
appal, disgust, offend, outrage, nauseate, scandalize

shop
noun a place where things are sold
▼ SEE BELOW

shore
noun land that borders a body of water » *The sandy shore was littered with shells.*
bank, beach, coast, foreshore, front, lakeside, sands, seaboard, seashore, shingle, strand, waterside, lakefront

*The sandy **shore** was littered with shells.*

short 1
adjective not lasting very long » *We enjoyed a short break in the countryside.*
brief, fleeting, momentary, short-lived
antonym: **long**

*Naomi arranged the Russian dolls from **short** to tall.*

short 2
adjective small in height » *Naomi arranged the Russian dolls from short to tall.*
little, small, diminutive, tiny, petite, squat
antonym: **tall**

short 3
adjective not using many words » *Kevin's speech was short and to the point.*
brief, concise, succinct, terse, abridged, laconic, pithy

shortage
noun a lack of something » *There was a shortage of bananas in the stores.*
dearth, deficiency, lack, scarcity, shortfall, want, insufficiency, paucity
antonym: **abundance**

shorten
verb to make something shorter » *Alexander shortened his name to Alex.*
abbreviate, cut, trim, abridge, downsize, truncate
antonym: **lengthen**

shout 1
noun a loud call or cry » *I heard a distant shout and ran to see what was going on.*
bellow, cry, roar, scream, yell

shout 2
verb to call or cry loudly » *Paul shouted downstairs to his brother.*
bawl, bellow, call, cry, roar, scream, yell

show 1
noun to prove something » *The experiment showed that oil is less dense than water.*
demonstrate, prove

show 2
verb to display a quality or characteristic » *Savannah's sketches showed real skill.*
demonstrate, display, indicate, manifest, reveal, evince, testify to

shop

noun a place where things are sold » *I went to the coffee **shop**.*

store
*I browsed in the **store**.*

boutique
*I bought smart clothes in the **boutique**.*

show ③
noun a public exhibition » *Our class went to see a show at the local theater.*
display, exhibition, presentation

show ④
noun a display of a feeling or quality » *Grandma gave all of us hugs and kisses in a big show of affection.*
air, display, exhibition, pose, pretence, semblance

show ⑤: show how
verb to do something to teach someone else » *Dad showed me how to play the game.*
demonstrate, instruct, teach

Dad **showed** me how to play the game.

shrewd
adjective showing intelligence and good judgment » *She was shrewd with money and saved most of it.*
astute, canny, crafty, perceptive, sharp, smart, perspicacious, sagacious

shrill
adjective high-pitched and piercing » *The bird's call was shrill and loud.*
penetrating, piercing, sharp

shrink
verb to become smaller » *Ron's sweater had shrunk in the wash.*
contract, diminish, dwindle, get smaller, narrow
antonym: **grow**

Ron's sweater had **shrunk** in the wash.

shut ①
verb to close something » *Someone had forgotten to shut the door.*
close, fasten, slam
antonym: **open**

shut ②
adjective closed or fastened » *Eva heard a sound coming from behind the shut door.*
closed, fastened, sealed
antonym: **open**

Pete was **shy** and found it hard to make friends at school.

shy
adjective nervous in the company of other people » *Pete was shy and found it hard to make friends at school.*
bashful, retiring, self-conscious, skittish, timid, fearful, timorous
antonym: **bold**

sick ①
adjective unwell or ill » *The doctor's waiting room was full of sick people.*
ailing, ill, peaked, run down, under par (informal)**, under the weather, unsound, unwell**
antonym: **well**

sick ②
adjective feeling as if you are going to vomit » *The stomach bug made Lily feel sick.*
ill, nauseous, queasy

sick ③: sick of
adjective (informal) tired of something » *Cora was sick of listening to the same music over and over again.*
bored with, fed up with, tired of, weary of

side ①
noun the edge of something » *Tyler sat up and dangled his legs over the side of the bed.*
border, edge
related word: *adjective* **lateral**

side ②
noun one of two groups involved in a dispute or contest » *Both sides had won the competition before.*
camp, faction, party, team

side with
verb to support someone in an argument » *Louise always sided with her sister when anyone was mean to her.*
agree with, stand up for, support, take the part of

sight ①
noun the ability to see » *My sight is so much better now that I wear glasses.*
eyesight, visibility, vision
related words: *adjectives* **optical, visual**

grocery store
I stocked up on cereal at the **grocery store**.

mall
I walked around the **mall** window-shopping.

big box store
I spent a long time deciding what to buy in the vast aisles of the **big box store**.

market
I bought fruit from a stall at the **market**.

A B C D E F G H I J K L M N O P Q R S T U V W X Y Z

sight ②
noun something you see
» *The fields of wild flowers were a beautiful sight.*
display, scene, spectacle

sight ③
verb to see something or someone » *We sighted a rare songbird on our walk in the woods.*
see, spot

sign ①
noun a mark or symbol
» *A heart is a sign that symbolizes love.*
character, emblem, logo, mark, symbol

sign ②
noun a notice put up to give a warning or information
» *The sign warned that the floor was wet and slippery.*
board, billboard, notice, placard, poster

*The **sign** warned that the floor was wet and slippery.*

sign ③
noun evidence of something
» *The green shoots of plants and flowers were a sign that spring was on its way.*
clue, evidence, hint, indication, omen, symptom, token, trace

signal ①
noun something that is intended to give a message
» *The signal lights flashed to warn that the bridge was opening.*
beacon, cue, gesture, sign

*Hayley **signaled** for a taxi.*

signal ②
verb to make a sign as a message to someone
» *Hayley signaled for a taxi.*
beckon, gesticulate, gesture, hail, motion, nod, sign, wave

significant
adjective large or important
» *The medicine had a significant effect on Evan's stomach bug, and he was feeling better in no time.*
considerable, important, impressive, marked, notable, pronounced, striking
antonym: **insignificant**

silence ①
noun an absence of sound
» *There was total silence in the room while the class took the exam.*
calm, hush, lull, peace, quiet, stillness
antonym: **noise**

silence ②
noun an inability or refusal to talk » *Mary maintained a respectful silence, keeping her thoughts to herself.*
dumbness, muteness, reticence, speechlessness, stillness, taciturnity, uncommunicativeness, voicelessness

silence ③
verb to make someone or something quiet » *The crying baby was silenced by the arrival of his father with the pacifier.*
deaden, gag, muffle, quiet, quieten, stifle, still, suppress

silent ①
adjective not saying anything
» *The class fell silent when the teacher entered the room.*
dumb, mute, speechless, taciturn, wordless, tongue-tied, uncommunicative

silent ②
adjective making no noise
» *The clock was silent because its battery was dead.*
hushed, quiet, soundless, still
antonym: **noisy**

silly
adjective foolish or ridiculous
» *The dog wore a silly hat.*
absurd, crazy, foolish, frivolous, goofy, idiotic, inane, ridiculous, stupid, asinine, puerile, witless

*The dog wore a **silly** hat.*

similar
adjective like something else
» *Our red dresses were similar.*
alike, analogous, comparable, like, uniform
antonym: **different**

similarity
noun the quality of being like something else
» *The similarity between the two paintings is striking.*
analogy, likeness, resemblance, sameness, comparability, congruence, similitude
antonym: **difference**

simple ①
adjective easy to understand or do » *The recipe had simple steps and was easy to make.*
easy, elementary, straightforward, uncomplicated, understandable
antonym: **complicated**

simple ②
adjective plain in style
» *Sarah wore a simple but stylish outfit.*
classic, clean, modest, plain
antonym: **elaborate**

simplify
verb to make something easier to do or understand
» *The teacher had to simplify her instructions as some of the students didn't understand them.*
make simpler, streamline

sin ①
noun wicked and immoral behavior » *The man asked for forgiveness for his sins.*
crime, evil, offense, wickedness, wrong, iniquity, misdeed, transgression, trespass

sin ②
verb to do something wicked and immoral » *I didn't mean to lie—I'm sorry I sinned.*
cheat, do wrong, go astray, misbehave, transgress

sincere
adjective saying things that you really mean
» *Ashley gave her sincere thanks for the thoughtful gifts.*
genuine, heartfelt, real, wholehearted
antonym: **insincere**

single ①
adjective only one » *Ruby kept the single sock in case the matching one turned up.*
lone, one, only, sole, solitary

*Ruby kept the **single** sock in case the matching one turned up.*

single [2]
adjective not married
» *Barry was single and enjoyed living on his own.*
unattached, unmarried

single [3]
adjective for one person only
» *Mom booked a single room at the hotel as Dad couldn't go.*
individual, separate

singular
adjective (formal) unusual and remarkable » *Mary had a singular smile—it lit up her whole face.*
exceptional, extraordinary, rare, remarkable, uncommon, unique, unusual

sinister
adjective seeming harmful or evil » *The bad guy in the book was a sinister character.*
evil, forbidding, menacing, ominous, threatening, baleful, disquieting, dark

situation
noun what is happening
» *Mr. Lee mistaking me for my brother was a funny situation.*
case, circumstances, plight, scenario, state of affairs

*The bears came in various **sizes**.*

size [1]
noun how big or small something is » *The bears came in various sizes.*
dimensions, extent, proportions

size [2]
noun the fact of something being very large » *The sheer size of the island meant that it would take weeks to travel its entire coastline.*
bulk, immensity, magnitude, vastness

skillful
adjective able to do something very well » *Kate had regular tennis coaching and was a skillful player.*
able, accomplished, adept, competent, deft, expert, masterly, proficient, skilled, adroit, dexterous
antonym: **incompetent**

skill
noun the ability to do something well
» *Completing such a complex task requires skill.*
ability, competence, dexterity, expertise, facility, knack, proficiency

skilled
adjective having the knowledge to do something well
» *The model was made by a highly skilled carpenter.*
able, accomplished, competent, experienced, expert, masterly, professional, proficient, skillful, trained
antonym: **incompetent**

skinny
adjective extremely thin
» *The boy ate like a horse, but was naturally skinny.*
bony, emaciated, lean, scrawny, slender, slim, thin, underfed, undernourished
antonym: **plump**

slander [1]
noun something untrue and malicious said about someone
» *It was a slander to say that someone else wrote her books.*
libel, scandal, slur, smear, aspersion, defamation, vilification

slander [2]
verb to say untrue and malicious things about someone » *She apologized for slandering the executive.*
libel, malign, smear, defame, traduce, vilify

sleep [1]
noun the natural state of rest in which you are unconscious
» *Heather woke up feeling rested after a good sleep.*
doze, forty winks (slang), **hibernation, kip** (Britain; slang), **nap, slumber, snooze** (informal), dormancy, repose, siesta

sleep [2]
verb to rest in a natural state of unconsciousness
▼ **SEE BELOW**

sleepy [1]
adjective tired and ready to go to sleep » *The cat was sleepy and curled up on the rug.*
drowsy, lethargic, sluggish, somnolent, torpid

sleepy [2]
adjective not having much activity or excitement » *We live in a sleepy little town.*
dull, peaceful, quiet

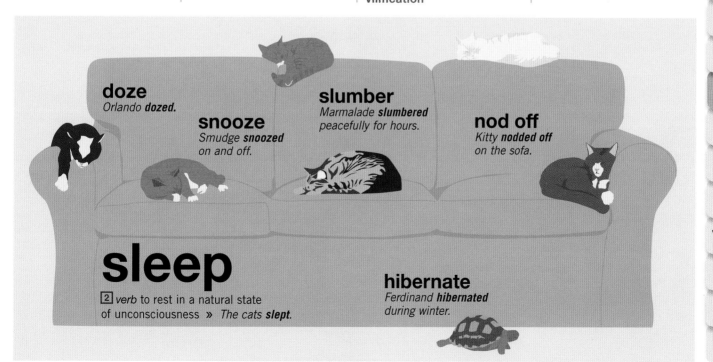

doze
*Orlando **dozed**.*

snooze
*Smudge **snoozed** on and off.*

slumber
*Marmalade **slumbered** peacefully for hours.*

nod off
*Kitty **nodded off** on the sofa.*

sleep
[2] *verb* to rest in a natural state of unconsciousness » *The cats **slept**.*

hibernate
*Ferdinand **hibernated** during winter.*

a b c d e f g h i j k l m n o p q r s t u v w x y z

A B C D E F G H I J K L M N O P Q R **S** T U V W X Y Z

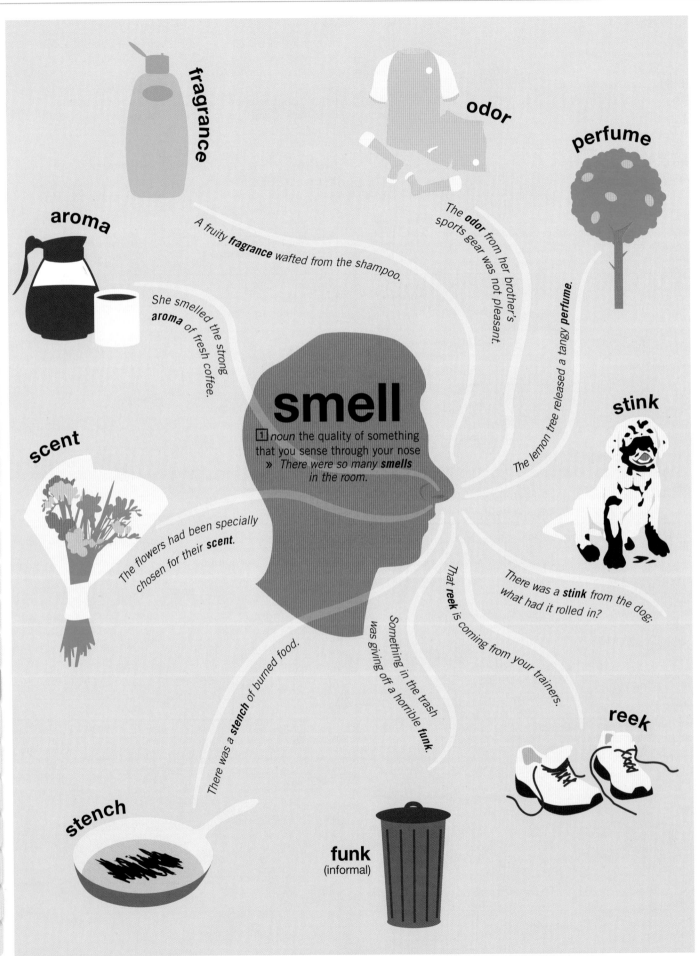

fragrance

odor

perfume

aroma

A fruity **fragrance** wafted from the shampoo.

The **odor** from her brother's sports gear was not pleasant.

She smelled the strong **aroma** of fresh coffee.

The lemon tree released a tangy **perfume**.

smell

1 *noun* the quality of something that you sense through your nose
» *There were so many* **smells** *in the room.*

scent

stink

The flowers had been specially chosen for their **scent**.

There was a **stink** from the dog; what had it rolled in?

That **reek** is coming from your trainers.

Something in the trash was giving off a horrible **funk**.

There was a **stench** of burned food.

reek

stench

funk
(informal)

*The woman was tall and **slender**.*

slender [1]

adjective thin and lean, not muscular » *The woman was tall and slender.*
lean, lithe, slight, slim, trim, svelte, willowy

slender [2]

adjective small in amount or degree » *The politician won the vote by a slender margin.*
faint, remote, slight, slim, small, inconsiderable, tenuous

slight

adjective small in amount or degree » *Tallulah found a slight dent on her phone.*
insignificant, minor, negligible, small, trivial, inconsiderable, paltry, scanty
antonym: **large**

slip [1]

verb to lose your footing and slide unintentionally » *Gavin slipped on the ice.*
skid, slide, slither, glide, skate

slip [2]

verb to go somewhere quickly and quietly » *Amy slipped away to her room while the others watched TV.*
creep, sneak, steal

slip [3]

noun a small mistake » *Levi worked hard to ensure there were no slips in the calculations.*
blunder, error, fault, mistake, slip-up, faux pas, imprudence, indiscretion

slogan

noun a short, easily remembered phrase » *"I want you for US Army," was a slogan used to enlist men into the army during World War I.*
jingle, motto

slope [1]

noun a flat surface with one end higher than the other » *The slope was so steep it was for expert skiers only.*
gradient, incline, ramp, declination, declivity, inclination

*The **slope** was so steep it was for expert skiers only.*

slope [2]

verb to be at an angle » *The bank sloped sharply down to the river.*
fall, rise, slant

slouch

verb to stand or sit with your shoulders and head drooping forward » *Dan slouched, so his dad told him to sit straight.*
bow, droop, loaf, loll, lounge, slump, stoop

slow

adjective moving or happening with little speed » *We made slow progress climbing the hill.*
gradual, leisurely, lingering, ponderous, sluggish, unhurried
antonym: **fast**

slow: slow down

verb to go or cause to go more slowly » *The car slowed down and then stopped.*
check, decelerate

slowly

adverb not quickly or hurriedly » *A tortoise walks very slowly.*
by degrees, gradually, unhurriedly
antonym: **quickly**

sly

adjective cunning and deceptive » *The sly fox is known for its crafty hunting techniques.*
crafty, cunning, devious, scheming, underhand, wily

small [1]

adjective not large in size, number, or amount » *Everything in the dolls' house was on a small scale.*
little, miniature, minuscule, minute, restricted, tiny
antonym: **large**

*Everything in the dolls' house was on a **small** scale.*

small [2]

adjective not important or significant » *Mom made small changes to the seating plan.*
inconsequential, insignificant, little, minor, negligible, petty, slight, trifling, trivial, unimportant

smart [1]

adjective (Britain) clean and neat in appearance » *My brother looked smart in his new school uniform.*
chic, dapper, dashing, dressy, elegant, neat, sharp, snappy, spiffed-up, spruce, stylish, modish, natty, snappy
antonym: **scruffy**

smart [2]

adjective clever and intelligent » *Eliza was smart and always got excellent grades at school.*
astute, bright, canny, clever, ingenious, intelligent, shrewd
antonym: **dumb**

smell [1]

noun the quality of something that you sense through your nose
◄◄ SEE LEFT

smell [2]

verb to have an unpleasant smell » *Do my feet smell?*
pong (Britain; informal)**, reek, stink**

smell [3]

verb to become aware of the smell of something » *Connie could smell the flowers as soon as she walked into the room.*
get a whiff (informal)**, scent, sniff**

smelly

adjective having a strong unpleasant smell » *Something in the garbage was so smelly.*
foul, reeking, stinking, fetid, malodorous
antonym: **fragrant**

smile [1]

verb to move the corners of your mouth upward because you are happy » *When Jon saw me, he smiled and waved.*
beam, grin, smirk

smile [2]

noun the expression you have when you smile » *Using an emoticon of a smile is a way of flagging up a joke.*
beam, grin, smirk

*Using an emoticon of a **smile** is a way of flagging up a joke.*

a b c d e f g h i j k l m n o p q r s t u v w x y z

A B C D E F G H I J K L M N O P Q R S T U V W X Y Z

*Pebbles have a **smooth** surface, worn down by the ocean waves.*

smooth

adjective not rough or bumpy
» *Pebbles have a smooth surface, worn down by the ocean waves.*
glassy, glossy, polished, silky, sleek
antonym: **rough**

smug

adjective pleased with yourself
» *Rory felt smug after he scored the winning goal.*
complacent, conceited, self-satisfied, superior

snag

noun a small problem or disadvantage » *The snag was that I had no way to get home.*
catch, difficulty, disadvantage, drawback, glitch, problem, downside, stumbling block

sneak ①

verb to go somewhere quietly
» *I like to sneak up on my brother and surprise him.*
creep, lurk, slink, slip, steal

sneak ②

verb to put or take something somewhere secretly
» *I sometimes sneak an extra banana from the fruit bowl.*
slip, smuggle, spirit

sneaky

adjective doing things secretly or things being done secretly
» *My cat took a sneaky mouthful of our tuna salad.*
crafty, deceitful, devious, dishonest, mean, slippery, sly, underhand, untrustworthy

snoop ①

noun a person who interferes in other people's business
» *The guy was a snoop and kept asking lots of questions.*
busybody, detective, eavesdropper, meddler, private detective, snooper, busybody

snoop ②

verb to interfere in other people's business
» *She snooped into my private locker.*
barge in, butt in, interfere, intrude, meddle, nose around, peek, peep, poke, pry, spy

soak

verb to make something very wet » *The spray soaked us.*
bathe, permeate, steep, wet, drench, saturate

*The spray **soaked** us.*

sociable

adjective enjoying the company of other people » *The girl was sociable and liked to spend time with her friends.*
friendly, gregarious, outgoing, companionable, convivial

society ①

noun the people in a particular country or region » *She comes from a traditional society.*
civilization, culture

society ②

noun an organization for people with the same interest or aim
» *He signed up to the school debating society to improve his public speaking skills.*
association, circle, club, fellowship, group, guild, institute, league, organization, union

soft ①

adjective not hard, stiff, or firm
» *Eric quickly fell asleep on the soft, comfy bed.*
flexible, pliable, squashy, supple, yielding, bendable, ductile, gelatinous, malleable, tensile
antonym: **hard**

soft ②

adjective quiet and not harsh
» *Oscar could just about hear the soft tapping at the door.*
gentle, low, mellow, muted, quiet, subdued, hushed, softened, toned down

software

noun computer programs used on a particular system
» *The computer's software needed updating.*
app, application, code, program

soil ①

noun the surface of the earth
» *The soil is full of nutrients that plants use as food.*
clay, dirt, earth, ground

soil ②

verb to make something dirty
» *The towel was soiled after he dried the muddy dog with it.*
dirty, foul, pollute, smear, smirch, smudge, spatter, stain, defile, sully
antonym: **clean**

solemn

adjective not cheerful or humorous » *Angela's speech was solemn and thoughtful.*
earnest, grave, serious, sober, somber, staid

solid ①

adjective hard and firm
» *The sculpture was carved from a block of solid ice.*
firm, hard

solid ②

adjective not likely to fall down
» *The solid tower had stood for hundreds of years.*
stable, strong, sturdy, substantial

solitude

noun the state of being alone
» *Jess needed solitude so she could finish writing her story.*
isolation, loneliness, privacy, seclusion

solve

verb to find the answer to a problem or question
» *We solved the big mystery.*
clear up, crack, decipher, get to the bottom of, resolve, work out

sometimes

adverb now and then
» *Stefan sometimes felt like bouncing on the trampoline.*
at times, every now and then, every so often, from time to time, now and again, now and then, occasionally, once in a while

soon

adverb in a very short time
» *I'll see you soon.*
any minute now, before long, in a minute, in the near future, presently, shortly
antonym: **later**

sophisticated ①

adjective having refined tastes
» *The new restaurant was fashionable and sophisticated.*
cosmopolitan, cultivated, cultured, refined, urbane

sophisticated ②

adjective advanced and complicated » *The airport had sophisticated eye-scanning security equipment.*
advanced, complex, complicated, elaborate, intricate, refined
antonym: **simple**

sore

adjective causing pain and discomfort » *The cut on Stephanie's finger was sore.*
aching, achy, inflamed, painful, raw, sensitive, smarting, tender

sorrow ①

noun deep sadness or regret » *The story was about a boy who overcame sorrow and lived happily ever after.*
grief, heartache, melancholy, misery, mourning, pain, regret, sadness, unhappiness, woe (formal)
antonym: **joy**

sorrow ②

noun things that cause sadness and regret » *Jim remembered with nostalgia both the joys and sorrows of his time in the navy.*
hardship, heartache, misfortune, trouble, woe (written), **worry, affliction, tribulation** (formal)
antonym: **joy**

sorry ①

adjective feeling sadness or regret » *I'm very sorry to bother you.*
apologetic, penitent, regretful, remorseful, repentant, conscience-stricken, contrite, guilt-ridden, shamefaced

sorry ②

adjective feeling sympathy for someone » *Renata felt sorry for the injured girl.*
moved, sympathetic

sorry ③

adjective in a bad condition » *The boat was in a sorry state after the storm.*
deplorable, miserable, pathetic, pitiful, poor, sad, wretched, piteous, pitiable

*The boat was in a **sorry** state after the storm.*

sort ①

noun one of the different kinds of something » *In the forest grew many sorts of trees.*
brand, breed, category, class, genre, group, kind, make, species, style, type, variety

sort ②

verb to arrange things into different kinds » *Rich sorted his notes and put them into three folders.*
arrange, categorize, classify, divide, grade, group, separate

sound ①

noun something that can be heard » *The sound of thunder rumbled in the distance.*
din, hubbub, noise, racket, tone
antonym: **silence**
related words: *adjectives*
acoustic, sonic

sound ②

verb to produce or cause to produce a noise » *The school sounded the bell to mark the end of lunch period.*
blow, chime, clang, peal, ring, set off, toll

sound ③

adjective healthy, or in good condition » *Everyone is safe and sound, thank goodness.*
all right, fine, fit, healthy, in good condition, intact, robust

sound ④

adjective reliable and sensible » *The teacher gave Arun sound advice about entering the poetry competition.*
down-to-earth, good, reasonable, reliable, sensible, solid, valid

sour ①

adjective having a sharp taste
▶▶ SEE RIGHT

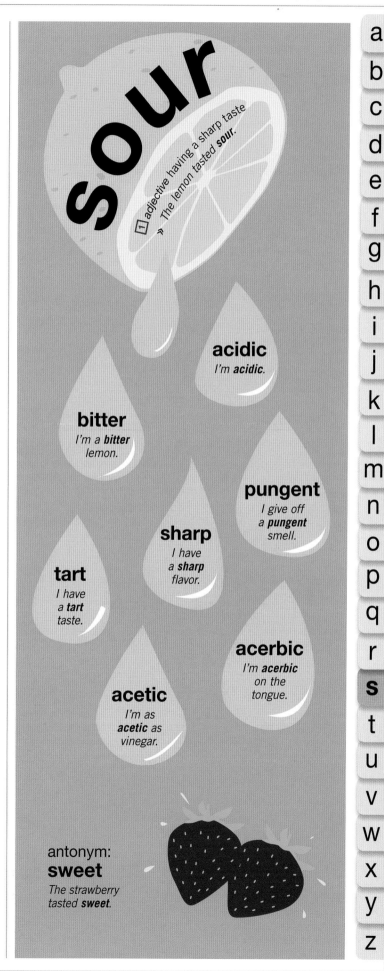

sour

① adjective having a sharp taste
» *The lemon tasted **sour**.*

acidic
*I'm **acidic**.*

bitter
*I'm a **bitter** lemon.*

pungent
*I give off a **pungent** smell.*

sharp
*I have a **sharp** flavor.*

tart
*I have a **tart** taste.*

acerbic
*I'm **acerbic** on the tongue.*

acetic
*I'm as **acetic** as vinegar.*

antonym:
sweet
*The strawberry tasted **sweet**.*

a b c d e f g h i j k l m n o p q r **s** t u v w x y z

sour [2]

adjective unpleasant in taste due to no longer being fresh » *Yuck, the milk's gone sour.*
bad, curdled, rancid

sour [3]

adjective bad-tempered and unfriendly » *The teacher had a sour expression on her face, so we knew we were in trouble.*
bitter, disagreeable, embittered, jaundiced, tart, unpleasant, unsavory

source

noun the place where something comes from » *The source of the river is in the mountains.*
beginning, cause, derivation, origin, originator, fount, fountainhead, wellspring

souvenir

noun something you keep as a reminder » *I bought a snow globe from the market as a souvenir.*
keepsake, memento, relic, reminder, token

I bought a snow globe from the market as a souvenir.

space [1]

noun an area that is empty or available » *The yard has plenty of space for a slide and swings.*
accommodation, capacity, room
related word: *adjective* **spatial**

space [2]

noun the gap between two things » *Fay squeezed into the small space between the table and chair.*
blank, distance, gap, interval

space [3]

noun a period of time » *Max and Josh received two pieces of good news in the space of a week.*
interval, period, span, time, while

spacious

adjective having or providing a lot of space » *The car was spacious enough for seven people to fit in it.*
ample, broad, expansive, extensive, huge, large, roomy, vast, commodious, sizable or sizeable

spare [1]

adjective in addition to what is needed » *Liz kept a spare pair of glasses in her bag.*
excess, extra, free, superfluous, surplus, leftover, supernumerary

spare [2]

verb to make something available » *Please could you spare us some change?*
afford, give, let someone have

spare [3]

verb to save someone from an unpleasant experience » *The teacher told us off but spared us her full lecture.*
let off (informal), pardon, relieve of, save from

sparkle

verb to shine with small bright points of light » *The water sparkled in the bright sunshine.*
flash, gleam, glisten, glitter, glow, shimmer, twinkle, radiate, scintillate

The water sparkled in the bright sunshine.

Jim wanted to speak to his best friend so he could tell her all about the trip.

speak

verb to use your voice to say words » *Jim wanted to speak to his best friend so he could tell her all about the trip.*
articulate, comment, converse, declare, explain, observe, pronounce, state, tell, affirm, assert, utter

special [1]

adjective more important or better than others of its kind » *They were celebrating a special occasion—it was his sister's 16th birthday.*
exceptional, important, incomparable, lone, one-off, significant, unequaled, unique
antonym: **ordinary**

special [2]

adjective relating to one person or group in particular » *You will have to wear special gloves when you work with chemicals in the laboratory.*
characteristic, distinctive, individual, particular, peculiar, specific
antonym: **general**

specify

verb to state or describe something precisely » *To avoid disappointment, please specify which size and color you would like the coat to be.*
be specific about, cite, designate, imply, indicate, name, note, spell out, refer to, state, stipulate

spectator

noun a person who watches something » *Spectators lined the route of the parade.*
bystander, eyewitness, observer, onlooker, witness, fan, viewer, watcher

speech

noun a formal talk given to an audience » *He delivered his speech in three languages.*
address, discourse, lecture, talk, disquisition, harangue, homily, oration

speed [1]

noun the rate at which something moves or happens » *The Formula One drivers increased their speed.*
haste, momentum, pace, rapidity, swiftness, velocity

The Formula One drivers increased their speed.

speed [2]

verb to move quickly » *The motorcycle sped along the road.*
career, flash, fly, gallop, hurry, race, run, rush, tear, hasten

spin

verb to turn quickly around a central point » *The wheels spun around as the bicycle gathered speed.*
gyrate, revolve, roll, rotate, turn, whirl

spirit [1]

noun the part of you that is not physical » *Leo had a strong spirit and was determined to complete the marathon.*
essence, life force, soul

spirit [2]

noun a ghost or supernatural being » *In the movie, a spirit haunted the house.*
apparition, ghost, phantom, specter, sprite

spirit [3]

noun liveliness and energy » *The young dog had so much spirit.*
animation, energy, enthusiasm, fire, force, passion, vigor, zest

*The young dog had so much **spirit**.*

spite [1] : in spite of

preposition even though something is the case » *In spite of the power cut, Akua did her homework on time.*
despite, even though, notwithstanding, regardless of, though

spite [2]

noun a desire to hurt someone » *Liam killed the mosquito out of spite.*
ill will, malevolence, malice, spitefulness, venom, malignity, rancor

spiteful

adjective saying or doing nasty things to hurt people » *It was spiteful to laugh at her.*
bitchy (informal), **catty** (informal), **cruel, malevolent, malicious, nasty, snide, venomous, vindictive**

splendid [1]

adjective very good » *I've had a splendid time.*
awesome, cracking (Britain; informal), **epic, excellent, fantastic, fine, glorious, great** (informal), **marvelous, superb, wonderful**

*The Taj Mahal looks **splendid**.*

splendid [2]

adjective beautiful and impressive » *The Taj Mahal looks splendid.*
glorious, gorgeous, grand, imposing, impressive, magnificent, superb

split [1]

verb to divide into two or more parts » *The team decided to split the prize money equally among all its members.*
break up, disconnect, diverge, fork, part, separate, disassemble

split [2]

verb to have a crack or tear » *Oh no! My pants have split and now there's a gaping hole.*
burst, come apart, crack, rip, slit, tear

split [3]

noun a crack or tear in something » *I can see through the split in the curtain.*
crack, fissure, rip, tear

split [4]

noun a division between two things » *There's a split between those who want to go outdoors and those who want to stay in and draw.*
breach, breakup, divergence, division, rift, schism

spoil [1]

verb to damage or destroy something » *She tried to keep the party a secret so as not to spoil the surprise.*
damage, destroy, harm, impair, mar, mess up, ruin, wreck

spoil [2]

verb to give someone everything they want » *Grandpa spoils us with more candy than we can eat.*
coddle, cosset, indulge, pamper, mollycoddle, overindulge

spoilsport

noun a person who spoils other people's fun » *I felt like a spoilsport for not joining in the game.*
downer, drag, fuddy-duddy, killjoy, party pooper, sourpuss, wet blanket

spooky

adjective eerie and frightening » *The old ruin was spooky.*
creepy (informal), **eerie, frightening, ghostly, haunted, scary, supernatural, uncanny**

spot [1]

noun a small round mark on something » *Dalmatians have a white coat with black spots.*
blemish, blot, blotch, mark, smudge, speck

*Dalmatians have a white coat with black **spots**.*

spot [2]

noun a location or place » *It was the perfect spot for a picnic.*
location, place, point, position, scene, site

spot [3]

verb to see or notice something » *Belinda spotted an owl in the tree.*
catch sight of, detect, discern, notice, observe, see, sight, spy, view

spread [1]

verb to open out or extend over an area » *He spread the picnic blanket on the grass for everyone to sit on.*
extend, fan out, open, sprawl, unfold, unfurl, unroll

spread [2]

verb to put a thin layer on a surface » *Melissa spread frosting on the cake.*
apply, coat, cover, overlay, plaster, smear, smother

*Melissa **spread** frosting on the cake.*

spread [3]

verb to reach or affect more people gradually » *Excitement is spreading through the school as the summer gets closer.*
circulate, grow, expand, increase, proliferate, travel

spread [4]

noun the extent or growth of something » *The spread of interest in the zoo brought new visitors each week.*
diffusion, expansion, extent, growth, increase, progression, proliferation, upsurge

squabble [1]

verb to argue about something trivial » *My brother and sister squabble about who gets to sit in the front seat of the car.*
argue, bicker, fall out, feud, fight, quarrel, row, scrap, wrangle

a b c d e f g h i j k l m n o p q r s t u v w x y z

A B C D E F G H I J K L M N O P Q R S T U V W X Y Z

squabble [2]

noun a minor argument » *We had a squabble about whose turn it is to do the dishes.*
altercation, argument, barney (Britain; informal), **disagreement, dispute, falling-out, fight, quarrel, row, spat, tiff, wrangle**

staff

noun the people who work for an organization » *The company's senior staff went to a meeting about new research.*
employees, personnel, team, workers, workforce

*The company's senior **staff** went to a meeting about new research.*

stage [1]

noun a part of a process » *Cycling is the second stage of a triathlon race.*
lap, period, phase, point, step

stage [2]

verb to organize something » *Area students have staged a fun run to help raise money for a new community center.*
arrange, engineer, mount, orchestrate, organize

stain [1]

noun a mark on something » *His T-shirt was covered in grass stains.*
blot, mark, spot

stain [2]

verb to make a mark on something » *The spilled drink stained the carpet.*
blemish, dirty, mar, mark, soil, spot, taint, tarnish, discolor, smirch

stale

adjective no longer fresh » *We fed the stale bread to the ducks and ate the fresh bread ourselves.*
flat, old, sour, stagnant, musty
antonym: **fresh**

standard [1]

noun a particular level of quality or achievement » *To join the club, you had to play tennis at a high standard.*
calibre, criterion, guideline, level, norm, quality, requirement

standard [2]

adjective usual, normal, and correct » *It is standard practice for schools to hold a parent-teacher conferences every year.*
accepted, correct, customary, normal, orthodox, regular, usual

standards

plural noun principles of behavior » *Our boss has high standards for his company.*
ethics, ideals, morals, principles, rules, scruples, values

star

noun a famous person » *The movie stars walked down the red carpet.*
celebrity, idol, luminary (literary)

*The movie **stars** walked down the red carpet.*

stare

verb to look at something for a long time » *Ed stared out of the window at the rain.*
gaze, look, gawp, goggle, ogle

start [1]

verb to begin to take place » *School starts again next week.*
arise, begin, come into being, come into existence, commence, get under way, originate
antonym: **finish**

start [2]

verb to begin to do something » *Susie started to read the book Judy had recommended.*
begin, commence, embark upon, proceed, set about
antonym: **stop**

start [3]

verb to cause something to begin » *The official started the race by firing the pistol.*
begin, create, establish, get going, inaugurate (formal), **initiate, instigate, institute, introduce, launch, open, pioneer, set in motion, set up,**
antonym: **stop**

*The official **started** the race by firing the pistol.*

start [4]

noun the beginning of something » *It was the start of a new era in the country's history.*
beginning, birth, commencement, dawn, foundation, inauguration, inception (formal), **initiation, onset, opening, outset**
antonym: **finish**

state [1]

noun the condition or circumstances of something » *The gardens were in a better state now that all the building work was finished.*
circumstances, condition, plight, position, predicament, shape, situation

state [2]

noun a country, especially in political terms » *The European Union is made up of a number of European states.*
country, kingdom, land, nation, republic, body politic, commonwealth, federation

state [3]

verb to say something, especially in a formal way » *Please state your full name and age.*
affirm, articulate, assert, craft, declare, express, put, say, specify, talk, word

statement

noun a short written or spoken piece giving information » *The school released a statement expressing delight over its students' achievements.*
account, announcement, bulletin, declaration, explanation, report, testimony

status

noun a person's social position » *Jamie was congratulated on his new status as the team's captain.*
position, prestige, rank, standing

*Jamie was congratulated on his new **status** as the team's captain.*

stay

verb to remain somewhere
» *Would you like to stay for dinner?*
hang around (informal), **linger, loiter, remain, stop, stopover, tarry, wait**

steadfast

adjective refusing to change or give up » *Jill was a steadfast supporter of animal rights and went on every protest march.*
constant, faithful, firm, immovable, resolute, staunch, steady, unshakable

steady ①

adjective continuing without interruptions » *There was a steady rise in temperature throughout the morning.*
consistent, constant, continuous, even, nonstop, regular, uninterrupted

steady ②

adjective not shaky or wobbling » *Tom held the ladder steady while Leo climbed up it.*
firm, secure, stable

*The surfers **steadied** themselves on the surf boards.*

steady ③

verb to prevent something from shaking or wobbling
» *The surfers steadied themselves on the surf boards.*
brace, secure, stabilize, support

steal ①

verb to take something without permission » *Did Elsa steal that orange from the fruit bowl or did she ask permission?*
appropriate, lift, nick (Britain; slang), **nip, pilfer, pinch** (informal), **rip off, swipe** (slang), **take, embezzle, filch, misappropriate, pillage, plunder, poach, thieve**

steal ②

verb to move somewhere quietly and secretly
» *Greg stole out of the class without the teacher noticing.*
creep, slip, sneak, tiptoe

steep ①

adjective rising sharply and abruptly » *The steep hill was difficult to climb.*
sheer, vertical
antonym: **gradual**

steep ②

adjective larger than is reasonable » *We noticed a steep rise in the price of bananas.*
excessive, extortionate, high, unreasonable, exorbitant, overpriced

steep ③

verb to soak something in a liquid » *Steep the vegetables in water to keep them fresh.*
immerse, soak, marinate

sterile

adjective free from germs » *Ted bandaged the cut with a sterile dressing.*
antiseptic, germ-free, sterilized

stick ①

noun a long, thin piece of wood
» *William threw a stick for the dog to fetch.*
bat, cane, mace, pole, rod, truncheon, twig, wand

stick ②

verb to thrust something somewhere » *Christine stuck her arm through the fence to pick flowers from the other side.*
insert, jab, poke, push, put, ram, shove, stuff, thrust

*Christine **stuck** her arm through the fence to pick flowers from the other side.*

stick ③

verb to attach
▼ SEE BELOW

stick
③ *verb* to attach
» ***Stick** the pictures into your scrapbook.*

attach
Attach it with tape.

bond
Bond the two paper surfaces.

fix
Fix the picture to the page.

glue
Glue the picture down.

paste
Paste the picture in.

Alphabet tab: a b c d e f g h i j k l m n o p q r **s** t u v w x y z

stick [4]

verb to become attached
» *Mud was stuck to the bottom of my boots.*
adhere, bond, cling, fuse

stick [5]

verb to jam or become jammed
» *The cat was stuck in her cat flap, but we finally got her out.*
catch, jam, lodge, snag

sticky

adjective covered with a substance that sticks to other things » *The bottom of Viv's shoe was sticky with chewing gum.*
adhesive, tacky, glutinous, viscid, viscous

*The bottom of Viv's shoe was **sticky** with chewing gum.*

stiff [1]

adjective firm and not easily bent » *The cardboard was stiff.*
firm, hard, rigid, solid, taut
antonym: **limp**

stiff [2]

adjective not friendly or relaxed
» *The lady was stiff and uncomfortable.*
awkward, cold, forced, formal, stilted, unnatural, wooden, constrained, standoffish

stiff [3]

adjective difficult or severe
» *The stiff training was not for the faint hearted.*
arduous, difficult, exacting, formidable, hard, rigorous

*The water on the lake was **still**.*

still

adjective not moving
» *The water on the lake was still.*
calm, inert, motionless, stationary, tranquil

stink [1]

verb to smell very bad
» *My breath stinks of garlic.*
pong (Britain; informal), **reek, rot**

stink [2]

noun a very bad smell
» *The stink of smelly cheese filled the house.*
funk, pong (Britain; informal), **stench, rancidity**

stock [1]

noun the total amount of goods for sale in a store » *The store counted how much stock it had in its storeroom.*
goods, merchandise (formal)

stock [2]

noun a supply of something
» *The store had a large stock of electrical equipment.*
reserve, reservoir, stockpile, store, supply

stock [3]

noun shares bought in an investment company
» *The reporter said stocks in the company were increasing.*
bonds, investments, shares

stock [4]

noun an animal or person's ancestors » *My family is of South American stock.*
ancestry, descent, extraction, lineage, origin, parentage

stock [5]

verb to keep a supply of goods to sell » *The store stocks a wide range of paint and other artists' materials.*
deal in, sell, supply, trade in

stock [6]

adjective commonly used
» *Dad's stock answer to every question was, "Ask your mother."*
hackneyed, overused, routine, standard, typical, usual

stockpile [1]

verb to store large quantities
» *My neighbor stockpiled cans of food when he heard there was a blizzard on the way.*
accumulate, amass, collect, gather, hoard, save, stash (informal), **store up**

stockpile [2]

noun a large store of something
» *Chris and Bill used the planks from the stockpile outside to make the new shed.*
cache, hoard, reserve, stash (informal), **stock, store**

*Chris and Bill used the planks from the **stockpile** outside to make the new shed.*

stocky

adjective short but solid-looking
» *The pygmy hippo is small but stocky.*
beefy, brawny, chunky, heavyset, solid, squat, stout, sturdy, stubby, thickset

stomach

noun the front part of the body around the waist » *David's T-shirt was too short and showed his stomach.*
abdomen, belly, gut, paunch, tummy (informal)

stop [1]

verb to cease doing something
▶▶ SEE RIGHT

stop [2]

verb to prevent something
» *The sudden downpour stopped the barbecue.*
arrest, break up, check, prevent, forestall, nip something in the bud

stop [3]

verb to come to an end
» *Elsie hoped that the rain would stop so she could ride her new bike outside.*
cease, come to an end, conclude, end, finish, halt
antonym: **start**

store [1]

noun a supply kept for future use » *The chipmunk added to its store of nuts.*
cache, fund, hoard, reserve, reservoir, stock, stockpile, supply

*The chipmunk added to its **store** of nuts.*

store [2]

noun a place where things are kept » *The farmer took the harvested wheat to the grain store.*
bank, cache, depot, resevoir, storeroom, warehouse, depository, repository, storehouse

stop

1 *verb* to cease doing something
» He **stopped** playing the piano when the doorbell rang.

cease
The baby **ceased** crying when she was fed.

cut out
Cut out that racket!

desist
Please **desist** from giggling when the teacher is talking.

discontinue
They **discontinued** selling his favorite pens.

quit
She **quit** playing the flute.

end
The conductor **ended** with a flourish.

antonym: **start**
Turn the key to **start** the car.

story

noun a tale told or written to entertain people » *We read a funny **story** together.*

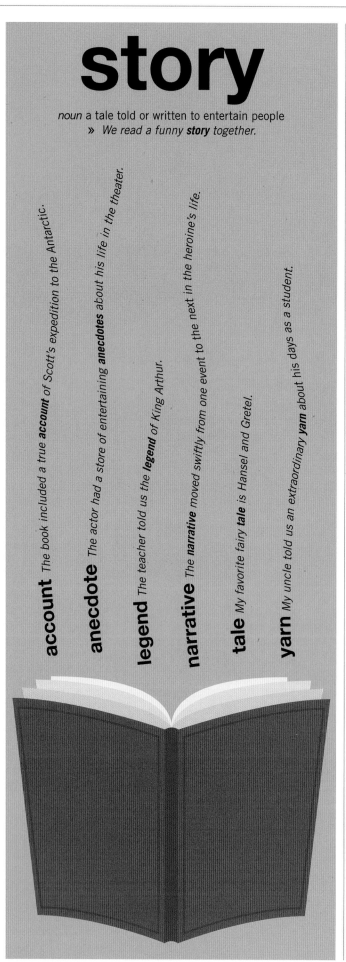

account The book included a true **account** of Scott's expedition to the Antarctic.

anecdote The actor had a store of entertaining **anecdotes** about his life in the theater.

legend The teacher told us the **legend** of King Arthur.

narrative The **narrative** moved swiftly from one event to the next in the heroine's life.

tale My favorite fairy **tale** is Hansel and Gretel.

yarn My uncle told us an extraordinary **yarn** about his days as a student.

store ③
verb to keep something for future use » *The photos are stored on your computer.*
hoard, keep, save, stash (informal), **stockpile**

story
noun a tale told or written to entertain people
◄◄ SEE LEFT

straight ①
adjective upright or level, not curved » *Hold your arms straight out to the side.*
erect, even, level, perpendicular, upright
antonym: **crooked**

*Hold your arms **straight** out to the side.*

straight ②
adjective honest, frank, and direct » *Andy's answer was straight and to the point.*
blunt, candid, direct, forthright, frank, honest, outright, plain, point-blank

straightforward ①
adjective easy and involving no problems » *The question seemed straightforward.*
basic, easy, elementary, routine, simple, uncomplicated
antonym: **complicated**

straightforward ②
adjective honest, open, and frank » *I liked his straightforward manner.*
candid, direct, forthright, frank, honest, open, plain, straight
antonym: **devious**

strain ①
noun worry and nervous tension » *The strain that Nadine had felt during her midterms was now gone.*
anxiety, pressure, stress, tension

strain ②
verb to make something do more than it is able to do » *The men strained to lift the bench.*
overwork, tax, overexert, overtax, push to the limit

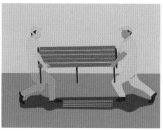

*The men **strained** to lift the bench.*

strange ①
adjective unusual or unexpected » *It was strange to bump into my old classmate.*
abnormal, bizarre, crazy, curious, extraordinary, funny, odd, peculiar, queer, uncommon, weird, out-of-the-way, unaccountable

strange ②
adjective new or unfamiliar » *We found it exciting to be traveling in a strange country.*
alien, exotic, foreign, new, novel, unfamiliar

strength ①
noun physical energy and power » *The bear pushed over a tree in an astonishing display of strength.*
brawn, might, muscle, stamina, brawniness, lustiness, sinew
antonym: **weakness**

strength ②
noun the degree of intensity » *The cheering and loud applause revealed the strength of feeling in the room.*
force, intensity, potency, power, vehemence, vigor
antonym: **weakness**

strengthen [1]
verb to give something more power » *The lateness of the trains strengthens the case for an improved railroad system.*
encourage, fortify, harden, toughen, hearten, invigorate
antonym: **weaken**

strengthen [2]
verb to support the structure of something » *Dad strengthened the treehouse with some timber beams.*
bolster, brace, fortify, reinforce, support
antonym: **weaken**

stress [1]
noun worry and nervous tension » *Louis didn't like the stress that came with taking major tests every semester.*
anxiety, hassle (informal), pressure, strain, tension, worry

stress [2]
verb to emphasize something » *The teacher stressed the importance of doing your best.*
accentuate, amplify, emphasize, reinforce, repeat, underline, dwell on, point up, underscore

stretch [1]
verb to extend over an area or time » *The boy stretched the elastic to fire the slingshot.*
continue, cover, extend, go on, hang, last, reach, spread

*The boy **stretched** the elastic to fire the slingshot.*

stretch [2]
verb to reach out with part of your body » *Megan stretched out her hand.*
extend, reach, straighten
antonym: **bend**

stretch [3]
noun an area of land or water » *We traveled along a smooth stretch of road.*
area, expanse, extent, sweep, tract

*We traveled along a smooth **stretch** of road.*

stretch [4]
noun a period of time » *My father often worked for eight-hour stretches.*
period, run, space, spell, stint, term, time

strict [1]
adjective very firm in demanding obedience » *The teacher was strict and we didn't dare talk in class.*
authoritarian, firm, rigid, rigorous, stern, stringent

strict [2]
adjective precise and accurate » *The referee had a strict interpretation of the rules.*
accurate, exact, meticulous, particular, precise, true

strive
verb to make a great effort to achieve something » *Mason strives to keep himself fit by running every day.*
attempt, do your best, do your utmost, endeavor (formal), make an effort, seek, try

strong [1]
adjective having powerful muscles » *Gorillas are terrifically strong.*
athletic, brawny, burly, muscular, powerful, strapping, well-built
antonym: **weak**

strong [2]
adjective able to withstand rough treatment » *Strong armor kept the knight safe during battle.*
durable, hard-wearing, heavy-duty, reinforced, sturdy, substantial, tough, well-built
antonym: **fragile**

Strong armor kept the knight safe during battle.

strong [3]
adjective great in degree or intensity » *Caroline had a strong following of supporters.*
acute, ardent, deep, fervent, fierce, intense, keen, passionate, profound, vehement, violent, zealous
antonym: **faint**

structure [1]
noun the way something is made or organized » *The science class learned all about the structure of a plant.*
arrangement, construction, design, makeup, organization, configuration, conformation

*The museum building is an imposing **structure**.*

structure [2]
noun something that has been built » *The museum building is an imposing structure.*
building, construction, edifice

struggle [1]
verb to try hard to do something » *We struggled up to the top of the mountain.*
strain, strive, toil, work

struggle [2]
noun something that is hard to achieve » *The marathon was a struggle, but Josh felt proud when he crossed the finish line.*
effort, labor, toil, work

stubborn
adjective determined not to change or give in » *Helen's stubborn refusal to give up is an inspiration.*
adamant, dogged, headstrong, inflexible, obstinate, tenacious, wilful, intractable, recalcitrant

stuck-up
adjective (informal) arrogant and conceited » *She was famous, but not stuck-up.*
arrogant, conceited, disdainful, haughty, proud, snobbish

study [1]
verb to spend time learning about something » *Billy enjoyed studying history.*
bone up on, cram, learn, memorize, read up on

a b c d e f g h i j k l m n o p q r s t u v w x y z

A B C D E F G H I J K L M N O P Q R S T U V W X Y Z

*The tourists **studied** the map to work out their best route.*

study ②
verb to look at something carefully » *The tourists studied the map to work out their best route.*
contemplate, examine, pore over, peruse, **scrutinize**

study ③
noun the activity of learning about a subject » *Mary threw herself into the study of ancient Egypt as she was going to see the pyramids.*
audit, delving, exploration, inquiry, investigation, lessons, research, school work, swotting (Britain; informal)

stuff ①
noun a substance or group of things » *"That's my stuff," Luke said, pointing to a bag.*
apparatus, belongings, effects, equipment, gear, kit, material, substance, tackle, things, paraphernalia

stuff ②
verb to push something somewhere quickly and roughly » *Martin stuffed the paper into the full recycling bin.*
cram, force, jam, push, ram, shove, squeeze, thrust

stuff ③
verb to fill something with a substance or objects » *The jar was stuffed with candy.*
cram, fill, load, pack

*The jar was **stuffed** with candy.*

stuffy ①
adjective formal and old-fashioned » *At first I found Aunt Jane rather stuffy, but we soon became great friends.*
dull, formal, old-fashioned, out of it, staid, strait-laced, futsy, old-fogeyish, **priggish, stodgy**

stuffy ②
adjective not containing enough fresh air » *It was hot and stuffy in the classroom as the windows wouldn't open.*
close, heavy, muggy, oppressive, stale, stifling, fetid, sultry, unventilated

stupid
adjective lacking intelligence or good judgment » *Mom told me off for making stupid jokes while she was talking to the new neighbors.*
airheaded, boneheaded, brain-dead, brainless, dense, dim, dim-witted, foolish, idiotic, inane, obtuse, asinine, crass, **fatuous**
antonym: **smart**

stupidity
noun lack of intelligence or good judgment » *Robert wondered at the bird's stupidity as it flew into the window for the third time.*
absurdity, brainlessness, dim-wittedness, folly, foolishness, inanity, silliness, imbecility

sturdy
adjective strong and unlikely to be damaged » *My sturdy boots protect my feet during long hiking trips.*
durable, hardy, robust, solid, substantial, stout, strong, well-built
antonym: **fragile**

*My **sturdy** boots protect my feet during long hiking trips.*

success
② *noun* a person or thing achieving popularity or greatness » *She's a business **success**!*

sensation

*Rory read about the latest sports **sensation** in the newspaper.*

celebrity

*The children were hailed as **celebrities** after appearing on TV.*

hit

*Stanley was an online **hit** with his blog.*

style ①
noun the way in which something is done
» *Mr. Preston's style of teaching made every subject seem interesting.*
approach, manner, method, mode, technique, way

style ②
noun smartness and elegance
» *Lena has such style, especially when she wears that evening dress.*
chic, elegance, flair, sophistication, taste, panache, savoir-faire

subdue
verb to bring under control by force » *Police were called in to subdue the protesters.*
crush, defeat, overcome, overpower, quell, vanquish

subject ①
noun the thing or person being discussed » *Maria was able to talk about a range of subjects, from pet care to philosophy and painting.*
issue, matter, object, point, question, theme, topic

subject ②
verb to make someone experience something
» *Chris was subjected to continual questions from his classmates, who were eager to hear more detail.*
expose, put through, submit

submit ①
verb to accept or agree to something unwillingly
» *I eventually submitted to my sister's nagging to borrow my dress, even though I knew she'd get it dirty.*
bow, capitulate, comply, give in, surrender, yield
antonym: **resist**

submit ②
verb to formally present a document or proposal
» *Jeff submitted his short story for publication in the school magazine.*
hand in, present, propose, put forward, send in, table, tender
antonym: **withdraw**

*Poisonous **substances** are labeled with a warning sticker.*

substance
noun a solid, powder, liquid, or gas » *Poisonous substances are labeled with a warning sticker.*
element, material, stuff

substitute ①
verb to use one thing in place of another » *You can substitute honey for sugar.*
exchange, interchange, replace, swap, switch

substitute ②
noun someone or something used in place of another
» *Nylon is sometimes used as a substitute for silk.*
deputy, proxy, replacement, representative, surrogate, locum, makeshift, stopgap

subtract
verb to take one number away from another » *Subtracting 3 from 5 leaves 2.*
deduct, take away, take from
antonym: **add**

succeed ①
verb to achieve the result you intend » *Lina succeeded as a professional musician.*
be successful, do well, flourish, make it (informal), **prosper, thrive, triumph, work**
antonym: **fail**

success ①
noun the achievement of a goal, fame, or wealth
» *Lil's success was unparalleled—no one had more awards than her.*
celebrity, eminence, fame, prosperity, triumph, victory, wealth, ascendancy (formal)
antonym: **failure**

success ②
noun a person or thing achieving popularity or greatness
▼ SEE BELOW

She's a **star**!
star

triumph

*The posters declared the movie a **triumph**.*

winner

*Nathan was a real **winner**, excelling in every sport he tried.*

a b c d e f g h i j k l m n o p q r s t u v w x y z

successful

adjective having achieved what you intended to do » *Carol was a highly successful artist.*
flourishing, lucrative, profitable, rewarding, thriving, top

sudden

adjective happening quickly and unexpectedly » *The sudden opening of the jack-in-the-box gave us all a shock.*
abrupt, hasty, quick, swift, unexpected
antonym: **gradual**

*The **sudden** opening of the jack-in-the-box gave us all a shock.*

suffer

verb to be affected by pain or something unpleasant » *Milo suffered an injury while playing ice hockey.*
bear, endure, experience, go through, sustain, undergo

sufficient

adjective being enough for a purpose » *Rick had sufficient time to write a good essay.*
adequate, ample, enough
antonym: **insufficient**

suggest 1

verb to mention something as a possibility or recommendation » *Clive suggested going out for ice cream.*
advise, advocate, propose, recommend

suggest 2

verb to hint that something is the case » *The girls' smiling faces suggested they had done well in the test.*
hint, imply, indicate, insinuate, intimate

suggestion 1

noun an idea mentioned as a possibility » *May I offer a suggestion for what to do next?*
plan, proposal, proposition, recommendation

suggestion 2

noun a slight indication of something » *There was a suggestion of a smile on Carl's face as they waited for the winner to be announced.*
hint, indication, insinuation, intimation, trace

suit

verb to be acceptable » *The house suits our needs.*
be acceptable to, do, please, satisfy

suitable

adjective right or acceptable for a particular purpose » *Rita's slip-on sandals were not suitable for running in.*
acceptable, appropriate, apt, fit, fitting, proper, right, apposite, befitting, pertinent, seemly
antonym: **unsuitable**

sulky

adjective showing annoyance by being silent and moody » *Kim was sulky because she hadn't been invited to the party.*
huffy, moody, petulant, resentful, sullen

*Kim was **sulky** because she hadn't been invited to the party.*

summary

noun a short account of something's main points » *Peter ended his essay with a three-point summary.*
brief, outline, review, rundown, summing-up, synopsis, abridgment, digest, résumé

sum up

verb to describe briefly » *Rudi summed up his week in one word: "Awesome!"*
recapitulate, summarize

superb

adjective very good » *The pilot had a superb flight with a perfect landing.*
breathtaking, excellent, exquisite, magnificent, marvellous, outstanding, splendid, superior, unrivaled, wonderful, superlative

superior 1

adjective better than other similar things » *The new software is superior to the old—much faster and with more functions.*
awesome, better, choice, exceptional, first-rate, surpassing, unrivaled
antonym: **inferior**

superior 2

adjective showing pride and self-importance » *The wealthy people in the mansion felt superior to their neighbors.*
condescending, disdainful, haughty, lofty, patronizing, snobbish, stuck-up (informal), supercilious

superior 3

noun a person in a higher position than you » *The assistant had to report to his superior.*
boss (informal), chief, controller, director, employer, big cheese (informal), head, leader manager, senior, supervisor
antonym: **inferior**

*The assistant had to report to his **superior**.*

supervise

verb to oversee a person or activity » *Wendy supervised more than 400 volunteers.*
be in charge of, direct, handle, keep an eye on, look after, manage, oversee, run, preside over, superintend

supplement 1

verb to add to something to improve it » *Mom supplemented the main course with a salad.*
add to, augment, complement, reinforce, top up

*Mom **supplemented** the main course with a salad.*

supplement 2

noun something added to something else » *The magazine was a free supplement that came with the newspaper.*
addition, appendix, complement, extra

supplies

plural noun food or equipment for a particular purpose » *Leila carried her supplies for the hike in a backpack.*
equipment, provisions, rations, stores

supply 1

verb to provide someone with something » *The company will supply all the equipment for the scuba dive.*
equip, furnish, give, provide, endow, purvey

supply 2
noun an amount of something available for use » *Our fridge contained a plentiful supply of food for the week.*
cache, fund, hoard, reserve, stash, stock, stockpile

support 1
verb to agree with someone's ideas or aims » *I support your idea for creating more bicycle lanes.*
back, champion, defend, promote, second, side with, uphold
antonym: **oppose**

support 2
verb to help someone in difficulties » *You should support your friends when they are feeling down.*
assist, encourage, help

support 3
verb to hold something up from underneath » *The pillars support the cathedral roof.*
bolster, brace, hold up, prop up, reinforce, buttress, shore up

*The pillars **support** the cathedral roof.*

support 4
noun an object that holds something up » *The metal supports will hold up the tent.*
brace, foundation, pillar, post, prop, abutment, stanchion

*The **supporters** wore team colors to cheer on their team.*

supporter
noun a person who agrees with or helps someone » *The supporters wore team colors to cheer on their team.*
adherent, advocate, ally, champion, fan, follower, sponsor, patron, protagonist

suppose
verb to think that something is probably the case » *I suppose John will be here by noon.*
assume, believe, expect, guess, imagine, presume, think, conjecture, surmise (formal)

supposed 1
adjective planned, expected, or required to do something » *You're supposed to ride your bike in the bicycle lane rather than on the sidewalk.*
expected, meant, obliged, required

supposed 2
adjective generally believed or thought to be the case » *What is it that Melissa is supposed to have said?*
alleged, assumed, believed, meant, presumed, reputed, rumored

suppress 1
verb to prevent people from doing something » *The teachers aimed to suppress bullying among the students.*
crack down on (informal), crush, quash, quell, stamp out, stop

suppress 2
verb to stop yourself from expressing a feeling or reaction » *Vikram suppressed a cry by turning it into a cough.*
conceal, contain, curb, repress, restrain, smother, stifle

supreme
adjective of the highest degree or rank » *The prime minister has supreme authority over the country.*
chief, foremost, greatest, highest, leading, paramount, preeminent, principal, top, ultimate

sure 1
adjective having no doubts » *Jonathan was sure that he was right.*
certain, clear, convinced, definite, positive, satisfied
antonym: **unsure**

sure 2
adjective reliable or definite » *The dark clouds were a sure sign that it was going to rain.*
definite, dependable, foolproof, infallible, reliable, trustworthy, undeniable

surprise 1
noun something unexpected » *Danny's gift to the teacher came as a delightful surprise.*
bombshell, revelation, shock, start

*Danny's gift to the teacher came as a delightful **surprise**.*

surprise 2
noun the feeling caused by something unexpected » *He let out a gasp of surprise.*
amazement, astonishment, incredulity, wonder

surprise 3
verb to give someone a feeling of surprise » *I was surprised by how many people came to the party.*
amaze, astonish, astound, jolt, stagger, stun, take aback, flabbergast

surrender 1
verb to agree that the other side has won » *I surrender! You have won the game.*
capitulate, give in, submit, succumb, yield

surrender 2
verb to give something up to someone else » *Marcus surrendered the ball to the puppy.*
cede, give up, relinquish, renounce, yield

surrender 3
noun a situation in which one side gives in to the other » *The blue team waved a white flag in surrender.*
capitulation, submission

*The blue team waved a white flag in **surrender**.*

surround
verb to be all around a person or thing » *The calf was surrounded by cows.*
encircle, enclose, encompass, envelop, hem in

a b c d e f g h i j k l m n o p q r s t u v w x y z

A B C D E F G H I J K L M N O P Q R S T U V W X Y Z

*The farm's **surroundings** were stunning.*

surroundings
plural noun the area and environment around a person or place » *The farm's surroundings were stunning.*
background, environment, location, neighborhood, setting, environs, milieu

survive
verb to live or exist in spite of difficulties » *We survived the intense heat by sitting in an air-conditioned cafe.*
endure, last, live, outlive, pull through

suspect 1
verb to think something is likely » *I suspect we'll have more to do after lunch.*
believe, feel, guess, suppose

suspect 2
verb to have doubts about something » *Troy suspected something was wrong when he saw Dylan had walked away.*
distrust, doubt, mistrust

suspect 3
adjective not to be trusted » *Peter's claims to be related to royalty were highly suspect.*
debatable, disputable, dodgy (Britain; informal), **doubtful, dubious, fishy** (informal), **questionable, shady, shaky, suspicious**

suspicion 1
noun a feeling of mistrust » *Having been bitten before, Carrie watched the parrot with suspicion.*
distrust, doubt, misgiving, mistrust, scepticism, qualm

suspicion 2
noun a feeling something is true » *I have a suspicion this route is the long way around.*
hunch, idea, impression

suspicious 1
adjective feeling distrustful of someone or something » *Elijah was highly suspicious as the fox approached the chicken coop.*
apprehensive, distrustful, doubtful, sceptical, wary

*Elijah was highly **suspicious** as the fox approached the chicken coop.*

suspicious 2
adjective causing feelings of distrust » *Brenda wondered why the lights were off—there was something suspicious going on.*
dodgy (Britain; informal), **doubtable, doubtful, dubious, fishy** (informal), **funny, problematic, questionable, shady** (informal), **suspect**

swap
verb to replace one thing for another » *The girls decided to swap coats for the day.*
barter, exchange, interchange, substitute, switch, trade

*After her dinner, Rosa loves to eat something **sweet**.*

sweet 1
adjective containing a lot of sugar » *After her dinner, Rosa loves to eat something sweet.*
cloying, sugary, sweetened
antonym: **sour**

sweet 2
adjective having a pleasant smell » *The air was filled with the sweet smell of roses.*
aromatic, fragrant, perfumed, sweet-smelling

sweet 3
adjective pleasant-sounding and tuneful » *The audience listened to the sweet sound of the children singing.*
harmonious, mellow, melodious, musical, tuneful, dulcet

sweet 4
noun (Britain) a sweet-tasting thing such as candy » *We were each allowed some sweets as a treat.*
bonbon, candy, confectionery

*We were each allowed some **sweets** as a treat.*

swerve
verb to change direction suddenly to avoid hitting something » *The girl on the bike swerved around the trees.*
swing, turn, veer

swift
adjective happening or moving very quickly » *The bird was swift in flight.*
brisk, express, fast, hurried, prompt, quick, rapid, speedy
antonym: **slow**

*The bird was **swift** in flight.*

symbol
noun a design or idea used to represent something
▶▶ SEE RIGHT

sympathy
noun kindness and understanding toward someone in trouble » *When Alan's friend broke his leg, he took care of him with great sympathy.*
compassion, empathy, pity, understanding

system
noun an organized way of doing or arranging something » *The new system is much more efficient than the old way of doing things.*
arrangement, method, procedure, routine, structure, technique, methodology, modus operandi

mark

A name badge is a **mark** of identification.

HELLO MY NAME IS

Andrew

token

A ring is a **token** of love and marriage.

sign

2×4=8

2 × 4 = 8 uses **signs** for multiplication and equals.

figure

The **figure** of a dove with an olive branch in its beak stands for peace.

logo

Companies use **logos** to make them instantly recognizable.

DK

emblem

A bald eagle is the American national **emblem**.

symbol

noun a design or idea used to represent something
» *The chemical **symbol** for the element oxygen is O.*

emoticon

He signed off with a happy-face **emoticon**.

representation

In Egyptian hieroglyphics, a lion is the **representation** for the letter "L."

a b c d e f g h i j k l m n o p q r **s** t u v w x y z

Tt

tact

noun the ability not to offend people » *The teacher corrected Ed's mistakes with great tact.*
delicacy, diplomacy, discretion, sensitivity

tactful

adjective careful not to offend » *John's questions were always tactfully worded.*
diplomatic, discreet, sensitive
antonym: **tactless**

take ①

verb to require something » *My sister takes two hours to get ready for the day.*
demand, require, need

take ②

verb to carry something » *I'll take your bag for you.*
bear (formal), bring, carry, convey (formal), ferry, fetch, transport

*I'll **take** your bag for you.*

take ③

verb to lead someone somewhere » *She took Ahmed to the bus stop to make sure he didn't get lost.*
bring, conduct (formal), escort, guide, lead, usher

take care of ①

verb to look after someone or something » *Abbey was asked to take care of the baby for the day.*
care for, look after, mind, nurse, protect, tend, watch
antonym: **neglect**

*Abbey was asked to **take care of** the baby for the day.*

take care of ②

verb to deal with a problem, task, or situation » *Darcy took care of cleaning up the house.*
attend to, cope with, deal with, handle, manage, see to

take in ①

verb to deceive someone » *I was taken in by the girl at the market—the apples she sold me were old and nasty.*
con (informal), deceive, dupe, fool, mislead, trick

take in ②

verb to understand something » *Tara took in everything the coach said, and her technique soon improved.*
absorb, appreciate, assimilate, comprehend, digest, get, grasp, understand

talent

noun a natural ability » *Jess had a talent for ballet.*
ability, aptitude, capacity, flair, genius, gift, knack

talk ①

verb to say things » *My parents talked about the trip they were planning.*
chat, converse, natter, ramble, gossip, say, state, mention

talk ②

noun a conversation » *The students had a long talk about the new teacher.*
chat, chatter, conversation

talk ③

noun an informal speech » *The visitor gave a talk about volunteering for charity.*
address, discourse, lecture, sermon, speech, presentation, oration

talkative

adjective talking a lot » *The boy was so talkative— he never stopped!*
chatty, communicative, long-winded

tall

adjective higher than average
▶▶ **SEE RIGHT**

tangle ①

noun a mass of long things knotted together » *There was a tangle of wires behind the television.*
jumble, knot, mass, mat, muddle, web

*There was a **tangle** of wires behind the television.*

tangle ②

verb to twist together or catch someone or something » *The kite became tangled in the tree's branches.*
catch, jumble, knot, twist

task

noun a job that you have to do » *Emily had the task of walking the dog.*
assignment, chore, duty, job, mission, undertaking

taste ①

noun the flavor of something » *I like the taste of fresh strawberries.*
flavor, tang

taste ②

noun a small amount of food or drink » *The chef had a taste of the sauce before it was served.*
bite, mouthful, sip

*The chef had a **taste** of the sauce before it was served.*

taste ③

noun a liking for something » *My aunt Jane has a real taste for adventure.*
appetite, fondness, liking, penchant (formal), partiality, predilection

tasteless ①

adjective having little flavor » *The vegetables were overcooked and tasteless.*
bland, insipid
antonym: **tasty**

tasteless ②

adjective vulgar and unattractive » *Decorating your bathroom gold is rather tasteless.*
flashy, garish, gaudy, tacky (informal), tawdry, vulgar
antonym: **tasteful**

tasty

adjective having a pleasant flavor » *The soup was extremely tasty.*
appetizing, delicious, luscious, palatable, flavorful, flavorsome, delectable, scrumptious, yummy
antonym: **tasteless**

tax ①

noun money paid to the government » *The amount of tax paid by each person was reduced this year.*
duty, excise, levy (formal), **tariff**

tax ②

verb to make heavy demands on someone
» *The difficult jigsaw puzzle taxed Dina's patience.*
drain, exhaust, sap, strain, stretch

*The difficult jigsaw puzzle **taxed** Dina's patience.*

teach

verb to instruct someone how to do something
» *Emma decided to teach the class the rules of the game.*
coach, drill, educate, instruct, school, train, tutor

teacher

noun someone who teaches something » *My English teacher inspired me to become a writer.*
coach, don, guru, instructor, lecturer, professor, tutor, educator, pedagogue

*The girls' basketball **team** won the championship again last year.*

team ①

noun a group of people
» *The girls' basketball team won the championship again last year.*
band, crew, gang, group, side, squad, troupe

team ② or team up

verb to work together
» *The teacher said we could team up with a classmate to work on the project.*
collaborate, cooperate, join forces, link up, pair up, unite, work together

tear ①

noun a hole or rip in something
» *I found a tear in my jeans.*
hole, ladder, rip, rupture, scratch, split

tear ②

verb to make a hole or rip in something » *The cat tore a hole in the curtains.*
ladder, rip, rupture, scratch, shred, split, rend, sunder

tear ③

verb to go somewhere in a hurry » *Mike tore down the road on his bike.*
barrel, blast, charge, dart, dash, fly, race, shoot, speed, zoom, bolt

tease

verb to make fun of someone
» *I teased my big sister about her new boyfriend.*
joke, josh, kid, make fun of, mock, ride, roast, taunt

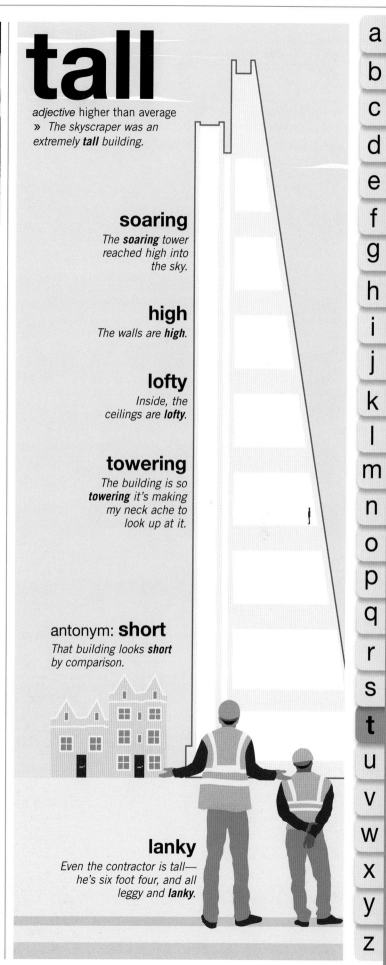

tall

adjective higher than average
» *The skyscraper was an extremely **tall** building.*

soaring
*The **soaring** tower reached high into the sky.*

high
*The walls are **high**.*

lofty
*Inside, the ceilings are **lofty**.*

towering
*The building is so **towering** it's making my neck ache to look up at it.*

antonym: **short**
*That building looks **short** by comparison.*

lanky
*Even the contractor is tall—he's six foot four, and all leggy and **lanky**.*

a b c d e f g h i j k l m n o p q r s t u v w x y z

A B C D E F G H I J K L M N O P Q R S T U V W X Y Z

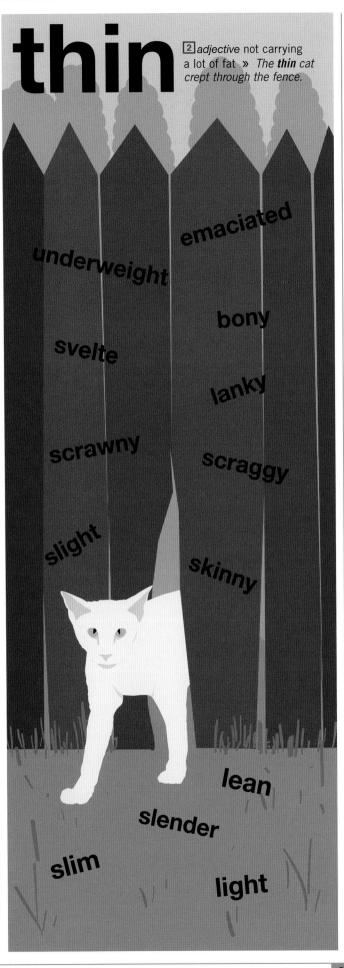

thin

[2] *adjective* not carrying a lot of fat » The **thin** cat crept through the fence.

underweight

emaciated

bony

svelte

lanky

scrawny

scraggy

slight

skinny

lean

slender

slim

light

telephone [1]

noun a device that allows you to speak to someone in another place » *Will you please answer the telephone?*
cellphone, mobile, mobile phone, phone

telephone [2]

verb (Britain) to contact by telephone » *Telephone me when you get home.*
call, contact, phone, ring, Skype®

tell [1]

verb to let someone know something » *Vanessa told us she was expecting twins.*
brief, fill in, inform, notify, acquaint, alert

tell [2]

verb to give someone an order » *The police officer told Jan to stop driving so fast on the highway.*
command, direct (formal), **instruct, order,** advise, call upon, request

The police officer **told** Jan to stop driving so fast on the highway.

tell [3]

verb to judge something correctly » *I could tell by her smile that my Grandma was pleased to see me.*
discern, see

temporary

adjective lasting a short time » *Fred took a temporary job for the summer vacation.*
fleeting, interim, momentary, passing, provisional, short-term, transient, transitory, impermanent, short-lived
antonym: **permanent**

Joe was **tempted** to eat lots of the cookies.

tempt

verb to persuade someone to do something » *Joe was tempted to eat lots of the cookies.*
bait, entice, lure, seduce

tend [1]

verb to happen usually or often » *I tend to wear jeans on the weekends.*
be apt, be inclined, be liable, be prone, have a tendency

tend [2]

verb to take care of someone or something » *The farmer tended the calves.*
care for, look after, nurse, take care of

tendency

noun behavior that happens often » *Dad has a tendency to talk too fast.*
inclination, leaning, propensity, predisposition, proclivity, proneness

tender [1]

adjective showing gentle and caring feelings » *My niece is a naturally tender and loving person.*
affectionate, caring, compassionate, gentle, kind, loving, sensitive, warm
antonym: **tough**

tender [2]

adjective painful and sore » *My ribs felt tender for days after I fell off my bike.*
aching, bruised, inflamed, painful, raw, sensitive, sore

*Al **tendered** his resignation after being offered a new job.*

tender [3]

verb to offer something such as an apology or resignation » *Al tendered his resignation after being offered a new job.*
extend, give, hand in, offer, submit

tense [1]

adjective nervous and unable to relax » *Anthony felt tense as he entered the classroom to take his final exam.*
anxious, edgy, jittery (informal)**, jumpy, nervous, uptight** (informal)
antonym: **calm**

tense [2]

adjective causing anxiety » *There was a tense silence as the judges prepared to reveal the winner of the contest.*
anxious, nerve-racking, stressful

tense [3]

adjective having tight muscles » *The doctor recommended a massage to help relax Matt's tense shoulders.*
firm, inflexible, rigid, stiff, strained, taut, tight
antonym: **relaxed**

term [1]

noun a fixed period of time » *Carlos took the job for a term of six weeks.*
cycle, duration, life span, lifetime, period, run, session, spell, stint, stretch, tenure, time, tour, duration, incumbency

term [2]

noun a name or word for a particular thing » *The scientific term for birds is aves.*
designation, expression, name, word

terms

plural noun conditions that have been agreed » *The terms of the deal were clear.*
conditions, provisions, proviso, stipulations

terrible [1]

adjective serious and unpleasant » *Dan suffered from terrible headaches.*
appalling, awful, desperate, dreadful, frightful (old-fashioned)**, horrendous, horrible, horrid** (old-fashioned)**, rotten**

terrible [2]

adjective of very poor quality » *Pat liked his haircut, but his mom thought it was terrible.*
abysmal, appalling, atrocious, awful, dire, dreadful, horrible, rotten
antonym: **excellent**

territory

noun the land that a person or country controls » *The map showed the territory belonging to each country.*
area, country, district, domain, dominion, land, province, state

*The map showed the **territory** belonging to each country.*

test [1]

verb to find out what something is like » *Stan went for a ride across the lake to test the boat.*
assess, check, try, try out

test [2]

noun an attempt to check or assess something » *He had routine eye tests.*
assessment, check, trial

texture

noun the way that something feels » *The rabbit's fur has a soft, smooth texture.*
consistency, feel

*The rabbit's fur has a soft, smooth **texture**.*

theft

noun the crime of stealing » *The squirrel's theft of the nuts meant there was none left for the birds.*
burglary, robbery, stealing, thievery, larceny, pilfering

theory

noun an idea that explains something » *The chemistry class performed an experiment to test the theory.*
assumption, conjecture, guess, hypothesis, premise, proposition, supposition, surmise (formal)

therefore

adverb as a result » *Candy contains sugar and is therefore bad for your teeth.*
accordingly, as a result, consequently, for that reason, hence (formal)**, so, thus** (formal)

thick [1]

adjective measuring a large distance from side to side » *It took Clarissa a couple of months to finish reading the thick book.*
broad, bulky, chunky, dense, fat, hefty, wide
antonym: **thin**

thick [2]

adjective containing little water » *The thick vegetable soup was delicious and filling.*
clotted, concentrated, condensed
antonym: **watery**

thick [3]

adjective grouped closely together » *The thick undergrowth in the forest was difficult to walk through.*
bristling, dense, close, crowded, impenetrable
antonym: **sparse**

thicken

verb to become thicker » *The fog thickened, making it hard to see.*
clot, condense, congeal, set, coagulate, jell
antonym: **thin**

thief

noun someone who steals something » *The security cameras in the store were there to deter thieves.*
burglar, cat burglar, crook (informal)**, mugger** (informal)**, pickpocket, robber, shoplifter, housebreaker, pilferer**

thin [1]

adjective measuring a small distance from side to side » *My grandpa cut the bread into thin slices.*
fine, narrow, slim
antonym: **thick**

*My grandpa cut the bread into **thin** slices.*

thin [2]

adjective not carrying a lot of fat
◀◀ SEE LEFT

a b c d e f g h i j k l m n o p q r s t u v w x y z

*Mary added more water to the gravy and now it was too **thin**.*

thin ③

adjective containing a lot of water » *Mary added more water to the gravy and now it was too thin.*
dilute or diluted, runny, watery, weak
antonym: **thick**

thing

noun a physical object » *What do you call that thing on the shelf?*
article, object

things

plural noun someone's clothes or belongings » *Mom looked in despair at Peter's things lying on the bedroom floor.*
belongings, effects, gear, possessions, stuff, chattels, gear, wares

think ①

verb to consider something » *Chris sat down to think about what she should do.*
consider, contemplate, deliberate, meditate, mull over, muse (literary), **ponder, reflect, cogitate, ruminate**

think ②

verb to believe something » *I think he goes to the same school as me.*
believe, consider, deem (formal), **hold, imagine, judge, suppose**

thorough

adjective careful and complete » *The vet gave the guinea pig a thorough examination.*
complete, comprehensive, exhaustive, full, intensive, meticulous, painstaking, scrupulous, all-embracing, in-depth

thought ①

noun an idea or opinion » *What are your thoughts on the subject?*
idea, notion, opinion, view

thought ②

noun the activity of thinking » *The girl was lost in thought and didn't hear the phone ring.*
consideration, contemplation, deliberation, meditation, reflection, thinking, cogitation, introspection, rumination

thoughtful ①

adjective quiet and serious » *Sam looked thoughtful as he tried to answer the question.*
contemplative, pensive, reflective, introspective, meditative, musing

*Sam looked **thoughtful** as he tried to answer the question.*

thoughtful ②

adjective showing consideration for others » *Lee was a thoughtful and caring man.*
attentive, caring, considerate, kind, solicitous, unselfish
antonym: **thoughtless**

thoughtless

adjective showing a lack of consideration » *Annie was thoughtless and always called very early in the morning.*
insensitive, tactless, inconsiderate, undiplomatic
antonym: **thoughtful**

threat ①

noun a statement that someone will harm you » *David said he was going to tell the teacher, but it was just an empty threat.*
menace, threatening remark

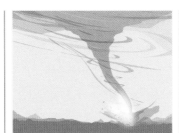

*The approaching tornado posed a **threat** to the crops.*

threat ②

noun something that seems likely to harm you » *The approaching tornado posed a threat to the crops.*
hazard, menace, risk

threaten ①

verb to promise to do something bad » *The teacher threatened to give us more homework if we didn't quiet down.*
make threats to, menace

threaten ②

verb to be likely to cause harm » *The new supermarket threatened to bring more traffic to the area.*
endanger, jeopardize, put at risk, put in jeopardy

thrifty

adjective careful not to waste money or resources » *Kristi was thrifty with money and always found the best bargains.*
careful, economical, frugal

thrill ①

noun a feeling of excitement » *The children loved the thrill of skiing at high speed.*
high (informal), **kick** (informal), **rush** (informal)

thrill ②

verb to cause a feeling of excitement » *I was thrilled to see everyone at the party.*
excite, give a kick (informal)

thrive

verb to be successful » *The children are thriving at their new school and getting excellent grades.*
do well, flourish, prosper

throw

verb to make something move through the air
▶▶ SEE RIGHT

thug

noun a very violent person » *Joe may look a bit like a thug, but he is very gentle.*
bandit, gangster, goon, hood, hooligan, tough

tidy ①

adjective arranged in an orderly way » *The teacher's desk was always extremely tidy.*
neat, orderly, shipshape, spick-and-span
antonym: **untidy**

tidy ②

verb to make something neat » *Krishnan tidied his room.*
spruce up, straighten
antonym: **mess up**

tie ①

verb to fasten something » *Mel tied her shoelaces.*
bind, fasten, knot, lash, rope, secure, tether, truss

*Mel **tied** her shoelaces.*

tie ②

verb to have the same score » *The two teams tied in the semifinal at the tournament.*
be level, draw

tie ③

noun a connection with something » *My family has close ties to the village.*
affiliation, affinity, bond, connection, relationship

tight 1
adjective fitting closely
» *My shoes are too tight and squish my toes.*
constricted, cramped, snug
antonym: **loose**

tight 2
adjective firmly fastened
» *There was a tight knot in the rope.*
firm, secure

*There was a **tight** knot in the rope.*

tight 3
adjective not slack or relaxed
» *Pull the string tight.*
rigid, taut, tense
antonym: **slack**

tilt 1
verb to raise one end of something » *Leonard tilted his chair back on two legs.*
incline, lean, slant, slope, tip

tilt 2
noun a raised position » *The tilt of the boat on the choppy seas made Max feel nauseous.*
angle, gradient, incline, slant, slope, camber, list, pitch

time 1
noun a particular period » *We enjoyed our time in Mexico.*
interval, period, spell, stretch, while

time 2
verb to plan when something will happen » *We timed our visit to coincide with the summer vacation.*
schedule, set

*The **timid** kitten hid from us.*

timid
adjective lacking courage or confidence » *The timid kitten hid from us.*
bashful, cowardly, nervous, shy, faint-hearted
antonym: **bold**

tiny
adjective very small » *We found a tiny frog in the yard.*
diminutive, microscopic, miniature, minute, negligible, teensy, infinitesimal, Lilliputian
antonym: **huge**

tire
verb to use a lot of energy
» *You'll tire yourself out in no time if you keep jumping on the trampoline.*
drain, exhaust, fatigue, enervate, wear out, weary

tired
adjective having little energy
» *I feel tired after my long day.*
drained, drowsy, exhausted, fatigued, sleepy, weary, worn out

*I feel **tired** after my long day.*

throw
verb to make something move through the air » *He went to **throw** the ball.*

pitch
*He **pitched** the ball to the batter.*

cast
*He **cast** the ball to the ground.*

sling
*He **slung** the ball into the distance.*

chuck (informal)
*He **chucked** the ball in the bucket.*

lob
*He **lobbed** the ball high over the net.*

fling
*He **flung** the ball across the field.*

hurl
*He **hurled** the ball toward the fielder.*

toss
*He **tossed** the ball to his little brother.*

a b c d e f g h i j k l m n o p q r s t u v w x y z

*We went on long bicycle rides **together**.*

together [1]

adverb with other people » *We went on long bicycle rides together.*
collectively, en masse, in unison, jointly, shoulder to shoulder, side by side

together [2]

adverb at the same time » *Three horses crossed the finish line together.*
as one, at once, coincidentally, concurrently, simultaneously

tolerable [1]

adjective able to be put up with » *The hotel was quite old and simple, but tolerable.*
acceptable, bearable
antonym: **unbearable**

tolerable [2]

adjective fairly satisfactory » *Bill is making tolerable headway with his essay and will finish it before the deadline.*
acceptable, adequate, okay or **OK** (informal)**, passable, reasonable, so-so** (informal)

tolerant

adjective accepting of different views and behavior » *Our teacher is tolerant of unruly behavior in the playground, but not in the classroom.*
liberal, broad-minded, open-minded, understanding, easygoing, forbearing, forgiving, lenient, permissive
antonym: **narrow-minded**

tolerate [1]

verb to accept something you disagree with » *Jen tolerates her children's laziness as long as they get their chores done.*
accept, put up with

tolerate [2]

verb to accept something unpleasant » *Henry tolerated his brother's messiness in the room they shared.*
bear, endure, stand

tomb

noun a burial chamber » *The pyramids in Egypt are ancient tombs.*
grave, mausoleum, sarcophagus, sepulchre (literary)**, vault**

too [1]

adverb also or as well » *It wasn't just me at the party. You were there, too.*
as well, besides, in addition, into the bargain, likewise, moreover

too [2]

adverb more than a desirable or acceptable amount » *Ling had a stomachache after eating too much candy.*
excessively, over-, overly, unduly, unreasonably

tool

noun a hand-held instrument for doing a job » *They had a garage full of gardening tools.*
implement, instrument, utensil

*They had a garage full of gardening **tools**.*

*I waited at the **top** of the cliff.*

top [1]

noun the highest part of something » *I waited at the top of the cliff.*
apex, brow, crest, crown, culmination, head, height, high point, peak, pinnacle, ridge, summit, zenith (literary), acme, apex, apogee
antonym: **bottom**

top [2]

noun the lid of a container » *Marie put the top back on the bottle.*
cap, lid, stopper

top [3]

adjective being the best of its kind » *Ivan was the team's top goal scorer.*
best, chief, elite, foremost, head, highest, lead, leading, preeminent, premier, prime, principal

top [4]

verb to be greater than something » *The temperature topped 40 degrees celsius.*
cap, exceed, go beyond, outstrip, surpass

top [5]

verb to be better than someone or something » *The world record was going to be quite difficult to top.*
beat, better, eclipse, improve on, outdo, surpass

total [1]

noun several things added together » *The school has a total of 1,776 students.*
aggregate, sum, whole

total [2]

adjective complete in all its parts » *There was total mayhem after the animals escaped from the zoo.*
absolute, complete, outright, unconditional, undivided, unmitigated, unqualified, all-out, profound

total [3]

verb to reach the sum of » *The money they raised for charity totaled $300,000.*
add up to, amount to, come to

touch [1]

verb to put your hand on something » *Please do not touch anything in the museum.*
feel, finger, handle

touch [2]

verb to come into contact with » *Amy lowered herself down until her feet touched the floor.*
brush, graze, meet
related word: *adjective* **tactile**

touch [3]

verb to emotionally affect someone » *I was touched by the stranger's kindness.*
affect, move, stir

touching

adjective causing sadness or sympathy » *The touching tale moved Anika to tears.*
affecting (literary)**, moving, poignant**

*The **touching** tale moved Anika to tears.*

touchy
adjective easily upset
» *Lucy was always touchy after an argument with her parents.*
easily offended, sensitive, oversensitive, thin-skinned

tough ①
adjective able to put up with hardship » *Marian is a tough and ambitious woman.*
hardened, hardy, resilient, robust, rugged, strong

tough ②
adjective difficult to break or damage » *The lid was too tough for Mark to unscrew.*
durable, hard-wearing, hardy, leathery, resilient, robust, rugged, solid, strong, sturdy
antonym: **fragile**

*The lid was too **tough** for Mark to unscrew.*

tough ③
adjective full of hardship » *The obstacle course was tough but fun.*
arduous, brutal, difficult, exacting, excruciating, hard
antonym: **easy**

trace ①
verb to look for and find something » *Sigrid was trying to trace her family tree.*
chase, follow, hound, locate, pursue, tail, track down, trail

trace ②
noun a sign of something » *Derek's keys had disappeared without a trace.*
evidence, footprint, hint, imprint, indication, record, residue, sign, suggestion, track, trail, whiff

trace ③
noun a small amount of something » *There was a trace of cinnamon in the muffin.*
dash, drop, remnant, suspicion, tinge, touch, vestige, iota, jot, soupçon

trade ①
noun the buying and selling of goods » *The country relies heavily on foreign trade.*
business, commerce

trade ②
noun the kind of work someone does » *Ed learned his trade while working as an apprentice.*
business, line, line of work, occupation, profession

trade ③
verb to buy and sell goods » *My parents have years of experience in trading clothes.*
deal, do business, traffic

trader
noun someone who trades in goods » *The bicycle trader helped me find the right bike.*
broker, dealer, merchant

tradition
noun a long-standing custom » *The tradition in the town was to hold a Christmas market every winter.*
convention, custom

traditional
adjective existing for a long time » *The family wore traditional Indian dress.*
conventional, established
antonym: **unconventional**

*The family wore **traditional** Indian dress.*

tragic
adjective very sad » *The book had a tragic ending— the hero dies.*
distressing, heartbreaking, heartrending

train
verb to teach someone how to do something » *We train our volunteers in first aid.*
coach, drill, educate, instruct, school, teach, tutor

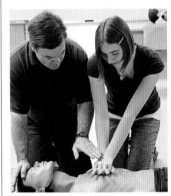

*We **train** our volunteers in first aid.*

transfer
verb to move something from one place to another » *It was easy to transfer the photos from the camera to the computer.*
carry, download, move, upload

transform
verb to change something completely » *The run-down building was transformed into a trendy café.*
alter, change, convert, reform, revolutionize

transparent
adjective able to be seen through » *Glass is transparent.*
clear, crystalline (literary), **sheer, translucent, see-through**
antonym: **opaque**

transport ①
noun the moving of goods and people » *Danny booked an all-inclusive vacation that included transport to the hotel.*
removal, shipment, transportation

transport ②
verb to move people or goods somewhere » *A bus transported passengers from the terminal to the plane.*
carry, convey (formal), **ship, transfer**

trap ①
noun a device for catching animals » *The net acted as a trap for catching fish.*
net, snare

trap ②
verb to catch animals » *Clara tried to trap the butterfly.*
catch, corner, snare

*Clara tried to **trap** the butterfly.*

trap ③
verb to trick someone » *She knew Kelly was trying to trap her into agreeing to swap shoes, but she kept refusing.*
dupe, trick, ensnare, entrap

trash ①
noun waste material » *The trash was collected every Monday.*
debris, garbage, junk, refuse, rubbish, waste

trash ②
noun something of poor quality » *The magazine was trash, but Denise still liked reading it.*
junk, garbage (informal)

travel
verb to take a trip somewhere » *Ben traveled through Europe by train.*
go, journey (formal), **make your way, take a trip, proceed, voyage**

a b c d e f g h i j k l m n o p q r s t u v w x y z

A B C D E F G H I J K L M N O P Q R S **T** U V W X Y Z

trip

1 *noun* travel to a place
» *Gary was saving up for his **trip** around the world.*

excursion
*We're going on an **excursion** to the old town.*

jaunt
*We're off on a **jaunt** to the seaside.*

journey
*It's a long **journey** across the US by bike.*

outing
*We're having a class **outing** to the castle.*

voyage
*We're going on a **voyage** across the ocean.*

tour
*The best way to see everything is to take a **tour**.*

expedition
*I'm excited about our **expedition** to the mountains.*

day out
*We're having a **day out** to the forest.*

trek
*He's going on a **trek** in the Himalayas.*

treacherous [1]

adjective likely to betray someone » *He was a treacherous character, betraying the hero's hideout to the enemy.*
disloyal, faithless, unfaithful, untrustworthy, traitorous
antonym: **loyal**

treacherous [2]

adjective dangerous or unreliable » *The vehicle traveled slowly along the treacherous mountain roads.*
dangerous, hazardous, perilous (literary)

*The vehicle traveled slowly along the **treacherous** mountain roads.*

treasure

verb to consider something very precious » *Friendship is something to treasure.*
cherish, hold dear, prize, value, revere, venerate

treat [1]

verb to behave toward someone in a certain way » *The manager treated all the players fairly.*
act toward, behave toward, deal with

treat [2]

verb to give someone medical care » *The doctor who treated me was kind and caring.*
care for, cure, heal, nurse

trendy

adjective (informal) fashionable » *I took my friend for smoothies at a trendy café.*
fashionable, hip, in (slang), **in fashion, in vogue, latest, stylish**

tribute

noun something that shows admiration » *The statue was a tribute to the former president.*
accolade (formal), **compliment, honor, praise, testimony**

trick [1]

noun something that deceives someone » *Josh liked to play tricks on his family.*
con (informal), **deception, dupe, fake out, hoax, ploy, ruse, hustle, swindle**

trick [2]

verb to deceive someone » *A magician tricks the audience into believing the unbelievable.*
con (informal), **deceive, dupe, fool, take in** (informal), **hoax, hoodwink**

*A magician **tricks** the audience into believing the unbelievable.*

tricky

adjective difficult to do or to deal with » *The family sat down to figure out the tricky problem together.*
complex, complicated, delicate, difficult, hard, problematic, puzzling, sensitive

trip [1]

noun travel to a place
◀◀ SEE LEFT

trip [2]

verb to fall over » *I tripped on the stairs.*
fall over, lose your footing, stumble

triumph [1]

noun a great success » *The band's final concert was a triumph, delighting their fans.*
success, victory, accomplishment, achievement, coup, hit, tour de force
antonym: **failure**

triumph [2]

verb to be successful » *The host country won the most medals and triumphed at the Olympics.*
come out on top (informal), **prevail, succeed, win**
antonym: **fail**

trivial

adjective not important » *The problem was trivial and could wait to be dealt with.*
insignificant, minor, negligible, paltry, petty, slight, trifling, unimportant, frivolous, inconsequential
antonym: **important**

trouble [1]

noun a difficulty or problem » *Luke was having trouble with his math homework.*
bother, challenge, difficulty, hassle (informal), **problem**

trouble [2]

verb to make someone feel worried » *The missing bag troubled Janet, since her keys were in there.*
agitate, bother, disturb, stress, worry

trouble [3]

verb to cause someone inconvenience » *Can I trouble you for some milk?*
bother, disturb, impose upon, inconvenience, put out

true [1]

adjective not invented » *The new action movie is based on a true story.*
accurate, correct, factual
antonym: **inaccurate**

true [2]

adjective real or genuine » *Alicia was a true friend who was always there for me.*
authentic, bona fide, echt, genuine, real
antonym: **false**

trust

verb to believe that someone will do something » *My parents trust me to do the right thing.*
count on, depend on, have confidence in, have faith in, place your trust in, rely upon

trusty

adjective considered to be reliable » *I bought my trusty old bike years ago, but it's still going strong.*
dependable, faithful, firm, reliable, solid, staunch, true, trustworthy

truth

noun the facts about something » *The documents revealed the truth about the mystery.*
fact, reality
related words: *adjectives*
veritable, veracious

try [1]

verb to make an effort to do something » *I tried my best on the test and received a satisfactory grade.*
attempt, endeavor (formal), **make an attempt, make an effort, seek, strive**

try [2]

verb to test the quality of something » *Howard tried the soup to see how hot it was.*
check out, sample, test, try out

*Howard **tried** the soup to see how hot it was.*

a b c d e f g h i j k l m n o p q r s t u v w x y z

A
B
C
D
E
F
G
H
I
J
K
L
M
N
O
P
Q
R
S
T
U
V
W
X
Y
Z

try ③

noun an attempt to do something » *After only a few tries, Mario played the piece of music perfectly.*
attempt, bash, crack, effort, endeavor (formal), **go** (informal), **shot** (informal)

tug ①

verb to give something a quick, hard pull » *The climber tugged hard on the rope to test that it was secure.*
drag, draw, haul, heave, jerk, pluck, pull, wrench, yank

*The climber **tugged** hard on the rope to test that it was secure.*

tug ②

noun a quick, hard pull » *Sam felt a tug at his arm.*
heave, jerk, pull, wrench, yank

tune

noun a series of musical notes » *Beth hummed a tune that had been stuck in her head for days.*
melody, strains, air, theme

turn ①

verb to change the direction or position of something » *Dan turned the car around so that they were facing in the right direction.*
rotate, spin, swivel, twirl, twist

turn ②

verb to become or make something different » *Your body turns food into energy.*
change, convert, mutate, transform, metamorphose, transfigure, transmute

turn ③

noun someone's right or duty to do something » *Tonight, it's my turn to cook.*
chance, go, opportunity

twist ①

verb to turn something around » *Dad twisted the strands of dough to make a loaf.*
bend, curl, twine, weave, wring, entwine, wreathe

*Dad **twisted** the strands of dough to make a loaf.*

twist ②

verb to bend into a new shape » *The bike was twisted out of shape in the accident.*
distort, mangle, screw up, contort, warp

twist ③

verb to injure a part of your body » *I've twisted my ankle.*
sprain, wrench, rick, turn

two-faced

adjective not honest in dealing with other people » *Jill is so two-faced. She talks about her friends behind their backs.*
deceitful, dishonest, disloyal, false, hypocritical, insincere, treacherous

type

noun a group of things that have features in common
▶▶ SEE RIGHT

typical

adjective having the usual characteristics of something » *Today was just another typical day at school.*
average, characteristic, normal, regular, representative, standard, stock, usual, archetypal, archetypical, stereotypical
antonym: **uncharacteristic**

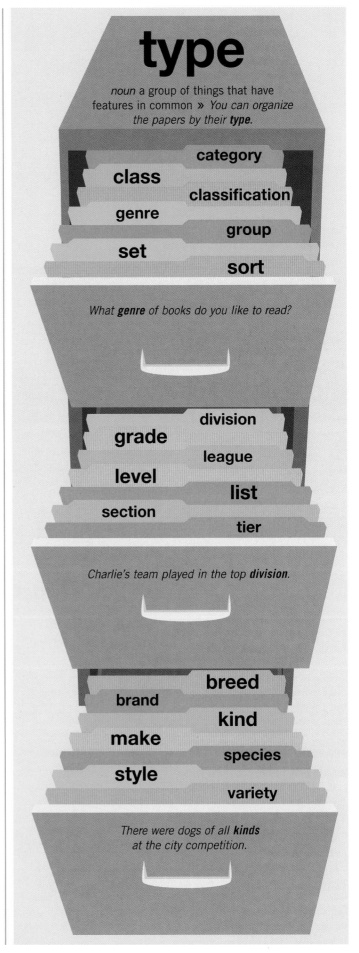

type

noun a group of things that have features in common » *You can organize the papers by their **type**.*

category
class
classification
genre
group
set
sort

*What **genre** of books do you like to read?*

grade
division
league
level
list
section
tier

*Charlie's team played in the top **division**.*

breed
brand
kind
make
species
style
variety

*There were dogs of all **kinds** at the city competition.*

Uu

ugly
adjective having a very unattractive appearance » *The fish was very ugly, with bulging eyes.*
plain, unattractive, unsightly, unlovely, unprepossessing
antonym: **beautiful**

ultimate [1]
adjective being the final one of a series » *It is not possible to predict the ultimate winner of the talent show.*
eventual, final, last

ultimate [2]
adjective the most important or powerful » *The ultimate goal of any tennis professional is to win a Grand Slam.*
greatest, paramount, supreme, utmost

ultimate [3]
noun the finest example of something » *The fancy hotel is the ultimate in luxury.*
epitome, extreme, height, peak

unaware
adjective not knowing about something » *She was unaware of the large spider dangling beside her.*
ignorant, oblivious, unconscious, unsuspecting
antonym: **aware**

unbearable
adjective too unpleasant to be tolerated » *The midday heat was unbearable.*
intolerable, oppressive, unacceptable, insufferable, unendurable
antonym: **tolerable**

unbelievable [1]
adjective extremely great or surprising » *Hugh showed unbelievable courage.*
colossal, incredible, stupendous

unbelievable [2]
adjective so unlikely it cannot be believed
▼ SEE BELOW

uncertain [1]
adjective not knowing what to do » *Jim looked uncertain after hearing Sam's insane plan.*
doubtful, dubious, unclear, undecided, irresolute, vacillating
antonym: **certain**

uncertain [2]
adjective not definite » *The injured player was facing an uncertain future.*
ambiguous, doubtful, indefinite, indeterminate, conjectural, undetermined
antonym: **certain**

unclear
adjective confusing and not obvious » *It is unclear exactly how much support Tia has for the new design.*
ambiguous, confused, vague
antonym: **clear**

uncomfortable [1]
adjective feeling or causing discomfort » *Sarah slept badly because her bed was uncomfortable.*
awkward, cramped, disagreeable, discomforting, painful
antonym: **comfortable**

uncomfortable [2]
adjective not relaxed or confident » *Talking about money made Mick uncomfortable.*
awkward, embarrassed, ill at ease, self-conscious, uneasy
antonym: **comfortable**

uncommon [1]
adjective not happening or seen often » *A lynx is an uncommon sight around here.*
exceptional, extraordinary, few, infrequent, out of the ordinary, rare, scarce, sparse, unusual, unprecedented
antonym: **common**

implausible
That's an implausible claim.

improbable
It's an improbable outcome.

inconceivable
It's inconceivable that'll happen.

incredible
It's incredible you think that.

preposterous
It's a preposterous statement.

unconvincing
It's unconvincing to say that.

unbelievable
[2] *adjective* so unlikely it cannot be believed
» *"Maybe we'll live on Mars." "And maybe pigs will fly," scoffed Dad. "**Unbelievable!**"*

a b c d e f g h i j k l m n o p q r s t u v w x y z

uncommon 2

adjective unusually great
» *Sue read Cecilia's letter with uncommon interest.*
acute, exceptional, extraordinary, extreme, great, intense, remarkable, unparalleled

unconscious 1

adjective in a state similar to sleep » *Frank banged his head and knocked himself unconscious.*
asleep, senseless, stunned, comatose, insensible
antonym: **conscious**

unconscious 2

adjective not aware of what is happening » *The fox was quite unconscious of their presence.*
oblivious, unaware, unknowing, unsuspecting
antonym: **aware**

uncover 1

verb to find something out
» *The journalist uncovered the truth behind the scandal.*
bring to light, disclose, expose, reveal, unearth

uncover 2

verb to remove the lid or cover from something » *When the seedlings sprout, lift the plastic to uncover the tray.*
expose, lay bare, open, reveal, unearth, unveil, unwrap

When the seedlings sprout, lift the plastic to uncover the tray.

The young children played with their toys under the table.

under

preposition at a lower level than something » *The young children played with their toys under the table.*
below, beneath, underneath
antonym: **above**

undergo

verb to have something happen to you » *My uncle had to undergo major surgery.*
be subjected to, endure, experience, go through, suffer

undermine

verb to make something less secure or strong » *I won't let you undermine me—I know I'm right.*
impair, sap, subvert, weaken
antonym: **strengthen**

understand 1

verb to know what someone means » *Do you understand what I'm saying?*
catch on (informal), **comprehend, follow, get, grasp, see, take in**

understand 2

verb to know why or how something is happening
» *Ria was too young to understand what was happening.*
appreciate, comprehend, fathom, grasp, realize, conceive, discern

understand 3

verb to hear of something
» *I understand your cousin hasn't been well.*
believe, gather, hear, learn

understanding 1

noun a knowledge of something
» *Kai has a good understanding of computers.*
appreciation, comprehension, grasp, knowledge, perception

understanding 2

noun an informal agreement
» *They came to an understanding that worked for both of them.*
accord, agreement, pact

They came to an understanding that worked for both of them.

understanding 3

adjective having a sympathetic nature » *My parents are very understanding.*
compassionate, considerate, sensitive, sympathetic

undertaking

noun a task that you have agreed to do » *Organizing the show has been a massive undertaking.*
affair, business, endeavor, enterprise, job, operation, project, task, venture

uneasy

adjective worried that something may be wrong
» *I was very uneasy about the plans to close the library.*
agitated, anxious, nervous, perturbed, worried, apprehensive, discomposed, restive
antonym: **comfortable**

unemployed

adjective not having a job
» *Henry is unemployed and looking for work.*
jobless, out-of-work, redundant
antonym: **employed**

uneven 1

adjective not the same or consistent » *Brooke drew six lines of uneven length.*
fluctuating, inconsistent, irregular, patchy, variable
antonym: **even**

uneven 2

adjective having an unlevel or rough surface » *The bikers raced over the uneven terrain with ease.*
bumpy, not level, rough
antonym: **level**

The bikers raced over the uneven terrain with ease.

unexpected

adjective not considered likely to happen » *Raj's win was completely unexpected—he was last in the semi-finals.*
astonishing, chance, surprising, unforeseen, fortuitous, unanticipated

unfailing

adjective continuous and not weakening as time passes
» *I admire Jan's unfailing cheerfulness, even in the most stressful times.*
constant, endless, unremitting

A B C D E F G H I J K L M N O P Q R S T U V W X Y Z

unfair
adjective without right or justice » *Joe said it was unfair that he wasn't allowed to go to the party.*
unjust, wrong, wrongful, inequitable, iniquitous
antonym: **fair**

unfamiliar
adjective not having been seen or heard of before » *Amber grew many plants that were unfamiliar to me.*
alien, exotic, foreign, new, novel, strange, unknown

unfriendly
adjective not showing any warmth or kindness » *The cats were unfriendly and hissed at each other.*
aloof, antagonistic, cold, disagreeable, hostile, unkind, icy, uncongenial
antonym: **friendly**

*The cats were **unfriendly** and hissed at each other.*

ungrateful
adjective not appreciating the things you have » *The guests were ungrateful and didn't thank us when they left.*
unappreciative, unthankful
antonym: **grateful**

unhappy
adjective feeling sad or depressed
►► SEE RIGHT

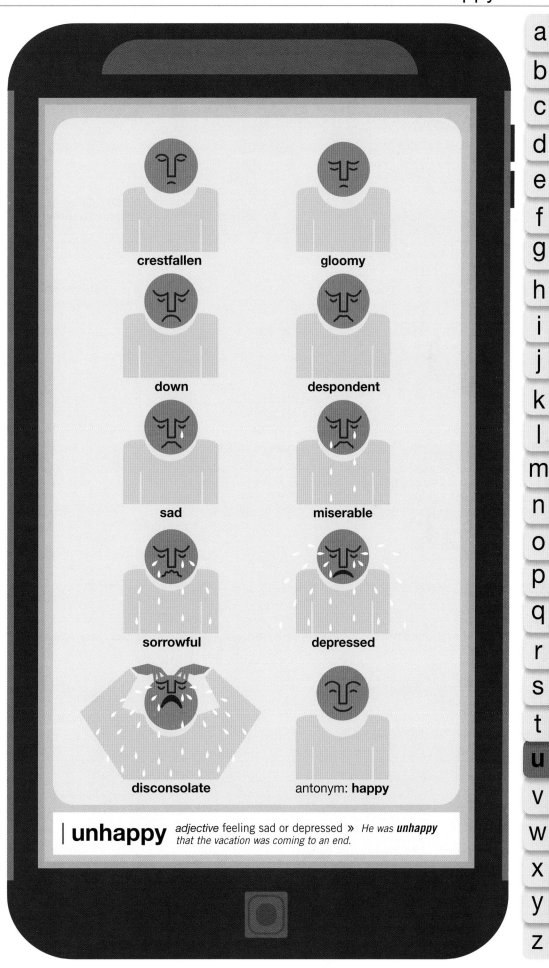

crestfallen

gloomy

down

despondent

sad

miserable

sorrowful

depressed

disconsolate

antonym: **happy**

| **unhappy** *adjective* feeling sad or depressed » *He was **unhappy** that the vacation was coming to an end.*

Dennis eats too much **unhealthy** food.

unhealthy ①

adjective likely to cause illness » *Dennis eats too much unhealthy food.*
bad for you, harmful, insanitary, noxious, unwholesome
antonym: **healthy**

unhealthy ②

adjective not well » *Ross looks quite pale and unhealthy.*
ailing, ill, not well, poorly (Britain; informal), **sick, sickly, toxic, unwell**
antonym: **healthy**

unimportant

adjective having little significance or importance » *The difference in their ages is unimportant and doesn't affect their friendship.*
insignificant, minor, paltry, slight, trivial
antonym: **important**

uninterested

adjective not interested in something » *I'm completely uninterested in politics.*
apathetic, bored, impassive, indifferent, nonchalant, passive, unconcerned
antonym: **interested**

union ①

noun an organization of people or groups with mutual interests » *Julie belongs to several different unions.*
association, coalition, confederation, federation, league

union ②

noun the joining together of two or more things » *We formed a union with another dance troupe.*
amalgamation, blend, combination, fusion, mixture, amalgam, conjunction, synthesis

We formed a **union** with another dance troupe.

unite

verb to join together and act as a group » *The rival bands united to perform a charity concert.*
collaborate, combine, join, join forces, link up, merge, pull together, work together
antonym: **divide**

universal

adjective relating to everyone or to the whole universe » *The programs have a universal appeal and are suitable for the whole family.*
common, general, unlimited, widespread, worldwide, omnipresent, overarching

unkind

adjective lacking in kindness and consideration » *It's very unkind to call anyone names.*
cruel, malicious, mean, nasty, spiteful, thoughtless
antonym: **kind**

unknown

adjective not familiar or famous » *Tim was an unknown writer before he won the book prize.*
humble, obscure, unfamiliar, unsung
antonym: **famous**

The two butterflies looked completely **unlike** one another.

unlike

preposition different from » *The two butterflies looked completely unlike one another.*
different from, dissimilar to, distinct from, divergent from (formal), **far from**
antonym: **like**

unlikely

adjective probably not true or likely to happen » *Sophia blamed her lateness on the unlikely excuse that there were no buses.*
implausible, incredible, unbelievable, unconvincing
antonym: **likely**

unsteady

adjective not held or fixed securely and likely to fall over
» *That bridge looks decidedly unsteady to me.*

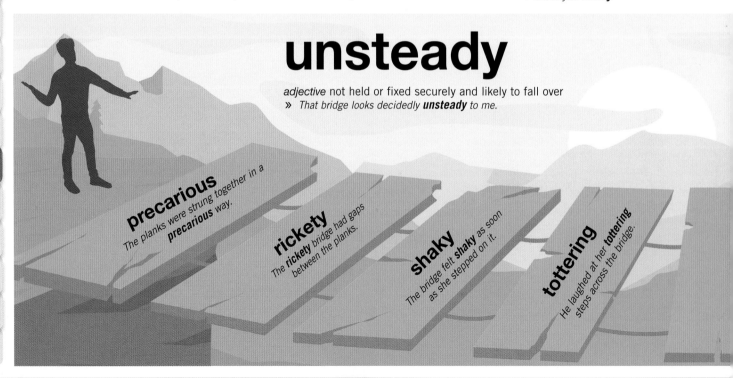

precarious
The planks were strung together in a **precarious** way.

rickety
The **rickety** bridge had gaps between the planks.

shaky
The bridge felt **shaky** as soon as she stepped on it.

tottering
He laughed at her **tottering** steps across the bridge.

unlucky

adjective having bad luck
» *Elias was unlucky not to score in the first half.*
cursed, hapless, luckless, unfortunate, wretched
antonym: **lucky**

unnecessary

adjective completely needless
» *My father considers taxis to be an unnecessary expense so we always take the bus.*
needless, pointless, uncalled-for
antonym: **necessary**

unpleasant 1

adjective causing feelings of discomfort or dislike
» *Dirty socks have a very unpleasant smell!*
bad, disagreeable, distasteful, nasty, repulsive, unpalatable
antonym: **pleasant**

unpleasant 2

adjective rude or unfriendly
» *He was thoroughly unpleasant to me earlier.*
disagreeable, horrid, objectionable, obnoxious, rude, unfriendly
antonym: **pleasant**

*The ginger cookies were **unpopular**, and everyone wanted the chocolate ones.*

unpopular

adjective disliked by most people » *The ginger cookies were unpopular, and everyone wanted the chocolate ones.*
detested, disliked, shunned, undesirable
antonym: **popular**

unpredictable

adjective unable to be foreseen
» *The weather in the mountains is unpredictable, one minute it's sunny and the next it's raining.*
chance, doubtful, hit and miss (informal)**, unforeseeable**
antonym: **predictable**

unsatisfactory

adjective not good enough
» *Emma's work was judged unsatisfactory by the teacher.*
disappointing, inadequate, mediocre, poor, unacceptable
antonym: **satisfactory**

unsteady

adjective not held or fixed securely and likely to fall over
▼ SEE BELOW

unsuitable

adjective not appropriate for a purpose » *Tom's attire was unsuitable for running.*
improper, inappropriate, unacceptable, unfit, inapposite, unseemly
antonym: **suitable**

*Tom's attire was **unsuitable** for running.*

*My bedroom is very **untidy**.*

untidy

adjective not neatly arranged
» *My bedroom is very untidy.*
bedraggled, chaotic, cluttered, jumbled, messy, unkempt, disordered, shambolic
antonym: **tidy**

untrue

adjective not true
» *The allegations that he lied were completely untrue.*
erroneous, false, fictitious, inaccurate, incorrect, misleading, mistaken
antonym: **true**

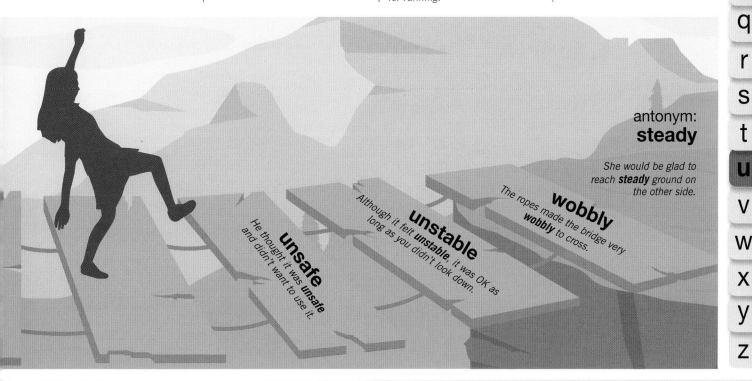

He thought it was **unsafe** and didn't want to use it.

Although it felt **unstable**, it was OK as long as you didn't look down.

The ropes made the bridge very **wobbly** to cross.

antonym: **steady**

She would be glad to reach **steady** ground on the other side.

a b c d e f g h i j k l m n o p q r s t u v w x y z

A
B
C
D
E
F
G
H
I
J
K
L
M
N
O
P
Q
R
S
T
U
V
W
X
Y
Z

*Baobabs are **unusual** trees with thick trunks and few leaves.*

unusual

adjective not occurring very often » *Baobabs are unusual trees with thick trunks and few leaves.*
curious, exceptional, extraordinary, rare, uncommon, unconventional, atypical, unwonted
antonym: **common**

unwell

adjective ill or sick » *Noah felt unwell and had to go home early.*
ailing, ill, poorly (Britain; informal)**, run-down, queasy, sick,** indisposed, under the weather
antonym: **well**

unwilling

adjective not wanting to do something » *Amelia was unwilling to get too involved in school politics.*
averse, grudging, loath, reluctant
antonym: **willing**

unwise

adjective foolish or not sensible » *It's very unwise to go out in the sunshine without wearing sunscreen.*
daft (Britain)**, foolish, idiotic, irresponsible, rash, senseless, silly, stupid,** imprudent, injudicious
antonym: **wise**

upkeep

noun the process and cost of maintaining something » *The school is raising money for the upkeep of the grounds.*
keep, maintenance, overheads, preservation, running

upset 1

adjective feeling unhappy about something » *Chloe was very upset when she heard the bad news.*
agitated, distressed, frantic, hurt, troubled, unhappy

*Chloe was very **upset** when she heard the bad news.*

upset 2

verb to make someone worried or unhappy » *The news about the missing dog upset me terribly.*
agitate, bother, distress, disturb, grieve, ruffle, discompose, faze, perturb

upset 3

verb to turn something over accidentally » *Aiden upset the coffee cup.*
capsize, knock over, overturn, spill

*Aiden **upset** the coffee cup.*

urge 1

noun a strong wish to do something » *Evelyn stifled the urge to laugh at her friend's singing.*
compulsion, desire, drive, impulse, longing, wish

urge 2

verb to try hard to persuade someone » *Saleh left early, despite being urged to stay.*
beg, beseech, implore, plead, press, entreat, exhort, solicit

urgent

adjective needing to be dealt with quickly » *The rescued sailors had an urgent need for food and water.*
compelling, immediate, imperative, pressing

use 1

verb to perform a task with something » *Use a sharp knife to cut into the lemon.*
apply, employ, operate, utilize, harness, ply

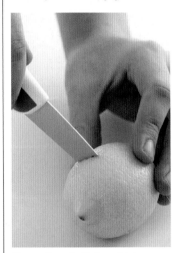

Use a sharp knife to cut into the lemon.

use 2

noun the act of using something » *There is rarely any need for the use of force.*
application, employment, operation, usage

useful

adjective something that helps or makes things easier » *This booklet contains a great deal of useful information.*
beneficial, effective, helpful, practical, valuable, worthwhile
antonym: **useless**

useless

adjective not suitable or useful » *My jacket was useless in the rain because it wasn't waterproof.*
futile, impractical, unproductive, unsuitable, worthless, disadvantageous, ineffectual, unavailing
antonym: **useful**

*My jacket was **useless** in the rain because it wasn't waterproof.*

usual

adjective done or happening most often » *You'll find Enzo sitting at his usual table, he's always there.*
accustomed, common, customary, habitual, normal, regular, standard

utter

adjective complete or total » *The teacher walked into the classroom to find a scene of utter chaos, with children running around everywhere.*
absolute, complete, consummate, out-and-out, outright, perfect, pure, sheer, thorough, total, unconditional, unmitigated, unqualified

Vv

vague

adjective not clearly expressed or clearly visible » *Uncle Bill was very vague about his job, so we didn't know what he did.*
hazy, indefinite, indistinct, loose, uncertain, unclear, ill-defined, indeterminate, nebulous
antonym: **definite**

vain ①

adjective very proud of your looks or qualities » *Sarah is so vain—she's always looking at herself in the mirror.*
conceited, egotistical, ostentatious, proud, stuck-up (informal), **narcissistic, swaggering**

vain ②

adjective not successful in achieving what was intended » *Danny made a vain attempt to stop the baby from crying.*
abortive, fruitless, futile, unproductive, useless
antonym: **successful**

vain ③ : in vain

adjective unsuccessful in achieving what was intended » *Sally tried in vain to open the locked door.*
fruitless, to no avail, unsuccessful, wasted

valley

noun an area of low-lying land between hills, often with a river or stream flowing through it » *There was a beautiful lake on the floor of the valley.*
dale, glen, hollow, vale

There was a beautiful lake on the floor of the **valley**.

valuable ①

adjective having great importance or usefulness » *Tim's experience as a mechanic was very valuable when the car wouldn't start.*
beneficial, helpful, important, prized, useful, worthwhile, cherished, esteemed, treasured
antonym: **useless**

valuable ②

adjective worth a lot of money » *Diamonds are valuable gems.*
costly, expensive, precious
antonym: **worthless**

valuables

plural noun the things you own that cost a lot of money » *Keep your valuables in a safe place.*
heirlooms, treasures

value ①

noun the importance or usefulness of something » *The fact that Maria spoke Spanish was of great value.*
advantage, benefit, effectiveness, importance, merit, use, usefulness, virtue, worth

value ②

noun the amount of money that something is worth » *The value of my stamp collection has risen by 50 percent.*
cost, market price, price, selling price, worth

value ③

verb to appreciate something and think it is important » *I really value all the help that Ashley gave me.*
appreciate, cherish, have a high opinion of, prize, rate highly, respect, treasure

value ④

verb to decide how much money something is worth » *Mom had her jewelry valued for insurance purposes.*
appraise, assess, cost, estimate, evaluate, price

vanish ①

verb to disappear » *The Moon vanished behind a cloud.*
become invisible, be lost to view, disappear, fade, recede
antonym: **appear**

vanish ②

verb to cease to exist
▼ SEE BELOW

vanquish

verb to defeat someone completely » *I read a gripping story about a knight who vanquished his enemies.*
beat, conquer, crush, defeat, destroy, overcome, rout, trounce

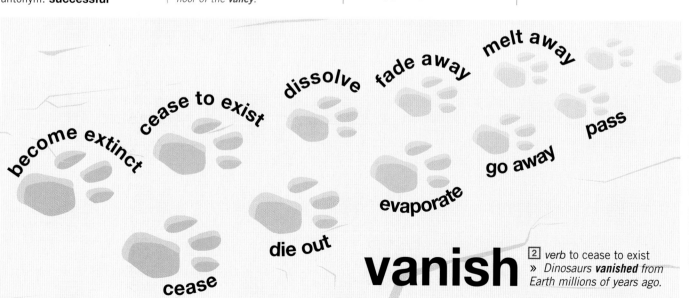

become extinct
cease to exist
dissolve
fade away
melt away
pass
go away
evaporate
die out
cease

vanish
② *verb* to cease to exist » *Dinosaurs* **vanished** *from Earth millions of years ago.*

a b c d e f g h i j k l m n o p q r s t u v w x y z

view

2 *noun* the things you can see from a particular place
» *What a beautiful* **view**!

landscape
The **landscape** *is stunning.*

aspect
Such a sunny **aspect**!

spectacle
Yes, all that sparkling water is quite a **spectacle**.

perspective
I have a great **perspective** *from here.*

variation
noun a change from the normal or usual pattern
» *There was no variation in Jim's mood from one day to the next—he was always grumpy.*
alteration, change, departure, deviation, difference, diversion

variety 1
noun a number of different kinds of things
» *An encyclopedia contains a wide variety of subjects.*
array, assortment, collection, medley, mixture, range, cross section, miscellany, multiplicity

variety 2
noun a particular type of something » *The café owner asked Carlos which variety of coffee he wanted.*
category, class, kind, sort, strain, type

Various *kinds of trees grow in the local park.*

various
adjective of several different types » *Various kinds of trees grow in the local park.*
assorted, different, disparate, diverse, miscellaneous, sundry, manifold

vary 1
verb to change to something different » *The weather here varies greatly from day to day.*
alter, alternate, change, fluctuate

vary 2
verb to introduce changes in something » *I try to vary my diet as much as possible.*
alternate, diversify, modify, permutate, reorder

vast
adjective extremely large » *We gazed at the Milky Way, one small part of our vast Universe.*
colossal, enormous, giant, gigantic, great, huge, immense, massive
antonym: **tiny**

We gazed at the Milky Way, one small part of our **vast** *Universe.*

The jury delivered their **verdict**: *he was innocent.*

verdict
noun a decision or opinion on something » *The jury delivered their verdict—he was innocent.*
conclusion, decision, finding, judgment, opinion

very
adverb to a great degree
» *I know Michaela very well.*
deeply, extremely, greatly, highly, really, terribly, exceedingly, profoundly, remarkably

veto 1
verb to forbid something
» *The government authorities vetoed the building plans.*
ban, forbid, prohibit

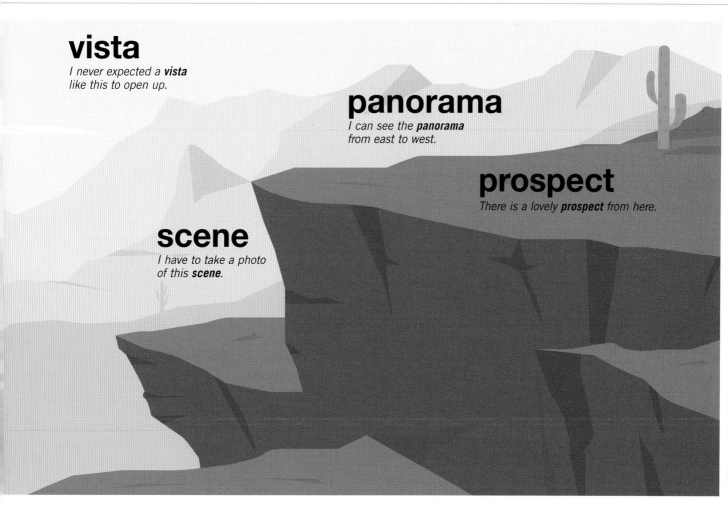

vista
I never expected a vista like this to open up.

panorama
I can see the panorama from east to west.

prospect
There is a lovely prospect from here.

scene
I have to take a photo of this scene.

---

veto ②
noun the act of forbidding or power to forbid something » *The governor issued a veto on the new legislation to raise taxes on gasoline.*
ban, prohibition

victory
noun a success in a battle or competition » *The team celebrated its fifth consecutive victory in the tournament.*
laurels, success, superiority, triumph, win
antonym: **defeat**

The team celebrated its fifth consecutive **victory** in the tournament.

Ben told me his **views** on football and I could hardly get a word in.

view ①
noun a personal opinion » *Ben told me his views on football and I could hardly get a word in.*
attitude, belief, conviction, feeling, opinion, point of view

view ②
noun the things you can see from a particular place
▲ SEE ABOVE

view ③
verb to think of something in a particular way » *Tina viewed the noisy kids as troublemakers.*
consider, judge, regard

viewpoint
noun an attitude toward something » *The parents had differing viewpoints on the new teacher.*
attitude, belief, conviction, feeling, opinion, perspective, point of view

violence ①
noun behavior which is intended to hurt people » *Nina absolutely hates seeing violence on television.*
assault, attack, barbarity, battering, beating, bloodshed, brutality, cruelty, force, savagery

violence ②
noun force and energy » *Amy was furious and slammed the door with great violence.*
fervor, force, harshness, intensity, severity

violent ①
adjective intending to hurt or kill people » *The violent criminals were sent to prison.*
bloodthirsty, brutal, cruel, murderous, savage, vicious
antonym: **gentle**

violent ②
adjective happening with great force » *Violent waves crashed against the rocks.*
powerful, raging, rough, strong, turbulent, wild, tempestuous, tumultuous

Violent waves crashed against the rocks.

a b c d e f g h i j k l m n o p q r s t u v w x y z

A B C D E F G H I J K L M N O P Q R S T U V W X Y Z

violent 3

adjective said, felt, or done with great force **»** *Jake was not expecting his chemistry experiment to give such a violent reaction.*
acute, furious, intense, powerful, severe, strong, forcible, passionate

virtue 1

noun the quality of doing what is morally right **»** *My grandmother reminded me that patience is a virtue.*
goodness, integrity, morality, probity, rectitude, righteousness

virtue 2

noun an advantage something has **»** *The players discussed the virtues of various hockey teams.*
advantage, asset, attribute, merit, plus, strength

virtue 3 : by virtue of

preposition because of **»** *Ben succeeds at school by virtue of hard work.*
as a result of, because of, by dint of, on account of, thanks to

visible 1

adjective able to be seen **»** *Wait until the green man becomes visible before crossing the road.*
clear, conspicuous, distinguishable, in sight, observable, perceptible
antonym: **invisible**

Wait until the green man becomes visible before crossing the road.

Jude ate the popsicle with visible enjoyment.

visible 2

adjective noticeable or evident **»** *Jude ate the popsicle with visible enjoyment.*
apparent, evident, manifest, noticeable, obvious, plain, conspicuous, discernible, patent

vision 1

noun a mental picture in which you imagine things **»** *My vision of the future includes flying cars.*
conception, daydream, dream, fantasy, ideal, image

My vision of the future includes flying cars.

vision 2

noun the ability to imagine future developments **»** *Lisa had a vision for her science project—it was going to be amazing!*
farsightedness, foresight, imagination, insight, intuition, perception, premeditation

vision 3

noun an experience in which you see things others cannot **»** *Lily was convinced her visions of ghosts were real.*
apparition, hallucination, illusion, mirage, phantom, spectre, chimera, phantasm, wraith

visit 1

verb to go to see and spend time with someone **»** *Sean visited his brother in Boston.*
call on, go to see, look up

visit 2

noun a trip to see a person or place **»** *Helen had recently paid her aunt a visit.*
call, stay, stop

vital 1

adjective necessary or very important **»** *As the top goal-scorer, Sam played a vital role in winning the game.*
central, critical, crucial, essential, important, indispensable, necessary, pivotal

vital 2

adjective energetic and full of life **»** *The dog was old, but it was vital and full of energy.*
active, dynamic, energetic, lively, spirited, sprightly, vivacious
antonym: **dull**

The dog was old, but it was vital and full of energy.

vomit

verb to have food and drink come back up through the mouth **»** *Any product made from milk made Andrea vomit.*
be sick, bring up, regurgitate

The staff took a vote on whether to move their office.

vote 1

noun a decision made by allowing people to state their preference **»** *The staff took a vote on whether to move their office.*
ballot, plebiscite (formal), **polls, referendum**

vote 2

verb to indicate a choice or opinion **»** *Many people voted for the new candidate in this year's election.*
cast a vote, go to the polls, opt, return

vote 3

verb to suggest that something should happen **»** *I vote that we go to the theme park.*
propose, recommend, suggest

vulgar 1

adjective socially unacceptable or offensive **»** *Adam was told off for using vulgar language in front of his little brother.*
coarse, rude, uncouth, improper, unrefined
antonym: **refined**

vulgar 2

adjective showing a lack of taste or quality **»** *My mom says it's vulgar to brag about how much money you have.*
common, flashy, gaudy, tasteless, tawdry
antonym: **sophisticated**

vulnerable

adjective weak and without protection **»** *In the wild, newborn animals are especially vulnerable to predators.*
exposed, sensitive, susceptible, weak, defenceless, unprotected

Ww

wait [1]
verb to spend time before something happens » *We waited all evening for Elizabeth to arrive.*
linger, pause, remain, stand by, stay

wait [2]
noun a period of time before something happens » *The passengers faced a three-hour wait for the next train.*
delay, interval, pause

wake
verb to make or become conscious again after sleep » *It was still dark when Fred woke early that morning.*
awake, come to, rouse, stir, waken

walk [1]
verb to go on foot
▼ SEE BELOW

*We'll have a quick **walk** while it's nice outside.*

walk [2]
noun a trip made by walking » *We'll have a quick walk while it's nice outside.*
hike, march, ramble, stroll, trek, constitutional, perambulation, saunter

walk [3]
noun the way someone moves when walking » *Although Sid was far away, I recognized him from his walk.*
carriage, gait, pace, stride

wander
verb to move around in a casual way » *The tourists wandered aimlessly around the village.*
cruise, drift, ramble, range, roam, stroll

want [1]
verb to feel a desire for something » *I want a red car, for a change.*
covet, crave, desire, wish

want [2]
noun a lack of something » *Phil started to feel weak from want of food.*
absence, deficiency, lack, scarcity, shortage, dearth, insufficiency, paucity
antonym: **abundance**

war [1]
noun a period of armed conflict between countries » *The war dragged on for five years.*
combat, conflict, fighting, hostilities, strife, warfare
antonym: **peace**
related words: *adjectives*
belligerent, martial

war [2]
verb to fight against something » *The two countries had been warring with each other for years.*
battle, clash, combat, fight

warm [1]
adjective having some heat but not hot » *It was a warm spring day.*
balmy, heated, lukewarm, pleasant, tepid
antonym: **cold**

warm [2]
adjective friendly and affectionate » *Jane has a warm and likable personality.*
affectionate, amiable, cordial, friendly, genial, loving
antonym: **unfriendly**

warm [3]
verb to heat something gently » *The sun came out and warmed his back.*
heat, heat up, melt, thaw, warm up
antonym: **cool**

warn
verb to give advance notice of something unpleasant » *I warned Sam that he might slip on the wet floor.*
alert, caution, forewarn, notify, admonish, apprise

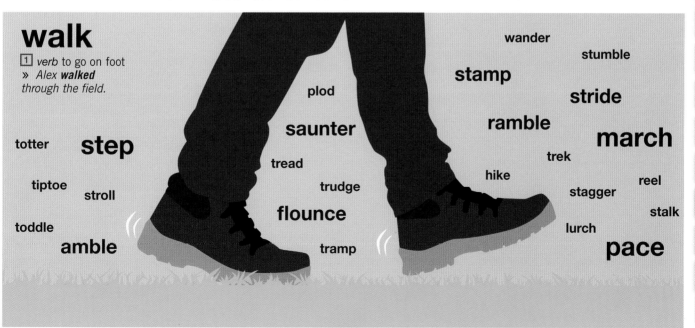

walk
[1] *verb* to go on foot » *Alex **walked** through the field.*

totter · step · tiptoe · stroll · toddle · amble · plod · saunter · tread · trudge · flounce · tramp · wander · stumble · stamp · stride · ramble · march · trek · hike · reel · stagger · stalk · lurch · pace

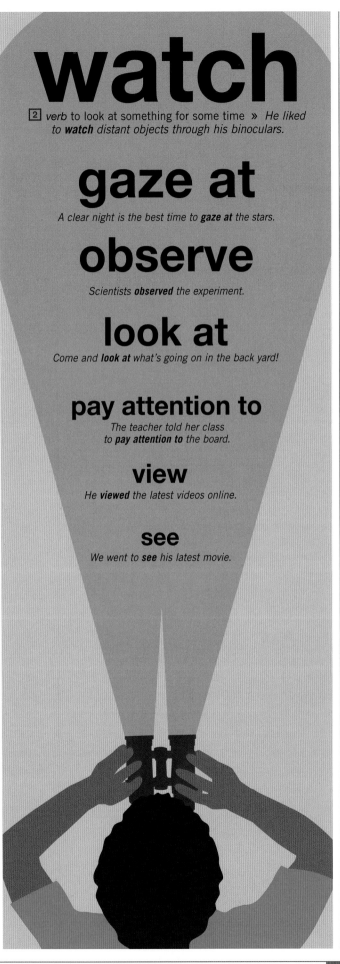

watch

[2] *verb* to look at something for some time » *He liked to* **watch** *distant objects through his binoculars.*

gaze at

A clear night is the best time to **gaze at** *the stars.*

observe

Scientists **observed** *the experiment.*

look at

Come and **look at** *what's going on in the back yard!*

pay attention to

The teacher told her class to **pay attention to** *the board.*

view

He **viewed** *the latest videos online.*

see

We went to **see** *his latest movie.*

warning

noun something that tells people of possible danger » *We had warning of the flood, so were able to protect our house.*
alarm, alert, caution, heads-up, notice, augury, premonition, presage

wary

adjective showing lack of trust in something » *Deer are usually wary of people.*
cautious, distrustful, guarded, suspicious, vigilant, chary, circumspect, heedful

Deer are usually **wary** *of people.*

wash [1]

verb to clean something with water » *Pete got a job washing dishes.*
bathe, cleanse, launder, rinse, scrub, shampoo

wash [2]

verb to carry something by the force of water » *Large clumps of seaweed were washed ashore by the waves.*
carry off, erode, sweep away

waste [1]

verb to use too much of something unnecessarily » *I wouldn't waste my money on junk like that.*
fritter away, squander, throw away
antonym: **save**

waste [2]

noun using something excessively or unnecessarily » *What a complete waste of money!*
extravagance, misuse, squandering, dissipation, misapplication

waste [3]

adjective not needed or wanted » *The floor was covered in waste paper by the time she finally decided what to write.*
leftover, superfluous, unused

wasteful

adjective using something in a careless or extravagant way » *He has a wasteful habit of leaving all the lights on.*
extravagant, uneconomical, improvident, profligate, spendthrift
antonym: **thrifty**

watch [1]

noun a period of time when a guard is kept on something » *Keep a close watch on the cake so the dog doesn't eat it.*
observation, supervision, surveillance, vigilance, watchfulness

watch [2]

verb to look at something for some time
◄◄ SEE LEFT

watch [3]

verb to look after something » *You must watch the baby carefully.*
guard, look after, mind (Britain), take care of

You must **watch** *the baby carefully.*

Watch out for the lamp post!

watch out

verb to be careful or alert for something » *Watch out for the lamp post!*
be alert, be watchful, keep your eyes open, look out

waterfall

noun a place where a river falls over a steep cliff » *The noise of the waterfall was deafening.*
cascade, cataract, chute, fall

wave ①

verb to move or flap back and forth » *The fans waved their soccer scarves in the air.*
brandish, flap, flourish, flutter, shake, oscillate, undulate

wave ②

noun a ridge of water on the surface of a lake or ocean » *The surfer paddled frantically to catch the wave.*
breaker, ripple, swell

wave ③

noun an increase in a type of activity » *He felt a sudden wave of panic at the thought of the exam the next day that he had not prepared for.*
flood, movement, rush, surge, trend, upsurge

way ①

noun a manner of doing something » *Freezing is an excellent way to preserve food.*
approach, manner, means, method, procedure, technique

way ②

noun the customs or behavior of a person or group » *I'll never get used to the way young people communicate.*
conduct, custom, manner, practice, style, idiosyncrasy, wont

way ③

noun a route taken to a particular place » *I can't remember the way.*
channel, course, lane, path, road, route

weak ①

adjective lacking in strength » *Carol felt weak after her illness.*
delicate, faint, feeble, frail, puny, sickly, wasted, debilitated, decrepit, enervated, infirm
antonym: **strong**

Carol felt weak after her illness.

weak ②

adjective likely to break or fail » *The loft had a weak floor, so we had to tread carefully.*
deficient, faulty, inadequate

weak ③

adjective easily influenced by other people » *He is a weak man who can't say no to those around him.*
powerless, spineless, indecisive, irresolute
antonym: **resolute**

weaken

verb to make or become less strong » *Dad's difficulty in keeping a straight face weakened his authority.*
diminish, fail, flag, lessen, reduce, sap, undermine, wane, debilitate, enervate, mitigate
antonym: **strengthen**

weakness ①

noun a lack of physical or moral strength » *His main weakness is his hot temper.*
defect, flaw, fragility, frailty, imperfection, vulnerability, Achilles' heel, debility, infirmity
antonym: **strength**

weakness ②

noun a great liking for something » *Jess has a weakness for chocolate.*
fondness, liking, passion, penchant, partiality, predilection
antonym: **dislike**

wealth ①

noun a large amount of money » *Mr. Brown used his wealth to build several new schools.*
affluence, fortune, means, money, prosperity, riches, substance

wealth ②

noun a lot of something » *She found a wealth of information about the artist.*
abundance, bounty, plenty, store, copiousness, cornucopia, plenitude, profusion
antonym: **shortage**

wealthy

adjective having plenty of money » *Isabella came from a very wealthy background.*
affluent, comfortable, opulent, prosperous, rich, well-to-do
antonym: **poor**

The guard was wearing a blue uniform.

wear ①

verb to be dressed in something » *The guard was wearing a blue uniform.*
be clothed in, be dressed in, don, have on, put on, sport (informal)

wear ②

verb to become worse in condition with use or age » *The walls of the old building were worn in places.*
corrode, erode, fray, rub, wash away, abrade, deteriorate

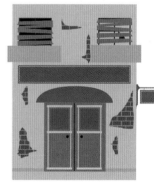

The walls of the old building were worn in places.

wear ③

noun the type of use which causes something to be damaged » *The old tires showed signs of wear.*
corrosion, deterioration, erosion, use, abrasion, fatigue

wear out

verb to make someone tired » *The past few days have really worn me out.*
exhaust, tire, weary

a b c d e f g h i j k l m n o p q r s t u v **w** x y z

A B C D E F G H I J K L M N O P Q R S T U V W X Y Z

weary
adjective very tired **»** *She sank to the ground, too weary to walk another step.*
drained, exhausted, fatigued, tired, tuckered out (informal)**, worn out**

weather
noun the condition of the atmosphere at a certain place and time **»** *What's the weather like today?*
►► SEE RIGHT

weird
adjective strange or odd **»** *I dreamed I could fly; it was really weird.*
bizarre, curious, extraordinary, funny, odd, peculiar, singular (formal)**, strange**
antonym: **ordinary**

well ①
adverb in a satisfactory way **»** *The interview went well, so I hope I get in.*
satisfactorily, smoothly, splendidly, successfully

well ②
adverb with skill and ability **»** *She draws well—I wish I had her talent and dedication.*
ably, adequately, admirably, competently, effectively, efficiently, expertly, professionally, skillfully, adeptly, proficiently
antonym: **badly**

She draws **well**—I wish I had her talent and dedication.

well ③
adverb fully and with thoroughness **»** *She washed her hands well to get rid of the paint.*
amply, closely, completely, fully, highly, meticulously, rigorously, thoroughly

well ④
adverb in a kind way **»** *My boss is a good man and treats his employees well.*
compassionately, considerately, favorably, humanely, kindly, with consideration

well ⑤
adjective having good health **»** *I'm feeling very well today.*
fit, healthy, in good condition, in good health, robust, sound, spry, strong, able-bodied, hale, hardy
antonym: **sick**

wet ①
adjective in rainy weather conditions **»** *It was a miserable wet day.*
humid, misty, rainy, showery
antonym: **dry**

It was a miserable **wet** day.

wet ②
adjective covered in liquid **»** *Keep that wet dog away!*
damp, doused, drenched, moist, saturated, soaked, waterlogged
antonym: **dry**

Wet your hands before applying soap.

wet ③
verb to put liquid on to something **»** *Wet your hands before applying soap.*
dampen, irrigate, moisten, soak, spray, water, drench, humidify, saturate
antonym: **dry**

whim
noun a sudden desire for or to do something **»** *At the very last minute, we decided on a whim to go to the zoo.*
craze, fad (informal)**, impulse, notion, urge, caprice, vagary, whimsy**

white
noun or *adjective*
Shades of white:
alabaster, bleached, chalky, ivory, milky, pearly, snowy

whole ①
adjective indicating all of something **»** *We spent the whole summer abroad.*
complete, entire, full, total, uncut, undivided

whole ②
noun the full amount of something **»** *I would love to explore the whole of Asia.*
aggregate, all, everything, lot, sum total, total

wicked ①
adjective very bad or evil **»** *Stealing that watch was a wicked thing to do.*
atrocious, bad, depraved, evil, sinful, vicious, egregious, iniquitous, nefarious

wicked ②
adjective mischievous in an amusing or attractive way **»** *She always felt wicked when eating chocolate in bed.*
impish, mischievous, naughty

wide ①
adjective measuring a large distance from side to side **»** *The river was too wide to cross.*
ample, baggy, broad, expansive, extensive, full, immense, large, roomy, spacious, sweeping, vast, voluminous
antonym: **narrow**

wide ②
adjective extensive in scope **»** *The pencils came in a wide range of colors.*
ample, broad, comprehensive, exhaustive, extensive, far-ranging, far-reaching, immense, inclusive, large, vast, wide-ranging
antonym: **narrow**

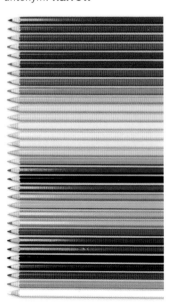

*The pencils came in a **wide** range of colors.*

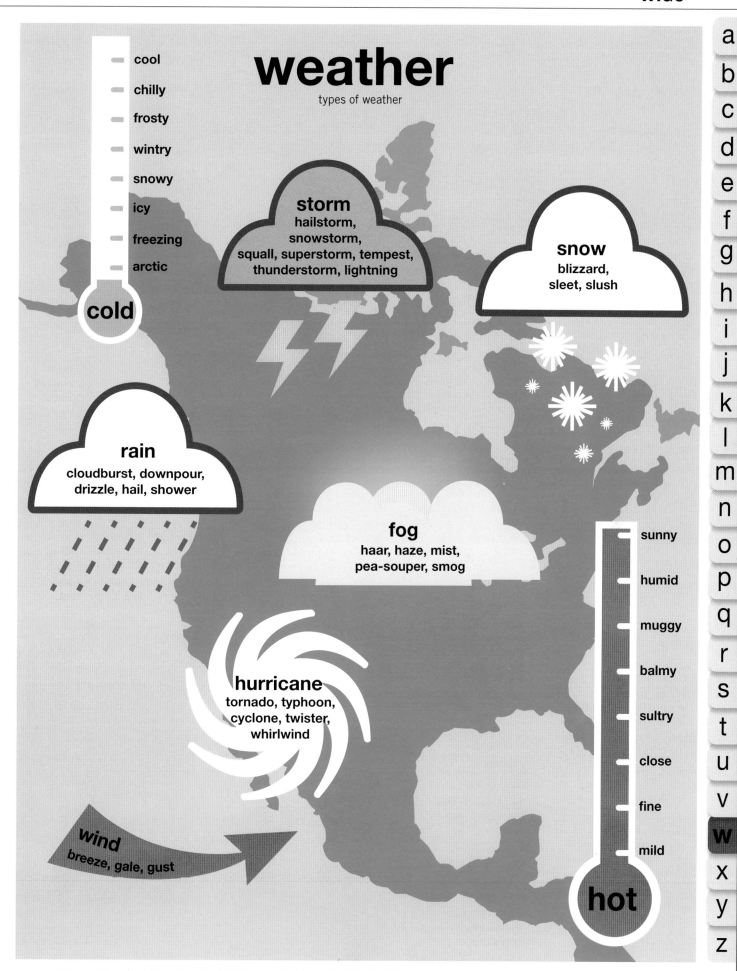

weather

types of weather

cold

- cool
- chilly
- frosty
- wintry
- snowy
- icy
- freezing
- arctic

storm
hailstorm, snowstorm, squall, superstorm, tempest, thunderstorm, lightning

snow
blizzard, sleet, slush

rain
cloudburst, downpour, drizzle, hail, shower

fog
haar, haze, mist, pea-souper, smog

hurricane
tornado, typhoon, cyclone, twister, whirlwind

wind
breeze, gale, gust

hot

- sunny
- humid
- muggy
- balmy
- sultry
- close
- fine
- mild

a b c d e f g h i j k l m n o p q r s t u v **w** x y z

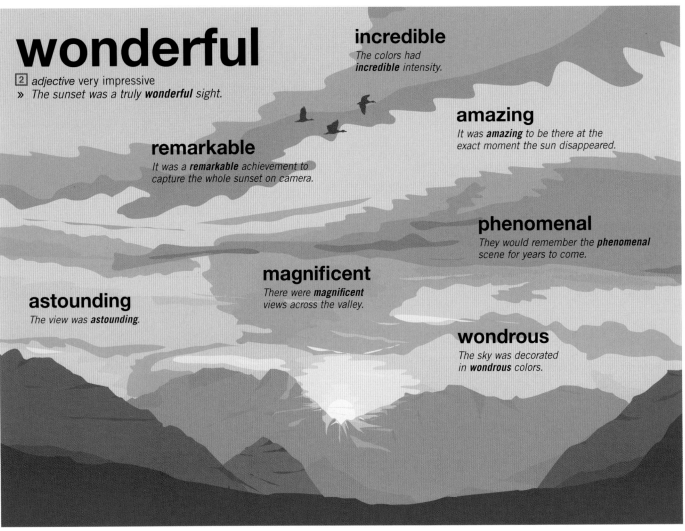

wonderful

2 *adjective* very impressive
» *The sunset was a truly **wonderful** sight.*

incredible
*The colors had **incredible** intensity.*

amazing
*It was **amazing** to be there at the exact moment the sun disappeared.*

remarkable
*It was a **remarkable** achievement to capture the whole sunset on camera.*

phenomenal
*They would remember the **phenomenal** scene for years to come.*

magnificent
*There were **magnificent** views across the valley.*

astounding
*The view was **astounding**.*

wondrous
*The sky was decorated in **wondrous** colors.*

---

wide 3
adverb as far as possible
» *The dentist asked Sal to open her mouth wide.*
completely, fully, right out

widespread
adjective existing over a large area » *Food shortages were widespread during the war.*
broad, common, extensive, pervasive, prevalent, rife

wild 1
adjective not cultivated or domesticated » *Michelle walked through a beautiful meadow of wild flowers.*
fierce, free, natural, uncultivated, undomesticated, untamed

*The boat held its course despite the **wild** weather.*

wild 2
adjective in stormy conditions
» *The boat held its course despite the wild weather.*
howling, raging, rough, stormy, violent

wild 3
adjective without control or restraint » *The birthday girl was wild with excitement.*
boisterous, rowdy, turbulent, uncontrolled, wayward, disorderly, riotous, uproarious

will 1
noun the strong determination to achieve something
» *His will to win was stronger than the pain in his leg.*
determination, purpose, resolution, resolve, willpower

will 2
noun what someone wants
» *Against her mother's will, she went out.*
choice, inclination, mind, volition, wish
related word:
adjective **voluntary**

will 3
verb to leave something to someone when you die
» *He had willed his fortune to his daughter.*
bequeath, leave, pass on

willing
adjective ready and eager to do something » *The children were willing to learn.*
agreeable, eager, game (informal), **happy, prepared, ready, amenable, compliant, desirous**
antonym: **unwilling**

*The children were **willing** to learn.*

*She **won** the tournament after defeating her closest rival.*

win ①

verb to defeat your opponents
» *She won the tournament after defeating her closest rival.*
be victorious, come first, prevail, succeed, triumph
antonym: **lose**

win ②

verb to succeed in obtaining something » *Her wonderful cooking won her a prize.*
achieve, attain, gain, get, secure

win ③

noun a victory in a contest
» *He has now suffered a run of seven games without a win.*
success, triumph, victory
antonym: **defeat**

winner

noun a person who wins something » *The competition winners all received prizes.*
champion, conqueror, victor
antonym: **loser**

wisdom

noun judgment used to make sensible decisions
» *Grandparents have wisdom that comes from experience.*
discernment, insight, judgment, knowledge, reason, astuteness, erudition, sagacity
antonym: **foolishness**

wise

adjective able to make use of experience and judgment
» *The professor is a wise old man.*
informed, judicious, perceptive, rational, sensible, shrewd
antonym: **foolish**

wish ①

noun a desire for something
» *Val's wish was to become an actress.*
desire, hankering, hunger, longing, urge, want

wish ②

verb to want something
» *Colin was bored and wished he could go home.*
desire, hunger, long, thirst, want, yearn

withdraw ①

verb to take something out
» *Tom withdrew some money from the bank.*
draw out, extract, remove, take out

*Tom **withdrew** some money from the bank.*

withdraw ②

verb to back out of an activity
» *He withdrew from the team.*
back out, leave, pull out, retire, retreat, disengage, secede

wither ①

verb to become weaker and fade away » *Support for the government has withered since they closed the libraries.*
decline, fade

*The sunflower **withered** from lack of water.*

wither ②

verb to shrivel up and die
» *The sunflower withered from lack of water.*
droop, shrivel, wilt

witness ①

noun someone who has seen something happen
» *The police appealed for witnesses to come forward.*
bystander, eyewitness, observer, onlooker, spectator

witness ②

verb to see something happening » *Anyone who witnessed the incident should call the police.*
be present at, observe, see, watch

witty

adjective amusing in a smart way » *He's so witty, I could listen to him for hours.*
amusing, brilliant, clever, funny, humorous, sparkling

woman

noun an adult female human being » *The audience was made up mostly of women.*
female, gal, girl, lady, madam, miss
antonym: **man**

wonder ①

verb to think about something with curiosity » *I wondered what the strange noise was.*
ask yourself, ponder, puzzle, speculate

wonder ②

verb to be surprised and amazed » *He wondered at her great confidence on stage.*
be amazed, be astonished, marvel

wonder ③

noun something that amazes people » *The migration of monarch butterflies is one of the wonders of nature.*
marvel, miracle, phenomenon, spectacle

wonderful ①

adjective extremely good
» *It's wonderful to see you.*
excellent, great (informal), **marvelous, superb, tremendous**

wonderful ②

adjective very impressive
◀◀ **SEE LEFT**

word ①

noun a remark » *I'd like to say a word of thanks to everyone who helped me.*
comment, remark, statement, utterance

*I'd like to say a **word** of thanks to everyone who helped me.*

word ②

noun a brief conversation
» *James, could I have a quick word with you?*
chat, conversation, discussion, talk

a b c d e f g h i j k l m n o p q r s t u v **w** x y z

word [3]

noun a message » *We've had no word from our neighbors since they went abroad.*
announcement, bulletin, communication, information, intelligence, message, news

word [4]

noun a promise or guarantee » *Phil gave me his word that he would be there.*
assurance, oath, pledge, promise, word of honor

work [1]

verb to do the tasks required of you » *I work 12 hours a day.*
labor, slave, slog away, toil
antonym: **laze**

work [2]

noun someone's job » *Vicky's work involves traveling abroad each week.*
business, craft, employment, job, livelihood, occupation, profession, calling, métier, pursuit

work [3]

noun the tasks that have to be done » *Sometimes George had to take work home.*
assignment, chore, duty, job, labor, task,

Sometimes George had to take work home.

worker

noun a person who works
▼ SEE BELOW

work out [1]

verb to find the solution to something » *It took us some time to work out the answer to the puzzle.*
calculate, figure out, resolve, solve

work out [2]

verb to happen in a certain way » *It worked out that we could get to the movie theater after all.*
develop, go, happen, turn out

worn-out [1]

adjective no longer usable because of extreme wear » *The marathon runner threw away her worn-out shoes.*
broken-down, tattered, threadbare, worn

worn out [2]

adjective extremely tired » *You must be worn out after the long trip.*
exhausted, fatigued, prostrate, tired, weary

*Rebecca was **worried** about her presentation the next day.*

worried

adjective being anxious about something » *Rebecca was worried about her presentation the next day.*
anxious, bothered, concerned, nervous, troubled, uneasy, overwrought, perturbed, unquiet
antonym: **unconcerned**

worker

noun a person who works » *He got a job as a farm worker for the summer.*

businesswoman

*The **businesswoman** ran a successful company.*

employee

*The store's **employees** had a competition to see who could serve the most customers.*

artisan

*Local **artisans** displayed their handmade goods, from bread to pottery.*

carpenter

*The **carpenter** created custom kitchens and furniture.*

worry [1]

verb to feel anxious about something » *Don't worry, I'll help you with your work.*
be anxious, brood, feel uneasy, fret

worry [2]

verb to disturb someone with a problem » *I didn't want to worry you with my homework.*
bother, concern, hassle (informal), **pester, plague, trouble,** unsettle, perturb

worry [3]

noun a feeling of anxiety » *Lack of money was a worry.*
anxiety, apprehension, concern, fear, misgiving, unease

worsen

verb to become more difficult » *My dog's behavior has worsened—now he's chewing on the furniture.*
decline, degenerate, deteriorate, go downhill (informal)
antonym: **improve**

worship [1]

verb to praise and revere something » *The ancient Egyptians worshipped many gods.*
glorify, honor, praise, pray to, venerate, deify, exalt, revere
antonym: **dishonor**

worship [2]

verb to love and admire someone » *Your little sister worships you.*
adore, idolize, love
antonym: **despise**

worship [3]

noun a feeling of love and admiration for something » *The emperor was used to the worship of his subjects.*
admiration, adoration, adulation, devotion, homage, praise, deification, exaltation

worthless

adjective having no real value or worth » *Why did you buy that worthless piece of junk?*
lousy, no-good, sub-standard, trivial, useless, valueless, negligible
antonym: **valuable**

write

verb to record something in writing » *Write your answers in pencil on the page.*
inscribe, record, take down

Write *your answers in pencil on the page.*

wrong [1]

adjective not correct or truthful » *The girl on the game show gave the wrong answer and was knocked out.*
false, faulty, incorrect, mistaken, unsound, untrue, erroneous, fallacious
antonym: **right**

wrong [2]

adjective morally unacceptable » *It's wrong to hurt people.*
bad, crooked, evil, illegal, immoral, unfair, unjust, paltry, poor, reprehensible, unethical
antonym: **right**

wrong [3]

noun an unjust action » *A great wrong had been done to him in the past.*
abuse, crime, grievance, injustice, sin

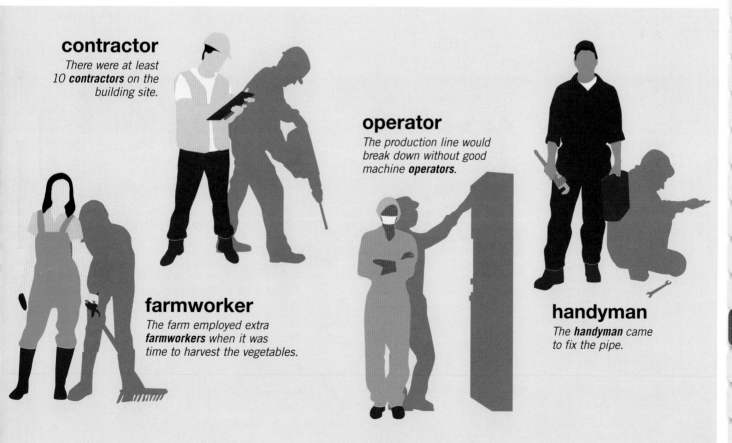

contractor
*There were at least 10 **contractors** on the building site.*

operator
*The production line would break down without good machine **operators**.*

handyman
*The **handyman** came to fix the pipe.*

farmworker
*The farm employed extra **farmworkers** when it was time to harvest the vegetables.*

a b c d e f g h i j k l m n o p q r s t u v **w** x y z

Yy

yell [1]
verb to shout loudly, usually because you are excited, angry, or in pain » *Tom yelled in delight on winning the handpainting competition.*
bellow, cheer, cry, cry out, roar, shout, scream, yell out

Tom yelled in delight on winning the handpainting competition.

yell [2]
noun a loud, piercing cry of fear, anger, or pain.
» *She let out a yell as something brushed past her in the haunted house.*
cry, howl, scream, screech, shriek, whoop

yellow
noun or *adjective*
Shades of yellow:
amber, canary yellow, citrus yellow, daffodil, gold, lemon, mustard, primrose, saffron, sand, straw, topaz

yes
interjection an expression used to agree with something or say it is true
▼ SEE BELOW

young [1]
adjective not yet mature
» *The campsite was full of young people.*
adolescent, immature, infant, junior, juvenile, little, youthful
antonym: **old**

The campsite was full of young people.

*Cats carry their **young** by the scruff of their neck.*

young [2]
plural noun the babies an animal has » *Cats carry their young by the scruff of their neck.*
babies, brood, family, litter, little ones, offspring

Zz

zero
noun nothing or the number 0
» *The temperature in the freezer was precisely zero.*
nil, nothing, nought

The temperature in the freezer was precisely zero.

zest ①
noun enthusiasm and energy
» *Grandma had great zest for life.*
appetite, eagerness, enjoyment, enthusiasm, excitement, gusto, joy, passion, relish

The added orange gave zest to the sauce.

zest ②
noun flavor » *The added orange gave zest to the sauce.*
flavor, piquancy, pungency, spice, tang, taste

zone
noun an area separated off for a purpose » *If you park in the free-parking zone you don't have to pay.*
area, district, locality, neighborhood, region

zoo
noun a large place where different types of wild animals are kept, usually enclosed, for people to see them
▼ SEE BELOW

zoom
verb to move very fast
» *The car zoomed past before I could see who was driving it.*
bolt, dart, dash, flash, hurry, race, rocket, rush, sail, scoot, soar, speed, streak, zip

The car zoomed past before I could see who was driving it.

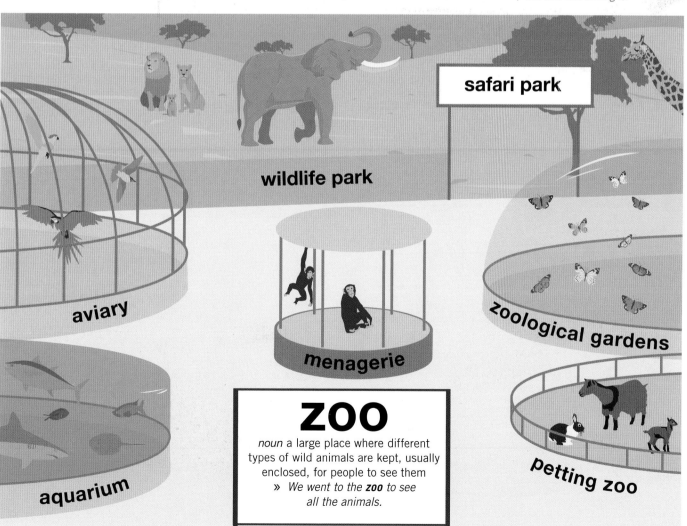

safari park

wildlife park

aviary

menagerie

zoological gardens

ZOO
noun a large place where different types of wild animals are kept, usually enclosed, for people to see them
» *We went to the zoo to see all the animals.*

aquarium

petting zoo

a b c d e f g h i j k l m n o p q r s t u v w x y z

Acknowledgments

Dorling Kindersley would like to thank the following people for their help in the production of this book:

Additional editorial assistance
Sugandha Agarwal, Nandini Gupta, and Sonia Yooshing

Additional technical assistance
Ruchi Bansal and Rachana Kishore

Picture agency credits
KEY: a-above; b-below/bottom; c-center; f-far; l-left; r-right; t-top.

The publisher would like to thank the following for their kind permission to reproduce their photographs:

2 123RF.com: Kanvag (bl). 6 123RF.com: Sergey Novikov (cra). 7 123RF.com: jahmaica (ca); Ksenia Raykova (cr); Luiscarceller (cla); Shao-Chun Wang (cb). Dreamstime.com: Justin Skinner (clb). 10 Dreamstime.com: Lasse Kristensen (bl). 11 Dreamstime.com: Ana Blazic Pavlovic (cla). 15 Dreamstime.com: Michal Bednarek (cla). 16 Dreamstime.com: Edward J Bock 111 (tr); Katrina Brown (tl). 18 Dreamstime.com: Photographerlondon (cb). 20 Dorling Kindersley: Anthony Posner. Hendon Way Motors (c). 21 123RF.com: Stephen Coburn (cl). Alamy Stock Photo: Fabian Bimmer (tr). iStockphoto.com: Eugenio Marongiu (br). 23 Dreamstime.com: Valentin Armianu (tc). iStockphoto.com: kirstypargeter (br). 24 123RF.com: Federico Rostagno / ilfede (br). 25 123RF.com: Maryna Pleshkun (cb). 26 123RF.com: gabe123 (bl). 27 123RF.com: Olga Chirkova (crb). Dreamstime.com: Mallivan (bc). 28 123RF.com: xalanx (clb). Dreamstime.com: Epicstock (tc). 29 123RF.com: auremar (ca). 30 Alamy Stock Photo: Horizon (cb/dog). Dreamstime.com: Nexus7 (cr); Stef22 (cb). iStockphoto.com: urbancow (tl). 32 Dreamstime.com: Gordon Miller (br); Photographerlondon (cl). 33 123RF.com: besjunior (c). Alamy Stock Photo: Martyn Williams (cra). Dreamstime.com: Brett Critchley (bc). 34 123RF.com: ptnphoto (cla). 37 Alamy Stock Photo: Bob Elsdale (br). Dorling Kindersley: Christopher Pillitz (cb). 38 Dreamstime.com: Nilanjan Bhattacharya (cr). 39 123RF.com: Anna Bizon / gpointstudio (c). Dreamstime.com: Tyler Olson (tr). 40 123RF.com: Ivan Kuznetsov (clb). Dreamstime.com: Jens Tobiska (cb). 41 iStockphoto.com: wakila (clb). 43 123RF.com: Comaniciu Dan (tr). Dreamstime.com: Branislav Ostojic (ca). Getty Images: Vasiliki Varvaki (cb). 44 Dreamstime.com: Breadmaker (cb). iStockphoto.com: wdstock (cr). 46 Dreamstime.com: Waihs (cr). iStockphoto.com: apCincy (bc). 47 123RF.com: Alexey Filatov (tc); Andriy Popov (cr). Alamy Stock Photo: moodboard (tl). 48 123RF.com: Cathy Yeulet (cr). Dreamstime.com: Razvan Ionut Dragomirescu (cb). 49 123RF.com: luchschen (tr). Dreamstime.com: Manfredxy (cb). 50 123RF.com: maridav (clb). 52 Dreamstime.com: Piksel (crb). 53 123RF.com: Thomas Fikar (clb). 54 Dreamstime.com: Nagy-bagoly Ilona (cla). 55 123RF.com: Karel Joseph Noppe Brooks (ca). Alamy Stock Photo: Ben Cranke (tr). 56 Dorling Kindersley: University of Pennsylvania Museum of Archaeology and Anthropology (cb). Dreamstime.com: Gustavo Andrade (tr). 57 Dreamstime.com: Eric Gevaert (tc); Ryan Stevenson (clb). 58 Dreamstime.com: Feverpitched (cb). 59 Alamy Stock Photo: Jamie Grill (cl). 60 Dreamstime.com: Jose Manuel Gelpi Diaz (bc); Redbaron (tc). 62 123RF.com: blueone (tc). Dreamstime.com: Isselee (crb); Michal Kaco (cb). 64 Dreamstime.com: Stefano Armaroli (cr); Paulus Rusyanto (cla). 65 Dreamstime.com: Thandra (cl). 67 Alamy Stock Photo: D Core / Ocean (c/sand castle). Dreamstime.com: Cristian Borod (c). 69 Dreamstime.com: Derektenhue (cra). 71 123RF.com: Zoran Orcik (tc). 73 Dreamstime.com: Jorg Hackemann (tc). 74 123RF.com: Stanislav Bokser (tc). 76 Alamy Stock Photo: Chris Robbins (c). 77 123RF.com: rawpixel (tc). iStockphoto.com: michaeljung (c). 78 123RF.com: Anthony Totah (tr). Dreamstime.com: Katarzyna Bialasiewicz (cb). 80 123RF.com: awrangler (cb). 81 Dreamstime.com: Gvictoria (ca). 82 123RF.com: Elena Moiseeva (c); Theartofphoto (cr). Dreamstime.com: Sean Nel (tc). 83 123RF.com: Taras Kushnir (clb); Quangpraha (tr). 84 123RF.com: Oleksii Sidorov (tr); Yarruta (clb); Tinna2727 (tc). 85 123RF.com: Cathy Yeulet (cb). Dreamstime.com: Gsphotography (clb). 86 123RF.com: Ian Allenden (tr); Tatsiana Yatsevich (ca). iStockphoto.com: Blackwaterimages (cb). 87 Dreamstime.com: Pixattitude (cr). 88 Dreamstime.com: Marianne Campolongo (c); Olga Vasilkova (cb). 89 123RF.com: Payphoto (tl). 90 123RF.com: Sonya Etchison (cr). 91 Dreamstime.com: Liubirong (ca). 92 Dreamstime.com: Olesia Bilkei (tc); Haveseen (cla); Photographerlondon (cb). 94 123RF.com: Dean Drobot (br). Dreamstime.com: Brett Critchley (cb). Getty Images: Robert Daly (bc). 95 123RF.com: Antonio Guillem (crb); Rubisco (clb). 96 123RF.com: Serezniy (cla). 98 Alamy Stock Photo: Duncan Usher (ca). Dreamstime.com: Marcel De Grijs (cr); Martin Novak (bl). 99 Alamy Stock Photo: Mandygodbehear (cl). 100 Dreamstime.com: Shae Cardenas (c). 101 Dreamstime.com: Jose Manuel Gelpi Diaz (cl); Denis Raev (tc). iStockphoto.com: Serge-Kazakov (cb). 102 Dreamstime.com: Pablo Caridad (bc); Jonathan Ross (bl). 103 123RF.com: Graham Oliver (tr). Dreamstime.com: Andreeacoman (cb). 104 Dreamstime.com: Jean Paul Chassenet (cla); Dmitry Kalinovsky (tc). 105 iStockphoto.com: Kaarsten (ca). Dreamstime.com: Katarzyna Bialasiewicz (crb). 109 iStockphoto.com: PeopleImages (cla). 110 123RF.com: Inspirestock International (Exclusive Contributor&#x (tc).

iStockphoto.com: Tagstock1 (cb). 112 Alamy Stock Photo: Capt.digby (c). Dreamstime.com: Piksel (tr). 114 123RF.com: Otnaydur (br); Pahham (tc). 117 Getty Images: Morsa Images (ca). iStockphoto.com: Betty4240 (c). 119 Dreamstime.com: Thierry Vialard (tc). 120 Dreamstime.com: Mato750 (cl); Paulus Rusyanto (cb). Alamy Stock Photo: Nik Taylor (clb). 126 Dreamstime.com: Robert Crum (c). 127 Getty Images: Dave King (tr). 128 Dreamstime.com: Voyagerix (tc). 133 Dreamstime.com: Mathew Hayward (tc). 134 Dreamstime.com: Tamara Bauer (br). 136 Dreamstime.com: Monkey Business Images (cla). 137 Alamy Stock Photo: Ian Allenden (cra). 138 Dreamstime.com: Monkey Business Images (tl); Wavebreakmedia Ltd (c). 139 123RF.com: Monika Wisniewska (crb). Alamy Stock Photo: IS-200703 (tc). Dreamstime.com: Wavebreakmedia Ltd (cb). 140 iStockphoto.com: FatCamera (cb). 143 123RF.com: Nagy-Bagoly Ilona (br). Dreamstime.com: Lamai Prasitsuwan (cb). 144 123RF.com: Dean Drobot (tc); Darrin Henry (cr). iStockphoto.com: Ljupco (fcr). 146 123RF.com: Hongqi Zhang (ca). Dreamstime.com: Lio2012 (bc). 148 Dreamstime.com: Sophiejames (ca). 149 123RF.com: Tiago Fernandez (crb). Dreamstime.com: Cheryl Casey (bc). 150 Alamy Stock Photo: Peter Bennett (crb). 151 iStockphoto.com: Jashlock (tr). 152 123RF.com: Roman Samokhin (crb). 153 123RF.com: Liorpt (br). iStockphoto.com: Xavierarnau (bl). 154 Alamy Stock Photo: SJH Photography (cra). 155 Dreamstime.com: Dastin50 (tr); Monkey Business Images (cb). 156 Dreamstime.com: Kiosea39 (clb); Kim Reinick (ct). 157 123RF.com: Nebojsa Markovic (cr). Alamy Stock Photo: Randy Green (ca). 158 123RF.com: Anelina (bl). Alamy Stock Photo: Tim Gainey (cb). 159 Dreamstime.com: Gale Verhague (c). 161 Alamy Stock Photo: ImageGB (crb); Vast Photography (tl). Dreamstime.com: Wavebreakmedia Ltd (c). 163 123RF.com: thamkc (crb). iStockphoto.com: deepblue4you (tl). 165 Dreamstime.com: Davidmartyn (cb). 166 iStockphoto.com: Kali9 (tl). 168 iStockphoto.com: Evemilla (tl). 170 123RF.com: Wavebreak Media Ltd (c). 171 Dreamstime.com: Ldprod (cb); Vladimir Mudrovcic (tr). 173 Alamy Stock Photo: Alexander Caminada (clb). Dreamstime.com: Błazej Łyjak (crb); Peanutroaster (c); Vadymvdrobot (tc). 174 Dreamstime.com: Djem82 (br). 175 Alamy Stock Photo: Simon Belcher (c). 176 iStockphoto.com: PeopleImages (ca). 177 123RF.com: Dean Drobot (ca). Dreamstime.com: Monkey Business Images Ltd (tc). 178 Alamy Stock Photo: Finnbarr Webster (c). 179 123RF.com: Viacheslav Nikolaienko (cr). Dreamstime.com: Mystock88photo (ca); Eva Vargyasi (bc). iStockphoto.com: PeopleImages (bl). 181 123RF.com: Wichan Sumalee (tr). iStockphoto.com: JackF (cl). 183 123RF.com: Leung Cho Pan (tl). Dreamstime.com: Monkey Business Images (crb). 185 Dreamstime.com: Helen Hotson (ca). iStockphoto.com: Eugenesergeev (cra). 186 Dreamstime.com: Steve AllenUK (cb). 187 123RF.com: Aleksandar Mijatovic (tc). Dreamstime.com: Jaromír Chalabala (crb); Joseph Golby (ca). 188 Alamy Stock Photo: Kim Karpeles (cb). iStockphoto.com: Wundervisuals (bc). 191 123RF.com: Vesilvio (tr); Anastasy Yarmolovich (bl). Dorling Kindersley: Fleur Star (bc). Dreamstime.com: Tsomka (cb). 192 123RF.com: Thanthima Limsakul (cla). 193 123RF.com: Pawel Kowalczyk (tc). 194 Dreamstime.com: Abdone (ca); Kungverylucky (tr). 195 Dorling Kindersley: Jerry Young (tr). 197 123RF.com: wckiw (cla). 197 Dreamstime.com: Michael Courtney (tc); Mario Kelichhaus (tr). 198 123RF.com: dolgachov (bc). Dreamstime.com: Corepics Vof (crb). 199 123RF.com: Iakov Filimonov (cl). 200 123RF.com: Jose Manuel Gelpi Diaz (bc); Wavebreak Media Ltd (crb). Dreamstime.com: Tatiana Dyuvbanova (tl). 201 123RF.com: (crb). Dreamstime.com: Puhhha (tc). iStockphoto.com: fstop123 (bl). 202 123RF.com: Kanvag (tc). Dorling Kindersley: Bethany Dawn Collection (c). 203 123RF.com: Volodymyr Nikulin (cl). Alamy Stock Photo: Hero Images (cl); Mike Kemp (ca). 204 123RF.com: paleka (br); tobkatrina (c). Alamy Stock Photo: Steve Hamblin (tc). Dreamstime.com: Nikita Rogul (cl). 207 Alamy Stock Photo: Adrian Sherratt (c). Dreamstime.com: Monkey Business Images (ca). 208 Alamy Stock Photo: moodboard (tl); Ellie Reed (c). 209 123RF.com: siraphat thanyaphuriwat (bl). 210 123RF.com: gopixa (clb). Dreamstime.com: Elena Elisseeva (c). 211 Dorling Kindersley: Peter Cook Photography (tc). 212 Alamy Stock Photo: Richard Green (cb). 214 123RF.com: belchonock (cl); Iakov Filimonov (cb). Dreamstime.com: Chris Lorenz (crb). 217 Dreamstime.com: Ampack (clb). 218 Dorling Kindersley: Stephen Oliver (c). Dreamstime.com: Tatonka (cl). 219 Dorling Kindersley: Pablo H. Caridad (c). 220 Dreamstime.com: Glenda Powers (bc). 221 Dorling Kindersley: Kateryna Levchenko (clb). Dreamstime.com: Luis Carlos Torres (tc); Lisa F. Young (cb). 222 123RF.com: Grosescu Alberto (tl). Alamy Stock Photo: Corina Marie Howell (tc). 224 123RF.com: Mykola Komarovskyy (bc). Dreamstime.com: Simone Van Den Berg (cr); Zuzana Randlova (ct). 225 123RF.com: Cathy Yeulet (cb). 226 Dreamstime.com: Diego Vito Cervo (tr). 228 123RF.com: Vladyslav Starozhylov (crb). 230 123RF.com: warrengoldswain (tl). Dreamstime.com: Alxcrs (tc). 231 Dreamstime.com: Lisa F. Young (ca). iStockphoto.com: subodhsathe (bc). 236 Alamy Stock Photo: Geoffrey Robinson (cr). 237 Alamy Stock Photo: Juniors Bildarchiv / F279 (cl). 239 Alamy Stock Photo: Jeremy Pembrey (c). 240 Dreamstime.com: Gstrange (ca). 242 Alamy Stock Photo: Christophe Lehenaff (bc); Chris Ryan (crb). 243 iStockphoto.com: Delpixart (br). 244 123RF.com: Ksenia Raykova (crb). Alamy Stock Photo: IE131 (tc). 246 123RF.com: pat kullberg (ca). iStockphoto.com: SolStock (br). 250 Dreamstime.com: Ed Francissen (cb). 251 123RF.com: Weerachat Chatroopamai (tc). 254 123RF.com: Cathy Yeulet (ca). Dreamstime.com: Vallorie Francis (tr). 255 123RF.com: klotz (cla). Dreamstime.com: Rotarepok (cra)

All other images © Dorling Kindersley
For further information see: www.dkimages.com